The Edible Landscape

The Edible Landscape

by
Tom MacCubbin

Waterview Press
Oviedo, Florida

The Edible Landscape. Copyright 1989 by Thomas J. MacCubbin. All rights reserved. No part of this book may be used or reproduced in any manner whatsoever without written permission from the publisher except in the case of brief quotations as part of articles and reviews. For information, please address Waterview Press, Inc., 169 West Broadway Street, Oviedo, Florida 32765. Telephone (407) 365-8500. E-mail oviedo@bellsouth.net.

Manufactured in the United States of America

First edition published November 1989 by Sentinel Communications Company.

Edited by Lynn O'Meara and Margaret Mott
Designed by Katie Pelisek
Illustrations by Mike Wright and Melissa Slimick
Horticultural illustrations by Gerald Masters
Landscape design by Paige Braddock
Maps by Peg Alrich
Illustration revisions by Ron Falkner

Revised edition published April 1998 by Waterview Press, Inc., an imprint of Charles B McFadden Co.

Cover photography by Doug Seibert of Esquire Photographers, Inc., Orlando
Cover design by Jan Smiley of 43 Vine Type & Design, Oviedo, Florida
Printed by BookCrafters, Fredericksburg, Virginia

Library of Congress Cataloging-in-Publication Data

MacCubbin, Tom, 1944-
    The edible landscape / by Tom MacCubbin. -- Rev. ed.
       p. cm.
    Rev. ed. of: Florida home grown 2. 1st ed. 1989.
    Includes index.
    ISBN 1-883114-09-8 (lib. bdg.). -- ISBN 1-883114-08-X (pbk.)
    1. Edible landscaping--Florida.   I. MacCubbin, Tom, 1944-
 Florida home grown 2.   II. Title
SB475.9.E35M325 1998
635'.09759--dc21   98-9368
                                                                     CIP

Paperback edition ISBN 1-883114-08-X
Library edition ISBN 1-883114-09-8

About the author

A NATIVE OF MARYLAND and horticulture graduate of the University of Maryland, Tom MacCubbin has been Orange County's urban horticulturist since 1972. He is an Extension Agent IV, which is equivalent to a full professor at the University of Florida.

In 1980 Mr. MacCubbin started the weekly television program *Florida Home Grown,* produced by WMFE-channel 24, and an offshoot of the show, *Florida Home Grown Live.* He also has launched *Indoor Gardens,* which is aired throughout the Southeast, and is a regular guest on WCPX-Channel 6. His syndicated radio program, *Better Lawns and Gardens,* can be heard on 22 stations throughout the state.

His name and face also are familiar to Florida gardeners through columns written for *The Orlando Sentinel,* talks on local radio programs, and frequent appearances at gardening clubs and civic organizations.

Throughout his career, Mr. MacCubbin has earned numerous accolades, including The Garden Communicator's Award from the American Association of Nurserymen. He has been named Best Horticulture Writer and Best Garden Editor by the Florida Nurserymen and Growers Association. In 1987 he received the Distinguished Service award from the National Association of County Agents. Epsilon Sigma Phi, the Extension Service honorary, awarded him its Distinguished Service Award in 1997.

When he is not busy advising Central Floridians on their horticultural problems, Mr. MacCubbin can be found cultivating his Seminole County garden with his wife, Joan.

Dedication

THE AUTHOR DEDICATES this book to the generations of Givvines, MacCubbins, Smiths and Underhills who have tilled and planted the land. Their success with crops and their shared knowledge now allows us all to reap bountiful harvests.

May these writings offer inspiration to future generations, especially younger family members Melanie Marie, Kristen, Melanie Lynn, Peter and Jeffrey that they, too, will know the pleasure of growing their own fruit and vegetables.

Acknowledgements

THIS BOOK is your guide to better gardening and a productive landscape thanks to the assistance of many.

Special thanks to longtime gardening friend and *Orlando Sentinel* editor Lynn O'Meara, whose encouragement and enthusiasm made this book a reality. Those long hours editing, plus advice and constructive criticism helped make this a gardening reference everyone can grow by.

Appreciation is expressed to Margaret Mott, who also loves the land, for editing the original manuscript and frequently adding a fresh viewpoint and suggestions for improvement.

Thank you, April Medina, for your many hours of proofreading.

Thanks also to Katie Pelisek for your design and layouts of the book, which invite easy reading and understanding of the concepts.

For many of the inside illustrations, the author thanks Mike Wright, who helped bring the garden to life.

Horticultural illustrations were created by Gerald Masters, and many cultural illustrations by Melissa Slimick. The author is deeply grateful for their artistic help that shows gardeners how plants grow.

The author is indebted to the many researchers and specialists of the Institute of Food and Agricultural Sciences at the University of Florida, Gainesville. Their training of the author as an extension agent and their frequent assistance make this a scientifically based planting guide. Many of the charts and tables found in this book were formulated from the IFAS publications.

Thanks to all who have worked on this revised edition, especially Stephen Combs, the publisher. It's his enthusiasm and dedication to each of the Florida Home Grown books that has kept them in print and available to help with your gardens. Also thanks to the staff of Florida's Radio Networks who encouraged the author to pen the revisions needed to bring you this updated version for your library.

Last but not least, thanks to my wife, Joan, for her love and encouragement that keeps this horticulturist enthused and willing to serve the residents of Florida. Her typing of the original manuscript was the beginning of this work and the start of your edible landscape.

Contents

Chapter	Page
1. Planning the edible landscape	1
2. First considerations	7
3. Matters of state — and what will grow	13
4. Starting from the ground up	21
5. Seed savvy for starting transplants	29
6. Grafting and other special techniques	37
7. Planting the formal vegetable garden	47
8. Watering — the essential chore	57
9. Maintaining the garden	63
10. Harvest time	71
11. Grow a taste of the exotic	77
12. Herbs — the fresher the better	93
13. Kindergardens	105
14. Citrus — how to grow the state crop	117
15. Deciduous fruit that can take the heat	129
16. Plant a grove of exotic flavors	147
17. Gardens for special places	163
18. How to control pests and diseases	175
Appendix I	189
Appendix II	275
Appendix III	283
Glossary	290
Index	293

XII.

Introduction

I HATE CHICKENS. I HAVE nothing against the birds, you understand. It was just the many Saturdays spent cleaning out coops that fostered a lasting resentment. Possibly, I do owe the hens a note of gratitude because much manure and corn-cob bedding was turned into the soil each spring to begin the garden.

Our 5-acre plot was pure Maryland clay — a good earth but hard to manage. I remember my dad planting a bushel of potato seed pieces one spring, only to dig a half-bushel of full-grown potatoes at the summer harvest.

This is where the chickens came in: The coop cleanings lightened the dense soil and added important nutrients. The hens' contributions made the difference between food and famine.

Today, chickens have disappeared from most home sites, but good gardeners still gather around manure piles. You can find them pitching in at the racetracks or boarding stables in search of the ingredients that will improve their garden soils.

It is important to learn good soil preparation techniques early in the gardening process, techniques that appear to work equally as well in Florida as in my native Maryland. Compost, peats, leaves and garden clippings can be as beneficial as manures if you know how to put them to use.

Florida sands can be quite productive, but gardeners must add all the ingredients essential to plant growth. Some say Florida gardening is a type of hydroponic culture where gardeners pour on the water and fertilizer, then watch the plants flourish. Many gardeners wish it were so easy.

Florida soils drain rapidly, but the pest problems build equally as quickly. First-time gardeners often are on a honeymoon of sorts: Everything just seems to grow right with only a minimum of effort. Then the insects seem to plant the "Free eats" sign, and while their insect buddies gather to devour the harvest, nematodes arrive and roam the soil, laying the groundwork to destroy roots of future plantings.

Enthusiasm: That's what it takes to grow a garden! However, enthusiasm quickly is shattered by the problems inherent with Florida soils.

My Florida garden was carved out of palmetto and slash-pine land where once only snakes frequented. The first plantings were great; the next were plagued by nematodes.

How did the nematodes get there? Who knows? But only after much fumigation and loads of organic matter was the garden once again productive.

Why is it that the easy-to-grow vegetables always seem to taste so bad? Perhaps because many gardeners new to Florida are unfamiliar with true Southern flavors. But then, gardening is an educational endeavor.

Gardening also is one good way to get the kids to eat their vegetables: How could they turn down a nice bowl of turnips, mustard greens or collards if they helped grow them?

Newcomers often assume citrus trees are native. How else could the fruit do so well? In Florida, it is the most carefree fruit imaginable. A few blemishes will have to be tolerated, but the trees really don't have to be sprayed. Before the freeze of 1983, almost every street corner in Central Florida had its productive citrus trees. How could the Spanish, who introduced the trees, ever have known how well the crop would flourish?

I wish apples, peaches and pears were as easy to grow. It's not that the trees have difficulty in Florida, only that pests plague the crops. Imagine the frustration of a backyard horticulturist watching Caribbean fruit flies laying eggs for which there are no ready controls. The alternatives are to spray to keep the pests away or to plant more citrus.

In addition to citrus, there are grapes, papayas, persimmons, mangoes and avocados to tempt new gardeners. Gardeners can plant a jungle of edible crops and fill the yard — without planting ornamentals. One local gardener counted 52 banana varieties, most of which produce edible fruit. The real secret to growing fruit is to obtain the necessary cultural information — before you plant.

As a teen-ager in Maryland, I grew transplants and other seedlings in my bedroom. I couldn't wait until the first seed catalog arrived each spring so I could place an order and start the seeds. Things were a lot different then — it was before plastics. Seed trays were fashioned from cardboard, and soil was used directly from the yard. With such crude techniques, it is a wonder anything grew.

Gardening has come a long way, and to have real success, planters must learn from experience. Formulate your own soil mix for growing seedlings. Not to brag, but my mix of peat and perlite is so simple and effective for plant culture, I don't know why it isn't on the market.

Maybe modern seeds are a bit finicky, but it takes near-sterile conditions to raise transplants. Fortunately, that's only one way to begin new plantings. Propagation by cuttings, layering and grafting can be equally rewarding.

This guide to edible landscapes is filled with scientific knowledge plus practical experience. Grow all your produce or just a little — the Florida way.

The Edible Landscape

1
Planning the edible landscape

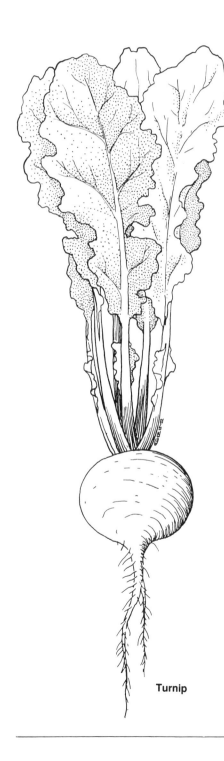
Turnip

TURN THE FRONT LAWN over to sweet potatoes and let pecans provide the patio shade. This could be the beginning of an edible landscape, where ornamental plantings take a back seat to crops that bear a harvest.

Don't waste the space if the plant is not edible. Ornamentals and fruiting crops require about equal time, water and fertilizer to grow. For your labor and investment, it is only reasonable to expect fresh produce from the landscape.

Feeding the family and stocking the freezer or pantry are just a few of the dollar-saving reasons for planting an edible landscape. Many gardeners also grow food for the fun of it. There is plenty of wholesome fresh air and exercise in tilling the soil and tending the crops. Planting a garden and managing fruit plantings can keep you outdoors just about every day of the year.

Gardeners are turning landscapes over to edible plantings for a variety of reasons:

• Crops are harvested fresh from the garden or orchard.
• Pesticides are known and carefully applied.
• Crops can be picked at the peak of ripeness.
• Varieties with the preferred flavor can be grown.
• Unusual and hard-to-find fruits and vegetables can be planted.
• There is personal pride from producing food and excitement in returning to the land.

As long as the spot receives plenty of sunlight, edible plantings can be grown over acres, on a few square feet of the patio or in containers. Even on a crowded balcony, one tall-growing tomato plant trained to a trellis can supply juicy, red-ripe fruit for the dinner table all spring, as well as a few surplus tomatoes for friends. A container-grown lime tree is sure to produce enough juice for pies and pitchers of limeade throughout much of the year.

Grow a pot of herbs in the sun on the windowsill — it may be all you need to season the family meals. These plants flourish almost anywhere there is some sun. Just about all are decorative and can be grown in containers and used as colorful accents on a patio table or at the entranceway to the home.

Edible substitutes

Gardens can be pretty and don't have to be hidden in the back yard. An eggplant patch is extremely ornamental — the plants open lavender flowers and bear decorative white or purple fruit. They are likely to attract as much attention as a bed of petunias.

Similarly, heads of ruby lettuce, pods of okra and swelling peppers are attention-getters to use in foundation plantings and entrance gardens. But filling the garden is just one step in planting the edible landscape.

Food-producing gardeners also must consider the trees needed to provide shade, screen views and reduce winds. This traditionally has been a job for the mighty oaks, maples and sweet gums, but fruit-bearing trees are capable substitutes.

For shade during the summer and warming sun in winter, plant the tall, wide-spreading pecan tree, a deciduous tree that can yield bushels of nuts.

Nothing beats an avocado, tamarind, loquat, longan, mango or white sapote for year-round shade. These trees provide shade comparable to that of magnolia, cherry laurel and camphor trees.

Small trees can add the excitement of flowers and fruit to the landscape. Get out of the habit of planting non-productive tabebuia, dogwood or fringe trees and add peach, pear, apple, citrus, persimmon or guava trees, which offer something for both the eye and stomach. These small trees also can compete with their ornamental cousins as view and traffic barriers. Many can be trellised or trained as espaliers for a special design effect.

Shrubs that grow as hedges or fill the foundation area with greenery also can be found among the edibles. Following are a few substitutes for familiar ornamental selections:

- Small shrubs. Skip the pittosporum, hollies and Indian hawthorn and select instead such edibles as pineapples, raspberries and blackberries.
- Medium shrubs. Substitutes for azaleas, junipers, thryallis and jasmine include high-bush blueberries, Surinam cherries and pomegranates.

Planting an edible landscape

- Locate vegetable garden in full sun.
- Trellis and train vining crops to save space and obtain maximum yields.
- Use as view barriers trees or large shrubs that can touch and maintain production at maturity.
- Use steppingstones, brick or mulch to form paths to major plantings.
- Mulch areas between plantings to conserve moisture, encourage root growth and maintain clean plant foliage.
- Plant low-growing perennials or shrubs to border gardens.
- Give hedged shrubs adequate room to grow and develop good yields.
- Place major plantings away from large-growing trees to avoid shade and root competition.
- Train upright, bushy shrubs near a wall to best use space.
- Allow adequate growing room for trees and large shrubs.
- Plant trees and shrubs that produce soft fruit away from walkways.
- Determine sun patterns before planting to ensure best exposures.
- Determine the need for evergreen or deciduous fruit trees.
- Set lower-growing shrubs near the front of the property to keep house visible.
- Minimize lawn and use majority of property for edible plantings.

Design that mixes edibles with ornamentals

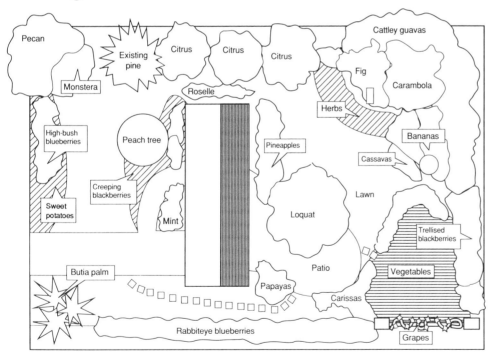

Gardens that provide a harvest plus fruit-bearing trees and shrubs surround an open recreational area. Create excitement with attractive flowers, fruit and foliage, including peaches, pineapples, papayas and cassavas as accents to an entrance or around patio. Many existing plants may need to be removed. A shade-giving pine or other non-edible tree might be left to give a mature look to the design.

• Large shrubs. Replace crape myrtles, camellias, powderpuffs and bottlebrushes with papayas, kumquats, figs and tropical apricots.

When you want to hide a blank wall, consider vines. Where flame vine, bougainvillea and confederate jasmine are common creepers, make substitutions with fruit producers. A few to train to a fence or send up a trellis include bunch and muscadine grapes, passion fruit, yams, chayotes and cucumbers.

For the purely ornamental effect, include in the landscape plants with a tropical look. A cluster of bananas or a monstera growing as a bushy vine will prompt conversation.

Where to start

Edible landscapes start on paper. All family members can participate in deciding where trees, shrubs, vines and a garden can fit in the existing landscape. Mom is sure to want an herb patch; dad, his vegetables; and the kids, a spot to experiment with a bean tepee or runaway pumpkin. Outline what exists around the home site, then fill in with edibles.

Map out the areas to be planted. It's not necessary to plan an entire landscape of edibles, but when the crops start coming in, the temptation to do so may be great. Perhaps the front yard or a section of the patio will get the treatment at first, and the plantings can be expanded later.

Here are a few techniques to stretch the available landscape space:

• Use square-foot and full-bed culture techniques to maximize production.

• Interplant quick-yielding crops between rows of slow-growing vegetables.

• Plant bush varieties of vining vegetables.

• Grow plants vertically in cages or on trellises.

• Seed leafy vegetables and root crops thickly; harvest and eat thinnings.

• Plant vegetables and herbs between young, developing trees and shrubs.

Landscape filled with edible plantings

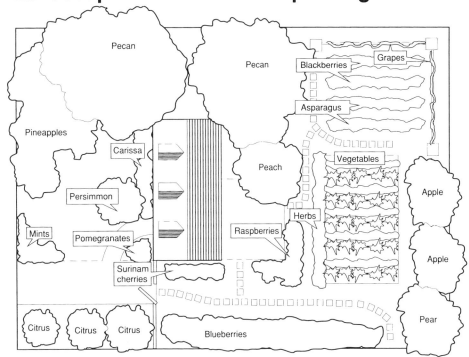

Fill front and back yard with edible plantings. Gardens grow up to the patio, making maximum use of often-barren space. Trees and shrubs provide seasonal color and fruit, replacing common but fruitless landscape ornamentals.

• Underplant trees and shrubs with shade-tolerant leafy crops.

• Fill pots and baskets with plants that grow tall, then fill in with others that creep over the sides.

• Selectively prune trees and shrubs to grow smaller-than-normal plants.

First, the trees

Plan and plant the trees first, because they will require years to grow. Trees produce the shade that can help with the air conditioning in summer and provide protection from northern winds during the winter.

Do, however, go lightly with the trees if vegetables and other sun-loving crops are to be planted. Trees grow in height and width, and just a few may produce all the shade that is needed.

Use these tips in positioning both large and small trees:

• Keep tall, spreading trees to the back or side of the property.

• Plant trees to the side of the home or front yard. Leave the front yard open to view.

• Where sun is needed for winter warmth, plant deciduous trees.

• Plant cold-tolerant and evergreen trees on the north and northwest sides of the landscape.

• Group small, low-branching trees together as a view barrier or to separate property lines.

• Use the more exciting small trees with colorful flowers or fruit for accents.

Double-duty shrubs

Next in the planning are the shrubs used as barriers and to divide the landscape. These often are the hedges that separate the neighbor's back yard from yours or screen out the objectionable views.

To serve these purposes well, edible plants must branch to the ground, grow dense and often be capable of being sheared. Some that form especially good barriers are the blueberry, Surinam cherry, feijoa and small citrus. Where an impermeable hedge is needed, consider blackberries supported by a trellis.

Barriers do not have to be formally sheared hedges. A cluster of shrubs often will block views and direct traffic movement when allowed to grow with only minor pruning. Edibles usually are much more productive if pruning is infrequent and the fruiting stems are preserved. Many will benefit from timely pruning once a year.

Accent the unusual

Select some of the more unusual shrubs for accent plantings staged against green background shrub clusters, hedges or trees.

As design elements in the landscape, accent plantings welcome visitors and produce excitement in the garden. They are the plants with pretty flowers, colorful fruit or unusual growth habits. Each view should have an accent plant or group of vegetation.

Accents do not have to be exceptional all the time, just for a portion of a season or two. Then another plant can take a turn. Many will add multiseason interest and should be given a position of prominence. Here are a few good edible accents to grow as shrubs:

- Feijoa — white flowers with red stamen in spring; gray-green fruit summer through fall.
- Cherry-of-the-Rio-Grande — white flowers in spring; red fruit in fall.
- Pitomba — white flowers in spring; yellow fruit in summer.
- Banana — flowers year-round; yellow fruit summer through fall.
- Pomegranate — orange-red flowers in spring; yellow to red fruit in summer.
- Blueberry — white flowers in spring; blueberries, late spring; bold leaf color, fall.
- Barbados cherry — pink flowers spring through fall; bright red fruit year-round.

An eye-catching accent could be a garden planted with fruiting tomatoes, heads of broccoli, leafy Swiss chard and stalks of corn. Any unusual-looking plant, including trellised chayotes and yard-long beans, will get a second glance. Frame the plantings with small shrubs, a grape arbor or backdrop of blueberries.

Don't let the enthusiasm for planting fill every section of the landscape. Leave plenty of space for walkways, and decide if you want a lawn or mulched open areas. It is also best to leave some room for recreational activities and plant around them.

With the accents in place and the open spaces defined, it is time to fill in the spaces left in the landscape. Often these are the voids near the foundation, along walks, to the rear of the property, and near the patio.

The fillers, called transition plantings by landscapers, can be annuals and perennials or additional shrubs. Here is the opportunity to fill in with the greenery of an herb garden or the creeping vine of a sweet potato. Leafy vegetables also would work, as would creeping blackberries.

What to plant

When planning what to plant, consider every spot — perhaps a planter beside the pool or pots on the patio. On the other hand, grow what will be eaten. Do not overplant. A few plants in pots may be enough to care for, yet yield fresh produce for the whole family.

Begin slowly. Read about crops before planting. Learn whether you want the obligations associated with good care.

Radishes, beans and turnips grow with minimal care, tomatoes take a little attention, and cantaloupes can be a real chore. Pears seem to grow with little spraying, but peaches and apples need constant pest-control programs.

How to plan a home landscape

Do:
- Draw every plant, fence, pool and patio to scale.
- Try several different designs.
- Plan for adequate lawn and shade areas.
- Create screens for privacy.
- Group plants together for dramatic effect.
- Leave room for future additions such as a pool or greenhouse.
- Study the characteristics of plants.
- Use low-maintenance plants.
- Get ideas from books and neighborhood walks.
- Plan for irrigation.
- Space plants for mature growth.

Don't:
- Plant trees within 15 feet of the house or septic tank.
- Scatter individual plants throughout the landscape.
- Place near the house plants with either a severe upright or rounded shape.
- Use tall-growing plants in front of windows.
- Plan to shear plants to keep them in bounds.
- Use too many plants.

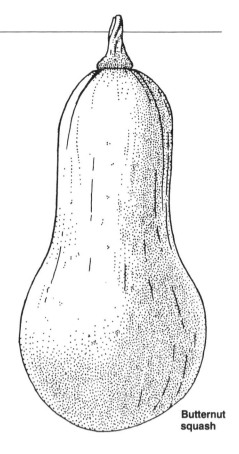

Butternut squash

Determining how much to plant always is a problem because crops are not equally productive. One pear tree can produce two or more bushels of fruit, but the banana produces only one stalk. Likewise, a 10-foot row of beans may give a few weeks worth of pickings while cauliflower yields a single head. Study the crops before you plant, then plan what the family can consume fresh or preserve.

Use yield tables to get an idea of what to expect from one tree, vine or a long row of vegetables. One watermelon may not be worth all the vines, but a trellis of grapes could yield fresh fruit, jams and juice. Where growing area is limited, consider fruits and vegetables that give the highest returns for the space available.

Learn mature heights and widths, then plant so each tree and shrub will have plenty of room to grow. Crowding can be a major reason the edible landscape becomes non-productive. Most plantings should be spaced so they barely touch at maturity and will not shade other sun-loving neighbors.

Finally, know that there will be failures. Each year, some crops will not meet expectations, while others yield bushels. As gardening becomes more intensive, both failures and successes are magnified.

Learn what went wrong. Dig up a problem plant and carry it to a cooperative extension service office or garden center for diagnosis. Follow recommendations and try again.

Vegetable crop yields

Type	Yield 100 feet
Asparagus	30 pounds
Beans, snap bush	45 pounds
Beans, snap pole	80 pounds
Beans, lima	50 pounds
Beets	75 pounds
Broccoli	50 pounds
Brussels sprouts	75 pounds
Cabbage	80 heads
Cantaloupe	75 melons
Carrots	100 pounds
Cauliflower	80 pounds
Celeriac	60 pounds
Celery	180 stalks
Chinese cabbage	80 heads
Collards and kale	150 pounds
Corn, sweet	10 dozen ears
Cucumbers	100 pounds
Eggplant	200 pounds
Garlic	40 pounds
Kohlrabi	100 pounds
Lettuce, head	100 heads
Lettuce, leaf	100 heads
Mustard	100 pounds
Okra	70 pounds
Onions	100 pounds
Parsley	40 pounds
Parsnips	100 pounds
Peas, English	40 pounds
Peas, Southern	80 pounds
Peppers	50 pounds
Potatoes	150 pounds
Potatoes, sweet	300 pounds
Pumpkins	100 pounds
Radishes	100 bunches
Salsify	100 pounds
Soybeans	20 pounds
Spinach	40 pounds
Squash, summer	150 pounds
Squash, winter	300 pounds
Swiss chard	75 pounds
Tomatoes	200 pounds
Turnips	150 pounds
Watermelons	40 melons

Fruit crop yields

Type	Yield per plant
Citrus	
Grapefruit	5-9 bushels
Kumquat	2-5 bushels
Lemon	3-6 bushels
Oranges	4-8 bushels
Persian lime	3-6 bushels
Tangelo	4-8 bushels
Tangerine	3-6 bushels
Deciduous	
Apple	2 or more bushels
Blackberry	2-6 pounds
Blueberry	6-10 pounds
Fig	10 or more pounds
Grape, bunch	10 pounds
Grape, muscadine	20 pounds
Nectarine	1-2 bushels
Peach	1-2 bushels
Pear	2 or more bushels
Pecan	up to 100 pounds
Persimmon	1 or more bushels
Plum	1 or more bushels
Tropical	
Avocado	1-2 bushels
Banana	5 or more bunches
Carambola	150-250 pounds
Guava	125-200 pounds
Loquat	50-100 pounds
Lychee	50-125 pounds
Mango	75-150 pounds
Papaya	8-15 pounds
Passion fruit	8-15 pounds
Pineapple	1 fruit

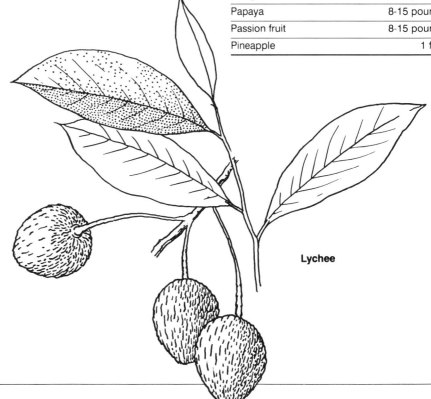

Lychee

2
First considerations

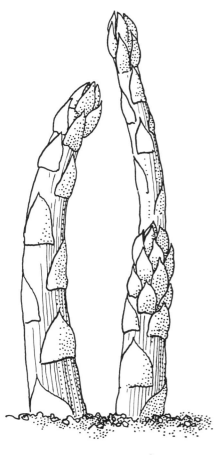

Asparagus

GOOD EATING IS JUST ahead. Transplanted herbs will yield a picking in a matter of weeks; squash and beans can be harvested in 60 days; papayas, about nine months; and fruit trees, just a few short years. All crops will be productive with some early planning.

Thoughts of a bountiful fruit and vegetable harvest lead gardeners directly outdoors to till and plant the landscape. But don't let the enthusiasm run out of control: Take time to consider what really is needed to have a great garden.

Use a sketch of the landscape to troubleshoot potential hazards to good plant growth, then fill in with plantings. By visualizing what is planned for the landscape, problems of crowding, inadequate light and water and inconvenient placement can be avoided before a crop is set in the soil. This step saves time and money by eliminating the chores of removing unwanted plantings later.

Room to grow

Plants are like people — they can take just a little crowding, but most need elbow room. The best harvests are produced when crops are given ample room to grow. Find out how much room you have to plant, then begin planning what to grow.

Quite often the back yard has room only for a vegetable patch, a few fruiting shrubs and a tree or two. Crowded plants grow lanky and are less likely to bloom or mature, turning the blossoms into fruit. Also think of the bees who must find the peaches, squash and blueberries to pollinate the flowers.

In general, trees should be located well beyond the garden. Competition from leaves and roots quickly limits vegetable production. Fruiting trees should be spaced so the foliage of the outer limbs will just touch and intermingle when the trees reach maturity.

The future size and shape of the tree determines the spacing. Peach trees need 15 feet between trunks; orange and avocado trees, 25 feet; and pecans, 50 to 60 feet. Don't crowd fruiting shrubs, either. As a general rule, space the plants a distance equal to half the expected height at maturity.

Growing room is needed for every crop. Crowded vegetable plant-

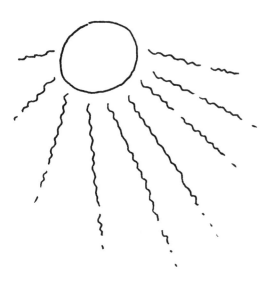

ings sometimes mean early harvests of young but immature greens, as from turnip or mustard. Consumption of the thinnings then allows room to produce the real crop.

Light triggers growth

Will the plants have enough light? Often the sun seems to shine everywhere except where it is needed. Unfortunately, gardens require sun. High yields usually are produced only in full-sun exposures. Some non-productive ornamentals may have to be eliminated to let the sun in for plants that will provide a a harvest.

Light drives the food manufacturing process in the plant. Yes, plants make their own food. Gardeners supply the basic water and nutrients, but the plants do the rest.

Green leaves absorb the sun's energy and manufacture a sugar that produces growth, including the greens, fruit and nuts eventually consumed. The more foliage on crops, the better the harvests are likely to be.

Very few crops are productive without plenty of light. Shaded foliage often is lanky and thin, stems twist and become distorted, and fruit that does form often has poor flavor. Leafy herbs and green-leaved vegetables are most likely to be the best survivors at the lower light levels.

Large-leaved vegetables tolerate lower light levels because of the surface size of the foliage, which absorbs the reflected sun. Cool-season crops of lettuce, collards, mustard and turnips often produce a harvest with half a day of sun, or in filtered shade under a tree, but the crop will be of lower quality. Herbs, including mint, oregano, chives and parsley, also will survive and produce a harvest in the shade.

Fruits, berries and plantings that form edible roots do well only in full sun; that is, six to eight hours a day of direct light. They may succeed in areas where some of the light is reflected off a building wall or filtered through leaves, but four to six hours of full sun is the minimum for most fruit and root crops.

Fruit trees, vines or shrubs often will grow in shade, but the more shade, the less fruit. A citrus tree crowded near a building or shaded by an oak often is barren on the shady side. An overshadowed peach tree will grow tall with spindly limbs. Blueberry bushes and grapevines grow wild in the woods, but produce much more fruit in full sun. All plants do best set out from buildings and allowed plenty of room from nearby plantings.

A location that has full sun in the summer may not have the sun it needs during the winter. As the seasons change, so do the lighting patterns. Gardens near trees or buildings are vulnerable to the differences in light levels, and it is difficult to plan ahead. Gardens as well as shrubs and greenhouses can be affected by shade.

During the early summer, the sun is directly overhead; in the winter the sun dips to the south. A tree or building that casts no shadow on the garden in the summer might be a major source of shade fall through spring. Many growers have moved the garden more than once before finding a location that is sunny year-round.

Avoid being a garden jockey by anticipating the movement of the sun. If the sun is overhead during the summer, check for factors that could cast shade in fall and winter. Are there trees nearby or a building next to where you want to plant the garden?

When planning the placement of a tree, think ahead 10 or 20 years and imagine how the shade could reduce the harvests from other crops. Trees and buildings on the north side of low-growing garden and shrub plantings normally will not obstruct the sun.

Don't let the fruit and vegetables starve for sun. Use these tips when planning the plantings:

• Determine seasonal sun patterns before planting.
• Keep most crops out in the sunniest areas.
• Allow the plantings room to grow to avoid future shading.
• Prune plantings that grow out of bounds and shade other crops.
• Place low-growing crops on the south side of major trees and buildings.
• Plan ahead, keeping tall plantings away from gardens and low-growing shrubs.

Drainage problems

In some locations, the problem is not enough drainage, perhaps after a heavy rain or during the wet summer season. Poorly drained soils may be dripping wet and sometimes can be squeezed like a sponge. A sour smell is often a first clue.

Gardeners often add gravel or rock in an effort to improve drainage. This is helpful only if the water has a place to go. A better solution is to grow plants above the water level. Shallow-rooted vegetables can be set in beds mounded 6 inches or more above normal ground level. On wide mounds, two or more rows of crops such as beets, turnips, carrots and lettuce can be planted close together.

Plants with deep roots — trees, shrubs and vines — need several feet of well-drained soil. Most trees, for instance, require at least 4 feet above the water table or consistently wet soil. For these plants, raised beds are a good solution. Railroad ties, landscape timbers or cement blocks can border a garden raised 6 inches to several feet above ground level. Fill the enclosure with a good planting mix to ensure good drainage.

Easy-access gardening

Locate the plantings where they can be enjoyed easily. Part of the fun of gardening is watching the progression of bloom to harvest. Crops crowded in the back yard or gardens inconvenient to cultivate certainly will not get tended.

Pest problems and harvests won't be missed if many of the trees, shrubs and vegetables are moved into the front yard, near the patio or along walks. You also will be reminded to do the pruning and supply the needed fertilizer.

Raised-bed gardens have become one way to organize planting thoughts and have made maintenance easier. They put crops in full view and make them easy to reach, while ensuring good drainage for plants.

Beds 4 feet wide can be cultivated from the sides, without stepping on the soil. Gardeners can sit on the sides to do the planting and weeding. Raised beds also have been elevated on legs to accommodate a wheelchair for the handicapped. Raised beds give a tidy appearance to the landscape and actually are neat, keeping soil off the paths and out of the house.

Any good garden soil can be added to a raised bed. Florida sand improves immensely with the liberal addition of organic matter, such as compost and peat moss. Garden soil may harbor insects, diseases and nematodes, so it may be necessary to fumigate such a mix before planting.

Equal parts of sphagnum peat moss and perlite make a loose, light substitute for raised-bed soil. The mix needs the addition of 2 pounds of dolomitic lime for every 100 square feet of bed surface to adjust the acidity for most crops. The lime can be worked in just before planting the bed but is better incorporated a week or two earlier to begin adjusting the acidity.

Fertilizer may be added at planting time, at a rate of 1 pound of 6-6-6 to each 100 square feet of bed area. Garden centers and wholesale-grower supply houses stock the ingredients for a soilless mix. Gardeners also can buy a prepared mix by the bag from garden centers or by the truckload from companies that supply commercial greenhouses.

Any area of the landscape that presents cultural problems requires special attention. Near the sea, for instance, plants need shelter from wind and spray. Salts will leach from sandy soil if fresh water is used for irrigation.

Some soils are so poor or rocky that the gardener must provide a growing medium in order for plants to survive. This is a situation made to order for gardening in pots or raised beds.

Successful gardeners direct their first efforts not to tilling the land but planning the plantings. Organize the areas that can be planted, then pick the crops to grow. Sketched out on paper, the trees, shrubs and gardens can be located and future growth anticipated.

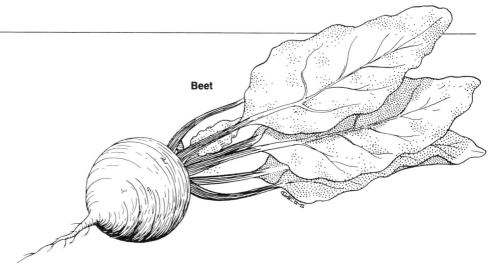
Beet

Raised-bed garden

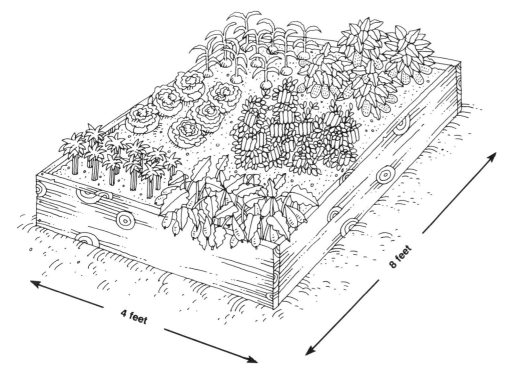

A small, raised-bed garden is ideal for the crowded landscape. The bed can be expanded to any length, but the 4-foot width makes it easy to tend the bed from the sides without stepping on the soil.

Learning about the land is next. As you will soon realize, Florida is a little different from most regions of the country but much more productive.

Vegetables need special consideration

Vegetable gardens need a spot all their own. They grow best in the open, away from trees and shrubs. Competition from larger plants not only takes away the light but robs vegetables of water and fertilizer. Tree and shrub roots also can harbor populations of nematodes, small roundworms that will multiply among the vegetables and damage the crops.

Trees and shrubs also complicate cultivation; tilling the soil can damage tree roots, and fumigation practiced near permanent plantings can kill trees and shrubs. Try to keep vegetable plantings at least several feet from the drip line of trees and shrubs.

Gardeners with limited planting space may have to intermingle vegetables with trees and shrubs. If this becomes necessary, make sure the soil is well-prepared and plant only the most vigorous, shade-tolerant crops.

In a Florida garden plot, row orientation is not important. In Northern gardens, where daily light levels are often low, rows are orientated north and south to give each side of the row equal exposure to the sun as it passes through the sky. In Florida's full sun there is plenty of light for all plantings in spite of row orientation.

Do, however, check to ensure taller vegetables do not shade the low-growing ones. Keep the large plants to the back and north end of the garden.

Gardeners sometimes attempt to shield plants from summer sun, believing that the bright light produces abnormal growth. Tomatoes set few fruit, lettuce plants bolt to seed, and beets wither because of the heat, not the light. Reducing the light levels with shade cloth or wood lathes further handicaps plants, causing survivors to grow lanky, unable to manufacture ugh food to grow fruit or roots.

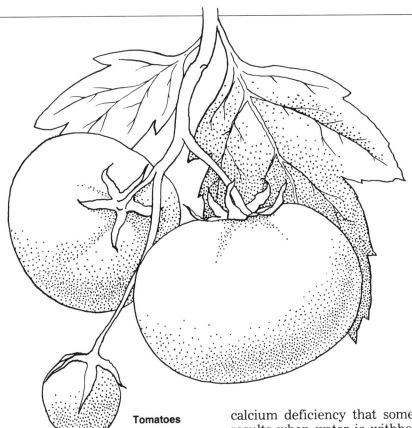
Tomatoes

Dry gardens are poor producers

Water is the second essential growth factor. Without periodic rains or irrigation, plants wilt and wither and harvests are reduced greatly.

Plants lose water as the moisture within leaf tissue and stems evaporates into the air. Actually, the plants lose the moisture for a good reason. Carbon dioxide needed for the food-manufacturing process enters openings of leaves, called stomata, and the water escapes as vapor. When water is scarce, the stomata close and much of the food-manufacturing ability of the plant stops.

Water also transports the nutrients needed for growth up through the stems of plants. Nitrogen, phosphorous, potassium and all the other elements needed for growth move into the roots, up the stems and are distributed throughout the plant. When water is scarce, the nutrients may not get delivered and some deficiencies result.

Blossom-end rot of tomato is a calcium deficiency that sometimes results when water is withheld too long from plants. The young tomatoes at the end of the vines are the last to get the calcium-rich moisture and often become deficient, with a brown, leathery dry rot at the base of the fruit. An even water supply could, in some cases, prevent this too-common cultural problem.

A good water supply also is responsible for food being dispersed and stored throughout the plant. Sugars, which are manufactured by the plant, move with the water in the stems to fruit and roots, which should produce the harvests.

When plants lack adequate moisture, they begin survival tactics. Many drop their fruit and thin the limbs of leaves — all of which takes away from the harvest. This is the sign of severe stress, which should be prevented. Plants can be permitted to curl some leaves and wilt a little, but never enter a stage of full wilt that will lead to reduction in growth and fruiting.

How to get the water to the garden is a consideration for early planning. Will there be a faucet nearby or will water have to be bucketed to the plantings? It's best to think of irrigation systems before the trees and shrubs are planted rather than disturb the roots later.

Modern gardeners are employing water-saving techniques. Drip irrigation and soaker hoses are replacing overhead systems and wasteful watering practices. Some home food producers use computers to turn the water on when needed. Planning for these conveniences early will save work in the future.

Too much water also has ill effects. First, it drives needed air out of the soil, and roots begin to decline. Soils should be thoroughly moistened then allowed to dry at least a little before being wet again. Soggy roots begin to rot rather quickly, and the plants decline.

Even when the soil dries quickly, too much water may have an adverse effect on the crop. Fruit near harvest often bursts with sudden surges of excess water. The fruit matures and, unable to take the pressure building inside, pops open. Extra water within the fruit also tends to dilute the flavors. The poorest-tasting cantaloupes and watermelons are produced when summer rains arrive early as the fruit is ripening.

Most Florida soils drain easily and do not retain water. In addition, the months of September through May, when most vegetables are planted and fruit is forming, are the dry season in Florida. Even well-mulched plantings will need irrigation once or twice a week.

Saltwater intrusion

Gardeners on the coast, and some inland growers, will need to be concerned with salt levels in their water. Water with salt levels reading above 1,000 parts per million (ppm) will kill beans, cucumbers, lettuce, mustard and tomatoes. Most fruiting trees, vines and berries cannot take more than 1,000 ppm. Beets and vegetables in the cabbage family will tolerate salt levels to 2,000 ppm and even more.

Salty well water calls for special irrigation techniques. Where available, fresh water from a city source can be used to supplement irrigation. If the well tests at 2,000 ppm, for example, watering half from the well and half with city water yields a level of 1,000 ppm, which most plants tolerate.

Salt-tolerant vegetables

Slight	
Beans	Cucumbers
Celery	Radishes
Moderate	
Carrots	Potatoes
Cauliflower	Squash
Lettuce	Sweet corn
Peas	
High	
Beets	Kale
Bell peppers	Spinach
Broccoli	Tomatoes
Cabbage	

Note: Tolerance at normal soil moisture level.

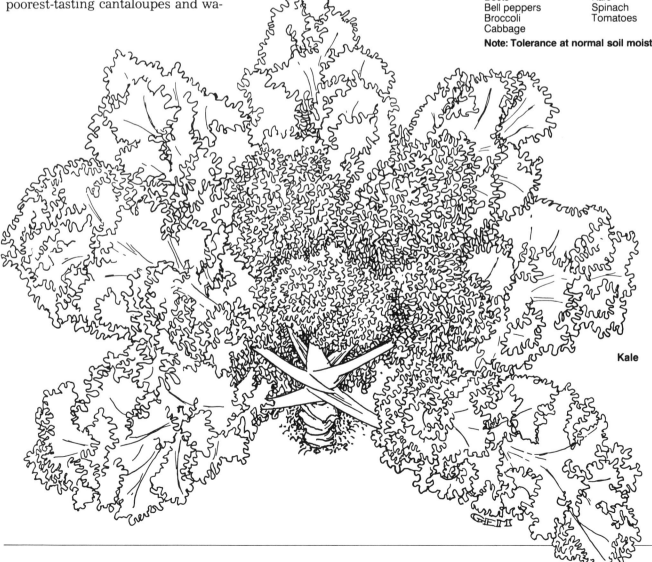

Kale

3
Matters of state — and what will grow

Cauliflower

GARDENING IN FLORIDA IS a new but wonderful experience. Twelve months of plantings and harvests await. After a brief orientation, you will be ready to plant the edible landscape.

Almost any crop imaginable can be cultivated somewhere within the state. For the most part the weather is warm and often humid — a subtropical-type climate with some moderating cool spells during the winter. In many areas, bananas flourish along with peaches, pears and tomatoes, but the dip in temperature also allows crops such as lettuce, turnips and cauliflower to grow.

The seasons seem long, and perhaps they are when compared to gardening in temperate climates. Cool-season vegetables grow from October to March in most areas of the state. Do realize that means two or three plantings of broccoli, months of lettuce and a radish crop every 25 days for six months. And there are two seasons for warm-weather plantings of vegetables, just to keep these crops on the table.

What is your favorite fruit? In Florida, most can be cultivated.

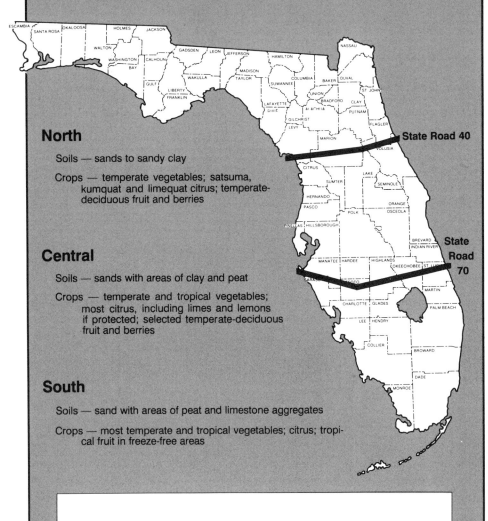

Florida facts

- Predominately sandy soils
- Temperate to tropical fruit and vegetables
- Heavy summer rains
- Dry periods fall through spring
- Saltwater intrusion in coastal areas

North

Soils — sands to sandy clay

Crops — temperate vegetables; satsuma, kumquat and limequat citrus; temperate-deciduous fruit and berries

Central

Soils — sands with areas of clay and peat

Crops — temperate and tropical vegetables; most citrus, including limes and lemons if protected; selected temperate-deciduous fruit and berries

South

Soils — sand with areas of peat and limestone aggregates

Crops — most temperate and tropical vegetables; citrus; tropical fruit in freeze-free areas

Tallahassee
Annual rainfall: 64.59 inches
Average first frost: Nov. 25
Average last frost: Feb. 28
Record high: 103°, June 1985
Record low: 6°, Jan. 1985

Jacksonville
Annual rainfall: 52.76 inches
Average first frost: Dec. 10
Average last frost: Feb. 18
Record high: 105°, July 1942
Record low: 7°, Jan. 1985

Orlando
Annual rainfall: 47.83 inches
Average first frost: Dec. 18
Average last frost: Feb. 15
Record high: 102°, May 1945
Record low: 19°, Jan. 1985

Miami
Annual rainfall: 57.55 inches
Frost: infrequent
Record high: 98°, June 1985
Record low: 30°, Jan. 1985

Grapes grow throughout the state, citrus, in most areas, and mangoes, in the consistently warm portions. No matter where you live there always is a good selection of fruit to be gathered from trees or bushes. It is possible to have fresh fruit almost every month of the year.

Florida offers non-stop gardening — a planter's paradise. When it's time to harvest one vegetable, another is popped into the ground. Avid gardeners take advantage of the year-round planting schedule, never allowing the soil to remain fallow for long.

The soil is a disappointment to many, but there are advantages to the mostly sandy planting sites. The fine, granular, non-adhering particles usually drain well and encourage far-reaching deep root systems. Nutrient levels in sand can be easily regulated. With scatterings of granules from the fertilizer bag, gardeners can promote or delay growth. Unless you overdo it, there is also little chance of too much watering.

The loose soils do present modern problems. Excessive moisture and nutrients that leach through the layers could pollute the water table below. One control is to carefully regulate the amount of water and fertilizer applied, adding just enough for the crop and not much extra.

Organic gardening techniques quickly will improve the Florida sands, just as they have helped the Northern clays. Adding organic matter gives water-holding ability to the soil and captures moisture for the crops. The organic matter also stores nutrients for the plants, so less fertilizer will be needed. Sand can be regulated and improved by mulching and growing cover crops.

What's neat about sands? For one thing, a gardener can make his own planting mix. There is reward in adding manures, grass clippings, compost and spoiled hay to the garden and seeing a rich earth develop. Many have taken pride in varying the ingredients to formulate that special soil.

Equally rewarding, however, is taking a large garden site and making the sandy land productive with only water and fertilizer. Many of the state's productive farmlands resemble beach sand.

If there is one bad feature of Florida farming, it must be the pests. The same insects and diseases known across the nation can be found in local landscapes, but often in greater numbers. Then there are the nematodes — little roundworms that live in the soil and knot plant roots.

It's not like every pest is out to get your crop, but you can expect some bugs to visit and feed. Take heart — many gardeners never have had to deal with devastating infestations. And if they do, it is a lesson learned about what to expect in the future.

Don't let the pests scare you from a great experience. First-time gardeners often do not see the pests people talk about. It is after constantly cropping the land that pest problems tend to build.

Good gardening techniques pay dividends in fewer plant pests. Try to rotate crops to another area of the yard. Build the soil up with organic matter, which stymies many insects, diseases and nematodes but encourages good bugs. Biological controls, handpicking and judicial use of pesticides give good pest relief if needed.

Florida varieties at first

Most Florida varieties of fruits and vegetables have been university-tested or proved effective producers by local growers. Much research has developed the best watermelons, grapes and papayas for home and commercial producers. Check extension service plant lists. For the first gardens, grow only what has been recommended.

Florida gardeners have attempted to grow most vegetables, berries and fruits at one time or another. Some have adapted better to the climate than others. Old favorites such as Delicious apples, Concord grapes and horseradish are likely to disappoint because they require a period of dormancy. If they struggle through without a chilly winter, they often fall prey to diseases and insects.

Varieties have been developed to thrive under regional conditions and to resist common pests. The list of varieties is expanding. In recent years, rhubarb, a seedless grape, several plums and blueberries have been added to the possibilities for most regions of the state.

Climate a guide to garden plantings

A first approach to the garden should include a survey of the local climate. A yearlong summary will set limitations for the crops that can be cultivated easily.

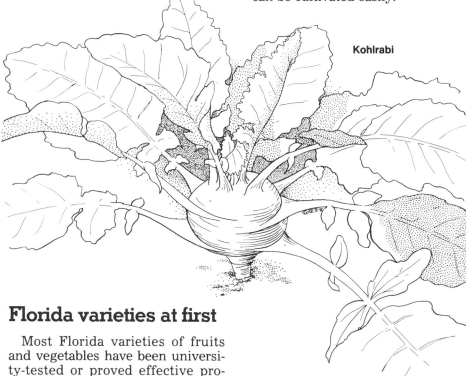
Kohlrabi

The state is a long one — about 900 miles from the Keys to the tip of the Panhandle. For planting purposes, Florida is divided into North, Central and Southern regions. Referring to these designations can help gardeners plan what to plant and know when what crops are likely to succeed.

During most years the temperatures in Tallahassee won't dip to the record low of 6 degrees set in 1985, but frost is just about certain. Find out when the first and last freezes can be expected in your growing area. These dates are averages that determine what crops can be planted when or what protection will be needed to extend the seasons.

In Orlando the fall tomato crop should be maturing by about Dec. 18. Consider any harvest after this date a bonus. Counting backward, this means the crop, which takes about 90 days for a reasonable harvest, will have to be planted during late summer. Planting guides help make these determinations, but the gardener must know when to expect a cold spell in order to be prepared to make a quick harvest or cover the crops.

Lucky are the residents who live in the most southern portions of the state — they seldom see a frost. Here is an area for the tropical plants that would be damaged by even a dip below 32 degrees. Even the record low for Miami is not too low — just 30 degrees. Tropicals are worth the risk. During cold weather, some quick covering of plant trunks or a little heat from irrigation sprinklers could save the crop.

Check when the last frost of the growing season can be expected. For Jacksonville it is about Feb. 18. This means spring crops should be planned for planting shortly after this date.

Another idea is to plant watermelons, cucumbers and other tender vegetables early, but be ready with buckets, baskets or cardboard coverings to serve as protection from late-season frosts and freezes. An early start may be worth the extra work when cold warnings are sounded because the plants will escape late-season pests or unfavorable growing conditions.

Although it may not seem ideal at first, having some cool to cold weather does have advantages. Deciduous fruit often needs the cool temperatures to break winter dormancy of flower and leaf buds, which begins spring growth. Peaches, apples, blueberries and pears are particularly sensitive to the amount of cold received. Even in North Florida, fruit varieties from more northern states may not grow properly. As plantings are made farther south in the state, select trees and bushes that grow without the winter cold. For some crops, including pears, plums and blueberries, there are no varieties for South Florida.

But don't worry — the tropicals that flourish in the southern portion of the state make up for the loss of more temperate-climate fruit. Mangoes, lychees, avocados, guavas and carambolas are just a few of the fruits South Floridians are sure to want to grow. Central Floridians may be able to squeeze in fruits from both the northern and southern areas during most years.

More regional particulars

■ SOUTH FLORIDA

Killing freezes are rare and most winters are frost-free in South Florida. Although the true tropics begin below the Keys, the climate is near-tropical. The soil is mainly sand, but some rockland and peat pockets exist.

Gardeners can grow lychee, jaboticaba, atemoya and Barbados cherry trees as well as the more familiar banana, citrus and pineapple.

Most vegetables are easy to grow in South Florida although a few, including asparagus, chard and rhubarb, require cool weather and seldom are successful.

Unusual crops familiar to this region include pigeon peas, chayotes and bitter melons.

■ CENTRAL FLORIDA

Stretching from near the Ocala National Forest southward to just above Lake Okeechobee, Central Florida combines qualities of tem-

Florida chilling hours

North — 350 to 650 hours   Central — 150-350 hours   South — 50-150 hours

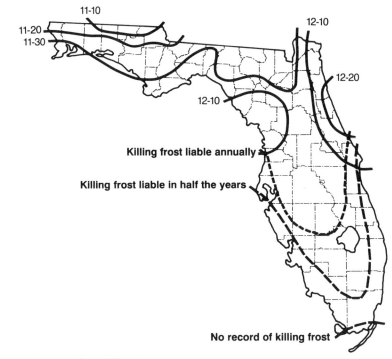

Average dates of first killing frost.

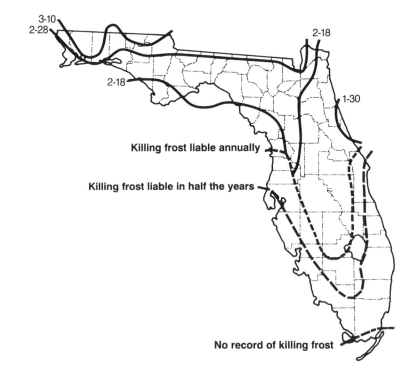

Average dates of last killing spring frost.

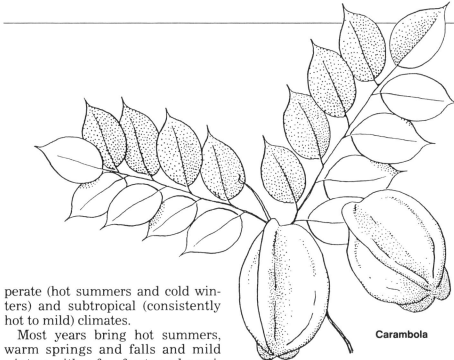
Carambola

perate (hot summers and cold winters) and subtropical (consistently hot to mild) climates.

Most years bring hot summers, warm springs and falls and mild winters with a few frosts and possible light freezes. Sandy soils predominate, but some garden sites are composed of peat or clay.

With careful selection of varieties, peaches, apples and pears can produce abundant harvests. Except for lemons and limes, citrus is a major crop, especially for the middle to southern portions of Central Florida.

Avocados, carambolas, pineapples, surinam cherries and papayas bear well after mild winters in many areas.

Almost all vegetables including tropical varieties can be cultivated.

■ NORTH FLORIDA

Winters with killing frosts and freezes are expected in North Florida, while summers can be as hot or hotter than the remaining portions of the state. Many years, severe weather fronts moving south appear to stall out in North Florida. In this region, seasonal changes are much more noticeable as leaves change color and eventually drop.

Soils typically are sand with some sandy clays. Deciduous fruits of peach, apple and pear flourish, although winters are too short to encourage plantings of cherries and walnuts. A few hardy citrus such as satsuma and kumquat survive, but the climate is too cold for other tropicals.

All temperate vegetables enjoy the long spring and fall growing seasons of moderate temperatures.

Rainy weather

Annual rainfall varies between 50 and 60 inches for most of the state. Much arrives during the summer, a period frequently termed the rainy season. From June through early September, monthly downpours can measure 10 or more inches. This often makes gardening a hot, sticky business. Flooding in low areas complicates the task, and the increasing humidity also encourages plant pests.

Many vegetable gardeners take a rest during the summer because of the heat, rains and pest problems. However, summer is a good time for experimenting with the crops that like these growing conditions. Tropicals flourish in the water and heat, having adapted to the insects and diseases. Other more familiar crops, including okra, sweet potatoes, cherry tomatoes and Southern peas, also are planted.

Rainfall drops drastically through spring. Often 2 inches or less accumulate each month. When the rain does arrive it is frequently a once- or twice-a-month downpour. In between storms, gardeners will have to plan for irrigation.

Spring typically is the driest season. Lengthening days and warming temperatures often accompanied by winds quickly deplete soil of moisture. When the weather is hot and dry, new plantings will need daily watering. Established gardens can exist for three to four days and trees or shrubs a week or more without irrigation.

During periods of lower rainfall, water-use restrictions often are mandated by the state's water management districts. Gardeners will be advised via the mass media when landscapes can be irrigated.

Conservation measures of mulching, drip irrigation and watering during the early morning hours will help reduce utility bills and conserve this natural resource.

Planting schedules

Florida planting schedules may take a little reorientation for gardeners from other regions. Crops are planted year-round, but the timing often is different from other areas of the country.

First-time as well as experienced planters will notice one of the nicest features of Florida gardening is the many vegetables and herbs that can be cropped more than once a year. Often they can be repeated another season or several times during the same season.

Quite often temperature is a major reason for sowing a crop at a particular time of the year. Some vegetables and herbs need a uniform, warm period to produce a harvest; others like it either hot or cold.

Time tomatoes for spring and fall plantings in North and Central regions, and one long period of fall through spring in the South. Corn must be carefully timed so the harvest is complete before the frost of winter or the pests of summer.

In Central Florida the spring plantings typically begin in February and fall plantings are made in August. On the other hand, okra needs the heat and can resist the summertime pests. In most areas okra is planted when the weather warms in spring and into the summer.

Arrival of the rainy season also can spoil the crop. Schedules often time watermelons and cantaloupes to completion before frequent showers begin. Tropicals malanga and dasheen need both the water and heat of a spring-summer growing season to produce their crops.

Pest problems often can be avoided by sticking to a time-tested schedule. As the hotter weather returns, so do many leaf spots and chewing insects. It's almost impossible to eliminate such persistent plant problems with pesticides. Careful timing helps the garden mature before the pests return.

Use planting schedules as a guide. The dates can be moved a little and crops planted somewhat earlier or later. Push spring planting dates into the cooler months if you are ready with frost protection. Alternatively, sow some cool-season crops during the hotter months but expect reduced production. Don't be afraid to experiment a little, especially with new varieties that may be a little more heat- or cold-tolerant.

Hop into gardening at any time of the year. If there is a most ideal time, for vegetables it's normally at the beginning of fall plantings. Summer is about over and the soil can be prepared for more than nine months of ideal planting time for the most familiar crops.

Summer is the season for growing a few tropicals, as well as preparing for future plantings. By midsummer, spring crops have finished growing and it's time to sow seeds of tomato, peppers and eggplant for fall transplants. Summer also is the best time to bake nematodes out of the soil with solarization techniques or to till the garden and fumigate. Every vegetable garden should be ready around the middle of August for fall crops that need an early start.

Anytime is ideal to add a tree, shrub, vine or other perennial to the landscape if it has been grown in a container. With water and consistently good care during the first few months, the new additions often grow vigorously and will yield a harvest before you know it.

The cool seasons are the best time for bare-root plantings dug from a friend's yard or bought at the garden center.

Right after the Christmas season, pecans, peaches, figs, apples, pears and others begin arriving from the nurseries for home planting. Get these plants fresh and waste no time adding them to the landscape. Keep the soil moist and the transplant should be successful.

Selecting a Florida home site is just the beginning of an edible landscape. Gardeners must become familiar with the climate, soils and varieties to be successful. Get ready to farm the four seasons to enjoy Florida gardening at its best.

Vegetables by season

Cool season (Late fall, winter)	Warm season (Early fall, spring)	Summer
Beets	Beans, snap	Boniato
Broccoli	Beans, pole	Calabaza
Cabbage	Beans, lima	Dasheen
Carrots	Cantaloupes	Okra
Cauliflower	Corn, sweet	Peas, Southern
Celery	Cucumbers	Potatoes, sweet
Chinese cabbage	Eggplant	Pumpkins
Collards	Okra	Roselle
Endive-escarole	Peas, Southern	Sweet cassava
Kale	Peppers, sweet	Tomatoes, cherry
Kohlrabi	Potatoes, sweet	Yard-long beans
Lettuce	Pumpkins	Yautia
Mustard	Squash, summer	
Onions	Squash, winter	
Parsley	Tomatoes	
Peas, English	Watermelons	
Potatoes		
Radishes		
Spinach		
Strawberries		
Turnips		

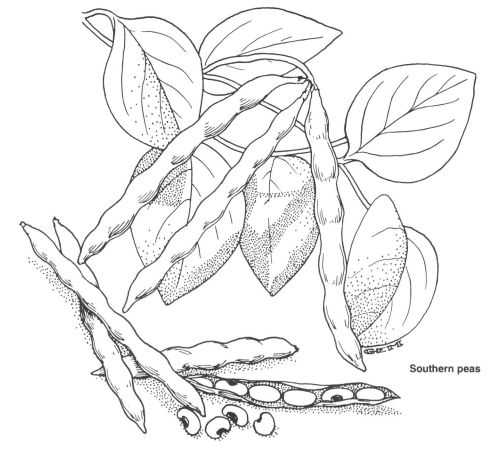

Southern peas

Fall garden

Staked tomatoes
Trellised snap beans
Summer squash
Sweet peppers
Cucumbers
Southern peas
Onion sets
Carrots
Sweet corn
Parsley

10 feet
20 feet

Winter garden

Trellised English peas
Broccoli
Butterhead lettuce
Mustard
Kale
Onion sets
Beets
Bulbing onions
Cauliflower
Leaf lettuce
Cabbage
Celery
Carrots
Collards
Crisp lettuce
Turnips
Radishes
Parsley

Spring garden

Trellised cucumbers
Tomatoes
Eggplant
Potatoes (planted in February)
Summer squash
Bulbing onions
Sweet peppers
Corn
Lima beans
Okra
Snap beans
Parsley

Summer garden

Trellised cherry tomatoes
Staked tomatoes from spring
Southern peas
Trellised yard-long beans
Sweet potatoes
Trellised Malabar spinach
Okra
Calabaza

Fall vegetables plantings begin the gardening year. Start in August and continue through September by planting the warm-season crops, which include tomatoes, beans, cucumbers and corn. Closely spaced rows and intensive culture techniques of double cropping and trellising make maximum use of space. When only a few plants are needed for harvest, plant portions of a row.

4
Starting from the ground up

Passion fruit

EDIBLE LANDSCAPES BEGIN with good soil preparation. Roots make up a major portion of the plant, living below the ground and absorbing water and nutrients needed for growth. The soil environment must be well-aerated, hold moisture and contain beneficial organisms to be considered healthy and satisfactory for plant growth.

Tilling the planting site is the first step in preparing a new garden. Loosen the earth and get the feel of what will support the crops to be cultivated. For many fruits, vegetables and berries, this will be your only opportunity to have a major influence on the environment where roots will grow for months or even years. Give plants the very best start with soil improvements that will make it easier to produce a harvest later.

Excluding the organic matter, soil primarily consists of small particles ranging in size from very coarse sand — the largest component — to finer sands, silt and clay — the smallest. The smaller the particle, the more moisture retained in the planting site and the larger quantity of nutrients held for root absorption.

Most gardens are planted in sand. Such soils are easy to dig, drain rapidly and give plants good support. But that is where the benefits end. Sands also are easy places for pests to thrive in because they are porous, almost devoid of nutrients and frequently dry.

Where soils are mainly sand, only a minimal water- and nutrient-holding ability exists. A typically moistened sand holds about half an inch of water in the upper 6 inches of soil, which is where a major portion of the root system grows.

During hot, windy weather this is enough moisture for about two days of growth. Plenty of water and fertilizer can make sands productive, but it is labor intensive and often expensive soil to farm.

Newly worked, sandy planting sites often can be considered almost sterile, with few major nutrients detectable through soil tests. One way to improve the soil is to add the smaller components of silt or clay. However, few gardeners are happy about hauling in and then mixing these heavy soil components into sandy soil.

In an effort to improve their plots, some gardeners order loads of topsoil but are shocked to find the trucks arriving with more sand. In many gardens, organic matter was scraped away or buried by bulldozers. But in Florida, even virgin lands have little topsoil, certainly not the rich clay or loam found on Northern farms and gardens.

The most common method for improving sandy soils is to add plenty of organic matter. Sources are readily available and often free for the hauling. Compost, leaves, stable manure and bedding, along with other organic residues will help tighten a loose, sandy soil and increase its moisture-holding capacity. Nutrients also are held by the particles of organic matter, which act as reservoirs of fertilizer to nourish growing plants.

Organic matter also encourages the growth of a multitude of beneficial insects, fungi and bacteria. Many seek out plant-threatening insects, diseases and nematodes. Others are involved with the breakdown of organic residues and release of nutrients to the plants.

A healthy soil improved with organic matter is alive with organisms that help plants grow, including bacteria that take nitrogen from the air and feed it to the legume-type crops. This means less fertilizer is needed to produce the crop. Also, don't forget earthworms, beneficial beetles and other insects that play important roles in building loose, well-aerated soil.

A good soil is filled with spaces that hold both air and moisture. Squeeze a handful. It should fall apart when lightly touched. An aqueous solution of water and nutrients flows from the soil through the roots to the stems and up the plant, supplying the basic components needed for growth.

Air is important because it supplies roots with oxygen needed for respiration, the burning of foods that drives the growth process within the cells. If the soil is kept saturated with water, the air is excluded and plant growth quickly ceases.

In search of the proper pH

One unseen factor in every soil is the acidity. Scientifically measured as the soil pH, acidity regulates nutrient availability and microbial activity. Crops growing at the improper pH often are chlorotic, less vigorous and non-productive.

Start the gardening year with a pH test. Acidity is recorded on a scale of 0 to 14. A pH of 7 is neutral. All readings below 7 are acid and all above, alkaline.

pH values for common substances

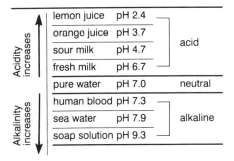

Acidity increases ↑	lemon juice	pH 2.4	acid
	orange juice	pH 3.7	
	sour milk	pH 4.7	
	fresh milk	pH 6.7	
	pure water	pH 7.0	neutral
Alkalinity increases ↓	human blood	pH 7.3	alkaline
	sea water	pH 7.9	
	soap solution	pH 9.3	

The pH of soils in Florida varies widely, so tests are necessary to determine the acidity of a particular garden spot. In many areas of the nation, lime routinely is added to the garden each year to sweeten — or make less acidic — the soil.

Most crops grow best when the soil pH is about 6.5 but will be productive in soils with pH ranges of 5 to 7. Blueberries are an exception, requiring an acid soil in the 4.5 to 5.2 range, and potatoes escape the disease scab when the pH is below 6.0.

For a soil test, gather samples from representative areas of the yard and garden, scooping soil from the surface to a 6-inch depth, then mixing together. A few scoops are adequate. Tests are performed at garden centers and through the county cooperative extension service.

Results may include a recommendation to add lime to raise a very acid pH to the slightly acid condition needed by most plants. Dolomitic lime or agricultural lime are suggested for use in gardens. These are ground limestone — slow-acting but effective in changing pH. They contain calcium carbonate; dolomitic lime also has magnesium carbonate. Both calcium and magnesium are necessary to healthy plants. Avoid hydrated, burnt or pickling limes, which react rapidly in the soil and can burn plant roots.

Alkaline soil with a pH above 7.5 may require sulfur, usually applied at a rate of a pound for each 100 square feet of planting area. Wetting, dusting and agricultural sulfurs are available from garden centers.

Treatments to alter soil pH are scattered over the garden and either worked or washed into the ground. It is best to till lime or sulfur into the soil several weeks before planting. If necessary, however, planting can begin the day applications are made. Changes in pH begin when the soil is wet. Test the soil again in a few months to gauge the extent of the change. Once the pH is satisfactory, a yearly test is sufficient.

Some soils resist change. If one or two applications of lime or sulfur do not change the pH, no more should be added. Organic soils often remain quite acid and lime rocks, alkaline. In these soils, pay special attention to minor nutrients — also called trace elements — such as iron, manganese and zinc. These nutrients can be applied separately or as part of a combination fertilizer product.

Dig in — with a dose of compost

Vegetable gardens should be dug to a depth of 4 to 6 inches. Traditional deep tilling is unnecessary. Because roots penetrate sand readily, a mixing of the upper layer is all that is needed to prepare the soil.

Additions of organic matter greatly improve sandy soil. Decomposing leaves, old hay and sawdust supply nutrients to plants and improve the soil's water-holding abilities.

Many gardeners like to make compost, well-decomposed organic matter ready to release nutrients when added to the soil. In sandy soil there can never be too much organic matter.

Plant trimmings, grass clippings, orange peels and vegetable scraps all can be heaped in a pile and left to decompose. Enthusiasts scour

Techniques for making compost

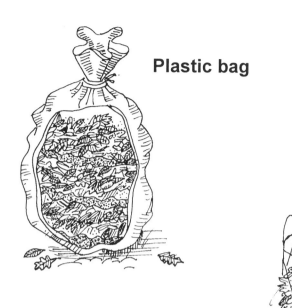

Plastic bag

Circular wire cage

Side-by-side bins

Attached bins make turning the pile an easier job. Left bin contains beginnings of compost; compost in right bin is almost ready to use.

Refuse
Soil and fertilizer
Refuse
Soil and fertilizer
Refuse

In-the-bag compost

Container: Large, sturdy plastic bag.
Organic matter: Materials that rot easily such as grass clippings, chopped leaves and plants.
Additional ingredients: 6-6-6 fertilizer, soil, 1 to 2 quarts water.

Pile organic material in the bag in 4- to 6-inch layers separated by light scatterings of soil and fertilizer. Add 2 quarts water if material is dry, less if it is moist. Tie the bag at the top and let sit. Every week or 10 days, turn the bag to mix the contents and speed composting.

Ready to use in four to six weeks.

Standard pile

Container: Open ground, wire cage, wood or concrete-block bin.
Organic matter: Leaves, grass clippings, small branches, kitchen scraps, straw or old hay.
Additional ingredients: 6-6-6 fertilizer, soil, dolomitic lime, water.

In piles or bins about 10-feet square, alternate 1-foot layers of organic material with 1-inch layers of soil and a scattering of fertilizer. A pound of lime may be added over each 100-square-foot layer for a non-acid compost. Repeat until the pile is 3 to 5 feet high.

After three or four weeks, turn the pile, mixing all ingredients. Ready to use in about another month.

Some gardeners keep two or more bins with compost in varying stages of decomposition.

Manure compost

Container: Open ground, wire cage, wood or concrete-block bin.
Organic matter: Leaves, grass clippings, small branches, kitchen scraps, straw or old hay.
Additional ingredients: Manure, superphosphate, dolomitic lime.

Make 1-foot-deep layers of organic material and cover with 4- to 6-inch layers of manure. Moisten thoroughly. Scatter 3 pounds of superphosphate and 1 pound of lime over each 100-square-foot layer. Continue layering until pile is 3 to 4 feet high. Turn the pile in three or four weeks.

Ready to use one month later.

Dry leaf compost

Container: Open ground, wire cage, wood or concrete-block bin.
Organic matter: Dry leaves — oak, maple, ash, elm or hickory.
Additional ingredients: Mineral mix of 4 pounds ammonium sulfate, 1 1/2 pounds superphosphate, 1 pound muriate of potash, 3 1/2 pounds limestone; soil; water.

Pile dry leaves 6 inches deep. Add a 2-inch layer of soil. For a pile about 10-feet square, scatter 1 quart of mineral mix over the surface and moisten the layer. Build to a height of 2 or 3 feet. Turn periodically.

Ready to use in three or four months.

neighborhoods for bagged leaves to add to their compost piles; inoculate the compost materials with microorganism-rich soil; and add nutrients to keep the fungi and bacteria working.

The simplest compost pile is a stack of organic matter gathered and allowed to decompose naturally. In Florida, the organic matter rots quickly and can become useful compost in about six months.

Speed the process by adding fertilizer and soil to the pile, keeping it moist and turning it occasionally. Compost piles usually are left uncovered with the tops slightly concave to hold extra water. Avoid keeping the pile sopping wet, however, because without space for air, decomposition slows down.

Mixing the pile helps decomposition and also discourages unwelcome animal visitors such as roaches and pill bugs, rodents or even a garden snake. Be sure to keep grease, meat scraps and bones out of the compost.

A compost pile can be enclosed with blocks, boards, wire or old bed springs. It can be made in a hole in the ground or in a strong plastic bag. Gardeners often keep two piles going, one in the making and the other ready to use.

In addition to being a soil enrichment, compost also can be used as mulch. A 3-inch layer at the base of trees, shrubs and plants conserves moisture as it breaks down into soil. When used in potting mixes, compost encourages good drainage, holds moisture and keeps the mix light. Equal parts of weed-free compost, soil and perlite make a good mix for outdoor planters, pots or container gardens.

Other soil types

Not all Florida gardens grow in sand. Soils may include chunky rocks, organic matter, clays and loamy sands. In terms of watering and fertilizing, treatments may differ. Rock soils, found especially south of Miami to Homestead, are well-drained and hold little in the way of nutrients. Treat like sands.

Organic peat soils need less attention. They often surround lakes or wetlands, may be wet themselves, and rarely need irrigation. Soil pH, which often is low, should not be adjusted with lime. These soils typically are naturally high in nitrogen and may hold nutrients from previous crops, so fertilizer should add little nitrogen.

Clays and sandy loams retain water and nutrients. Water and fertilize less frequently than sands. Like most soils, they benefit from the addition of organic matter.

Nutrients from manures

Although compost improves soil structure and adds nutrients, it is not always available in quantity, so additional nutrients often are needed. Manures are one good source. Different kinds supply varying amounts of usable fertilizer. In general, poultry manure is high in nutrients; cow, horse and pig are lower. The manure nutrient table gives nutrient values of manures plus recommended amounts to incorporate with garden or orchard soil before planting.

Manures often are low in available phosphorus. Superphosphate, rock phosphate or bone meal may be added as manure is dug in. Use 2 to 3 pounds for cow, horse and pig manure, or 1 to 2 pounds for poultry or sheep manure, for each 100 square feet of garden.

A layer of manure also can be

Nutrient values of common compost materials

Material	Percent nitrogen	Percent phosphorus	Percent potassium
Banana skins	—	3.25	41.76
Cantaloupe rinds	—	9.77	12.21
Castor bean pomace	5.00	2.00	1.00
Cattail reeds	2.00	.81	3.43
Coffee grounds	2.08	.32	.28
Corncobs	—	—	50.00
Corn stalks and leaves	.30	.13	.33
Crabgrass, green	.66	.19	.71
Eggs, rotten	2.25	.40	.15
Feathers	15.30	—	—
Fish scraps	2.0-7.50	1.5-6.0	—
Grapefruit skins	—	3.58	30.60
Oak leaves	.80	.35	.15
Orange culls	.20	.13	.21
Pine needles	.46	.12	.03
Ragweed	.76	.26	—
Tea grounds	4.15	.62	.40
Wood ashes	—	1.00	4.0-10.00

Nutrient values of manures

Type	Percent nitrogen	Percent phosphorus	Percent potassium	Pounds per 100 square feet
Cow	.55	.15	.50	25
Duck	1.10	1.45	.50	12
Goose	1.10	.55	.50	12
Hen	1.10	.90	.50	12
Hog	.55	.30	.45	25
Horse	.65	.25	.50	25
Sheep	1.00	.75	.40	12
Steer or feed yard	.60	.35	.55	25
Turkey	1.30	.70	.50	12

The numbers of a fertilizer analysis indicate the percentage of, in order, nitrogen, phosphorus and potassium. In a 6-6-6 formulation the numbers can be added together for a total of 18% nutrients in the bag or 18 pounds in a 100-pound bag. Minor nutrients that might include iron, boron, zinc and manganese often are added with the fertilizer.

spread under trees and shrubs or along vegetable rows to feed developing crops. As a side dressing in a vegetable garden, for instance, spread 5 pounds of cow, horse or pig manure or 3 pounds of poultry or sheep manure along 100 feet of row. Apply three or four weeks after planting.

Other fertilizers

Most growers add chemical fertilizers to the garden before planting and apply supplemental feedings throughout the season. Sandy, rock and clay soils need a balanced fertilizer that supplies equal portions of the major nutrients nitrogen, phosphorus and potassium. Organic soils contain nitrogen and need only phosphorus and potassium. The following are recommendations for fertilizer to be incorporated into a prepared planting site:

- Sand, rock or clay soil: 2

Plant food content of natural and organic fertilizer materials

Material	Percent nitrogen	Percent phosphorous	Percent potassium	Availability	Acidity
Basic slag	—	8.0	—	quick	alkaline
Bone meal, raw	3.5	22.0	—	slow	alkaline
Castor pomace	6.0	1.2	0.5	slow	acid
Cocoa shell meal	2.5	1.0	2.5	slow	neutral
Compost	1.5-3.5	0.5-1.0	1.0-2.0	moderate	acid
Cottonseed meal	6.0	2.5	1.5	slow	acid
Dried blood	12.0	1.5	0.8	moderately slow	acid
Fish emulsion	5.0	1.0	1.0	moderate	acid
Fish meal	10.0	4.0	0	slow	acid
Fish scrap	5.0	3.0	0	slow	acid
Greensand	—	1.0	6.0	very slow	—
Ground rock phosphate	—	33.0	—	very slow	alkaline
Guano, bat	10.0	4.0	2.0	moderate	acid
Guano, Peru	13.0	8.0	2.0	moderate	acid
Horn and hoof meal	12.0	2.0	—	—	—
Milorganite	6.0	2.0	—	—	—
Peat and muck	1.5-3.0	0.25-0.5	0.5-1.0	very slow	acid
Seaweed	1.0	—	4.0-10.0	slow	—
Sewage sludge	2.0-6.0	1.0-2.5	0.0-0.4	slow	acid
Soybean meal	7.0	1.2	1.5	slow	very slightly acid
Tankage, animal	9.0	10.0	15.5	slow	acid
Tankage, garbage	2.5	1.5	1.5	very slow	alkaline
Tobacco stems	1.5	0.5	5.0	slow	alkaline
Urea	45.0	—	—	quick	acid
Wood ashes	—	2.0	4.0-10.0	quick	alkaline

Note: Urea is an organic compound, but because it is synthetic, it is unlikely most organic gardeners would consider it acceptable.

pounds of 6-6-6 or 1 pound of 12-12-12 per 100 square feet.

• Organic soils: 1 pound of 0-12-20 per 100 square feet.

Supplemental feedings depend on crop and soil type. The vigor and color of the crop should help determine nutrient needs: If vegetables start to turn pale green, fertilize.

In general, gardens in sandy soils should be fed every three or four weeks. Crops grown in soils high in organic matter or clay may need additional feedings at four- to six-week intervals.

Some crops get nutritional help from soil bacteria. Bean roots, for example, grow in association with rhizobium, which take nitrogen from the air. As a result, the plants need less in the way of supplemental feeding. These bacteria are plentiful in Florida soils and seed inoculation, usually performed in the North, is not needed. Bacterial growths appear as easy-to-detach, small, yellowish-brown balls along the roots and should not be confused with nematode enlargements of the roots.

Nematodes: No. 1 pest

Nematodes are a major pest problem. The microscopic roundworms invade root tissue and cause galls, or knots, to form. The roots swell and lose their ability to remove water and nutrients from the soil. The expanding root system often is stunted and the plant begins to decline.

Symptoms of nematode damage mimic nutrient and water deficiencies. Leaves turn yellow, and plants become stunted and susceptible to disease. Gardeners can dig around vegetables, trees and shrubs to check root for evidence of root knot nematodes.

Other nematodes affect crops, but the root-knot nematode is by far the most common. Most treatments for nematodes have to be performed before planting — once the crops are in the ground there is very little a gardener can do. Sometimes extra attention to the plant's cultural needs can help reduce the affect of the pests.

Check the planting site before tilling a vegetable garden: The roots of remaining crops or weeds may indicate infestations. Large swollen roots of okra or small balls on the root growth of carrots indicate the presence of nematodes.

Trees, shrubs and vines all are vulnerable. Figs and papayas become severely dwarfed with few controls available. Some plants including peaches can be grafted onto nematode-resistant roots. A few varieties developed for Florida have built-in nematode resistance — it's best to check before you plant.

Presently all fumigants previously labeled for use in the garden are no longer available or are restricted in their use to professionals only. This leaves gardeners with mainly cultural techniques to help control the root damaging roundworms.

Just good soil preparation can help slow the nematode activity. Adding lots of organic matter to the garden prior to planting can help increase beneficial organisms that affect the harmful nematodes. These alone cannot be counted on for total control.

Some companies also offer natural organic products that affect nematode survival in the soil. University tests are not conclusive but you may want to give the products a try following label recommendations.

Gardeners can help reduce nematodes in the soil through the use of soil solarization. This technique heats the soil to temperatures above the survival level for nematodes. Normally only the upper 4 to 6 inches of soil are affected, so do not disturb the soil after the treatment is completed and plant immediately.

A few other techniques may help.

Root-knot nematode damage on roots

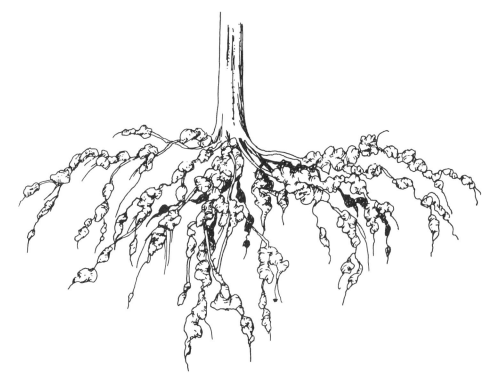

Swollen roots are a sure sign nematodes are affecting crop performance. The knotted roots reduce water and nutrient uptake. Plants are likely to wilt; leaves yellow and decline.

Nematode control before you plant

Nematodes, the villains of the vegetable patch, are getting the hotfoot treatment from backyard farmers. These farmers are using solar power to bake nematodes and other garden pests out of the soil.

Microscopic nematodes cannot be seen by the unaided eye, but gardeners can easily detect the damage. At first the plants appear in need of fertilizer and may show signs of wilt, but the real damage is observed when roots are checked. Affected vegetable roots are abnormally swollen, often twisted and gnarled by the root knot nematode. The crippled root systems are unable to absorb water and nutrients needed for growth and production, and the plants often become dwarfed and non-productive.

Soil solarization is a worthy alternative to chemical treatment. The best time of the year to employ this technique is the summer. First rake and till the soil until the earth is smooth, without clods or root fragments. Water it well, because moisture will help conduct the heat deep into the ground. Cover the garden area with a clear plastic tarpaulin and seal the edges into the earth with soil.

The benefits of soil solarization can only be obtained by careful maintenance of the plastic. Use clear polyethylene that lets the sun through to strike the moist soil and heat the earth. Black plastic becomes hot above the soil and does not work as well. The entire garden area, including paths, should be covered. Keep the plastic in place until the garden is ready to plant.

If the cover is left undisturbed four weeks or more, temperatures in the soil will reach more than 120 degrees to a depth of about a foot. When the soil gets that hot for that long, the nematodes die.

Sometimes when the planting season is fast approaching, gardeners don't have time to utilize solarization techniques. Also, the weather may be too cool to heat the soil up to the high temperatures needed to control pests. Don't worry; there are still some nematode controls available.

A chemical nematicide may be available for home landscape use. Many can only be used for agricultural purposes and some require permits to apply in landscapes. Check with your extension service for the most recent list of synthetic and natural chemicals for nematode control by gardeners.

Another control possibly best used with small plantings is replacing the nematode infested soil. Adding fresh compost or potting soil to the root zone where you would like to grow a few squash or pittosporum would give the plants a fresh nematode-free start.

With plants that are extra sensitive to nematodes including impatiens and coleus, sink the plants, pot and all, in the garden. Also, wherever possible select nematode resistant varieties for yards and gardens.

One is crop rotation where susceptible plantings are alternated with plantings that do not have a major nematode problem or are not affected by the same nematodes. Regretfully, this is difficult for people who have small gardens. Often these smaller planters have to resort to replacing some or all the soil in the planting site to produce the susceptible crops.

Perhaps it's just an observation, but nematode activity appears to be less aggressive during the cooler months. The cool season crops usually give some production even in infested soils. Enjoying the benefits of fall through spring plantings may make you successful even in problem soils.

Certain plants may help control nematodes. Solid beds of French marigolds, hairy indigo, crotolaria and some varieties of Southern peas have been somewhat effective.

These plants often are referred to as trap crops. They cause the nematodes to hatch, but because they are not host plants, the roundworms starve. Best test results have been with hairy indigo grown as a cover crop during the summer.

The garden must be planted entirely to the one crop, and weeds, which could harbor nematodes, must be eliminated. Planting of a trap crop followed by soil solarization gives an extra measure of nematode control.

Gardeners who plant only one or two seasons traditionally sow a cover crop to keep nutrients from washing out of the soil. Cover crops take up the nutrients as they grow. As they near maturity, plants are mowed and plowed under as green manure. Decomposition releases nutrients stored in the plants.

Choose a cover crop wisely so as not to increase nematode populations. Ryegrass will cover the garden quickly in cool seasons. For the hot season, use legumes such as hairy indigo, or Southern pea varieties Iron or Clay. These legumes not only resist nematodes but also can cause a decrease in populations. They also add organic matter and store nitrogen for future crop use.

5
Seed savvy for starting transplants

STARTING FROM SEEDS IS A dollar-saving, fun way to begin the edible landscape. Most vegetables, herbs and a few tropical plants can be sown in containers or directly in the ground to begin the next planting. You control what varieties will grow, selecting the very best for flavor, yield and pest resistance.

Radicchio

Begin the edible landscape using the most basic of horticultural skills. Whether it is a broccoli plant or a papaya tree, it is exciting to carry a germinated seed to the transplant stage then on to production.

Transplants from the nursery provide a quick start for the garden, but the varietal selection is often limited. One section of seedlings simply may be marked "cabbage," rather than Gourmet, Marion Market or King Cole — varieties recommended for Florida.

Gardeners in search of fancy herbs, unusual vegetables and tropical fruit often must start these plantings from seeds because transplants rarely are offered for sale. Seeds are fun and easy to sow. Most produce transplants in four to six weeks.

Garden centers are a good source of fresh seeds, but mail-order companies typically offer a more extensive selection. Seeds also can be found at some grocery and hardware stores. Seeds should be packaged and tested for the current or upcoming year.

In Florida, seed racks are replenished with fresh seeds at least once a year, typically during the summer. These seed packets will be marked for planting the following year. This just means the seed is extra fresh. Good germination should be assured if the packets have been kept dry and at normal room temperatures.

It is not important to find locally grown seed; depending on the crop, conditions for growing many seeds are better in the western United States or abroad.

It is important, however, to choose at least some varieties that have been tested and are recommended by the Institute of Food and Agricultural Sciences at the University of Florida for growing in the state. These often demonstrate extra vigor, improved pest resistance and are likely to do well.

Soil matters

Fresh seeds are full of vigor, ready to germinate in a warm, moist growing medium. However, germinating seeds are vulnerable to many pests, the worst of which are fungal rots that attack tender roots and shoots. These rots cause a condition called damping off, which can prevent seedlings from emerging or enable them to grow only a few inches tall, then wither and die. Soil gathered from the yard is likely to contain organisms that cause damping off, as well as weeds, insects and nematodes.

Garden soil can be used if it is first sterilized. To sterilize, wet the soil then spread it in a shallow pan and bake for 30 minutes at 160 degrees Fahrenheit. Place a small pan of water in the oven to prevent organic matter in the soil from drying. Allow the soil to cool before planting in it. Although this process is relatively inexpensive, the baking soil smells terrible, and most gardeners opt for seeding in a soilless mix.

Soilless seedling mixtures can be bought at garden centers or from mail-order companies, but the mixes are easy to make at home. Main ingredients are sphagnum peat moss and vermiculite; dolomitic lime often is used to adjust the pH. Fertilizer either can be added to the mix or applied after the seedlings sprout.

Mix 1

2 quarts sphagnum peat moss
2 quarts horticultural vermiculite
½ tablespoon dolomitic lime

Begin fertilizing plants immediately after germination.
Formula makes enough mix to fill half a flat or three 6-inch pots.

Mix 2

1 bushel sphagnum peat moss
1 bushel horticultural vermiculite
1 cup dolomitic lime
1 cup 6-6-6 with minor nutrients

Thoroughly mix all ingredients. Store extra mix in a clean trash can or plastic bag. Avoid contaminating the mix with other soils or dirty pots.
Formula makes enough mix to fill eight flats or 45 6-inch pots.

How to sow

Plant seeds in shallow containers. Young plants need little room, and an inch or two for roots is ample during the first few weeks of growth. Innovative gardeners make seeding trays from egg cartons, cottage cheese containers, and fast-food salad, burger and hot dog packaging.

Containers must provide for drainage; egg cartons need only a quarter-inch hole per section, but a cottage cheese container will need several holes. A fast-food salad tray makes a good miniature greenhouse, with the bottom used for seeding and the clear top used to retain moisture. Both top and bottom will need a few holes. Soft materials can be punctured with a knife, while brittle containers may need to be drilled against a block of wood.

Recycled pots, market packs and seeding flats also can be used but first should be cleaned of loose soil and potential pests. Soak previous-

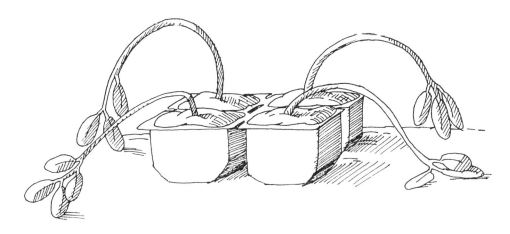

Damping off is a condition that causes seedlings to rot at the base. It is prompted by using infected soils, keeping seedlings too wet or providing poor air circulation. Correct growing conditions. Treat with a fungicide spray labeled for vegetable seedling rots.

ly used clay and plastic containers for 10 minutes in a solution of one part laundry bleach to 10 parts water, then brush clean. Wear gloves while working with the bleach solution and allow containers to dry before using.

Fill containers with planting mix to within half an inch from the top to allow space for watering; wet thoroughly.

Before sowing, determine how many transplants are needed. Germination is usually 80 to 90 percent. Where only a few plants are needed, count out and sow one or two seeds to a small pot, section in a market pack or cell in an egg carton to save time needed for transplanting later. Plants should be ready to move to the garden four to six weeks after germination.

If many seedlings are needed, sow a whole tray or large pot with one variety. Space seeds to give each ample room to grow. While moving the seed packet across the surface, watch the seeds drop; even-handed sowing makes for easier transplanting in a few weeks.

Cover large seeds with growing medium to a depth equal to that of their thickness. For seeds the size of sand grains or smaller, simply scatter over the growing medium and gently water.

Moisture triggers germination, but light also is needed by some crops. The seed packet should outline specific cultural requirements.

Where light is not a factor, hold in moisture by covering the container with another pot or tray, a sheet of damp newspaper, a pane of glass or a plastic bag. If the covering is transparent, keep trays out of direct sun or the seeds will bake.

Seeds germinate rapidly in warm locations. A south-facing window with good ventilation, a warm kitchen, a greenhouse or any bright spot where temperatures remain between 60 and 80 degrees is ideal.

During winter when night temperatures can drop dramatically, containers can be set over heating cables, which are available from garden centers and mail-order nurseries for about $10. The thermostatically controlled cables keep soil temperatures at 70 to 75 degrees. Germination time may be cut in half, and increased seedling vigor helps combat the disease problems that beset slow-growing plants.

Check daily for signs of growth and for moisture; water if the soil begins to dry. Many seeds are quicker to emerge than the gardener expects. In warm, moist conditions seeds of cabbage, collards and broccoli germinate in three to four days; tomatoes and eggplants emerge in five days. Pepper plants should appear in 10 days and parsley, 14.

Tall and lanky, weak-stemmed seedlings are caused by too-low light levels or too-high temperatures. Move to a full-sun location when seedlings emerge. Lanky growth may be a problem with cool-season crops germinating during hot weather.

Seedlings normal in size but with a pale green color suffer from lack of adequate fertilizer. Feed weekly with a fertilizer solution; double the frequency to encourage vigorous seedlings.

Remove the covering as soon as green shoots appear; young plants need full sun or bright light.

During the cooler months or when plants need protection, seedlings can be raised indoors. Pick a southern window or under a bank of fluorescent lights for the best growing area.

In the window, allow the seedlings to have full sun. Developing plants will lean toward the light and should be turned periodically to reduce stretching. During warmer days, open the window to let in cool air to prevent excessive heat build-up that will encourage quick growth and weak stems.

A shop-type fluorescent fixture provides adequate light for eight to 10 pots or two flats of seedlings. The lights must be positioned about a foot above the top of the seedlings to ensure adequate exposure. Keep the lights on for 12 to 14 hours a day. Grow seedlings under lights only for the time needed to produce a transplant ready for a container or the garden. Vegetables and herbs that grow tall and lanky under lights do not transplant well.

Seedlings grown outdoors or in the greenhouse generally are the most durable. The direct sun exposure as well as gentle winds and rains toughen the seedlings, making the transition to larger containers or the garden easier. Care for young plants grown indoors and outdoors will be the same.

Care of seedlings

Fragile, young seedlings can grow rapidly. Within a week, true leaves follow the first pair of seed leaves. Root systems are shallow during early growth, so it is essential the soil is kept moist. Water gently from a fine nozzle, sprinkling can or misting bottle.

As the seedlings grow, check once or twice a day for moisture. When the soil surface feels a bit dry, water until moisture appears from the drainage holes. If the soil stays constantly wet, the root and stem rots that cause damping off multiply. Also make sure that ventilation is good — heat and humidity encourage disease. Add a fan to increase air movement in rooms with poor ventilation.

Seedling protection

Germinating seedlings get exposure to sun while being supported on wooden platform. Plastic cover draped over top and secured along the sides provides protection from wind and rain.

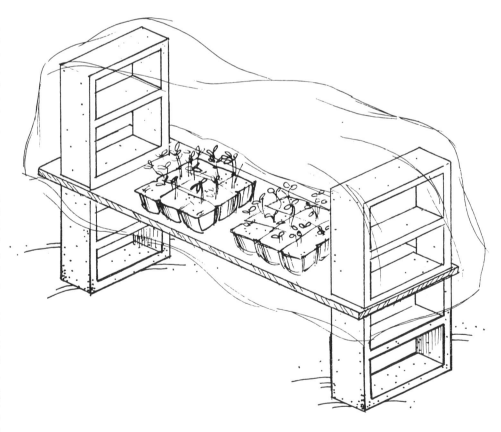

A board, concrete blocks and a plastic cover create a good growing area that offers protection from wind and rain for transplanted seedlings.

If the seeding medium lacked nutrients, begin fertilizing a few days after plants emerge. Use either houseplant fertilizer or a formula made specifically for young plants. A 20-20-20 formula mixed at a rate of a teaspoon to a gallon of water can be used once a week. Feed immediately after watering thoroughly. A medium enriched with nutrients before seeding will not need additional feedings for two to three weeks.

Transplant time

Seedlings started as groups in flats or large pots will be ready to transplant into individual containers in about two weeks. This may seem early, but if a plant has only a few leaves and a shallow root system, the move is easy. When plants are more than an inch or so tall, roots will be intertwined; separation at this stage will injure the plant and slow future growth.

Recycled market packs, small pots or egg cartons are suitable containers for transplants. Clean containers and check for drainage. Maintain all efforts to keep growing conditions free of pests.

A seeding mixture can be used for young transplants, but many growers prefer a chunkier medium to ensure drainage. The following mix is good, especially for plants that will remain in containers for a long time:

Transplant mix
---
2 quarts sphagnum peat moss
2 quarts horticultural perlite
½ tablespoon dolomitic lime
Enough water to moisten the mix
Combine ingredients and you are ready to pot.

To transplant, gently loosen the seedlings from their container. The plants should pull apart easily if some attempt had been made to space seeds when sowing. A few roots will be broken and torn, but seedlings are tough at this stage. Hold each plant by a leaf — some gardeners use tweezers — for the move to an individual space or container.

Thoroughly water the potted-up transplants and place in full sun. If the weather is hot, transplants may need some shade for a day or two. Almost overnight, however, the seedlings that sagged after transplanting perk up and stand tall, ready to grow.

Seedlings need direct sun to grow compact and strong. The south window that worked well for germination is no longer satisfactory. If it is the only space available, turn seedlings frequently to prevent them from becoming lopsided. Fluorescent light also is second-best. A shop light suspended a foot above the container will produce adequate transplants, but they will be soft and slightly stretched.

The best location for developing plants is in full sun, outdoors or in the greenhouse. Outside, a clear plastic cover fixed a few feet above the plants will let in the light but protect the seedlings from storms. Leave two or more sides open for good ventilation.

Water to keep the soil moist. When the surface begins to dry, water. Transplants will use more water

Grow your own transplants

Fill pots with growing medium. Sow seeds.

Transplant plants from pot.

Plant seedlings in egg cartons or other containers to grow.

as they grow, so check several times a day to be sure the soil is moist but not soggy.

Fertilize regularly with a 20-20-20 or similar formula. Encourage good growth with a weekly application of a solution of a tablespoon of fertilizer mixed with a gallon of water.

During warm weather, when the plants are growing particularly rapidly, fertilize at half the rate but twice as often — half a tablespoon of fertilizer to a gallon of water applied twice a week.

Keep plants in full sun to prevent stretched and lanky growth. Most seedlings escape pests, but watch for and treat insects and diseases as needed.

A stocky new plant is ready for the garden after two to four weeks in the transplant container. Plants grown outdoors or in a greenhouse can go directly into the ground. Plants propagated under light or in windows will need hardening off, a process of gradually adjusting the plants to outdoor conditions.

To harden off plants, expose them to a half-day of morning sun and bright light in the afternoon for several days. Then move containers to full sun and natural breezes for the final adjustment. A week or two of hardening off will assure a good transplant for the garden.

Trees from seeds

Growing trees from seeds is a long-term project and few fruit trees are grown from seed. For home gardeners, seed propagation is a temptation nevertheless. Who hasn't started an avocado by suspending a seed pit over water? When planted outside, however, these plants often turn out to be sensitive to cold or require a long time before producing the first harvest.

Citrus seeds have about a 75 percent chance of producing a tree that bears fruit identical to that of the parent. Seedling trees, however, tend to be taller, thornier and take longer — eight or nine years — to bear fruit.

Fruit grown from seed typically is tropical — coconut, jaboticaba, mamey, sapote and papaya. Most have not been grown commercially and fewer specific varieties have been

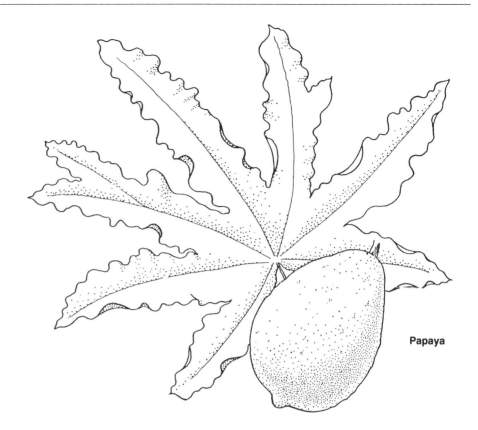
Papaya

developed. A named variety of any plant probably has been produced from cuttings, tissue culture, air layers or grafts. Some method of asexual propagation is necessary to keep plants true to type.

Fruit trees generally are produced by grafting a desirable top to a particular rootstock, one known to improve fruit production or pest resistance. Certain varieties of citrus, loquats, mangoes, apples and avocados come relatively true from seed, and rootstocks for these commonly are grown from seed.

Seeds of temperate-zone fruit, including nectarines and peaches, may need a moist, cold storage period, called stratification, before germination will occur. Soak the seeds in water for a few hours, then place in a plastic bag of moist peat moss or growing medium. Refrigerate for a month or more before planting in pots or in the ground.

In most ways, growing trees and shrubs from seed is similar to growing vegetables, but the type of planting medium is less important. Using a coarser transplant mix from the start is quite satisfactory. Sow in pots or in a prepared garden site. Scatter small seeds over a shallow tray of soil and plant large seeds individually in 6-inch or larger containers. Keep seeds warm and moist for germination to begin.

Like vegetables, seedling trees and shrubs need full sun to grow stocky and compact. Encourage green, healthy foliage with frequent watering — as often as once a day when the plant begins to fill the pot. Fertilize either with a liquid fertilizer at a rate of a tablespoon of 20-20-20 to a gallon of water applied in place of watering every week or two or by adding a slow-release fertilizer to the planting medium. Slow-release fertilizers will feed the plants for several months every time they are watered.

Gardeners with the time, space and willingness to experiment can grow seedling trees to fruiting size. Otherwise, when stems are about pencil thickness or a bit larger, it is time to think about grafting.

While you wait

While seedlings are growing, prepare the garden site. Tilling and fumigation or solarization will require the same time as growing most vegetables and herbs. Seeds also can be sown while the garden is

How to save seeds for another season

Don't toss out the half-sown packet of seeds — save it for another season. Seeds, which contain living embryos just waiting to grow, can be stored until another crop is needed.

Sometimes there are failures and replanting is necessary. Often just a few weeks after planting a row of beans or radishes, it is time to sow another. Saving the leftover seeds is one way of reducing the costs of an edible landscape.

Seeds from a few non-hybrid crops, often called open-pollinated varieties, can be harvested from fruit left on the vine and allowed to mature, then stored for another season. When grown as pure stands, these varieties come true from seed and can be counted on to produce more fruit that resembles that of the parent plant.

Hybrids, however, are produced from crosses of plants that may not be completely alike in looks or yields. When seeds from the fruit of hybrids are saved and later sown, many of the offspring will be different from the crop that produced the seed. It is best to buy fresh hybrid seed when the supply is exhausted.

Sometimes saved seeds produce garden treasures when sown. Squash seeds that have been collected, dried, then later planted may result in an unfamiliar harvest. Bees carrying pollen between squash in your garden and that of a neighbor may have produced some crosses of their own. The result is a sort of hybrid that gives a new variety once the seed is sown. Such unusual fruit can be a pleasant surprise and is edible.

When seed is to be saved from the garden, allow the fruit to mature on the plant. Normally there is a color change: Bean pods brown, peppers turn bright red and squash skin becomes golden yellow — signs of the full development of the embryo within the seeds. When this occurs, the fruit can be picked, the seeds extracted and air-dried in the shade, then stored or planted.

Most seeds can be stored for several years if kept in cool, dry conditions. Jars with tight lids are ideal containers, but more modern gardeners now use plastic food-storage tubs or self-sealing bags. To reduce moisture in the containers, some gardeners add a handful of dry milk powder wrapped in a paper towel. This absorbs much of the moisture that could encourage growth or a deterioration of the seeds.

Claim a shelf in the refrigerator to store the seeds. Cool temperatures in the high 30s to low 40s are ideal. Do not place the seeds in the freezer, which could damage them. Date the seeds and use the oldest ones first.

productive. It requires four to six weeks during warm months and a few weeks longer during winter to produce a transplant from quick-growing varieties.

Keeping containers full of ready-to-transplant seedlings means the edible landscape never will stand idle. When one crop finishes, pop in another to maintain production and constant supply of food.

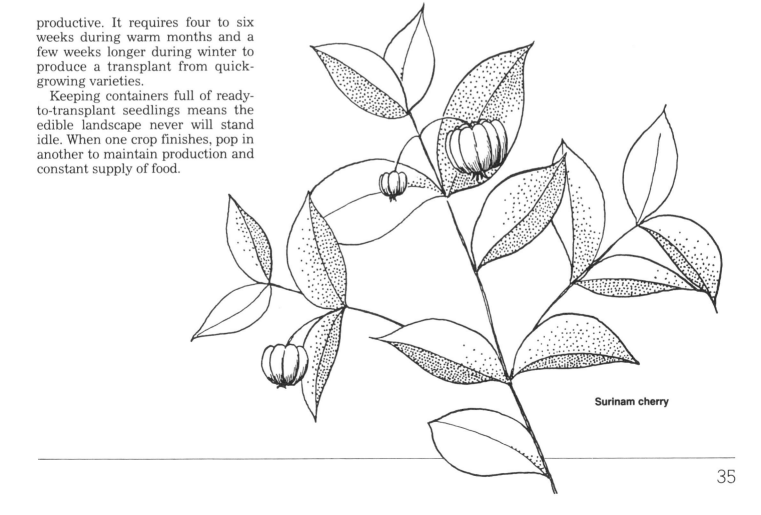

Surinam cherry

6

Grafting and other special techniques

GROWING A PLANT FOR the edible landscape that is just like its parent sometimes takes a special approach to propagation. This is where techniques including grafting, cuttings, layering and other vegetative propagation methods can ensure the desired variety.

A peach pit sown in the ground may not grow into a tree that ripens the same time as the parent tree or has the needed disease tolerance. Likewise, citrus sown from seed often is disappointing.

Vegetative propagation takes the guesswork out of growing plants for the landscape. Will the avocado tree produce fruit just like the one from which it came? You normally know for sure only if the new plant comes from a bud or limb of the parent tree. Most fruiting trees, shrubs and vines are reproduced using what are called vegetative techniques.

Propagation using growing plant portions including buds, stems and small limbs also can produce a bearing plant quicker than seeding methods. With grapes it is often just a matter of rooting a stem with several buds, then growing and training the new vine for a few years before production begins.

Grafted trees including citrus, mangoes, apples and peaches could be producing desirable fruit in four to five years. When such fruiting plants are propagated from seed, add at least a year or two of growing time, then it is still a guessing game as to what the produce will look like and how it will taste.

Grafting methods are based on scientific information about how plants grow to heal wounds and form a union of plant parts, but the technique really is an art. Not everyone has the nimble fingers and experience to become good at grafting. Successful grafters seem to have an instinct for what is likely to work — the trait of an artist.

Luckily, many plants such as citrus and grapes are forgiving, and grafting can be a rewarding experience for the beginner. Leave the more difficult-to-graft trees such as pecan, sapote and macadamia for the professional or those who have had many other successes.

Grafting unites two portions of closely related plants, splicing them together. Many types of grafts exist, but only a few that usually are successful for the beginner will be discussed here.

All methods of joining plant por-

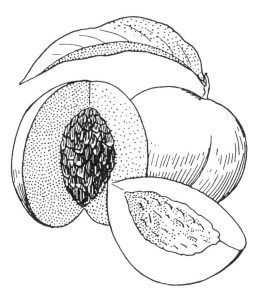

Nectarines

tions are forms of grafting, but when only buds are used for the new variety, the technique is called budding. The techniques of budding normally are treated differently from other grafting methods.

Grafting is somewhat like making a jigsaw puzzle: The gardener cuts a pair of complementary pieces freehand and fits them together as closely as possible. Cuts must be clean and sure — no whittling allowed. Selecting promising material to work with and choosing the best place to make cuts calls for an understanding about plants.

Home gardeners usually learn to graft out of necessity. Professional help rarely is available. A skilled grafter works at a nursery and has little time to spend with hobbyists. To have just one tree in the landscape grafted is relatively costly. Backyard gardeners may have only one tree to deal with, so they may need to learn to do their own grafting.

If a favorite citrus has been frozen to the ground, for instance, the fastest way to restore it may be to graft a new top on the shoots coming up from the established system. Grafting also can be a way of adding new and better, or perhaps just different, varieties to an established tree.

Major limbs of a tree can be cut back and replaced through grafting with new varieties that will grow to produce a better harvest. Only the growth from the addition will produce the new variety, of course; the rest of the tree remains its old self. Some gardeners like to make cocktail trees by grafting a number of varieties to a single trunk.

When to graft

Grafts can be made any time of year but are most successful when the plants are breaking into new growth. During this stage the plants are vigorous and wounds made during grafting will heal rapidly.

Manuals often suggest grafting when the wood slips. Grafting works with the cells that initiate growth and this tissue, called the cambium, lies immediately under the bark of a tree or shrub. When the cells are dividing rapidly, the bark slips or peels easily from the stem, which is a good indication the plant is in a growth phase.

The best time for grafting varies with the tree or shrub. Deciduous trees typically are grafted just before and during early spring growth. Citrus and other evergreen trees usually send out new growth several times in a year. Any of these times — late winter, early summer, early fall — are good.

Tools

The only tools needed for grafting are a sharp knife and strips of plastic. Successful grafting requires clean, smooth cuts. A serrated kitchen knife won't do. Some gardeners use razor blades or X-acto knives, but most professionals prefer a knife made specifically for grafting or budding. These knives are available at garden centers, hardware stores and from mail-order companies.

The plastic bandages a new graft. For small grafts, the wrapping can be cut in strips half an inch wide and 10 to 12 inches long; for larger projects, a whole plastic bag is used. The wrapping prevents movement and keeps the union dry.

Making the graft

The plant providing the roots is called the stock. It can be a seedling or an older, established tree. To the new, grafted plant it may contribute vigor, a strong root system, adaptability to poor soils and resistance to nematodes, insects or diseases. The stock plant is wanted only for its roots. Once the graft is established, all other growth from the stock — at the roots, on the trunk below the graft or along remaining limbs — is removed.

A new top sprouts from the scion, a small piece of stem or a single bud from another plant. The scion variety determines the variety of the new, grafted plant; it is what makes a tree a Dancy tangerine, Curtis pecan or Flordabelle peach.

■ **BEGIN WITH BUDDING**

Budding is the simplest form of grafting and usually the most forgiving of mistakes made by beginners. Touching the cut portions or not properly wrapping the plant parts together may have little effect on the union of the two plant portions.

The term budding comes from the taking of a bud from a desirable variety such as a Dancy tangerine or Anna apple and placing it on a desirable rootstock of the same species. Budders work with small portions of the desirable variety, which is one reason the attempts often are so successful.

As the budding is performed, there may be an opportunity to place more than one bud on the rootstock to maximize the chances of success. Bud wounds begin to heal quickly, and in a matter of a

Chip bud graft

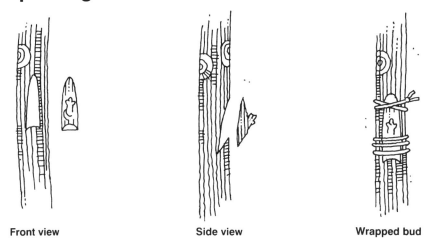

Front view   **Side view**   **Wrapped bud**

Chip bud is fitted under flap of tissue on plant stock.

Side-veneer grafting

Trim foliage and small limbs from base of stock plant.

Make downward cut through stem and into wood.

Cut into stem to remove chip of stem and wood tissue.

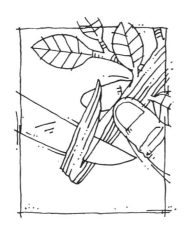

Cut scion stem with 2 or 3 buds to match prepared stock.

Insert scion into stock plant.

Wrap with plastic strip and allow plant to heal.

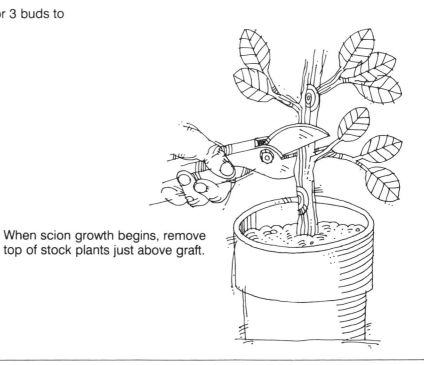

When scion growth begins, remove top of stock plants just above graft.

inch down the stem. Hold the split stem open with one end of the clefting tool or screwdriver to prepare the stock for the scion portions.

Scions are prepared from short stems containing two or three buds. Cut the stems to form a wedge with a 1- to 2-inch-long taper. Make one side of the wedge a bit narrower than the other. Insert the scions into the split section of the stock, one on each side of the stem with bark tissue matched as closely as possible. Allow the split portion of the stock to close by putting pressure on the scion portions, then the graft is ready to wrap.

A modified cleft graft can be used on grapes. A small stock stem is split and only one scion is inserted. Select a scion about the same size as the stock, prepare and wedge into the stock portion. Bark areas should match on at least one side of the stems.

For all grafts, the edges are where wound healing occurs. Wrap the scion in place. Wait for signs of healing or growth before removing the wrap. As growth begins, the top of the stock can be removed.

■ SIDE-VENEER GRAFT

The side-veneer graft is useful when stems are about the same size, or when the stock is a little bigger than the scion wood. Make a slightly slanted cut 2 or 3 inches downward through the bark and slightly into the wood of the stock. Make a second cut across the base of the first, forming a notch, and remove the section of plant tissue.

Take a scion with two or three buds about the same size or slightly smaller than the stem of the stock. Cut a slice on a slant down one side of the scion to match the stock. Make another slanted cut across the base to make a wedge that will fit into the notch in the stock. Place the scion in position. Make sure the bark and cambium make contact on at least one side.

Fruit propagation techniques

Plant	Budding, grafting	Cutting, layering, suckering	Seeds
Temperate fruit			
Apple	shield bud, whip graft		stratify 8-9 weeks*
Blackberry		softwood cutting, simple layering	
Blueberry		softwood cutting, suckers	
Fig	shield bud	hardwood cutting, air layering	
Grape, bunch	cleft graft	hardwood cutting	
Grape, muscadine		softwood cutting, simple layering	
Loquat	shield bud, side-veneer graft, cleft graft	air layering	common for ornamentals and rootstocks
Nectarine	shield bud		stratify 3-4 weeks*
Peach	shield bud		stratify 3-4 weeks*
Pecan	budding, whip graft, cleft graft		plant immediately after harvest or stratify 8-16 weeks
Persimmon	chip bud, whip graft, cleft graft		
Tropical and subtropical fruit			
Avocado	chip bud, side-veneer graft		common for rootstocks
Banana		suckers	
Barbados cherry	side-veneer graft, cleft graft	hardwood cutting, air layering	common for rootstocks
Carambola	side-veneer graft	air layering	common for rootstocks
Citrus	shield bud, chip bud, cleft graft	hardwood and semihardwood cuttings, air layering	common for rootstocks
Coconut			place on side, bury halfway
Eugenias	side-veneer graft, cleft graft		common
Guava	chip bud, side-veneer graft	softwood cutting, air layering	common
Jaboticaba	side-veneer graft		common
Longan	side-veneer graft	air layering	common
Lychee	side-veneer graft	air layering	
Macadamia	side-veneer graft, cleft graft		common for rootstocks
Mamey sapote	chip bud, side-veneer graft		common
Mango	chip bud, side-veneer graft		common for rootstocks
Papaya		softwood cutting	common
Pineapple		suckers	
Sapodilla	side-veneer graft		common
Sugar apple	shield bud, side-veneer graft		common

* Stratify by providing a period of cold, moist storage before planting. Propagated for rootstocks.

Cuttings

Many plants will grow roots from a piece cut from the parent plant and stuck in soil. Plants that do well on their own roots often are started from cuttings. Three types are used:

- Softwood: Cuttings 4 to 6 inches long are taken from the tips of plants, usually just after new growth has begun to toughen, May through June.

- Semihardwood: Cuttings 4 to 6 inches long are taken from plants when the spring flush of growth has matured but is still green, usually July through September.

- Hardwood: Cuttings 6 to 12 inches long are taken from dormant wood. Remove from the plant just below a node, the area where the leaves join the branch, late fall through winter.

Collect softwood and semihardwood cuttings in early morning when stems and leaves are full of moisture. Protect from drying by covering them with layers of wet newspaper or by soaking in a pail of water. Strip leaves from the lower half of the stem and dip the bottom inch or two in a rooting powder. Place the cuttings in pots or shallow trays filled with moist sand or vermiculite.

Cuttings usually are inserted about 2 to 3 inches into the rooting medium. Try to place a node — the area where leaves were attached — below the surface because plants often root from these nodal zones. If cuttings are placed fairly close together, preferably with leaves just touching, they help one another create a humid atmosphere. A 6-inch pot will hold six or more carefully spaced stems.

Mist with water several times daily until rooting begins. Many gardeners like to use a spacious, clear plastic bag as a miniature greenhouse. Keep cuttings in a humid, bright area protected from full sun.

Rooting may take two weeks for succulent plants and 10 to 12 weeks for woody trees and shrubs. Give the stems a gentle pull from time to time. When a small, well-branched root system has formed, the young plants are ready for potting. Pot into pest-free soil or potting mixture, and place transplants in filtered shade for several days to recover from shock.

Trees and shrubs should be grown in containers until they reach the sizes of similar plants found at a nursery. They then can be planted in more stressful, open-ground conditions. Water and fertilize to encourage growth during this developmental period.

Treat hardwood cuttings with rooting powder and tie in small bundles. Turn the bundles upside down, place in a box or container, and cover with peat moss or loose soil. Some propagators simply bury the cuttings in the ground upside down, digging them out in late winter to check for signs of growth.

In the box or the ground, the cuttings begin healing the wounds by forming callus, a yellowish-white lumpy tissue. When callus has formed but before roots begin to form, place the cuttings in the garden or plant in a pot in the normal, upright position to root and grow while the weather is still cool. Cover all but the top bud of the cutting with soil.

Cuttings

Take small cuttings — 4 to 6 inches.

Strip leaves from the lower half of the stem and dip in rooting powder.

Stick cuttings into pot with moist sand or vermiculite.

Layering

Many plants form roots where a stem or branch lies against the ground. When this occurs naturally, it allows plants to spread out in thickets. Gardeners can use this rooting tendency to obtain a few transplants.

■ SIMPLE LAYERING

Bend a branch until it touches the ground or a pot of soil and peg it to the ground or bury it with soil just behind the tip. Rooting is encouraged by making a shallow, slanted cut through the bark on the bottom side of the limb where it touches the ground and applying a little rooting powder to the wound. Roots usually begin to form in six to eight weeks.

When the rootball is about the size of a fist, sever the new plant from its parent branch and move pot or plant to a permanent location. The new plant may need staking to hold it upright.

■ AIR LAYERING

Another way to encourage trees and shrubs to form roots along their trunks or branches is by air layering. This process works on older parts of plants, not just young, growing tips. Air layering usually is performed at least 12 inches from a tip.

Start by removing leaves from a 4- to 6-inch section of branch, then wound the plant to stimulate rooting. One way is to make a long, shallow slanting cut up through the bark. Hold the cut open with a bark chip or toothpick. Another method is to girdle the stem with two shallow cuts made an inch apart. Cut across and remove the ring of bark between the two cuts.

Immediately apply a light coating of rooting powder to the exposed plant tissue with a fine brush or the tip of a knife. Too much powder can delay rooting. Before the wound has a chance to dry, enclose the area in moist sphagnum moss. Garden centers often sell small bags of this water-absorbent, stringy material. Take two handfuls of damp sphagnum moss and place them on either side of the wounded stem.

Enclose the moss in plastic film or aluminum foil. Sandwich, newspaper or bread bags are ideal. Extend the wrapping above and below

Simple layering

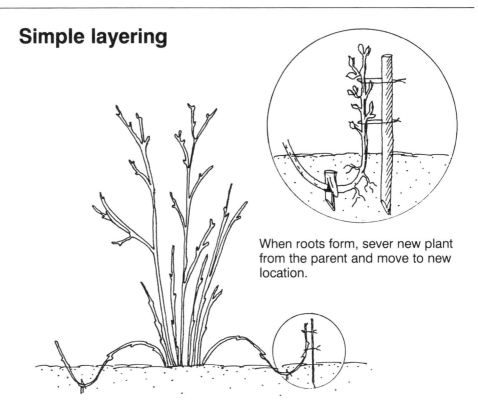

When roots form, sever new plant from the parent and move to new location.

Bend limbs down to the soil and bury or peg area behind the tip to prompt rooting.

Sucker removal

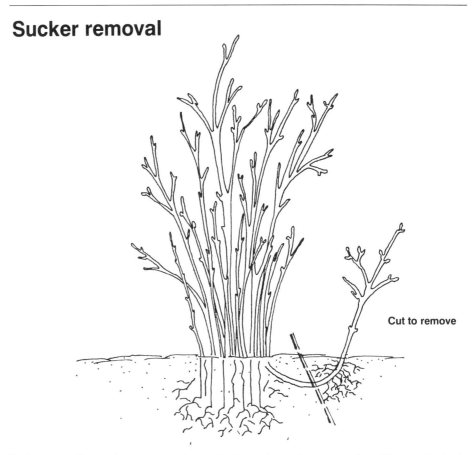

Cut to remove

Sucker growth produces new plants that can be cut, removed and transplanted to containers or garden.

the ball of moss to seal in moisture. Seal both ends with twine, rubber bands or twist ties.

The time it takes for roots to form depends on the time of year, the type of plant and the age of plant material. Most trees and shrubs require several months.

Periodically look for roots. When five or six roots can be seen, remove the new plant by cutting across the stem or branch below the ball of moss and roots. Do not remove or disturb the moss. Plant moss and all in a pot or prepared bed. Air layers can be planted as deeply as necessary to give the new plant adequate support.

Suckers and offshoots

A few fruiting plants that are not grafted still send up shoots or suckers from the roots. Often a new shoot, together with a nice clump of roots, can be cut from the original plant. This is perhaps the cheapest, easiest way to obtain a new transplant. Plants that multiply by suckers and offshoots include bananas, pineapples, blackberries and blueberries.

Suckers and offshoots often form near the base of the plant or grow underground as rhizomes and send up shoots a few inches to several feet away from the main limbs. Allow the new stems to grow at least 6 inches tall and form a sizable root system before digging the new plant. Dig around the plant, then sever the offshoot from the underground stem with the blade of a sharp shovel or a pair of pruners.

Move the new plant to a permanent planting site. Provide the same care as would be given a new tree or shrub. The plant also can be placed in a container and allowed to grow for transplanting later. Keep container-grown plants moist, in full sun and feed every two or three weeks with a liquid fertilizer during the growing season until a permanent location is prepared.

Suckers and offshoots from grafted plants may not produce desirable trees or shrubs. When new plants rise from below the grafted portion, the growth will be from the rootstock. New plants for grafting or budding can be grown from these shoots.

Air layering

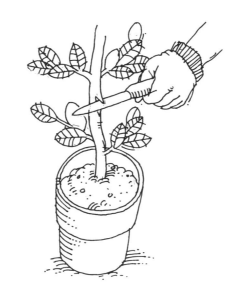

Make a long, slanting cut upward and insert a toothpick or bark chip.

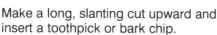

Apply rooting powder to the cut and wrap with moist sphagnum moss.

Enclose with plastic or aluminum foil.

After rooting takes place, cut just below the moss ball. Do not disturb the moss ball.

Move the new plant to a pot or prepared garden site.

7
Planting the formal vegetable garden

Chinese cabbage

PLANTING A FORMAL GARden is a traditional way of beginning an edible landscape. The large or small areas mapped out into square, rectangular or circular planting sites quickly are filled by the gardener with seeds or transplants of herbs and vegetables.

With the formal garden, every plant is placed in its own spot. There are designated walkways and rows that come to an abrupt but well-marked end. For many this is the only way to grow a garden, but for those unfettered by past traditions it is time to examine other ways of locating plantings to make better use of space.

First, investigate intensive cultivation techniques of square-foot gardening, in which rows are eliminated, or wide-bed plantings that devote more of the garden area to crops. Also determine where raised beds might better serve the needs of the gardener when located within easy reach, off a patio or at the entrance to the house.

The only rule to where gardens should be located is that most plantings need full sun. Many plantings can be temporary additions between new trees that for the first few years will not create major shade. Here the plantings can be scattered about to give a pleasing but perhaps less-organized look than that of a formal garden. A single fruit tree by the door with clusters of rosemary, radishes or a creeping squash forms an attractive garden spot.

Window boxes, urns and even in-ground planters can be filled with vines and bushes that produce good things to eat. Here is a place for a small-fruited watermelon vine that creeps across the patio or a colorful container of chard. Don't let a space go to waste if it could be planted with an edible crop.

How to cope with difficult situations

Even in shady areas, some leafy crops will grow. This could be an ideal spot for mint, oregano or parsley. Some gardeners have produced fair crops of onions, beans, lettuce, collards and turnips in filtered sun or areas with four hours of direct sun and the rest of the day with bright light or minimal shade.

Also remember deciduous trees typically provide shade spring through fall but during the remaining months let the sun in for quick crop production. How about devoting the space near these trees to a late fall and winter planting of beets, broccoli or carrots that will mature before the new tree leaves appear in spring?

Plantings under trees and around shrubs do present some special problems. The soil cannot be tilled deeply without risking major root damage to the plantings. Nematodes also can build up faster when the area is heavily cropped.

Keep these soils in the best of shape by adding plenty of organic matter, which tends to repel pest problems in the ground. Frequent additions of a compost or mulch layer will create new planting zones so as not to disturb tree or shrub roots when herbs or vegetables are added under and beyond the spread of tree limbs.

Fumigation and even soil solarization techniques may be too damaging to use under trees and shrubs. If soil-borne pests become a major problem, avoid planting the area for a season or two. The area also could be devoted to container-grown crops that would not sink roots into the soil.

Container gardens give the plants a root zone free of major pests. Buy the soil or make your own. A good mix is composed of equal parts peat moss and perlite, with half a tablespoon dolomitic lime added to each gallon of prepared mix. Quite often the soil is used for more than one season and several different vegetables can be grown together in the same pot.

Grow a single tomato plant, but don't forget to add a border of chives or a cascading cucumber. A few climbing beans can be trellised in a container with peppers filling the rest of the pot.

Do give the root systems plenty of room to grow. Container sizes start at a gallon or two and can end up being large tubs or special decorative planters. Containers are movable and can be positioned for best sun exposure throughout the year or brought indoors when cold weather approaches.

Container gardens do take a little extra care. Watering may have to be daily during the hot, dry seasons, but a timer-regulated drip-irrigation system could be used to make the work easier. Also, plan on feeding the plantings at least weekly, although use of a slow-release fertilizer in the soil mix can minimize this chore, too.

When to plant

Planting is almost as much fun as harvesting. Many gardeners say that as each seed or young plant is set in the ground, they almost can taste roasted corn, plump tomatoes,

sweet cantaloupes and zesty collards.

Timing is everything to successful planting. For many vegetables, there is only a small window of opportunity during which they can be started in the soil, grow for the months required to produce crops, and be harvested before the weather changes and production fades.

Tomatoes are a good example. Varieties that produce full-size fruit are particularly sensitive to temperature. They will set fruit only when flowers open in temperatures between 55 and 85 degrees. In South Florida, where the weather remains warm from fall through spring, tomatoes can be grown during all but the hot summer months.

In Central and North Florida, however, tomato plants must be set in the ground during August for a fall harvest. Wait any longer and cool weather may arrive before the plants form fruit or the harvest succumbs to the first frost. For a spring harvest in these regions, plants must be in the ground by March to ensure fruit set before summer heat slows production.

Other crops for which timing is critical include peppers, eggplants, cantaloupes and watermelons.

Planting times are more flexible for crops that mature quickly or ones less sensitive to temperature. Radishes, carrots and turnips can be planted October through February in most parts of the state. Do not, however, attempt to grow them late spring through summer. Out-of-season sowings result in tops but few or immature roots. Leaves are bitter and the plants are quick to flower and go to seed.

To be successful, gardeners must adjust planting schedules to the flow of their own seasons. Check planting guides for each vegetable, then be sure to plant on time.

Garden designs

Gardens come in all sizes — big, small and in-between. In the crowded landscape the garden may have to take a sharp bend or form a semicircle. Gardens literally can be fitted into any space.

Do, however, keep in mind that plants need room to grow. If plantings are too cramped, the results

Planting a row

Sow seeds in a row at depth and spacing suggested by guides or seed packets.

could be lots of tops and a few roots from radishes, or just a small picking of bush beans.

Gardeners have been plotting and planting for years to develop the techniques that give the best production from gardens. Manipulations of row length and width plus crop-planting intensities also are designed to get the best harvest from a specific space.

Long rows

Given plenty of room, planting in rows is the favored production technique. These gardens are well-organized and allow the use of mechanical equipment. There is no doubt what is the seeded crop and what are the weeds: The seedlings that look alike in the rows should be kept, and all other vegetation should be hoed out.

Long rows are best adapted to the big gardens where rototillers keep the rows clean and wagons can be pulled between the crops to gather harvests. Gardeners do not have to be as careful to note what might be stepped on next. The crops also get maximum production space. Beans can have the full 3 inches between plants and 18 to 30 inches between rows, as recommended on many seed packets. The plants grow to maximum size and production potential.

With this method garden space is sacrificed for convenience. Where necessary, it is easier to spray one crop without also treating another. During harvest, the nearby crops are not disturbed. Gardeners also can plant many of the vining crops without being concerned about trellising. The row planting techniques may use more water and fertilizer, but with drip irrigation and feeding only in the row, even these wastes can be minimized.

Plant the whole garden in long rows and divide rows into sections of different vegetables. For instance, half of a long row could be planted with tomatoes and the rest divided between beans and squash.

Some crops should be planted in blocks. Plant corn in at least three or four side-by-side rows so the wind will blow the pollen among the stalks and pollinate the ears. If cucumbers, squash and melons are kept close together, the bees that do the pollinating can work the entire patch.

Problems with soils or drainage can influence the way rows are made. If conditions are particularly damp, mound the soil along a row to encourage water to move down and away from the growing crops. Hollows between rows then serve as drainage ditches.

Raised beds

Some gardeners enjoy mounding beds and planting crops above normal ground level for the sake of appearance. The technique becomes a form of raised-bed gardening and eliminates some of the stooping that goes with performing garden chores. It also provides a neat garden — a look backyard farmers admire.

Formal raised beds can be mounded piles of soil a few inches to a foot or more high. Many are enclosed with landscape timbers or treated lumber. The technique gives a neat, packaged look and blends into patio designs.

Raised beds often are preferred because they organize the garden. One bed can be devoted to tomatoes and Southern peas, while another is devoted to beans or even a shrubby crop of blackberries or a peach tree.

When wooden, brick or even concrete block edges give form to the bed, the gardener has a sitting area available that can make planting or weeding a bit easier. In addition to the appearance and some ease of culture, the main reason for raised beds is the excellent drainage that gardeners in the lowlands surely need.

Soil for raised beds often is formed from the sand of the landscape and enriched with organic matter. When native soils are used, inherent problems of the land — including weeds and nematodes — also may be incorporated into the garden.

Gardeners with small raised beds can blend their own planting mix from compost, peat moss and perlite or coarse, clean sand to ensure pest-free planting sites. Large and small raised beds adapt well to any of the common spacing techniques, including those used for long rows.

Wide rows

Even gardeners with lots of space are interested in high yields. Single-row crops are easy to maintain but take a lot of room. Because crops tolerate a bit of crowding, wide-row plantings often are made.

In the simplest wide-row planting, the gardener makes beds 2 to 4 feet wide, as long as needed, and either level or mounded up to 6 inches high. Seeds of a single crop are scattered over a section of the row to create a plot of planted garden. Seeds are sown more thickly than usual and thinned to normal spacing as the crop begins to grow.

Wide rows use space economically by devoting less of the garden to pathways. Weeding is more of a chore when plants are young, but as they grow, the vegetables create a dense cover and weeds are shaded out. Wide rows work well with leafy green and root crops, including carrots, turnips, mustards, beets, onions and radishes. Some growers stagger their planting times to achieve even better use of space.

Double cropping

Both commercial and home growers use double cropping to obtain maximum production from their garden space. Crops may be planted at ground level or in raised beds.

Vegetables are seeded in two or more closely spaced rows 6 to 12 inches apart, and the several rows are treated as one. Carrots, lettuce, spinach, beets, mustards, collards and turnips respond well to this treatment.

Plantings may be of a single variety or different rows may be different. If they are different, plant similarly sized vegetables together. Plant a row of beets with one of carrots, or combine mustards and collards in a single row. Within rows, plant seeds at normal spacing. Begin harvesting when plants are young to prevent crowding.

Double cropping

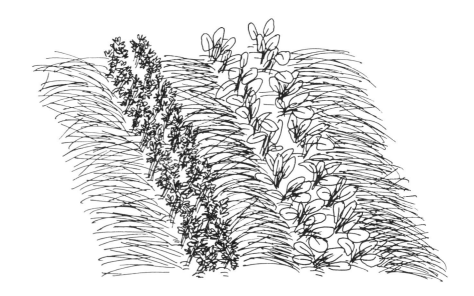

Multiple rows of the same or similar crops are planted in the space that normally would be devoted to a single row. Each of the rows is spaced about 6 inches apart.

Square-foot garden

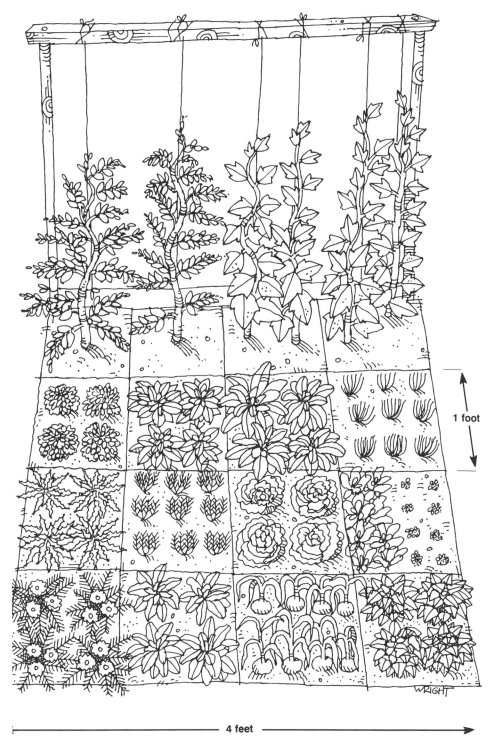

Square-foot gardening techniques use all available space. Rows are eliminated and each square foot of garden bears a harvest from 1 or more plants to maximize production.

Small plots

Planting schemes based on geometry truly are intensive: They aim to use all available land. Every bit of space is planted except a few walkways.

Square-foot gardens can be surprisingly productive. Sites 4 feet by 4 feet or 8 feet by 8 feet can help feed a family. This technique divides a garden into individual square feet of space. An area 4 feet by 4 feet will have 16 squares for planting. How many plants in each square is determined by the amount of room needed by the specific crop planted in it to produce a harvest.

A single square, for example, can contain one staked tomato, four lettuce or bean plants, one pepper plant or 50 radishes.

See the small-plot spacing chart for placement of additional vegetables.

Positioning of seeds or plants within in the square also depends on the crop. Where a single plant occupies a square, set the seed or transplant in the middle to allow room to grow in all directions. Several plants in the same square may be planted in rows, smaller squares or at random.

For example, to fill a square with four bean plants, divide the area into smaller squares and plant one seed in the middle of each.

Root crops often are sown at extremely close spacings. A square foot can accommodate 50 carrots or radishes or 20 turnips or onions. These seeds can be scattered across the square or sown in small rows. Harvest early by thinning out young plants for use as tender greens or roots, creating room for the rest to mature.

The French intensive method sets plants in hexagonal patterns within wide rows. Plants are seeded or transplanted at recommended spacings in a six-sided configuration, then an additional plant is placed in the center.

In an effort to use every bit of land, gardeners similarly have planted the corners of triangles, squares or rectangles, then added a plant or two in the middle.

Trellises add a third dimension to

a garden and are useful to gardeners seeking more space. Rather than allowing vine crops to sprawl across the garden, send them upward on a trellis. Cages also can be used to take advantage of vertical space and keep crops from sprawling over the ground. Many plants can be grown in cages, including tomatoes, eggplants and melons.

In addition to space-saving planting techniques, gardeners have an additional resource: the many recent introductions of dwarf varieties and bush forms of plants that once grew only as vines. While these space-savers, as they are called, take less garden room, the harvests may be somewhat smaller than those from their full-size relatives.

Fertilize first

Seeds store enough energy to germinate, but when a plant begins to grow it will need nutrients from the surrounding soil. The most successful gardeners don't wait until a plant shows signs of stress before they fertilize; rather, they incorporate food into the soil before planting so it is ready when the developing plants need it.

Lime and organic sources of nutrients such as compost and manure are best added several weeks to a month before planting, and before any planned fumigation. Most of the value of organic additions to the soil depends on microorganisms to break down residues and release nutrients. A few weeks will give the microorganisms time to work.

Some chemical fertilizers undergo some transformation in the soil before plants can use them to grow, but many granular fertilizers need only to be moistened by rain or irrigation. Absorption by roots begins minutes after application of liquid fertilizers. Because the nutrients quickly become available to plants, apply chemical fertilizers the week — or day — of planting to keep nutrients from leaching away in rains.

Fertilizing techniques abound. Some gardeners dig a row, lay fertilizer along the bottom, add a layer of soil, then plant the crop. Others spread fertilizer in small trenches dug on either side of the planned

Geometric

Geometric planting patterns make maximum use of garden space. Gardeners use simple designs to fill wide beds with vegetables.

French intensive

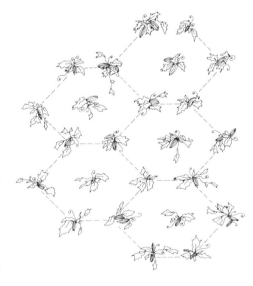

The French intensive gardening technique makes maximum use of wide beds by planting the corners of hexagons, then adding another plant in the center.

row. These techniques take time but work well. Just be sure that young roots will not be in direct contact with concentrated fertilizer or the plants will burn.

Other growers scatter fertilizer over the entire garden area, either by hand or with a spreader. This technique wastes fertilizer on pathways and other areas that won't be planted, but it guarantees each plant some fertilizer and avoids the danger of burn. Broadcasting works well in small plots, especially where intensive gardening techniques are practiced.

For the least amount of waste, put fertilizer exactly where it will be needed. At planting time, scatter dry fertilizer down the row, across the wide bed or over each square foot of land. The fertilizer may be worked into the soil or incorporated as the crop is planted. As long as fertilizer is applied at suggested rates, the normal turning of the soil that occurs when a row is planted or a transplant set will mix the fertilizer adequately with the soil and avoid burning roots.

A single application of fertilizer never can last the season, so make the preplant feeding moderate. With whatever formula selected, follow label instructions and lean to the side of caution. For sandy, rocky or clay soils, use a balanced fertilizer. Apply 6-6-6 at a rate of 2 pounds per 100 square feet of bed area or for each 100 feet of row. A 12-12-12 analysis, which is twice as concentrated, would be applied at half the rate.

Organic — peat or muck — soils can do without the nitrogen. For these soils, apply a 0-12-20 or similar formula at the lower 1-pound rate.

Liquid fertilizers are another option. Without bothering about manure or granular fertilizers beforehand, the gardener can mix a water-soluble 20-20-20 formula at a rate of 1 tablespoon to a gallon of water and sprinkle over 25 feet of row. If the garden soil is damp, liquid fertilizer will penetrate the upper few inches.

Sowing seeds

At times, Florida soils appear to consume seeds. Many sowings result in paltry germination. Often the gardener is at fault, using old seeds that were stored carelessly.

Seeds also may have been sown too deep or left to dry out. Other times, the weather turns too cold or too wet and the seeds rot in the ground. Perhaps here more than most places it is important to follow basic principles when sowing seeds.

Every seed contains an embryonic plant ready to grow when given the right conditions. First, soil must be free of competition, loose and moist. Rocks are rarely a problem, but insects, clods, or chunks of turned-under plants can hinder seedlings. The smaller the seed, the more important it is to have well-worked soil before planting.

Seeds can be sown in rows, groups or scattered across the garden. Scattering allows little control over planting depth. As the term suggests, seeds are tossed across prepared soil and either raked in or covered with another scattering of soil.

Scattering seeds works best with crops that germinate quickly. Seeds for greens or roots that will be gathered young can be tossed over the earth with little concern for spacing. Mustard, kale, radishes, collards, kohlrabi, leaf lettuce and turnips, which are usually up and growing within a week, are good candidates. Scattering can be used in wide-row, square-foot and container gardens.

Planting in rows gives order to the garden and is preferred for most crops. Seeds can be planted at specified depths. Seedlings emerging in a row easily are distinguished from weeds. Cultivation, watering, fertilizing and harvesting are easier when the plants are in neat rows.

The most reliable way to keep rows straight is to use as a guide a string stretched the length of the row. With experience, gardeners can set their sights on a tree or post and make a row straight toward it.

Mark each row with a label listing vegetable, variety and date. Keeping track of what did well and how long it took helps in selecting varieties for another season. Although it seems impossible at planting time, memory soon fades. Also mark the end of a row with a blank label, stake or stick to make it clear where not to step while the plants are emerging.

Labels can be bought from garden centers and catalogs or cut from household bleach containers. Although it is tempting to try the latest permanent marking pen, pencil usually lasts longer.

Make a seeding trench the depth suggested on seed packets or planting guides. It does not have to be exact, but keep it close. Fresh, vigorous seeds will poke up through a little deeper soil cover, but shallow rows may allow the seeds to dry out or fail to give adequate support to young roots.

Vegetable spacings for small plots

Vegetable	Plants per square foot	Comments
Beans	4	a sure producer
Beets	16	thin greens when small
Broccoli	1	may need staking
Brussels sprouts	1	may need staking
Cabbage	1	produces a single head
Cantaloupe	1	trellis
Carrots	50	thin; use small roots
Cauliflower	1	produces a single head
Corn, dwarf	2	plant several blocks
Cucumbers	1	trellis
Eggplant	1	may need staking
Endive	4	make successive plantings
Garlic	6	plant late fall
Kale	4	harvest individual leaves
Kohlrabi	4	make successive plantings
Leeks	40	thin; use small plants
Lettuce	4	make successive plantings
Mustard greens	12	harvest when young
Onions	20	thin for scallions
Parsley	4	harvest individual leaves
Peanuts	1	keep soil loose
Peas	4	grow bush varieties
Peppers	1	may need staking
Potatoes	1	plant spring or fall
Potatoes, sweet	1	sprawling plants
Radishes	50	thin; use small roots
Rutabaga	9	use large, mature roots first
Spinach	16	harvest individual leaves
Summer squash	1	use fruit when young
Swiss chard	4	plant early fall
Tomatoes	1	trellis or stake
Turnips	20	thin and use tops when young
Watermelon	1	trellis

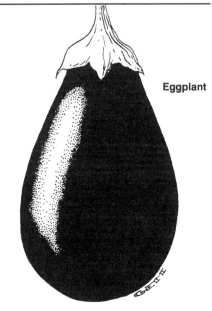

Eggplant

Sandy soil dries rapidly, which may not affect such crops as beans, corn and radishes, but with seed that is slow to germinate or when the soil is very dry, dribble a hose or sprinkling can down the row before planting.

Spread seed down the row at the spacings suggested on the packet or in planting guides. Experience soon teaches that in every row some seeds fail to grow, leaving skips. Sowing a little thickly often results in the desired spacing. Where young plants come up in a crowd, some can be transplanted to fill gaps in the rows. Use a narrow trowel and keep the roots as intact as possible.

After seeding the row, cover to the proper depth. Some gardeners combine equal parts of peat moss and either vermiculite or perlite, and use the mix to fill the seeding trench. This mixture defines the row, will not compact and holds a little extra moisture around the seeds.

Slow-germinating seeds can be covered to hold in moisture using the old-board trick. Lay a board, a piece of cardboard or sections of wet newspaper over the row. Check frequently to be sure the soil remains moist; remove the covering at the first sign of growth.

Group plantings

Without quite remembering why, gardeners may recall that cucumbers, melons, pumpkins and squash traditionally are planted in hills. Seeds are planted three or four together, an inch or so apart, in hills spaced 4 to 6 feet apart. In places with wet and chilly springs, mounding the soil improves drainage, and a bit of buried manure heats the soil and stimulates germination as it decomposes.

Most Florida soils need no help with drainage and usually are warm. The old spacing still groups plants conveniently, however, and helps increase production in a small space. For a group planting, plant several seeds 2 or 3 inches apart. Follow seed packets or planting guides for instructions on planting depth. Space the groups according to the growth habit — bush or vining — of the plants.

Setting out transplants

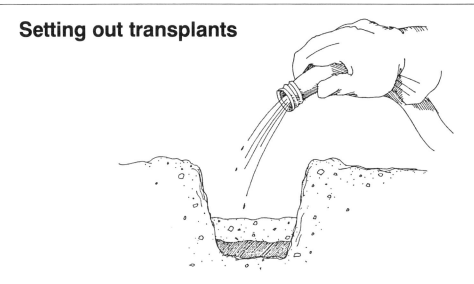

Add water or starter solution to transplant hole.

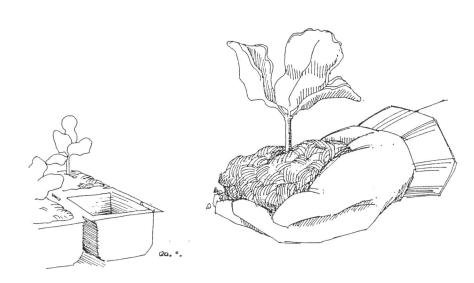

Remove transplant and surrounding soil from container. Avoid disturbing the roots.

Add soil to fill in around the roots. Additional water is optional.

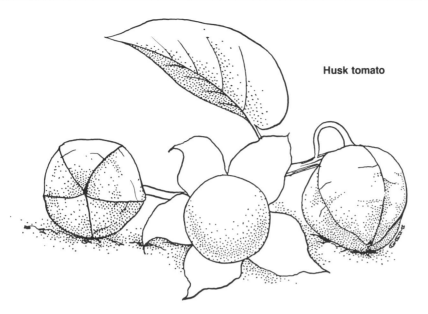
Husk tomato

Planting transplants

Transplants ready for the garden are 4 to 6 inches tall and have grown several sets of true leaves. The best transplants are compact and stocky. When buying plants, reject any that have grown lanky or are yellowish. Plants that are not green probably have been sitting too long awaiting sale.

Tap a transplant out of its container. Roots should be white to yellowish. Many brown roots or roots wrapped tightly together indicate plants have dried out or grown old; they will be slow to produce. Leave cauliflower, broccoli and lettuce in containers too long and they will try to mature in the small pots. They never will produce anything but small heads, even if they later are given plenty of garden room.

Before the days of market packs and peat pots, most transplants were sold freshly pulled from a bed and bundled in quantities of 25 or 50 plants. Cabbage, collards, onions, sweet potatoes, strawberries and tomatoes often still arrive this way at garden centers. Bare-root transplants should appear fresh and bright green, with moist, white-to-yellowish roots.

Set transplants in a row, in a group or individually, depending on the crop. Prepare the planting site as for seeding, with a light scattering of fertilizer. For bare-root plants, hardy and able to take some abuse, the classic technique is to:

- Open a hole with a shovel by sinking the blade in the soil, lightly moving the handle back and forth.
- Pour water or starter solution in the hole.
- Pop the plant in the ground.
- Close the hole with a foot.

Many an acre has been planted using this technique; most plants survive.

Today, with small gardens and container-grown plants, gardeners tend to baby young transplants. New arrivals suffer less shock; plants grown in pots may suffer none. Given water, they perk up and start growing right away.

Shading a transplant

Palmetto fronds pressed cut end into the ground cast shade on new transplants. Protecting the transplants from drying heat for just a few days will give them a head start.

Begin by making a hole with a trowel or shovel. Make the hole several times wider and deeper than the root ball of the plant going in the ground. Many gardeners fill the hole with water or a nutrient-enriched transplant solution. For a homemade formula, mix 1 to 2 tablespoons of a granular 6-6-6 fertilizer or a teaspoon of 20-20-20 water-soluble fertilizer to a gallon of water.

Set the plant in the hole, even if the hole is filled with water. Filling in the hole with soil makes it mud, so this technique is called puddling or mudding in. More water is not required, but many gardeners irrigate again.

Try not to transplant when the sun is directly overhead, especially when the weather is hot. Late afternoon is the best time. In any case, plants may need protection for a day or two from the hot afternoon sun. A palmetto frond pushed in the ground makes a good shade and often is right at hand. A leafy branch, a bushel basket propped on a stick or a board or a piece of cardboard also can give temporary shade.

Transplant shock is greatest for lanky plants, plants grown indoors or bare-root transplants. These need extra shade and water.

Care after planting

Water prompts growth of seeds and transplants. Keep the soil extra moist, at least for a week with transplants, and until seedlings display several true leaves.

At first, water may be needed every day, but do not maintain this schedule too long. As plants begin good root growth, reduce waterings to once every few days. Plants can withstand slight wilting. In fact, it may encourage new root growth. Too-frequent watering promotes shallow root systems and washes nutrients from the soil.

After the first week, be a little stingy with the water, stretching the interval between waterings. A mulch will help conserve moisture and speed establishment. Fertilizer applied in soil preparation and transplant solution sustains plants for the first few weeks.

8
Watering — the essential chore

FROM THE MOMENT A SEED or transplant is set in the ground, its survival depends on receiving adequate water from rainfall or irrigation. Vegetable plants are water hogs, especially during hot, dry weather. Watering is a gardener's most important chore. If the soil dries out, the garden will shrivel quickly unless it is watered.

Water may be drawn from lakes, wells or municipal systems. Water quality is not a problem for most gardens. Only in coastal areas of saltwater intrusion and inland regions where underground pockets of saline solutions contaminate the available resources will gardeners have to be concerned with plant safety.

Wells normally are the source of salty water. Many plants cannot tolerate salt levels in irrigation water much above 1,000 parts per million. If you can taste salt in the water, it should be suspected of causing plant injury. Beets, cabbages and loquats are quite tolerant of salty water, but blackberries, blueberries and bananas will shrivel with the first few sprays.

Salt-contaminated water can be used when combined with good quality water to give safe concentrations. A blend of municipal water and saline well water is one way of helping to meet the crops' moisture needs.

Pumpkin

Where water sources are suspected of being contaminated, have a sample tested by the local cooperative extension service office.

Water can be delivered to the plants through oscillating wands, pulsating sprinklers, soaker hoses and drip systems. Any method that wets the soil is fine for the plants. However, water is a valuable resource and should be conserved.

Hand watering

Hand watering to sprinkle the foliage or wet the surface of the soil is the least effective method of irrigating the garden, yet gardeners often are seen out in the early evening with a finger over the hose, spraying the plant foliage. Most are not patient enough to do a good job of wetting the soil to a depth of several inches.

Sprinkling the plants with water tends to be an every-night affair. This technique encourages development of shallow root systems and a dependency on frequent waterings. Watering vegetables in the early evening hours also can encourage disease problems by excessively wetting the foliage.

However, hand watering often is the best technique for container plantings. Gardeners easily can see when the pots or planters are filled with water and moisture is draining from the holes in the container bottoms. They also can detect by touch or soil color which containers need watering so just the right moisture level is maintained.

Container plantings sometimes need daily waterings during the hot, dry months. A thorough soaking every few days is all that is needed when the cool season arrives.

An alert gardener is the best judge of soil-moisture levels for containers, but drip irrigation has been adopted to make the job a bit easier for busy gardeners.

Overhead irrigation

Overhead sprinklers, inexpensive and easy to install, are the standard way to water the garden, but they are not very efficient. Much of the water evaporates before being used

Sprinkler types

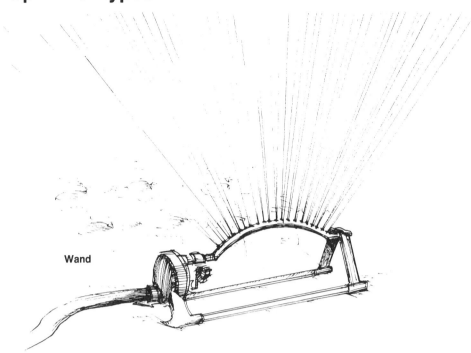

Wands gently apply water to the crops and can be placed where needed. The overhead irrigation does waste water to evaporation.

Impulse sprinklers can be adjusted to irrigate small plantings or large beds. Strong sprays of water from the heads may damage plants or splash soil on the foliage.

Adjust soaker hoses to distribute water near the base of vegetables. The hoses can be positioned easily throughout the landscape to water trees and shrubs.

by the plants because foliage and soil are wet indiscriminately.

Oscillating wands mimic a gentle rain as they sweep back and forth. Foliage seldom is disturbed and soil is not likely to splash up on growing crops.

Pulsating sprinklers can be custom-tailored to the needs of an individual site. Sprinkler heads can be placed at ground level or on posts; sprays can be set to large or small droplets. Full-force spray can damage foliage and flowers, so position these sprinklers with care. Adjust the flow to a medium droplet size that hits both plant and soil gently. Foliage and fruit splashed with sand mean more work washing at harvest time.

Soaker hoses are similar to other forms of overhead irrigation except that water sprays out in fine streams from slits or holes in a hose. The water usually rises slightly above plants, wetting foliage, flowers and fruit as it moistens the soil. Some water is conserved because hoses are placed where water is needed. Most of the water is distributed close to the surface, reducing evaporation.

Drip irrigation

Drip irrigation works like a leaky faucet in a situation where a leaky faucet is exactly what's wanted. It applies water over and around roots.

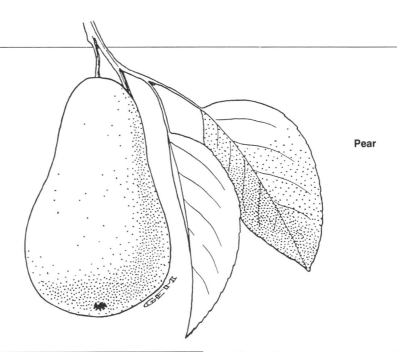

Pear

It is almost inconceivable such small drops can water rapidly growing plants, but drips do make gallons and, in time, wet an increasingly large area. The water spreads out under the surface, going wide and deep to moisten roots. Little moisture is lost to the atmosphere, sprinkled over sidewalks or wasted on weeds. The result is savings on water bills and wise use of a precious resource.

The soaker hose, in which slits in a hose spray water to a select area of the garden, is a forerunner. Soaker hoses operate under high pressure, however, and waste water to the air. Picture a soaker hose just barely seeping water and you have the drip concept.

Do's and don'ts of watering

Do:

- Water when top half an inch to inch layer of soil begins to dry.
- Apply half an inch or more of water.
- Moisten soil thoroughly.
- Use mulches to stretch time between irrigations.
- Water after fertilizing.
- Water at least a few hours before applying pesticide.
- Water vegetables during early morning hours.

Don't:

- Water daily after seeds and transplants are established.
- Water just to wet the foliage or the soil surface.
- Water unplanted soil.
- Water before fertilizing unless soil is very dry.
- Water immediately after applying pesticide.
- Irrigate to wet the whole plant. (Wet foliage leads to disease.)
- Water late in the day, so that foliage and fruit are wet overnight.

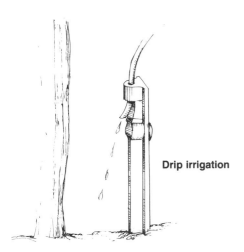

Drip irrigation

A steady flow of water droplets wets the soil in the root zone of crops. Moisture spreads out underground to dampen the root system. More than 1 dripper may be needed per plant.

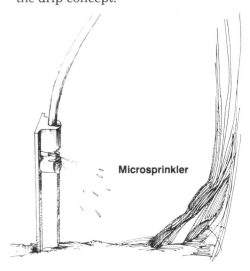

Microsprinkler

Microsprinklers save water by wetting soil around the base of plantings. Several sprinklers may be needed around large trees and shrubs.

Drip irrigation

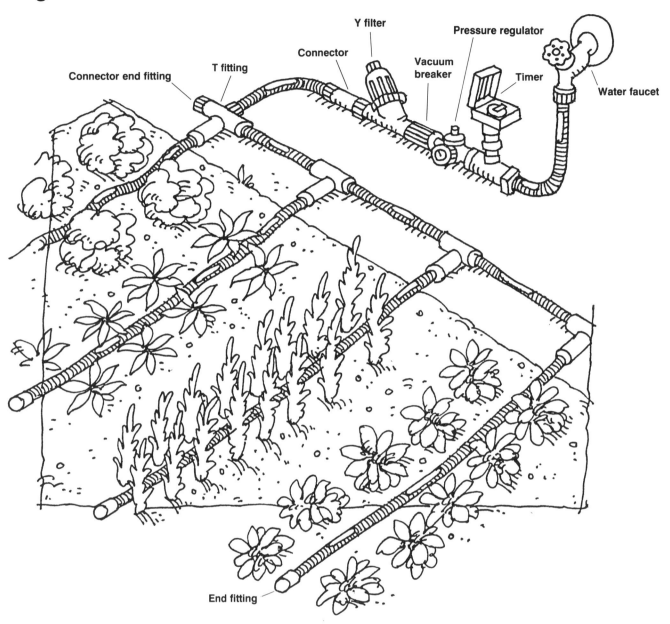

Drip irrigation systems put the water where it is needed — at the base of the plants. A timer can be installed to turn the system on while you are away. Systems run for about an hour, until the soil is moist.

A drip irrigation system consists of a plastic hose for a supply line and a number of emitters that apply water near plants, drop by drop. Emitters are more than slits in the pipe. Each meters a specific flow of water from the supply line. Some are spaghetti-size tubes with open ends; others appear to be miniature faucets. Each is a water miser, supplying moisture only where crops are to grow.

Drip irrigation is easy to install, although some systems take time. Lay the plastic water pipe near growing plants or along the garden row. Products packaged for home use let the gardener place the emitters along the supply line. A tool is provided to punch holes in the supply pipe so the emitters can be inserted near each plant or planned planting.

Agricultural systems, with the emitters already installed in the supply line, are simpler to install. In five minutes or less, a hundred feet of system can be hooked up to the water system and be ready to use. The only problem is that emitters may not be where they are needed unless plantings are carefully planned ahead.

Like other systems, drip irrigation usually is turned on as the soil dries and plants begin to show signs of stress. Moistening the soil in the root zone takes an hour or more; then the system is turned off until needed again.

A few systems operate continuously, dispensing a drop of water every three to four seconds. For these, calculate 12 gallons of water a day to keep a hundred feet of garden row moist.

Cost? Outlay truly is just a drop in the bucket. Simple systems start at $10 per hundred feet of row and run to $50 for some prepackaged systems. It pays to shop around, and do-it-yourselfers definitely come out ahead. The conservation of water, as mentioned already, keeps operating costs minimal.

Such a unique watering system does have a few drawbacks. Emitters can plug, although installing a filter in the supply line usually will prevent clogs. Fertilizing is more difficult. To supply fertilizer through the lines requires a sophisticated system, so most gardeners must rely on conventional irrigation or rain to wash fertilizer into the soil.

Microsprinklers or minisprinklers are another way to deliver water only where it is needed. Water volume is low — these sprinklers use only a few gallons per hour — and distribution is limited to fan or full-circle patterns. Often they are used to moisten the soil under one big plant or along a portion of a row.

Like drip emitters, microsprinkler or minisprinkler heads are inserted in a plastic supply line. Often the heads can be pressed into a puncture in the line; others are glued or screwed in place. Using them to thoroughly wet the soil normally takes 45 minutes to an hour.

Microsprinklers often are used in combination with drip emitters to give the best possible coverage.

When to water

Irrigation timing depends on plant needs. In general, water when the top half an inch to inch of soil begins to dry. Frequent checks will help the grower spot drooping leaves or other signs of plants in distress.

Thick-leaved cabbage, collards and broccoli will not dry out as fast as plants with thin, large leaves such as squash, cucumbers and pumpkins. Young plants, or vegetables with root problems such as nematodes, may need frequent watering.

Established trees and shrubs with deep and far-reaching root systems usually can go a week or more without rain or other irrigation. Planting in improved soil and adding mulch helps stretch the time between waterings to the maximum.

When irrigation is needed, be sure to thoroughly moisten the soil. Do not, however, just let a hose run by the tree or shrub for an unlimited amount of time. Use an overhead, drip or similar system that effectively wets the root zone and then allows the soil to dry.

The best time of the day to water is between 4 a.m. and 6 a.m. There will be little wind to blow the water from sprinklers onto walks and buildings, less evaporation and some dew may be washed off the plants to add additional moisture to the soil.

Extending waterings into the normally dry morning hours or starting before the dew forms at night can keep the plants excessively wet and encourage disease problems.

Wet the soil thoroughly each time; avoid just wetting the surface. Theoretically, half an inch of water will moisten sandy soil 6 inches deep. Hard-to-wet organic soils, clays, or gardens with a heavy mulch may need as much as an inch of water to wet the same depth, but will hold the moisture longer.

It will not hurt crops to wilt a little. The big, thin leaves of squash, melons and similar crops frequently droop during the heat of the day.

Plants normally recover as afternoon temperatures drop and the sun becomes less intense. Sustained wilting may indicate irrigation is needed, however, so check for dry soil.

Mulches help retain moisture. Whenever possible, cover soil with 2 to 3 inches of organic matter — sawdust, compost, leaves or old hay. Even newspaper or plastic can be used.

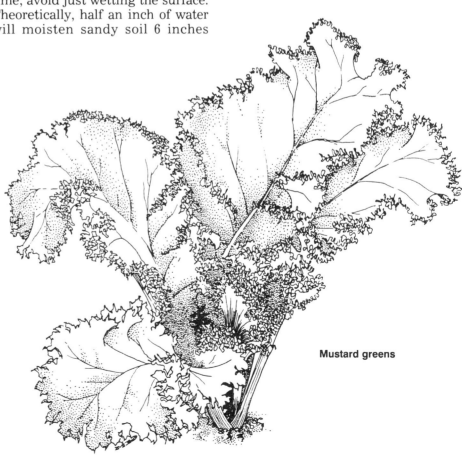

Mustard greens

9
Maintaining the garden

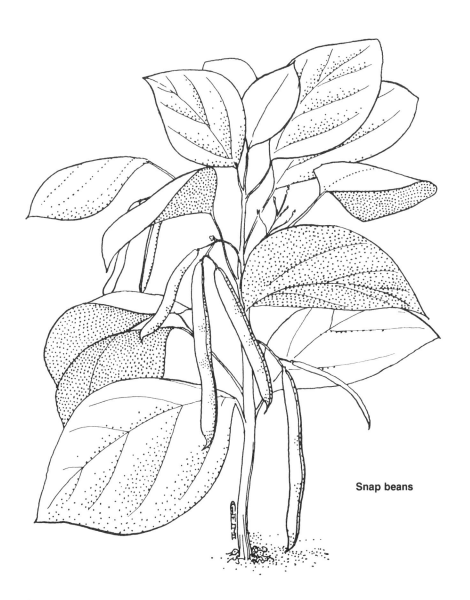

Snap beans

THE TIME BETWEEN PLANTing and harvest is when many gardeners lose their plants. The great enthusiasm generated for tilling and planting dwindles as plants begin to grow. Maintenance — watering, fertilizing, pulling weeds, directing growth, just checking plant needs — can be tedious.

Daily garden visits are the surest way to achieve rewarding harvests. The needs of plants can change drastically in a few days. Soil dries and pests invade overnight. A small effort made during a daily visit to hoe a few weeds, destroy some insect eggs, or tie a wandering shoot to a trellis can save hours later in the week. Garden visits also help the gardener harvest crops at their best. Beans, corn, tomatoes and melons reach their peak, then quickly spoil.

Watering

Without moisture, plantings shrivel and die. Even if crops are drought tolerant, the lack of adequate water means fewer harvests and inferior-quality fruit and vegetables.

Some wilting cannot be avoided and appears to be beneficial. When plants are under a little stress, roots tend to grow out a bit farther or deeper into the soil. The plant is not looking for water, as many believe, but the effect of the added growth may be more water absorption by the new roots.

Many plants wilt or curl their leaves during the heat of the day. This is a defensive maneuver that conserves moisture while the plant is excessively hot and would not be able to carry on normal growth processes anyway.

Maintenance watering means supplying moisture when the root zone begins to dry. In sandy soils during hot, dry conditions, this may mean frequent, every-other-day irrigation. Well-prepared soils enriched with organic matter or clay soil will hold a reserve of moisture. Here watering often can be delayed for four or more days, even during the hotter, drier months.

When plants are watered, give them a good soaking. After watering, the soil should be thoroughly moistened in the upper 4 to 6 inches. Normally, between half an inch and an inch of rain or watering is adequate to wet the soil if applied over a period of about an hour.

Fertilizing

Water and fertilizer together nurture a healthy garden. Many gardeners are accustomed to clay or loam soils where one or two applications of fertilizer last a season. Like moisture, nutrients are held in these heavier soils for plants to draw on. In sandy soils, nutrients leach away with the water. As rapidly as they are lost, nutrients must be replaced for the garden to be productive.

Adding clay to sandy soils helps hold nutrients in place, but most gardeners prefer to improve their soil by adding organic materials — leaves, manure or vegetation — that rot quickly. Over the years, liberal additions of organic materials will help build soil that holds moisture and supplies nutrients.

Meanwhile, supplemental feedings keep plants vigorous and productive. When plants grow reluctantly or start turning yellow, fertilizer may help. Do, however, avoid overfeeding. If plants are green and vigorous, wait a little longer. Too much fertilizer can burn plants. Tomatoes and beans given too much fertilizer grow lots of rich, green foliage but little fruit.

Vegetables growing in porous, well-drained soil should be fed frequently. Usually a balanced fertilizer, a 6-6-6 or similar analysis, is applied every three to four weeks throughout the growing season at a rate of 1 pound to each 100 square feet of garden or 100 feet of row.

Do not stop feeding at the first sign of fruit. Continue to feed the plants to encourage ongoing production.

Vegetables growing in clay soils will need less fertilizer. One supplemental feeding four to six weeks after planting usually will be sufficient to produce a crop.

Similarly, crops growing in organic soils may need little additional fertilizer; use foliage color and plant vigor as a guide. In gardens where the soil is sand enriched with organic matter, one or two addition-

Fertilizing techniques

Side dressings put the fertilizer near the root systems for rapid use by plants.

Surrounding a plant with a light fertilizer application conserves nutrients when treating a few or widely spaced plants.

A scattering of fertilizer is quick and distributes nutrients over the entire root system. Wash fertilizer off foliage and avoid spreading fertilizer on walkways and unplanted areas.

al feedings at intervals of three to four weeks usually will suffice.

Leafy vegetables may need only nitrogen to grow large, tender foliage. Scatter a quarter of a pound to half of a pound of nitrate of soda or similar source of nitrogen down 100 feet of row every three or four weeks to get the best production from cabbage, kale, collards, lettuce and spinach.

Root crops such as sweet potatoes, potatoes, beets, carrots and turnips often benefit from an extra dose of potassium. Spread a quarter of a pound of muriate of potash down each 100 feet of row once or twice during the growing season.

Dry fertilizer can be applied in many ways — scattered over the entire garden, down a row or ringed around individual plants. To ensure successful supplemental feedings:

• Avoid feeding when foliage is wet.

• Water after feeding to remove particles from foliage.

• Use small amounts or light concentrations of fertilizer.

• Keep fertilizer away from plant stems.

• Spread fertilizer over the root zone.

Animal manures used in place of chemical fertilizer are best applied as a side dressing. The manures that sometimes also contain animal bedding are placed next to the rows so the roots can absorb the nutrients.

Spread up to 5 pounds of cow, horse or pig manure or up to 3 pounds of poultry or sheep manure along 100 feet of row and water to begin washing the nutrients into the soil. Side dressings can be made three or four weeks after planting and repeated as needed to maintain growth.

Manure also can be applied around tree, shrub and vine plantings to encourage crop production. Use the manure and bedding as a mulch that also feeds the plantings. The side-dressing rates can be used in mulching every 100 square feet of the edible landscape. Apply once during the late winter, midspring and midsummer seasons.

Water-soluble fertilizers often are useful as a quick boost for vegetables. Liquids or crystals mixed with water are applied as frequently as once a week. Follow label directions for best results. The nutrients, easily distributed by a gardener with a sprinkling can, are readily available to plants.

Gardeners wishing to avoid strictly chemical fertilizers can use fish emulsions or manure teas. Fish emulsion, typically of a 5-1-1 analysis, is mixed with water and sprinkled around plants as a liquid feeding. Feed every two to three weeks or as needed.

Manure tea is made by seeping a quantity of manure in a barrel of water. The amount of manure is not exact, nor is the quantity of water. Start with a barrel or tub that holds 5 to 10 gallons of water. Place several shovels full of manure in a porous cloth sack. Soak the sack of manure in the water until the water becomes the color of weak tea. Use as a liquid feeding every few weeks or as needed.

Many gardeners use a combination of feeding techniques. Granular products or manures supply the main nutrients, and liquids are applied to correct minor deficiencies or quickly boost growth. Liquids are particularly handy when plants are grown in containers. Applica-

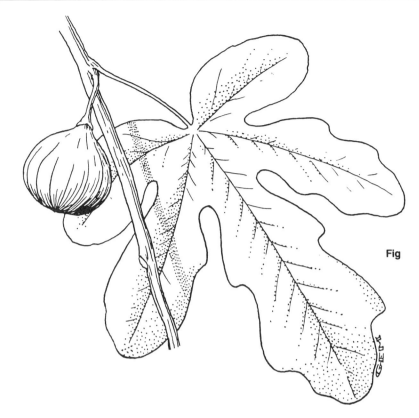

Fig

tions can be made weekly when plants are young and reduced to an every two- to three-week schedule as flowering and harvest time arrives.

Foliar feeding, a technique of spraying plants with dilute liquid fertilizer, rarely is part of a regular maintenance program. Rather, it is used to provide a special boost or to compensate for deficiencies in minor nutrients such as iron, manganese and zinc. Follow label instructions when making these special applications.

Mulching

Spread a layer of organic matter across the surface of the garden to conserve moisture, keep soil temperatures uniform and prevent weeds. Mulches can be applied before planting or added after the crops are up and growing. If applied after tender vegetables and herbs are set in the ground or seeds have germinated, care must be taken to avoid mechanical injury to the crops as the layer is formed.

Compost makes an ideal mulch. Its loose consistency allows air and water to penetrate into the soil. The deteriorating organic matter also holds a wealth of major and minor nutrients that are slowly released to the plantings.

Other good mulches include animal bedding with manure, leaves, bark, pine needles and grass clippings. Even a few sheets of newspaper, a plastic tarp, old rug or strips of cardboard can be used for mulch. Do be sure water can penetrate through the mulch so moisture and fertilizer reach the plant roots.

Plastic sheeting needs to be perforated to assure good water movement down to plant roots. Even leaves and grass clippings can repel moisture. Usually a 2- to 3-inch layer of these organic materials is adequate. If the mulch becomes matted, rake to loosen the surface layer.

A bale of hay or straw can be used as a quick mulch. A fresh-from-the-farm bale could be full of weed seeds or grains, so make the mulch layer a little thicker than normal to suppress weed growth. Be prepared to rake organic matter periodically to disturb any grains or grasses that might try to grow. Bales are available year-round at most feed stores. A bale is enough to mulch a few hundred square feet of garden.

Ignore stories that some mulches are bad for the garden or will rapidly change the acidity of the soil. Most decomposing organic matter

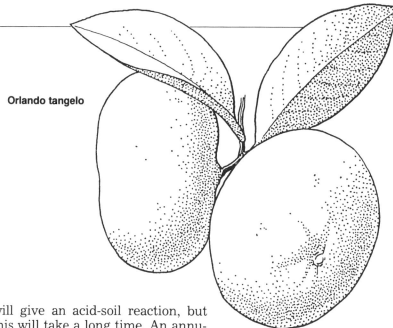

Orlando tangelo

will give an acid-soil reaction, but this will take a long time. An annual test of the soil to determine pH will allow plenty of warning that the soil acidity is changing and can be corrected before the next planting. Of all the ingredients that could be added to the compost or mulch layer, walnut leaves are one that might be avoided because of associated toxic properties.

Mulches are applied to almost every garden planting except citrus. Mulch, weeds or any debris gathered around the trunks can contribute to foot rot, a fungal disease common to citrus. Gardeners who would like to conserve moisture should keep the soil within a few feet of the tree trunk free of mulch, then apply a thin organic layer out over the remaining portion of the root system.

Weeding

Few people enjoy weeding, yet in every edible landscape there are bound to be errant growths most call weeds. A weed is really just a plant out of place, but if it competes with crops for moisture and nutrients, it should be prevented or removed.

Weeds also harbor insects and can serve as a source for disease-causing inoculum. A few weeds may have to be tolerated, but most should be kept out of the garden and away from trees, shrubs and vines.

Cultivation is an ancient way of eliminating weeds. Many have visions of the farmer cultivating the fields or hoeing a row of potatoes. Weeding is work; preventing the growth is easier.

Soil fumigation or solarization before planting will control many weed seeds before they germinate. The garden preparation must begin weeks in advance to take advantage of the treatments.

Use mulch to keep weeds in check. Several inches of organic matter spread around plantings can eliminate most hoeing and weeding by hand.

One method of minimizing weeds is to cover the soil with perforated plastic, several sheets of newspaper or modern landscape fabrics. When

Mulching

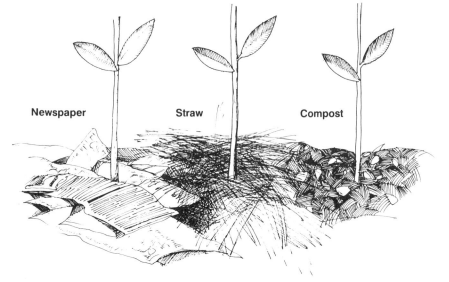

Organic matter of all types can be used to form a mulch layer to keep plantings moist, soil temperature even, and to control weeds.

the coverings are in place the weeds will have difficulty sprouting. Add a covering of organic matter and the site is decorative and well-protected from weeds.

With mulch in place, water and fertilize as usual. Do not take up the mulch. Water and apply fertilizer over the top layer. It may appear the fertilizer has not entered the soil because the carrier for the nutrients may remain on the surface of the mulch. However, the nutrients are washed off the carrier and into the soil with the first rain or irrigation.

Some weeds will have to be pulled or hoed out. Try to eliminate the weeds when they are young. Weeds with small root systems pull easily and will not disturb crops when they are removed. As garden crops grow tall and spread out, they shade germinating weed seeds and less control is needed.

Container-grown plantings usually have few weeds, but some seeds may be blown in and here, too, some hand-pulling may be needed. Use of a weed-free prepared potting mix is one way to avoid weed problems. If unwanted growths are expected, try fitting landscape fabric or sheets of perforated plastic around the plants to cover the soil. Where needed, a thin layer of mulch also could be added.

Sky-high plantings

Another maintenance task is to provide plants with appropriate support. Many vining plants will be just as productive given a fence or trellis to climb. Some yield more, and produce is clean and easy to reach.

Even some bush plants are better grown with support. Fewer branches are broken and crops like eggplants, tomatoes and peppers are more visible. Growing a sprawling plant in an upright fashion also saves considerable garden space.

Just an 18-inch stake next to a tall-growing plant provides reassurance it won't fall over during the next rainy or windy day. Plants loaded with fruit often appear to topple easily. Set the stake in the ground just a few inches from the main stem. Then place several ties around the stake, main stem and

Staking

A single stake will support floppy, low-growing plants that might be injured by winds or abundant productions.

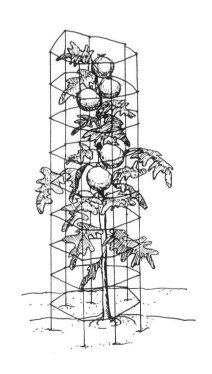

A wire cage gives the best support for well-branched or tall-growing plants. Use wire with wide openings to make maintenance and harvest easy.

limbs to secure the plant. Leave the ties a bit loose to allow some gentle movement.

Ties can be bought at a garden center, but it is cheaper to make your own. Cut rags into 12-inch lengths or longer or use panythose cut into appropriate lengths and widths for extra-strong ties.

Trees and shrubs also may need support. Stakes commonly are placed near trunks to secure the tree during the first year of growth. The ties should allow some movement but prevent major upheavals. A wire cage may be needed for tropical raspberries and a trellis for some varieties of blackberries.

Plants need help and guidance to climb a support. Many grow upward, but only a few have tendrils or other means of holding on, and even plants with holdfasts may be dragged down by the weight of their developing crops. Melons may need a special support for each fruit — a cloth sling, a net bag or a small wooden shelf.

Tie growth securely in place, making provisions for future growth. Avoid a major tangle by directing shoots early. Positioning and tying stems make for a shapelier plant, one that best covers its trellis or fills its support.

The simplest support, a stake pounded into the soil, works best with a fairly low-growing, single-stemmed plant that is likely to become top-heavy. Tie the plant in place as it grows up the stake.

Another simple support can be made from a few poles and a rope. Sink bamboo, saplings, or 2-by-2s several feet into the soil and zigzag the rope between them to make a rough ladder for the plants to climb. This trellis is quick to assemble and economical; although the rope usually must be thrown away after a season, the poles often can be used again.

Take advantage of a chain-link fence if possible; if none exists, construct an inexpensive garden fence by stapling chicken wire to poles sunk at least 2 feet deep. Although not a permanent installation, it can be placed exactly where needed and moved easily. A chicken-wire fence can last for years.

Sturdy cages for tomatoes are made from concrete reinforcement wire mesh. The wire is heavy gauge and the holes of the mesh are about 5 inches by 6 inches, big enough to easily fit a hand through.

Building supply companies sell long rolls 5 feet wide. A 5-foot length makes a cage 18 inches in diameter. After placing it over a transplant, stake the cage to the ground to help the future fruit-laden plant withstand a windy day.

Support systems can become elaborate. Cucumbers and beans, for example, quickly mount wooden latticework tacked to rigid pole supports. Vining squash will readily fill an overhead arbor. Gardeners should consider the site and decide whether to construct a permanent, decorative trellis, arbor or gazebo. Those who do should protect their investment of time and money by using treated or rot-resistant lumber.

Pest patrol

Make every trip into the landscape a pest patrol. It is only by watching for plant abnormalities that insect, disease or cultural problems are spotted. When leaf spots, moving bodies and declining plant portions are detected early, the pests often can be eliminated and the harvest saved.

When a few insect eggs are detected or small colonies are spotted, cut off and destroy the beginning infestation. Diseases that can spread rapidly can be controlled on plants of the same variety if the initial infection is detected.

When pests are suspected, thoroughly search the foliage and stems. Beginning stages of insect infestations and diseases may be prevalent on the lower as well as upper sides of leaves. Sometimes a magnifying glass is needed to check plants for the first feeding of mites and other small insects.

Some plant problems begin underground. Often when a plant wilts or grows slowly, the roots are having difficulties. The problem could be as simple as compacted soil that resists root growth or as damaging as nematodes causing galling, which inhibits moisture and nutrient intake. Dig around the plants to make this diagnosis.

If problems are not easily diagnosed, help is available at garden centers and extension service offices. Take fresh, representative samples of the affected plant for examination. Include leaves, stems and roots, especially if the entire plant appears affected. A pint of soil also can be taken for analysis. Gather soil samples from the surface and down about 6 inches. The diagnosis of plant problems will be only as good as the samples taken for examination.

When pest or cultural problems are detected, act quickly to apply controls. Many insects and diseases multiply rapidly. Mites can double in population overnight and caterpillars become full grown in a few days. When conditions are right, the brown rot fungus of peaches can produce the familiar mushy spots overnight. Whether the controls are biological, chemical or mechanical, for the best results they need to be applied when problems are first detected.

Cold protection

Many warm-season vegetables as well as tropical fruits are damaged when temperatures approach 32 degrees. Citrus trees are a little tougher, with most varieties tolerating temperatures into the upper 20s. Only lemon, lime and Temples are extremely cold-sensitive and need protection at about 30 degrees.

Gardeners often are caught off guard by freeze warnings and typically resort to using sheets, quilts, plastic or even trash cans to provide quick plant protection. These covers protect against mild frosts but let extended freezing temperatures in to injure plants. Covers are most effective when supported above foliage and should be removed during early morning hours, before the sun begins to penetrate and damage plants. Better cold protection requires some advance planning.

Providing heat to warm trees, shrubs and vegetables gives maximum cold protection. The heat of a light bulb or two may be just enough to ward off the cold when entrapped under a cover. These semipermanent structures can be fashioned from cloth or plastic and supports. The tentlike structure should extend above and beyond the plant foliage. Leave the top or sides open for ventilation until the cold protection is needed.

Water from microsprinklers has been shown to be the best heat source. Even though the water freezes, heat is liberated and conducted to the plant surface. Small amounts of water are needed — about 10 gallons per hour sprayed over the trunk and lower limbs.

Protection must be provided to keep the wind from blowing the water around, which would reduce the effectiveness of the technique. Water can provide cold protection even when temperatures dip into the low 20s. Caution: Strong winds and failure to apply water evenly during the entire freeze period and until ice melts can cause major plant injury.

Pineapple

Cold weather protection

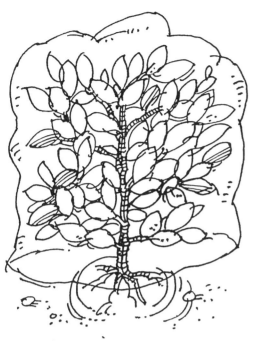

Good: Sheets, quilts or plastic

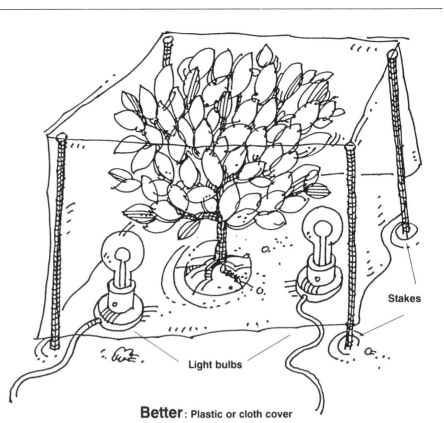

Better: Plastic or cloth cover

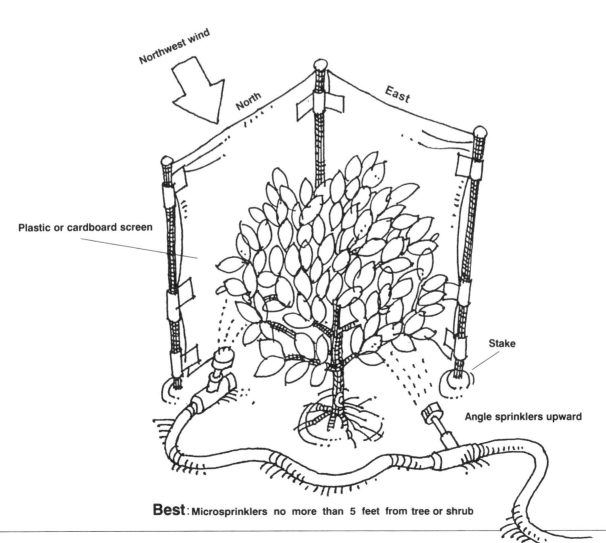

Best: Microsprinklers no more than 5 feet from tree or shrub

10
Harvest time

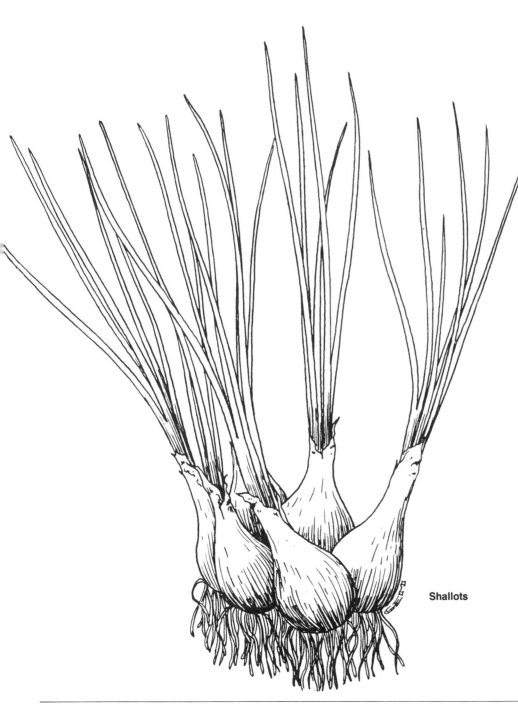
Shallots

ASSEMBLE BOXES AND BASkets to gather the fruits of your labors — it's harvest time. Crops that were just a vision when planning and planting the edible landscape may be maturing on the tree or in the garden. Learning when the crop is ripe is just as important as understanding how to plant.

A few crops, including carrots, sweet potatoes and citrus, can remain in the field until ready to be used, but cantaloupes, peaches and tomatoes should be picked at the peak of ripeness. Crops that store on the plant for only a short time usually are susceptible to rot organisms or plant pests all too ready to help with the harvest.

With herbs, leafy greens and many root-forming vegetables, harvest time can be any time there is enough of the vegetable to consume. Pick just a little mint foliage to flavor a drink or trim the tops of young chives to spice a salad. Small carrot roots can be stir-fried, and young beets can be cooked tops and all for an early garden treat.

It's good planning to have tender greens just a few weeks old to serve at the table. The first mustard or

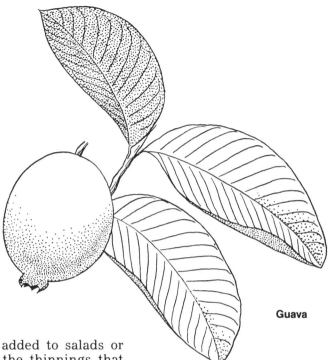

Guava

turnip greens added to salads or boiled can be the thinnings that leave room for more plant growth. Spring onions often are young stems that were planted close together and pulled early.

A few fruiting vegetables are ready to eat at any stage. Summer squash and cucumbers can be picked when the fruit first plumps out. They are extra tender, with small seed cavities. Small squash can be fried whole and the little cukes, pickled.

Most gardeners will allow a majority of the fruit to grow to a near-mature size as long as the skin and seeds remain soft. Be careful, however, as the difference between a young fruit and a too-mature vegetable can be just a few days.

Most fruit tastes best when harvested near full maturity. Cantaloupes are supersweet and fully ripe when they perfume the garden and turn yellow-orange. Harvest when the plant stem cracks and the fruit can be released from the vine with gentle pressure. These crops ripen overnight and must be gathered from the field.

The pineapple is another fruit that leaves little doubt when it's harvest time. The ripe fruit is exceptionally fragrant and begins to turn yellow. Other types of fruit that signal harvest time by a change in color include peaches, apples, grapes, guavas and bananas.

A number of crops keep you guessing. An unknown avocado variety may produce big fruit that for months appears to be ready to pick. But when are they fully mature? Because avocados do not soften on the tree, the fruit will have to be sampled throughout the growing season. Begin testing when similar trees in the neighborhood are ready to be harvested. Bring a fruit indoors, allow it to soften, then taste. This is one fruit that stores well on the tree and can be picked as needed over a period of one or two months.

Harvesting citrus seems simple, but the changing of color can be used only as a guide. The satsuma, a mandarin-type fruit, ripens early in the fall but may remain quite green. Yellow grapefruit often is quite bitter during late fall but extra-sweet in the spring. Rely on a taste test to determine harvest time.

Don't rush to harvest all the citrus early. Many gardeners miss the best flavor the crop has to offer by picking at the first hint of sweetness. Store some of the fruit on the tree and allow it to mature for full flavor. Like many types of fruit, citrus does not sweeten after it has been picked.

Hints from the grocery

Learn what ready-to-eat fruit and vegetables look like by visiting the grocery store or neighborhood produce stand. Commercial growers may not be able to harvest and ship produce at the peak of ripeness because it might spoil in transit, but

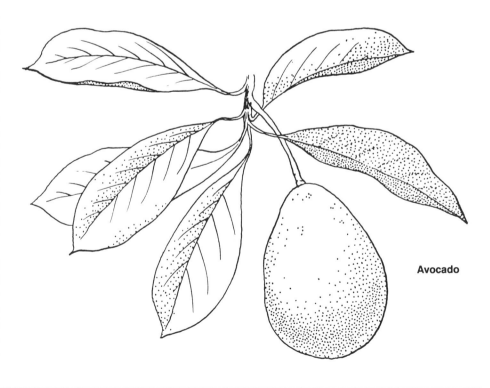

Avocado

examining the items offered for sale will provide an idea of the stage at which a crop is edible.

Store-bought tomatoes often tend to be green. Melons are picked before the flesh has softened and sugars have developed. These vegetables typically are of a usable stage, but gardeners can harvest their crops when produce is at its peak.

Use the store displays as a guide to size and color — to determine how big and how developed a head of cauliflower or broccoli should be when cut, or what a good-sized head of lettuce and a bunch of celery looks like.

Tomatoes allowed to grow on the plants until they are bright red will have fuller, richer flavor. Vine-ripened honeydews and cantaloupes will have an aroma, freshness and a taste never found in the store.

Use the information provided with the profiles of vegetables and fruit in Appendix I and experiment to find the peak of perfection for each.

More vegetable tips

Greens are edible almost from the start. Leaves can be thinned when just a few inches high or left to grow to a foot or more. Greens may grow beyond tenderness to become tough and bitter. Experiment to find the best stage.

Mustards, kale, collards, spinach and similar greens can be cut a leaf at a time or as an entire plant. Most gardeners prefer to harvest individual leaves at tender stages, allowing the plant to continue to grow.

Some growers believe that cold, especially a light frost, improves the flavor of greens. Sugars accumulate in leaves as the weather turns cool, and the flavor appears to remain mild.

The harvest time of some crops differs with varieties. With squash, for example, summer varieties are ready to eat as fruit forms. They are at their prime until the skin toughens and the seeds become large and hard.

Winter squash, on the other hand, can be consumed when young but develops its best flavor as the fruit matures. When the skin becomes thick and hard, the crop is ready to harvest. Winter squash may change

Harvest time for vegetables

Young to mature stages	
Beans, snap	Mustards
Beets	Onions
Cabbage	Okra
Carrots	Parsley
Celery	Peas, edible-pod
Chinese cabbage	Peppers
Collards	Pole beans
Cucumbers	Radishes
Endive/Escarole	Spinach
Kohlrabi	Squash, summer
Lettuce	Turnips

Mature stages only	
Broccoli	Potatoes, sweet
Cantaloupe	Pumpkins
Cauliflower	Squash, winter
Corn, sweet	Strawberries
Eggplant	Tomatoes
Peas	Watermelons
Potatoes	

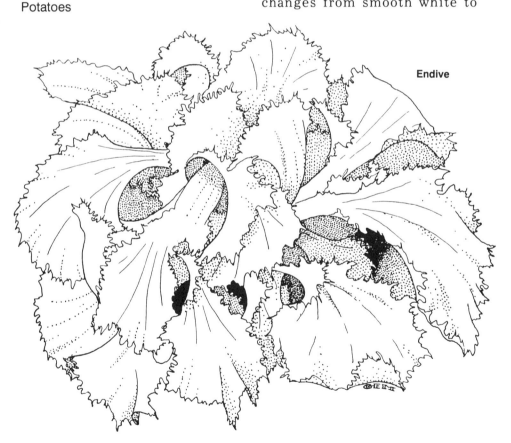
Endive

color, from a bright and shiny green to a dull green, or to yellow or orange. Often fruit is harvested only when the vines begin to die.

Melons, too, should remain on the vine to mature. Cantaloupes practically harvest themselves, as previously noted.

With other melons, a change of color helps determine ripeness. Honeydews are ready to eat when greenish fruit changes to ivory-green, often with a tinge of yellow. Casaba melons turn from green to gray-green. Melons also may develop a sweet aroma as they ripen.

Deciding when a watermelon is ripe can be a tricky task. Experienced farmers just look for an overall change in color and a slight flattening of the fruit, but most gardeners need better guidelines to pick watermelons that are red to the rind.

Thumping melons works only with some varieties. The idea behind thumping is that green melons give a ring when rapped, while ripe melons echo with a dull thud.

For further evidence, roll the melon over and check the belly. As the melon matures, the underside changes from smooth white to rough yellow and begins to feel a bit like sandpaper.

Finally, when the stringlike tendril on the vine nearest the watermelon dries and turns from green to brown, it is a sure sign the melon is ripe. When the indications all agree, it is harvest time.

Summer squash

For many types of fruit, a color change is a signal to the wildlife in the neighborhood to pick their share. Birds swoop down on grapes and blueberries at the first hint of purple. A net may be needed to protect the produce.

A color change also signals it is time to start sampling the fruit. Conquistador grapes turn a light blue or purple at first, but become deep purple and slightly soft when sweet and fully ripe.

Some types of fruit are tricky. Many papayas turn bright yellow when ready to harvest, while others remain green with only a tinge of yellow. Here, a softening of the skin signals it is time to harvest.

Astringent varieties of persimmons will cause the mouth to pucker if not picked when fully mature. Wait until fall when the fruit softens and turns bright orange to almost red.

Knowing the season a variety ripens is a big help in determining the time to pick. Try to keep a varietal name with the tree, shrub or vine. It is especially helpful in judging the time to pick citrus, avocados and mangoes.

Flowering crops present other dilemmas. Another stop by the grocery store may be helpful. The ideal time to harvest broccoli or cauliflower is immediately before the tiny buds open on the heads. When harvested too young, the crop is tasty but it is easy to overcook the heads and there is less to eat. Once the blooms begin to open, the heads will be edible but a little tough.

It is important to harvest crops at or just before peak maturity. Insects, birds and other pests may be waiting for vegetables to ripen. To avoid worm and bird damage, tomatoes may be picked when pink. Collecting squash and cucumbers a little early may prevent pickleworm damage.

To achieve the best harvests:

• Cut leafy crops early in the morning, when they are plump and full of moisture.

• Quickly refrigerate tender crops before they wilt or lose flavor.

• Leave corn on the stalk until the last minute. Have the water boiling or the fire ready to roast.

• Mulch plants to keep soil off edible leaves and fruit.

• Inspect the garden daily. Harvest frequently to discourage pests and to enjoy crops at their prime.

Tree-ripened fruit

Fruit of most woody trees, bushes and vines usually is picked near the peak of ripeness. Ideally, the crop is left on the plant to the last moment to gain sweetness and flavor. With many crops, pest problems or physiological decline determines how soon the fruit must be harvested.

Peaches cannot be left on the tree once the skin softens or brown rot and fruit flies will begin to damage the crop. Pears ripen during the hot summer and begin to break down internally if left to turn yellow on trees. Here it is best to pick the fruit just as the color change begins to prevent the internal browning.

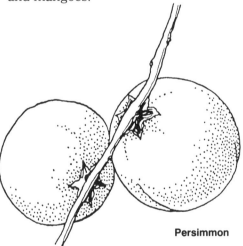
Persimmon

Cold weather strategy

Grab the covers to try and keep out the frost. Just a sheet or layer of newspaper can prevent a light frost from damaging tomatoes, beans or cucumbers. Covering with a layer of mulch also traps some heat and holds out the cold.

Gardeners trying to get the most out of a season are bound to run into a sudden cold spell when the crops are in danger of being lost to the cold. If the plants can't be protected, harvest.

Young beans, small squash and little cucumbers are usable. Harvest the green tomatoes to make pickles or preserves. The entire plant can be pulled and hung in a protected area, where the fruit will ripen gradually.

Winter crops of peas, carrots and beets can be damaged by a hard freeze. Root crops can be saved by mounding soil up along the row, but vining plants will need cover.

Often during a severe cold spell, the only way to prevent crops from freezing is to provide heat from a light bulb or other source. Even if the plantings are hurt by the cold, many will grow back and begin new production as the weather warms.

Most fruit ripens before cold weather is expected, but some citrus varieties mature between fall and spring and can be harmed by an arctic blast. Most trees and fruit can withstand temperatures into the high 20s.

If colder weather is predicted, harvest the ripe fruit, but remember that citrus does not improve in flavor once it is picked. It generally is best to leave the fruit on the tree even if a freeze is expected. First of all, the weather may not become as cold as predicted. If the fruit does freeze and become damaged, it will still be edible for some time — often, weeks.

Frozen citrus can be eaten and processed into juice. When a fruit survives a period of extreme cold but looks, smells and tastes good, most growers consider it edible. Citrus that drops to the ground after a hard freeze normally is not eaten.

With many fruiting plantings, the cold is likely to affect the next year's production by damaging dormant or opening buds. It may be necessary to protect with covers or irrigation to save trunks and lower limbs.

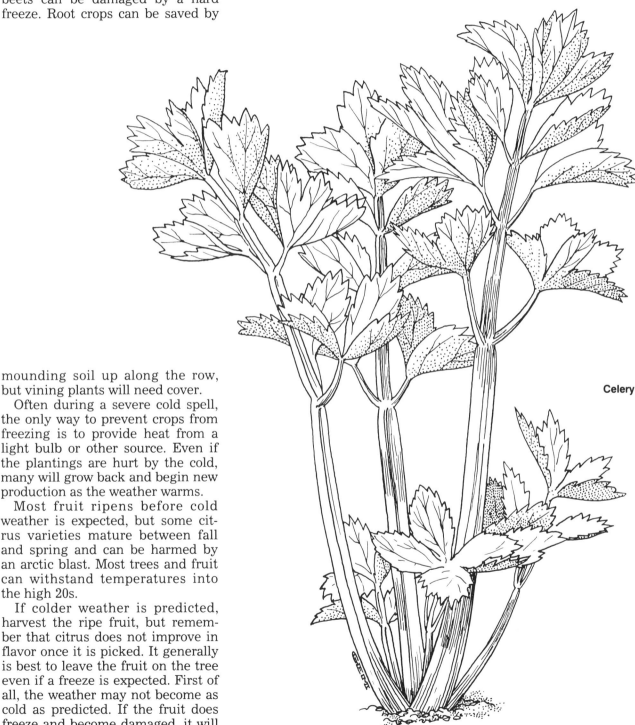

Celery

11
Grow a taste of the exotic

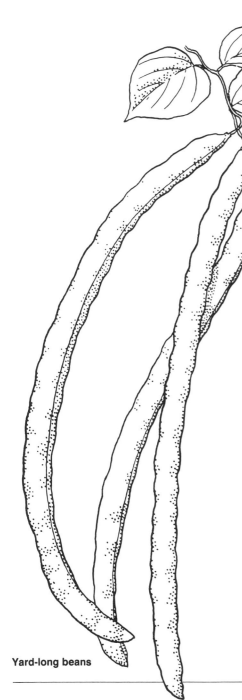

Yard-long beans

A WORLD OF EXOTIC VEGEtables can be right outside the door just for the planting. Grow the familiar crops but leave room to experiment with unusual vegetables.

New greens, beans and melons from around the world join the list of crops harvested in Florida as newcomers bring seeds and cuttings of many ethnic favorites. Among them, any gardener will find sights and tastes worth cultivating.

Crops from the tropics adapt well to the state's long growing season. They frequently need 10 months or more of warm to hot weather to produce a harvest. With all that time to grow, many exotic vegetables run rampant, developing extra-long vines or oversized leaves. They can take lots of space and may need to be confined to a trellis.

Vegetables that can take the heat are welcome. Familiar vegetables fade in summer's soaring temperatures and high humidity, but tropical plants flourish. Gardeners in central and northern areas can grow many selections spring through fall, while South Floridians enjoy production year-round.

Many greens also have been added to home plantings during the cool season. With increased interest in stir-fry cooking and in unusual salads, American seed companies are introducing new selections from Europe and Asia. Seed racks display a range of unusual greens to be sown directly in the garden or in containers for transplants. Many grow rapidly and produce a harvest in a matter of weeks.

The new vegetables with novel tastes often are relatives of old favorites. This makes production easier because growing conditions and principles will be similar.

Timing is the most important element; plants that require a long growing season need an early start. Stay aware of crop development and check harvest times to pick vegetables at their peak. A firm hand in guiding or pruning may be needed to keep the garden from becoming a jungle.

Fruit and seeds for these crops may be difficult to find. Check with gardening neighbors, who may save part of a favorite crop to replant.

Garden centers sometimes sell locally produced roots and transplants, and many catalogs feature specialty crops. Fruits and roots found in ethnic markets may be the start of a new planting.

Also, through the Florida Market Bulletin, a free publication of the state Department of Agriculture and Consumer Services, home and commercial growers offer all kinds of unusual plants for sale. For a copy, write Florida Market Bulletin, 545 East Tennessee Street, Tallahassee, Fla. 32308.

Calabaza

Suppliers of calabaza, also called Cuban squash or Cuban pumpkin, often promise fruit as big as car tires. This is a slight exaggeration, although 40-pound pumpkins have been harvested.

Calabazas, a type of winter squash, grow four or five to the vine and usually average 5 to 10 pounds. They resemble a slightly

Calabaza

flattened pumpkin and are mottled gray-green and cream.

Calabazas are good keepers, as suggested by the winter squash designation. They last many months in cool, dry storage, often through the winter.

The orange-colored flesh can be made into pies or mashed like sweet potatoes. Blossoms can be dipped in batter then fried, and the seeds can be toasted for snacks.

Most growers start seeds saved from a calabaza used for a meal, but seeds are available from specialty companies. Varieties LaPrimera and Marian Van Atta are recommended for Florida.

Calabaza grows spring through summer in cool regions and year-round in South Florida. As with other winter squash, production requires lots of room — vines can grow 40 feet long. Sow seeds 4 feet apart. Many gardeners add manure to each planting site. Water and fertilize like winter squash; the first fruit will be ready to harvest in 90 to 100 days.

The calabaza is one of the most heat-tolerant members of the cucurbit family. Plantings have few pest problems. Powdery mildew may affect foliage; it can be controlled with fungicides labeled for squash.

Cassava

The swollen root of the cassava plant is high in starch and used much like potatoes. Tapioca is made from cassava roots. The many names for this 6- to 8-foot-tall perennial include tapioca plant, manioc, manihot, yuca and sweet potato tree.

The species is divided into types producing bitter and sweet roots. All contain some quantity of toxic hydrocyanic (prussic) acid in the outer bark covering the roots. The sweet roots contain less of the acid.

It takes eight to 11 months of warm weather to produce a crop of usable roots, which grow five to 10 to a plant.

Begin new plantings with stem cuttings 10 to 12 inches long. Set the stems horizontally, 4 feet apart and 4 to 5 inches deep in a prepared garden site. New shoots and roots develop from buds along the stems. Plants like a moist, mulched soil and feedings every four to six weeks.

At harvest time, which is in the fall, the roots are several feet long and up to 3 inches in diameter. Cut the top of the plant and pull the roots to dry or use. The roots have a short storage life and should be used soon after harvest. Leave a plant growing or save several stems from which to make cuttings for new plantings when spring weather arrives.

Cassava root is washed and peeled before cooking. Boil in salted water to which is added a tablespoon of vinegar. When soft, the roots are drained and used.

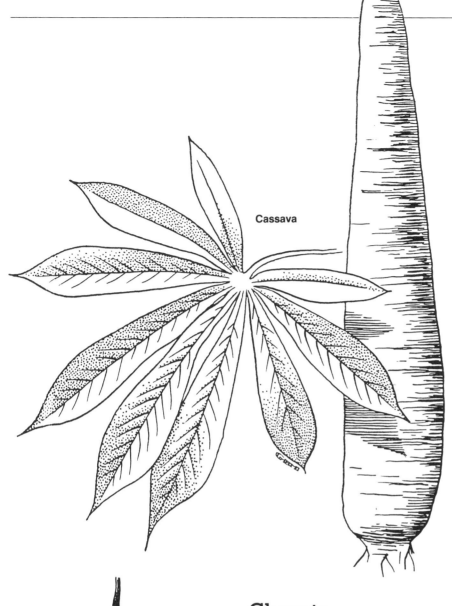

Cassava

Chayote

Chayote is becoming a common vegetable in Florida. Although a trellis is preferable, the vines can climb to the tops of tall trees to produce an early fall crop of pear-shaped fruit. A starchy, rootlike tuber, also edible, forms underground, but the fruit is more popular.

The vine often dies during winter, but roots, with buds just below the soil line, survive to start next year's crop. Nicknames include mango squash, vegetable pear and mirliton. Recommended varieties include Florida Green and Monticello White.

A single successful chayote plant may produce three to four bushels of fruit, with individual fruit weighing up to 3 pounds. They are eaten creamed, buttered, baked, pickled or in salads. Chayotes can be found in markets when in season to be cooked or to start a home planting.

Chayote fruit contains a single seed. To begin production, plant an entire fruit with the stem end at, or slightly below, ground level. Although the practice is common, chayotes are better not allowed to climb trees. Pick a head-high trellis or fence to hold the burgeoning vine.

One plant usually is all a garden can hold, often yielding as much as the family can handle as well.

The vines grow during the long days of summer. When shorter days arrive in late summer and early fall, the plant begins to flower. Fruit is ready to harvest by October.

Because day length is a factor, street lights or spotlights near the garden may delay or inhibit flowering and fruit production.

Nematodes are a major pest. In areas where high populations of nematodes are expected, treat the soil before planting.

Cocoyam

The tropical-looking cocoyam, also known as yautia and malanga, sends up big, elephant-ear leaves from the base to make a plant more than 5 feet tall.

The leaves resemble those of the dasheen, but the vegetables can be distinguished by the way in which the leafstalk connects to the leaf. In the dasheen, the connection is about in the middle, under the leaf; with the cocoyam, it is near the V-shaped notch.

The edible parts of the cocoyam are tubers, really sections of stem that enlarge underground. The tubers are washed, peeled and cooked. Yellow-fleshed varieties are more nutritious than Irish potatoes, and all are eaten boiled, baked, mashed and fried, as well as in soups, salads and stews.

A cocoyam plant will produce one large tuber and a number of smaller ones. Replant a whole tuber to grow new shoots and roots or cut a large one into pieces, each containing four or more buds or eyes, to start new plants.

Space the seed pieces 18 to 24 inches apart and 3 to 4 inches deep.

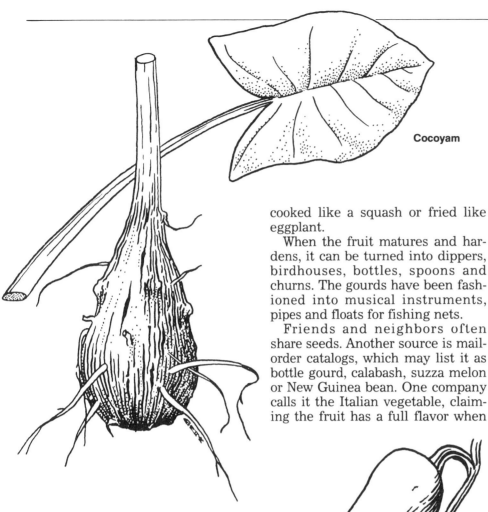

cooked like a squash or fried like eggplant.

When the fruit matures and hardens, it can be turned into dippers, birdhouses, bottles, spoons and churns. The gourds have been fashioned into musical instruments, pipes and floats for fishing nets.

Friends and neighbors often share seeds. Another source is mail-order catalogs, which may list it as bottle gourd, calabash, suzza melon or New Guinea bean. One company calls it the Italian vegetable, claiming the fruit has a full flavor when cooked and served with a tomato and herb sauce.

After the initial planting, gardeners may never have to plant another seed. Volunteer plants keep popping up to produce this rampant climber with hairy leaves, which may be up to 12 inches across.

Flowers are white; as usual with plants in the squash family, separate male and female flowers are produced on the same plant.

There is no great secret to growing cucuzzi gourds. The plants adapt to any bit of land where the seed falls. Some gardeners like to grow them over the compost pile, giving them ample nutrients, moisture and room to spread.

Dasheen

The large, round or heart-shaped leaves of the dasheen resemble their relative, the ornamental elephant ear. While many people grow this plant for food, others just enjoy the look of the foliage. The dasheen plant, which is also called taro, looks like the cocoyam.

Dasheen requires at least seven months of frost-free weather to produce a crop. In cooler regions of the state, plant at the end of winter to have a crop mature by October or November.

To start a new planting, set tubers 3 inches deep in rows 2 feet apart. Give them moist, enriched soil, and keep them moist and mulched to promote vigorous plant growth and tuber development. A feeding every four to six weeks is recommended.

When the tubers begin to form, around August, the foliage starts to decline. By fall, which is digging time, only a few leaves will remain.

Plants produce a central corm that usually weighs 1 to 2 pounds, but sometimes reaches as much as 8 pounds. Clusters of small tubers weighing just a few ounces surround the corm.

All portions are edible, with a delicate nutty flavor. To prepare, peel the tubers, boil for 20 to 30 minutes until soft, then serve like potatoes.

The leaves are edible if they first are cooked to remove an acrid, unpleasant flavor. Add a pinch of bak-

Although total production can take many months, harvesting on a limited scale can begin early. Dig and check for early maturing tubers in four to six months; harvest a few that show white on the tips.

Wait to gather the majority of the crop when plants begin to decline and leaves yellow around the edges. Plants need moist but well-drained soil, so enrich the garden with organic matter and use mulch.

Cucuzzi

The cucuzzi gourd has yet to become a popular vegetable, but it certainly attracts attention, swinging from tall trees or scrambling across backyard arbors.

This is the whopper of the gourd family, often growing 3 feet long and 3 inches in diameter. Gardeners are not quite sure how to handle these 15-pound giants, but most hold one like a Hercules club or swing it like a Louisville slugger.

Younger fruit, about 10 inches long and with fuzz still on it, can be

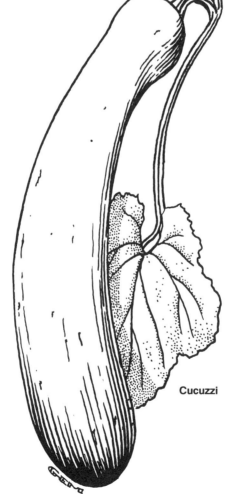

ing soda to boiling water, and cook the leaves until tender, about 15 minutes. Rinse with boiling water before serving as a green.

The large corms can be forced into growth in the dark to produce blanched, tender shoots said to have a mushroom flavor.

Garlic

Garlic may be a bit of a stinker, but it grows well in cool-season gardens throughout Florida. Fear of its pungent odor and taste limits most consumers to just a few bulbs a year. This is barely a month's supply for enthusiasts, who may use garlic whole, smashed, diced, powdered or in salts.

Curiosity usually prompts the first home planting. It is exciting to watch a single clove develop waist-high, onionlike foliage in eight months and produce a new segmented bulb.

Most garlic is used in cooking, but organic gardeners keep plants and extracts handy to discourage pests that threaten the vegetable patch. Superstitious folks reach for garlic to ward off evil spirits.

Garlic for the home garden includes common and elephant types. Growth patterns are similar, but the two are of different species. As the name implies, elephant garlic produces large bulbs, often two to three times the size of the common type. Elephant garlic also has a milder flavor.

Garlic bulbs form soft divisions called cloves. Plant individual cloves saved from previous crops, obtained at food stores, garden centers or ordered from other producers.

Common garlic does not produce fertile seeds and is reproduced only by the division of cloves.

To grow all varieties of garlic, begin by improving the soil in June. Fortify sandy soil with manure, cover crops and compost in preparation for a fall planting. Also incorporate an organic fertilizer, which will not leach from the soil before planting time.

Garlic can be planted October through January, but mid- to late fall is the best time. Wide-row intensive planting in raised beds is the best technique.

Make beds about 42 inches wide to allow room for seven garlic cloves across the bed spaced 6 inches apart. Place a teaspoon of bone meal at each planting site and push each clove about 2 inches into the loose, well-tilled soil.

Cloves germinate erratically. Chilling at 38 degrees Fahrenheit for a few weeks before planting appears to improve the stands.

Garlic is not a crop gardeners can sit back and watch grow. Plantings need a thorough watering about every three days to keep the soil moist. They need fertilizer every other month until a month before harvest. Apply 10-10-10 or a similar analysis at the rate of 1 pound to 100 square feet of bed.

Garlic cannot compete with weeds. Control weeds by mulching with an inch of compost or rotted horse manure immediately after planting.

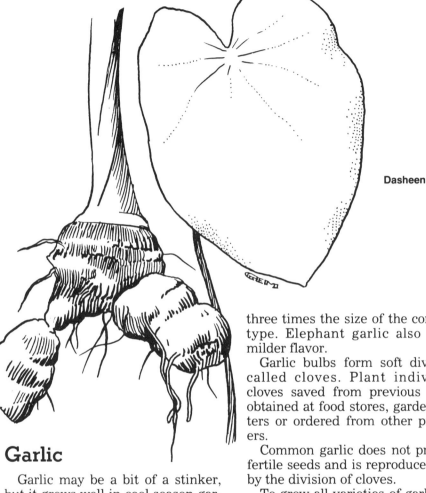

Dasheen

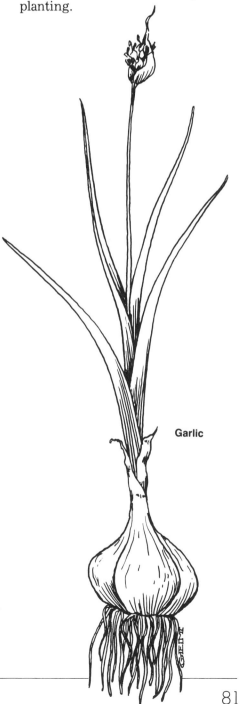

Garlic

As the plants begin to grow, weed the beds and incorporate the initial layer of mulch into the soil. Apply a second layer of mulch 2 inches deep, which should last the remainder of the growing season.

About February each elephant garlic sends up a tall, flowering spike. The white to purplish blooms would produce seed if left to mature. Snap them out to encourage the bulbs to divide. Walk the rows daily to break off the developing stalks and ensure a better harvest.

Other garlic types produce flower heads infrequently and should be removed when present.

Although it tastes wonderful straight from the garden, much of the crop will need to be dried and stored.

Garlic tells you when it is harvest time. In May, the leaves start to yellow and eventually collapse near the ground. When this happens, loosen the bulbs with a pitchfork and shake off the soil.

Hang the stalks upside-down to dry for three weeks, then cut the roots back to the bulbs, shorten the tops to 4 inches, and continue drying for another three weeks. Bulbs won't separate into individual cloves until they are dried. Store in a dry, cool location.

Horseradish

Gardeners who enjoy hot sauce may wish to try growing horseradish. The name is derived from the Latin *radix* for root, and horse refers to the strong flavor. The plant is a perennial member of the mustard family that likes cool, temperate climates.

Culture of horseradish is best attempted in the northern and cooler central portions of the state.

Root portions are planted during the early spring in 3- to 5-inch deep furrows made in an organic-enriched soil. Space the roots 24 inches apart and position segments horizontally with a little soil over the basal end. After all root cuttings are planted, fill the row with soil. A dozen or so plants usually are enough for the average family.

Keep the soil moist and feed every three to four weeks with a 6-6-6 or 5-10-10 fertilizer.

As the plants grow and leaves reach 8 inches in height, a cultural process called lifting must be performed to grow smooth roots free of side growths. Remove soil from the upper end of the main root and trim away small side roots. When trimming is completed, mound the soil up to its original level. Repeat the procedure in a few weeks.

Roots normally are harvested during the late fall, but the Florida crop often will be harvested at the end of spring — except in cooler northern portions of the state — to avoid summer heat stress. Dig a trench next to the rows and gradually remove the horseradish root, trimming away the tops and lower side shoots. Store in the refrigerator in a dark-colored bag to prevent the roots from turning green.

In warmer areas of the state, horseradish plants can be grown in containers. Give the plantings a full-sun exposure during the cooler months and a shady spot for the summer. Propagation usually is from saved root trimmings or purchased transplants. Seeds seldom are used.

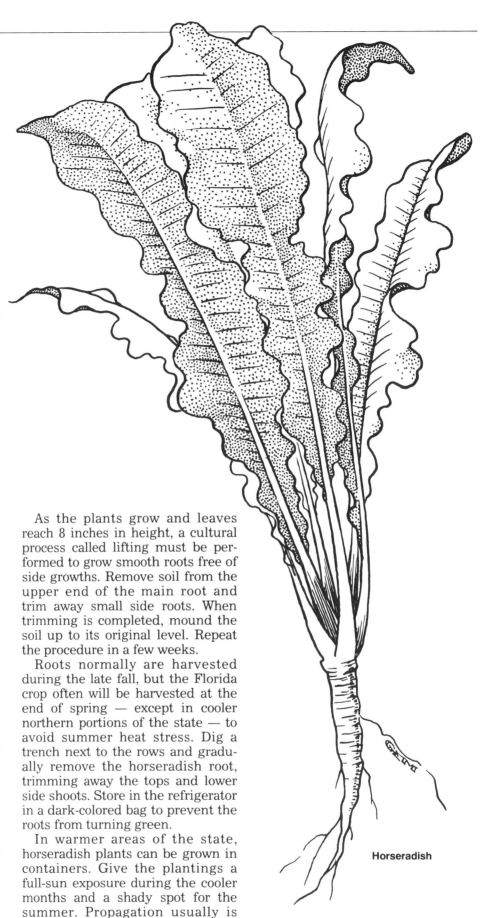

Horseradish

An oil within the root gives sauces and purees a biting taste. Peel the roots, then grate or boil.

Husk tomato

Until it is ripe and ready to pick, fruit of the husk tomato is hidden by a green, papery covering that gives rise to the common name, Chinese lanterns. The plant also is called ground cherry and tomatillo.

When ripe, the edible fruit swells the husk and softens, turning from green to yellow or sometimes orange, depending on species.

Plants can be heavy bearers. One plant can produce 2½ pounds of husk tomatoes, which can be eaten fresh, fried, baked, stewed or mixed with salads and soups. Ten plants should supply a family of four.

Husk tomatoes are grown like ordinary tomatoes. Start seeds in pots or nursery beds. Because seed may be difficult to find, save some from a previous crop. For a first-time start, check catalogs or buy fruit at the market and use the seeds.

Plants do well in most soils but produce more fruit when well-fertilized and watered. Staking is recommended because the plants grow more than 40 inches tall.

Plants started in March will begin fruiting by summer. Husk tomatoes store poorly, so use them shortly after harvest.

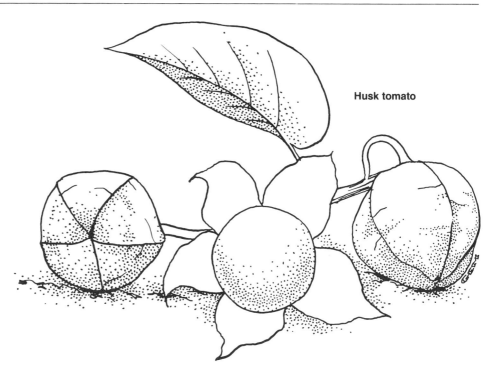

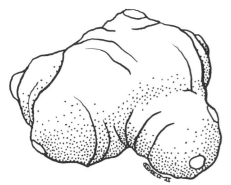

Jerusalem artichoke

Early explorers found the American Indians enjoying the native Jerusalem artichoke. The name is a bit confusing because the plant is neither from the Holy Land nor a true artichoke. The thistlelike globe artichoke, or true artichoke, has done poorly in Florida gardens.

Girasole, the Italian name for this crop meaning turning toward the sun, may be more appropriate because the Jerusalem artichoke is a member of the sunflower family and responds to strong light sources.

These broad-leaved plants grow spring through fall, 6 to 10 feet tall, and produce a crop of knobby tubers underground. The yellow-petaled flowers with dark centers produce small seeds that birds enjoy.

Start with Jerusalem artichokes bought from the grocery store, garden center or mail-order company. Plant the tuber whole or cut into sections that contain several buds. Set pieces 2 inches deep and 2 feet apart in an enriched soil.

A good site gives plants a moist, well-drained soil and full sun. Feed every three to four weeks with a balanced fertilizer.

The new tubers that form underground at the base of the main stem will be ready to harvest in about 130 days. Sneak a peek. The crop can be dug when tubers are about an inch in diameter and 3 to 4 inches long. They can be left in the ground until needed, or dried and stored in a cool location.

Slice or grate small Jerusalem artichokes and add them to salads. Eat large tubers raw or cook like potatoes. The taste is sweeter but very similar; the calorie count is much lower. Diabetic patients find them useful in controlling insulin levels because Jerusalem artichokes are low in starch.

Jicama

Leaves, flowers and seed pods of the vining jicama or Mexican potato are poisonous, but the underground tubers are edible. Cut and sliced, they have the consistency of water chestnuts and frequently are used in salads.

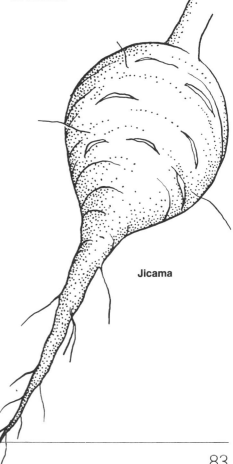

Don't judge jicamas by the taste of those found in grocery stores. They often are dry and bland-tasting, a poor introduction to the vegetable. When fresh, the large, flat to rounded tubers have a sweet, apple taste.

Seeds of jicama can be saved from a previous planting or bought from a few mail-order companies specializing in tropical vegetables. In north and central areas, planting begins in the spring as the weather warms; farther south, jicama can be planted year-round.

Sow seeds an inch deep near a trellis for a harvest in 120 days. Give them plenty of room because vines can grow 20 feet high. Space plants 12 inches apart. Provide a moist soil and feed every four to six weeks. Pinch off the purple blossoms to encourage the growth of large tubers; harvest in the fall.

Luffa

Luffa gourds easily could pass for an ornamental vine that also happens to produce 2-foot-long, strongly ribbed fruit.

The immature, tender fruit is eaten as a cooked vegetable similar to okra or summer squash. Mature fruit develops a fibrous interior that makes a good scrubbing cloth or sponge. Some descriptive common names for luffa fruit include Chinese okra, vegetable sponge and dishcloth gourd.

Luffas grow much like cucumbers or squash. Save seeds from a previous crop or buy packets from garden centers or mail-order companies. Start seeds when the weather warms.

Sow three or four to a cluster near a fence, trellis or arbor where the vines can be left to grow up to 15 feet long. Growth is rapid and will need just a little direction.

Keep the soil moist and apply a mulch over the root system. Feed lightly every three to four weeks.

Edible fruit will appear in about three months. A mature fruit takes almost five months. It can be turned into a sponge a couple of ways:

• Pick green but firm luffa gourd and wash in a weak bleach solution. Submerge the fruit in water for several days until the outer covering and the central pith can be removed by brushing. Rinse several times and air-dry before using.

• Allow the gourd to dry on the vine. Strip off the dry skin and submerge the fruit in water for several days to remove the fleshy portions. Change water frequently.

Allow the gourd to dry and remove the seeds. Hang the sponge-like remains in the sun to bleach or use a solution of hydrogen peroxide. Dry the sponge before using.

Malabar spinach

When true, cool-season spinach won't grow, gardeners have a substitute that can take the heat. The tropical Malabar spinach produces a vine that needs a trellis or fence to climb. It will produce edible greens throughout the summer, usually continuing until frost.

The plant also is called Indian spinach, Malabar nightshade or Ceylon spinach. Varieties Rubri and Basella Malabar Red Stem are aimed specifically at home growers.

Start seeds indoors for an early planting or sow directly in the soil to give a final spacing of 10 to 12 inches apart. Plants will grow 6 feet or more in height, with thick green leaves on red stems. Both the leaves and young stems can be cooked like spinach or mixed with salad greens.

New plants can be started from stem ends taken from established

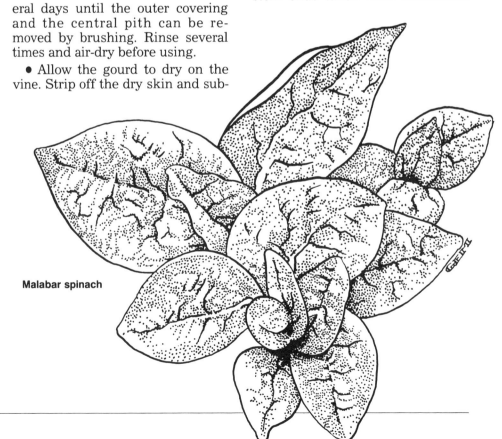

vines. Several plants can feed a family of four.

Grow in full sun to light shade; some growers believe afternoon shade is beneficial. Plants adapt to poor soil, but keep the soil moist to encourage the young, tender shoots. Feed every four to six weeks.

Momordica

Covered with what appear to be bumps and warts, this funny-looking fruit in the momordica family has the appetizing names of Chinese cucumber, balsam pear and balsam apple. All grow on perennial vines that usually are grown as annuals; they produce a harvest in three or four months.

Balsam apple is smaller, about 3 inches long at maturity, and is round or oblong. It also turns bright orange and splits open when ripe. Boil immature fruit and serve as a vegetable.

Treat them like cucumbers. Space seeds or seedlings 2 feet apart near a trellis. Vines will grow 10 feet or more, with ornamental foliage and flowers.

For all three species, fruit is bitter but palatable when young. Harvest before the fruit reaches mature size — about 8 inches long — and the skin toughens; older fruit is extremely bitter and tough.

Chinese cucumbers are light green and hollow. Remove the seeds before using the fruit in soups.

The balsam pear also is called bitter melon or La-Kwa. Its deeply furrowed fruit grows 4 to 6 inches long. When fully mature, it turns yellow-orange and splits open to reveal seeds with a reddish pulp. Immature fruit is boiled as a vegetable.

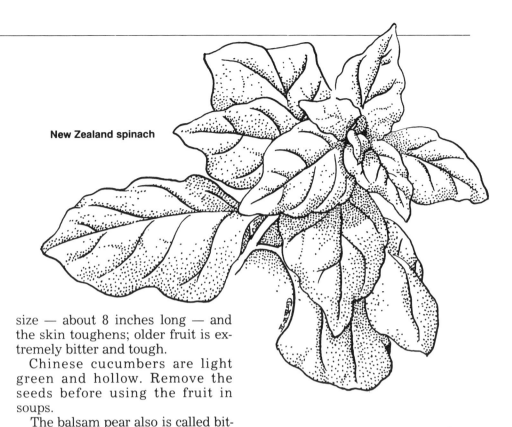

New Zealand spinach

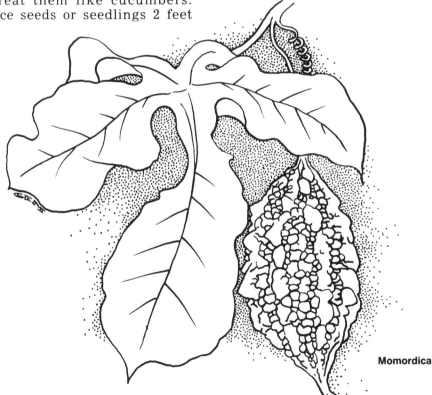

Momordica

New Zealand spinach

Heat-tolerant New Zealand spinach can be eaten spring through summer. A continual harvest of the tender, 2 to 3 inches of tip growth can begin about 60 days after planting.

Plant New Zealand spinach whenever the weather is warm. The seeds are slow to germinate and benefit from being soaked overnight in water.

Sow three-quarters of an inch deep and aim for a final spacing of 12 to 15 inches apart because plants grow 2 feet tall and equally as wide.

When the plants are a foot tall, begin cutting new shoots to eat for an early harvest and to encourage new growth.

Only young plant portions are harvested; older stems and foliage have a strong flavor. Young greens have a mild flavor and are cooked like spinach or added to salads.

Plants are tolerant of heat and drought but do better when given adequate water and fertilizer. Keep the soil moist and feed with a balanced fertilizer every three to four weeks. Some afternoon shade may be a good idea in the summer heat.

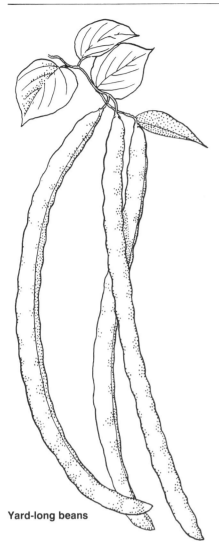
Yard-long beans

Novelty beans

To be assured of a good harvest, plant a row of beans. Easy to grow, they should be one of the first crops for the beginner. Snap beans, limas and Southern peas are the most familiar, but the legume family contains many bushes and vines with edible pods and seeds.

The beans and bean relatives that grow in Florida come from around the world. Snap beans and limas are from South America; Southern peas originated in Africa. Broad beans are native across Europe and Asia, while the Mediterranean region provides garbanzo beans and garden peas.

Some beans were growing in the New World when the colonists landed. Native Americans, early practitioners of companion planting, taught the colonists to grow pole beans with their corn.

The Indians also had a way to maximize germination of their lima or butter beans: They planted seeds in shallow pots of moist soil and set them in the cooling ashes of a fire to sprout before being transplanted to the fields.

All beans require similar treatment. Most prefer warm weather, growing spring through fall in North Florida and year-round in Central and South Florida. When cold damages the crop, gardeners turn the plants under to improve the soil and plant again when temperatures rise.

Beans prefer loose garden soil. Feel free to add lots of organic material to clay or sandy soils and adjust acidity to a pH of around 6.5. Sow most seeds an inch or two deep and keep the soil moist. Seeds normally germinate rapidly, within seven to 10 days. Mulches help extend the period between waterings and keep the soil temperatures even.

Beans need only water, light and infrequent feedings; a complete fertilizer applied before planting may be all that is needed because legume roots establish a symbiotic relationship with rhizobium bacteria in the soil. The bacteria take nitrogen from the air, which the bean roots use. In return, the roots supply the bacteria with sugars.

Culture of all legumes is similar, and specific hints can be found in Appendix I under beans and Southern peas. For additional hints on other beans, check the table on bean and bean relatives.

When you select a new bean variety, note the type of growth habit

Novelty beans and bean relatives

Type	Other names	Type of growth	Spacing, rows	Spacing, plants	Planting depth	Comments
Broad	horse bean, tick bean, Windsor bean, fava bean, pigeon bean	erect bush	36-48	3-4	1-2	Grow during the cool season. Snap pods when young, shell when mature; snapped and shelled beans may be cooked together.
Dry	Many varieties, including navy, pinto, cranberry, red kidney, great Northern, Jacobs cattle	bush or vine, depending on variety	18-30, bush 40-48, vine	2-3, bush 3-6, vine	1-2	Plant early spring or late fall. Pull plants with maturing pods and hang in sheltered, airy place to dry.
Garbanzo	chick pea, common gram, gram pea	low bush	24-30	3-4	1-2	Plant in spring; grow four to five months. Harvest and dry beans when pods start to mature.
Jack, sword	chickasaw lima bean, coffee bean, horse bean	vining bush	40-48	3-6	1-2	These similar beans produce large, 10- to 14-inch-long pods. Harvest when young to snap and cook. May be mildly toxic if eaten in large quantities.
Mung	green gram, black gram, moyashi	bush	30-36	2-3	1-2	Mostly eaten as sprouts of dried seeds. Young green pods can be snapped and cooked.
Scarlet runner	scarlet conqueror, fire bean, red giant	vine	40-48	3-6	1-2	Snap and steam until tender or shell and cook like limas.
Winged	goa bean, princess bean	vine	40-48	3-6	1-2	Plant late summer or early fall. Harvest pods when young, 4-5 inches long; snap to cook. Tuberous roots are edible raw or cooked.
Yard-long	asparagus bean, Peru bean, snake bean	vine	36-48	8-12	1-2	Harvest young pods 12-15 inches long to snap and cook.

Note: All spacings measured in inches.

and spacing needed for best yields. Most can be cultivated during the spring and fall, but a few have more specific planting times.

Pigeon pea

Tolerant of drought but sensitive to cold, the pigeon pea is a special challenge in the cooler regions of Florida. It is one crop that may not yield a harvest by the time fall frost arrives. The plant is a short-lived perennial. In warm regions it produces a continual crop for two to three years.

Pigeon pea plants grow as 3- to 8-foot-tall bushes. With luck, seeds sown in spring will flower by October and produce an early winter harvest. Plant rows 3 to 4 feet apart and thin seedlings to 12 to 18 inches apart.

Soil can be poor as long as it is well-drained, and plants need only minimal care. Provide a starter fertilizer and water when the soil begins to dry.

Peas can be shelled and cooked green, or dried for later use. Save seeds for future plantings or buy from mail-order companies.

Pokeweed

Pokeweed is a native wild plant growing throughout Florida in a wide range of soil conditions. Birds often distribute the seeds, which germinate after passing through the bird's digestive system. Pokeweed seldom is cultivated; most is gathered from the wild.

Pokeweed is a perennial plant. It survives periods of unfavorable growing conditions as a large, poisonous taproot.

The new shoots that emerge from the soil in spring are edible. Gather 6-inch shoots like asparagus, but be careful not to cut any portion of the poisonous root.

Young shoots contain oxalic acid and should be boiled before using. Most cooks rinse and boil the shoots in several batches of water to remove any bitter flavor before eating.

Home plantings can be started from roots transplanted from the wild. A fall planting should yield a good spring harvest. Keep the soil moist and fertilized to encourage production of tender shoots.

Remember to leave room for the mature plant, which will grow about 4 feet tall and wide. It is a somewhat sprawling but dramatic plant, with red stems and purple berries.

Plants can be started with seeds saved from the berries. Seeds extracted from the pulp should be dried and treated to encourage germination.

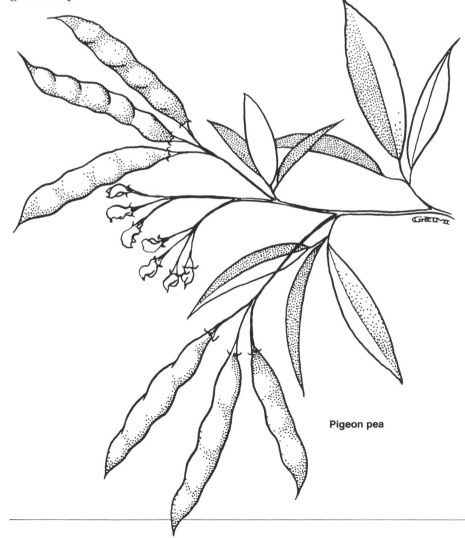

Acid soaks have been used by professional propagators to eat away layers of the thick, outer coat. Home gardeners can rub the seeds between layers of fine sandpaper for a few minutes to reduce the thickness of the seed coat.

Seeds germinate in about two weeks. The first crop of new shoots can be harvested the following spring.

Radicchio should be ready to harvest 65 to 70 days after transplants are set in the garden. Head size is quite variable; harvest when a firm, usable head forms.

Four varieties of radicchio have been tested for home and commercial production in Florida. All showed variability in head size, susceptibility to bolting and appearance.

Overall, varieties Augusto and Otello appear to be slightly superior to Cessna and Giulo. Seeds are available from garden centers and mail-order companies.

Radicchio

For a tangy gourmet taste, add radicchio to a salad. This Italian chicory resembles a small cabbage. The heads are a compact 3 to 5 inches in diameter, and deep red in color, with contrasting white veins.

Plantings are cold hardy, surviving temperatures in the upper 20s without damage. They need cool weather to be productive. Seed should be sown between September and December to produce transplants for the garden. From seed to transplant requires between four and six weeks.

Radicchio grows well in improved sandy soil. If possible, enrich the soil with organic matter. Add fertilizer to the planting site. Plant in single rows or space-saving wide beds. Allow 10 inches between plants, with rows as close as 14 inches. Mulch to conserve moisture and keep the foliage clean. Rows can be side dressed with additional fertilizer at three- to four-week intervals.

Roselle

Most people wouldn't think of eating an ornamental hibiscus, but roselle, a tropical species, is a favorite of many West Indians. Just mention that it is ready and there will be plenty of takers.

Also called sorrel, roselle is not to be confused with French or wild sorrel of the *Rumex* genus, often used as a green for salads or soups.

Sow roselle seeds, available from mail-order companies specializing in tropical vegetables, to grow a food crop as well as an attractive landscape planting.

The green leaves and red stems of this edible hibiscus, often called the Florida cranberry, can be trained to form a temporary hedge. Seeds sown in spring will produce plants up to 9 feet high by fall.

New beds of roselle also can be started with cuttings from established plants. They root rapidly in vermiculite. When the root balls are

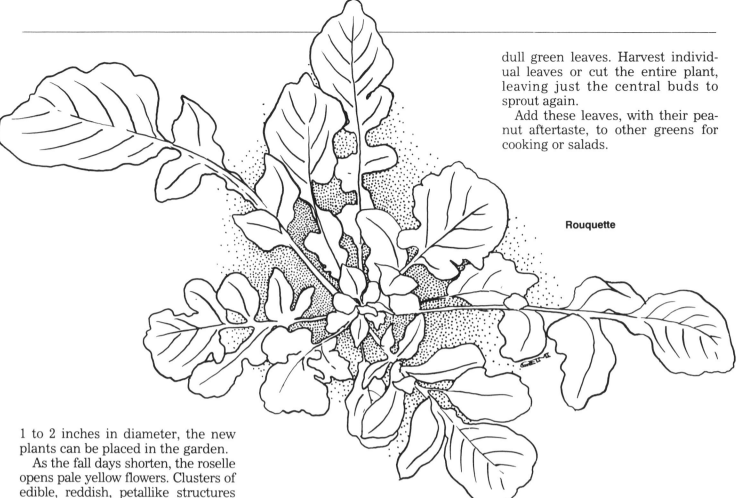

Rouquette

dull green leaves. Harvest individual leaves or cut the entire plant, leaving just the central buds to sprout again.

Add these leaves, with their peanut aftertaste, to other greens for cooking or salads.

1 to 2 inches in diameter, the new plants can be placed in the garden.

As the fall days shorten, the roselle opens pale yellow flowers. Clusters of edible, reddish, petallike structures develop beneath the bloom.

About 15 days after the flower fades, harvest the crop to make jelly, juice, tea and holiday drinks. Prepared roselle products have a cranberry taste without the bitterness.

New, tender leaves also are harvested and prepared like spinach or mixed with salads.

Rouquette

This low-growing member of the mustard family also is called true rocket, rocket salad and arugula. It was used in salads as long as 2,000 years ago.

Ancient Egyptians and Romans believed it to be an aphrodisiac. Early writers cautioned cooks to mix it with lettuce or purslane for, eaten alone, "it causeth headache and heateth too much."

Grow this annual in winter. The cool temperatures will slow the production of flower shoots and prolong the useful life of the plant. Plants can withstand light freezes and, if killed back by frosts, will grow back from the central crown of leaves.

Seeds often are available from companies specializing in herbs. Sow thickly in the garden; later, thin plants to 3 or 4 inches apart.

Feed and water regularly to maintain production of the deeply cut,

Seminole pumpkin

The native Seminole pumpkin, once cultivated by Florida Indians and harvested by early explorers, is gaining new popularity as a summer-season vegetable. It is a type of winter squash distinguished by its thick skin and good keeping quali-

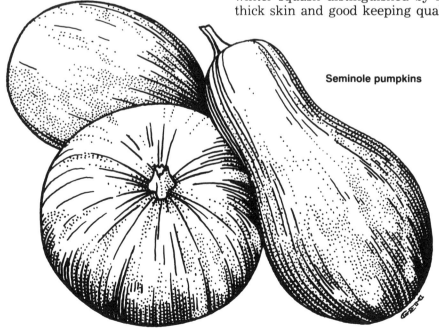

Seminole pumpkins

ties. Sweet-tasting, it is served baked, boiled or steamed.

Seeds seldom are found at garden centers but often are saved from the best fruit and shared between neighbors.

Sow where the plants can run on the ground or climb a trellis. The vines are vigorous and root at the joints when left in contact with the soil. Plantings can be made spring through summer for continuing production.

Fertilize lightly or the garden may yield lots of vine and few squash. Once every four to six weeks is enough.

Although the plants tolerate drought, moist soil and a mulched root system result in better production.

Fruit, borne up to 15 to a vine, is buff-colored and 6 to 8 inches in diameter. It is ready to harvest in 95 days. The vines will continue to grow, however, often until the first frost.

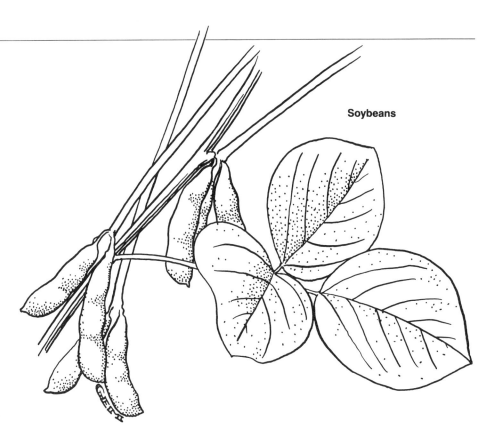

Soybeans

Soybeans

Although not commonly grown in home gardens here, soybeans have been cultivated in the Orient for several thousand years. They are eaten fresh, as a green shelled bean, or dried and stored for future use.

A few varieties have been tested for Florida. Good producers include Verde, Disoy, Bansei, Giant Green and Prize.

Plant in early spring, in single or double rows. Sow seeds 1 inch deep and 2 to 3 inches apart. A starter fertilizer, used at planting, may be all that is needed because, like other legumes, soybeans obtain nitrogen from the air with the help of soil bacteria. Bean plants improve the soil in which they are grown. If they turn yellow during early stages of growth, scatter an additional feeding down the row.

Soybean bushes grow tall but need no special support. They tolerate drought but make better growth when the soil is kept moist. The green beans will be ready to shell in about 105 days. Complete the harvest while the pods are in the mature green stage to prevent fungus diseases from damaging the crop.

Tamarillo

Tomatoes don't really grow on trees but the tamarillo, a fruit that looks very similar, does. National companies have marketed seeds as a sensationalized garden vegetable, sometimes calling it the tree tomato.

Most plantings, however, have been started with seeds exchanged between gardeners or from sources listed in the *Florida Market Bulletin*.

Egg-shaped and pointed at the ends, tree tomatoes grow in clusters of three to 12. They may ripen yellow, orange, red or purple, with those most like a tomato being the most popular.

The fruit has a tough outer skin with an unpleasant flavor. Peeled, it has the mild taste of a slightly underripe tomato, with a slight resinous aftertaste and aroma.

Use like tomatoes: fresh, in salads or sandwiches; or cooked, baked, or added to soups or stews.

Plants easily are propagated from cuttings or seeds. To obtain the more popular colors of fruit, select seeds carefully. To increase the likelihood of red fruit, collect seeds from red fruit with a black seed

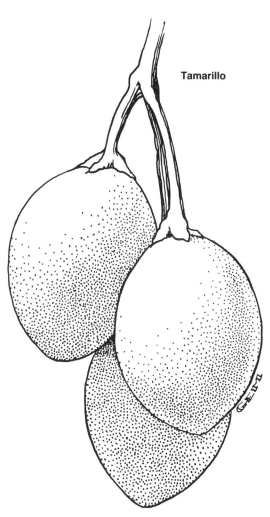

Tamarillo

pulp surrounding the seeds; for yellow fruit, choose seeds from yellow fruit with yellow seed pulp.

The trees are large, up to 10 feet tall and can have more than one trunk. Given a porous, enriched soil, they grow well in a subtropical climate, but they need protection when temperatures fall below 30 degrees.

Treat like perennials. Feed every six to eight weeks with a light scattering of 6-6-6 or similar product during the warm months. Keep the soil moist with frequent waterings and a thick layer of mulch.

The first year, top the trees when they reach 3 to 4 feet tall. Thereafter, prune yearly to remove older limbs and encourage the new growth on which the fruit is produced.

Fruiting begins in about two years and may continue for four to six years. A blossom requires about three months to turn into a ripe fruit. Clip the fruit from the tree, leaving a short stem behind.

Vegetable spaghetti

Boiled or baked until tender, the vegetable spaghetti makes a good low-calorie substitute for pasta. Loosen the yellow-orange flesh and you might swear that it was spaghetti, ready for the sauce. It has enough squash flavor, however, that it tastes fine with nothing more than butter.

This garden curiosity is a type of winter squash, which means the fruit, also known as spaghetti squash, spaghetti gourd and Manchurian squash, stores for months. Most fruit weighs about 2 pounds and measures 10 inches long and 5 inches across.

Culture is similar to other bush-producing squash. Plant during the warm season in northern and central areas, and September through March in South Florida. Sow seeds in clusters of three or four in a prepared garden site. Space the clusters 3 feet apart.

Separate male and female flowers will be borne on the same plant, but not necessarily together at first, so there may be a little wait before pollination occurs and fruit production begins. Fruit will mature in 80 to 100 days. Harvest when fruit stops

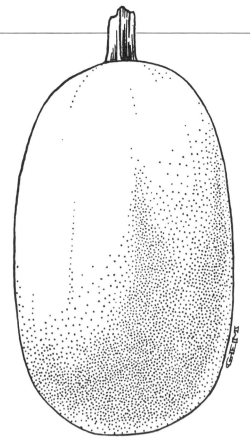
Vegetable spaghetti

enlarging and has turned deep yellow.

Pests common to squash, including mildew, fruit rots and pickleworms, also will attack this species. Check Appendix I and control as needed with the appropriate pesticides.

Yam

Yam plants will run rampant in the garden before producing a harvest. The heart-leaved vine climbs rapidly up an arbor, fence or even a nearby tree. Even though both are vines, have heart-shaped leaves and produce underground crops, true yams should not be confused with sweet potatoes. Botanically, they are quite separate.

Wild yams are a familiar sight in Florida, but only the garden varieties produce edible tubers. The white yam is the most popular, but Japanese, Guinea and Tongo yams also are grown. Most weigh from 3 to 8 pounds. Sometimes an exceptional tuber, up to 60 pounds, is produced.

Whatever the size, production time for yams is 10 to 11 months, which limits the crop to central and southern portions of the state.

When the new crop is harvested around December, the starchy tubers, similar to the potato in food value, are ready to peel, boil or bake, and enjoy.

Plant in late winter or early spring. Use small tubers whole or cut large tubers into 4- or 5-inch sections, called seed pieces.

Yams like a loose, rich soil. Space the seed pieces 18 inches apart and 2 to 3 inches deep near a fence or trellis. Mulch the planting site and keep the soil moist.

The vines respond well to infrequent feedings. Apply a light scattering of a balanced fertilizer every six to eight weeks. The tubers keep best in the ground; harvest when ready to use.

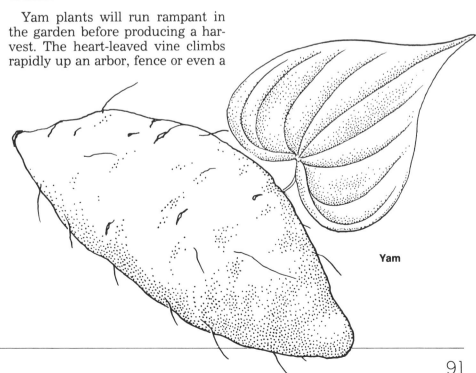
Yam

12
Herbs — the fresher the better

Horehound

EVEN IF HERBS WEREN'T the quickest way to bring interesting flavors to the most ordinary foods, some gardeners would grow them just for the delightful aromas they bring to the landscape. Brush by a sweet basil plant and the spicy, clovelike scent evokes memories of the finest Italian dishes. Crush a mint leaf and imagine how much a small sprig could enhance a pitcher of iced tea.

Cooks, crafters and flower arrangers all prize the sweet smells and flavor-enhancing attributes of herbs. If fresher is indeed better, nothing could be handier than herbs ready to be picked as needed from the garden.

Herbs are woven intricately into the history of medicine. Traditional remedies depended heavily on herbs. In classical Rome and ancient Egypt, rue was believed to cure baldness and inebriation. Later, rosemary was used to ward off witches. Through the ages, nearly every herb imaginable has been turned into a love potion.

Folklore suggests teas made from basil, oregano and thyme have a calming effect; lemon balm, sage and thyme help cure colds. Sweet marjoram, mints and rosemary may give relief from a headache. A pennyroyal tea poured over Fido is even reputed to chase away fleas. Try any remedy at your own risk; little scientific evidence supports their use.

Cooks, on the other hand, have plenty of reasons to rediscover herbs. Herbs contribute great subtlety and variety of taste to cooking. For people who must eliminate salt from their diet, the use of herbs may more than compensate and serve as a healthful substitute.

Even the smallest balcony garden can accommodate an herb garden — just fill the pockets of a strawberry jar with a cook's sampler of parsley, thyme, rosemary, tarragon and basil. Gardeners with more space can intermingle herbs with vegetables — planting basil near the tomatoes it accents so well; teaming cucumbers with dill — or set aside a small plot exclusively for herbs.

Gardeners in Florida have anticipated difficulties with herbs and most haven't even tried to grow their own. Home growers who bring enthusiasm to the task can be successful, given just a bit of advice.

Windowsill gardens

Bright, sunny locations are best for herbs. The ideal window faces south, so plants receive a full day of sun.

Be choosy about the herbs to be grown in a confined space. Many grow tall and would be inappropriate companions indoors. Mint, chives, oregano, parsley and others that stay compact or drape from a pot are best.

Often a windowsill serves as temporary quarters. A container-grown herb cultivated outdoors in full sun can be handy as a temporary kitchen plant until it begins to decline in the lower light indoors. Then it is time to go back outdoors to rejuvenate in the sunshine.

For a successful windowsill garden:

- Give plants maximum sun exposure.
- Turn plants periodically so all sides receive equal sun.
- Water when the soil starts to dry.
- Fertilize every month or two.
- Move declining plants outdoors to allow them to rejuvenate.
- Frequently cut and use sprigs and leaves to keep growth from becoming lanky.

Balcony plantings

Balconies, decks and patios are ideal for herb culture. When plantings are near the kitchen door, fresh sprigs are gathered easily for cooking. A small pot or a tub of herbs enhances any outdoor garden.

Containers are movable. Plants can be repositioned seasonally to take advantage of the changing sun exposures. While many herbs, including mints, chives, ginger, marjoram and thyme, survive in light shade, sunny locations typically are best. Container gardens can be treated like patio furniture, even brought inside before guests arrive to serve as decorations for the home. No one has to know that the plants, too, are just visiting.

Put herbs on display. Many make good substitutes for purely ornamental foliage. They can be a topic of conversation. Have visitors who ask about the fern-leaf plant or creeping greenery pinch a leaf and the mood for the visit is set.

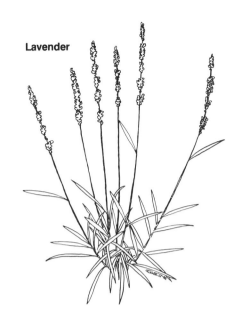

Lavender

Pots, tubs and planters

Gardeners who have tried and failed with herbs probably planted them in the ground. Here, the ability of the soil to consume plantings can be frightening. Beginners should skip planting herbs in the garden and enjoy success in containers.

When herbs are grown in pots and tubs, the gardener is in control. Potting mixes start out relatively free of pests, and the gardener can regulate the water, adjust the feedings and move the plants to the best sun exposure. Only when plants have grown big and strong in containers should anyone even want to consider planting in the ground.

Any container can hold herbs, but small pots eventually look silly. The small containers often sold as windowsill herb planters hardly hold a few sprigs or seedlings. At best, they are starting places for plants that will grow tall or spill over the sides. If tiny samples of herbs are all that is wanted, plan to replace the plantings frequently.

Containers 6 inches or more in diameter are better. Most herbs have shallow roots, so pots 4 to 6 inches deep are adequate, but containers can be much bigger. Some people like to plant strawberry jars with a variety of plants. Others use planter boxes, half-barrels or old bathtubs. The largest containers accommodate an entire garden — a gourmet's delight stuffed with all the herbs needed for cooking and crafts.

In planting large containers, remember herbs come in all sizes. Keep shorter, creeping species to the sides and tall varieties in the middle. Some herbs are annuals, so be ready with replacements to fill holes when plants grow old and die. Because herbs grow year-round in Florida, a bit of planning keeps them available constantly.

Soil for containers should be of the highest quality — a porous but moist, pest-free blend. It is best to buy or prepare a potting mix. Garden soil is loaded with potential weeds, insects and diseases that can damage new plantings.

Mix equal portions of peat moss and perlite, available at garden centers, for a great medium for growing herbs. Add half a tablespoon of dolomitic lime to each gallon of prepared medium. Give herbs known to like lime, such as lavender, rosemary, sage, tarragon and thyme, a full tablespoon of dolomitic lime to each gallon. This prepared soil is ready to use as soon as mixed. Fill containers to within an inch of the top and pop in the herbs.

Like other container-grown plants, herbs need ongoing attention. Check daily for moisture. Container-grown plants often need to be watered daily during the warm seasons, so it is important to check both morning and late afternoon. When the soil is dry or the pot feels light when lifted, it is time to water.

A small pot of herbs that dries out rapidly may need to be transplanted to a larger container where more soil will hold water longer and allow more roots to grow, giving the plant more endurance.

During winter and rainy seasons, or for plants growing indoors, daily watering may not be necessary.

Feed regularly for the best growth. When plants are growing outdoors or in bright areas, use a 20-20-20 fertilizer every week, mixed at the rate recommended on the label. In reduced light or during cool weather, fertilize less frequently.

Alternatively, use time-release fertilizers to feed potted plants for a period of months. Scatter the capsules or pellets over the soil surface; they will dissolve a little every time the plant is watered.

Outdoor herb gardens

Dill grows like a weed, but sage may need to be mollycoddled in the garden. In-ground culture is not intrinsically difficult but can be disappointing if the soil is not well-prepared. Weeds, insects and diseases often lurk in old garden sites, ready to spoil new plantings.

Start by considering the specific conditions required by different plants. Some like it wet, while others prefer a slightly alkaline soil. Give a plant exactly what it needs and it will flourish.

Full-sun locations usually are best, but many gardens with four to six hours of sun yield a great harvest. Find a permanent location, prepare the soil well, and perennial herbs will grow for years. A corner of the vegetable patch, the border of a flower bed, or a garden on its own — any can be a successful spot for herbs.

Begin by thoroughly tilling the planting site. Small gardens can be turned with a shovel; a rototiller helps with a big bed. Dig down at least 4 inches.

If the new garden site is an old lawn, turn the sod under to speed its decomposition and to add organic matter to the soil.

Add plenty of organic material to build a loose soil that will hold moisture. The decomposing materials also provide nutrients and help reduce nematode activity.

Good additions include compost, peat moss, peat humus, stable bedding and manure, lawn clippings, leaves and kitchen scraps. Work any or all into the garden. The better it is mixed, the more quickly decomposition occurs and new soil forms. Wet the soil well to start the microorganisms working.

This is a good time to check soil pH and determine soil acidity. Garden centers and the cooperative extension service will test pint-size soil samples. Gardeners can perform the test at home using commercially available kits.

Most herbs prefer a pH ranging from 6.0 to 7.0, but do note those that like a pH in the 7 to 7.5 range. Where adjustment is needed, adding lime usually will make the soil less acidic — raising the reading on the numerical scale — and sulfur will increase acidity, indicated by a lowering of the pH number. Both sulfur and dolomitic lime are available at garden centers.

As a rule of thumb, 2 pounds of lime per 100 square feet will raise the pH of sandy soil about one unit, and a pound of sulfur will decrease the pH one unit. Some naturally alkaline or acidic soils resist a pH change and may be changed only with difficulty. Such soils may not be suitable for specific herbs; grow them in containers instead.

When organic materials and pH adjustments are well-mixed in the soil, avoid future trouble by dealing with potential pests, especially nematodes. Gardeners who know they have problems should fumigate or use solarization techniques. These treatments will help stamp out other insects, diseases and weeds in advance.

In first-time garden sites, the big problem usually is weeds. Once the garden is growing, hand-pulling and mulching take care of most weeds. Most insects will take some time to discover the herb patch. When they do, many can be hand-picked or sprayed.

Fertilize the garden with a 6-6-6 or similar fertilizer just before planting. Scatter 1 to 2 pounds over each 100 square feet of garden. There is no need to mix the fertilizer with the soil; it will be incorporated with planting.

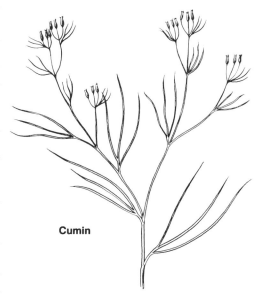
Cumin

At last, the plants

Finally it is planting time. Only a few herbs, including basil, chives and dill, are sown directly in the garden. Most soils dry out rapidly and herb seedlings have a difficult time because they often are tiny when young.

Move most herbs into the garden as divisions, plants moved with a clump of soil from an existing bed, or seedlings grown big and strong in market packs or containers.

Herbs seem to go through cycles of popularity. One kind may be everywhere at one time and others, difficult to find. Nevertheless, check garden centers for potted plants that will grow quickly in the garden. Especially for beginners, the instant rewards make this source a good one.

Most store racks and mail-order companies offer seeds of many kinds of herbs. Some start easily and in just a few days, while others require weeks to even germinate. Although some herb seeds are easy to handle, many are small and hard to sow. A few principles should help:

• Sow seeds in small trays or pots, not in the ground.

• Use a seeding mix of peat moss and vermiculite.

• Keep the mix moist. Cover the container with wet newspaper, plastic bags or another container.

• Check daily for germination; expose to full sun when first seedling emerges.

• Once seedlings are growing, allow medium to dry slightly, then water thoroughly.

• Feed seedlings weekly with a half-strength solution of 20-20-20 or similar fertilizer.

• Plant seedlings in the garden when they are about 4 inches tall.

Many herbs can be started from cuttings. Some will root in water, but because those roots slowly adapt to soil, it is not the best way to start transplants.

Choose a container big enough to hold cuttings spaced 2 to 3 inches apart, and fill it with vermiculite. Take tip cuttings 4 to 6 inches long and insert stems an inch or two into the medium.

Keep the cuttings in filtered sun and out of the wind while they root. Increase the humidity by periodically misting the plants. Some may wilt the first few days, but most recover rapidly, producing transplants in six to eight weeks.

When cuttings form root balls an inch in diameter, move to individual containers. They will be ready for the garden or larger pots in another four to six weeks.

Another way to acquire an herb is to share in a friend's collection. A whole plant isn't necessary. With a sharp knife or shovel, simply slice a good start — including leaves, stems and roots — from an established planting. Fill in the resulting hole with soil.

The new division is ready to plant. Give it improved soil and it will become established quickly, with little transplant shock.

Care of the garden

Mulch reduces weeds and supplies some of the nutrients needed for growth; above all, it helps retain moisture for shallow-rooted herbs. A 2- to 3-inch-thick organic layer of compost, wood chips or old hay is ideal. As the mulch decomposes, periodically renew the layer.

Flavorful, often tender herbs need water and fertilizer on a regular basis. Some, like mints, thrive in extra-moist soil while others are happy with normal garden irrigation. All will grow well if the soil is kept moist; water when the surface starts to dry.

Water frequently, perhaps every two or three days, during hot, dry months. When winter arrives, water once or twice a week.

Fertilize to encourage growth. During warm seasons, herbs grow vigorously and need frequent feeding. Lightly scatter a 6-6-6 or similar fertilizer around the herbs every two to three weeks. Use less than a pound per 100 square feet of bed.

When growth slows due to cooler weather or if older plants are declining, a monthly feeding is adequate.

Pests

Herbs have few devastating pests. Those they do have tend to be insects that suck juices or chew leaves and move on without killing the plant.

This is fortunate because few pesticides have been developed for use on specific herbs, and everyone — gardeners, county agents and consultants — is legally bound to use products only as labeled. Restrictions are particularly important where food plants are concerned.

To control insects and diseases on herbs, take advance precautions by using sterile potting mixes or treating in-ground sites for nematoes before planting. Once the plants are growing, most control is limited to handpicking, rubbing off or washing away pests.

Herbs seldom rot unless the soil compacts or fails to drain after rain or irrigation. Choose a planting medium that drains well and a location that does not puddle or collect water. Leave the saucers off outdoor containers to allow water to drain out of the soil.

When big bugs attack, handpick as many as possible. Grasshoppers, stink bugs and caterpillars can be destroyed underfoot or dumped in a can of kerosene or alcohol. It is an old-fashioned approach that works.

Sticky boards work well with leaf miners, whiteflies and other flying insects. The bold yellow color attracts the insects and a surface emulsion traps them in place. See Chapter 18 for instructions on how to make sticky boards.

Soap can be a good insecticide. Even a mix made at home, one part soap to 40 parts water, frequently will control smaller pests such as aphids. Soaps are contact products and need only be sprayed, drenched or rubbed on foliage long enough to control the pest; then they can be rinsed off with water.

Soaps may kill plants as well as pests. If using a commercial product, be sure to follow label recommendations. Test each herb individually, and test a product for a few days before any major treatment.

Quite a few young caterpillars succumb to the *Bacillus thuringiensis* organism, which works dramatically when it works at all. Vulnerable caterpillars usually stop feeding within a day and are controlled in less than a week.

Extracts of the bacteria, available under several brand names, are considered insecticides and must be used as labeled.

When pesticides seem to be applicable, read the label carefully. To prevent burning foliage or leaving a persistent residue, note mixing instructions. Most herbs are eaten, so pay special attention to the time that must elapse between spraying and harvest.

Be careful to keep separate equipment for insecticides and fungicides, and don't use it to water or fertilize.

Gathering and storing

For the best flavor and appearance, gather herbs when they are to be used. Cut tender basil leaves when making tangy tomato sauce, pick parsley to garnish the cold cuts and gather dill to put the punch in the pickles. Collect as much as needed and leave the plant to continue growing.

Herbs often produce abundantly, more than can be used all at once. Many cooks take the opportunity to preserve a little for times when the garden is less productive.

Freezing is easiest. Collect firm, fresh leaves and newly opened flowers early in the morning, just as the dew begins to dry. Wash away any dust and sand, and pat dry between towels. Seal in a plastic bag, leaving as little surrounding air as possible, and place in freezer until ready to use.

Drying herbs can give satisfying results. A good location is bright and well-ventilated but out of direct sun. Results are better when the drying is fast, so choose a warm spot and, if possible, a less humid time of year.

Bundles of herbs can be hung upside-down from a line. If dried inside a paper bag that is open at the bottom, they'll also be protected from dust.

Another method is to strip leaves from stems and dry on a screen covered with cheesecloth. Space the leaves to allow air to circulate. Figure on drying herbs for about 10 days before storing.

Containers should be airtight to seal moisture out and flavor-rich oils in. Good cooks recommend storing dried herbs as whole leaves or big pieces, waiting to crumble or grind until time to use.

The most up-to-date cooks dry herbs in microwave ovens. To try this, begin by rinsing herbs. Shake off excess moisture. Place no more than four or five sprigs between two paper towels and cook for two or three minutes.

Herbs should be brittle and flaky when removed from the oven. Some may need another 30 seconds or so cooking time before they are ready to store.

Some herbs can be preserved in vinegars, including basil, rosemary, sage, tarragon and thyme. One simple method is to place a handful of clean herbs in a saucepan and cover with cold cider or wine vinegar. Heat the mixture, but do not let it boil. Cool; transfer to another container, seal with a non-metallic lid, and let seep for about a week.

Strain the vinegar and use to flavor salad dressings and sauces.

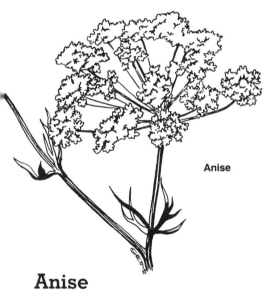

Anise

A relative of parsley with a licorice flavor, anise grows about 2 feet tall. It makes a willowy plant with attractive white flower heads. Rub the leaves to release the pleasing fragrance.

Gardeners use the leaves fresh or collect the seeds when they begin to dry. Either leaves or seeds are used for a brisk tea and in confectionery products.

Seeds can be sown year-round in frost-free locations. They are best planted a few to a small pot and later thinned to individual plants that can be transplanted with a ball of soil to the garden.

Space transplants 18 inches apart in the garden or grow one plant in a 6-inch pot.

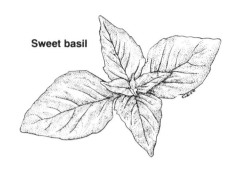

Basil

Release the sweet, spicy smell of basil by brushing the plant. Lemon and camphor-scented varieties add to gardeners' enjoyment. Basil may be green or purple, and its leaves may be flat or ruffled, quite broad, or small and narrow.

Plants are easy to grow during warm weather and, if grown in pots, can be protected from extreme cold during winter. Sow several seeds in a tray to transplant or just one or two to remain in a pot. Seeds germinate well and a packet always yields plenty of basil. Space plants 12 inches apart in the garden or one to a 6-inch container.

Pick to encourage branching and new growth. Basil is best used fresh and must be fresh to make pesto, which can then be frozen, but it also can be dried to use later in sauces, soups and vegetable dishes. In Italian cooking, basil and tomatoes are considered to have a special affinity.

Bay laurel

The bay leaves used in cooking come from this special herb, native to the Mediterranean region and not to be confused with local, native trees. The crown of honor for winners in the original Olympic games was a wreath of laurel leaves.

Slow-growing and tricky to cultivate, a plant can require seven months just to root from a cutting. Bay laurel must be protected from cold, so it is best grown in containers. Older plants can make beautiful specimens.

Home growers prize their plants and feel the rewards are worth the effort. This is one herb that has more power fresh than dried. When the harvest is from a home planting, try using just half a leaf in spaghetti sauce or stew.

Seeds and small plants can be ordered from mail-order companies.

Grow in filtered sun during extremely hot weather and in full sun when temperatures are cool. Protect

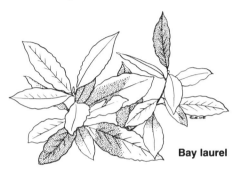

from freezes during the cold winter season by bringing indoors, where it needs as much light as possible.

Borage

Borage is ornamental in the garden, with fuzzy, broad green leaves and blue to purple spikes of color. Sow seeds fall or spring. It is easy to grow and survives in poor, dry soils. If possible, make the pH slightly alkaline, above 7.0.

Plants grow about 2 feet tall and should be spaced 18 inches apart in the garden. Harvest tender young leaves and use fresh. Add flowers and foliage as a garnish and sprinkle over salads, where they add a cool, cucumber taste. Blossoms also can be brewed into a mild tea.

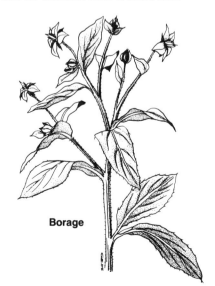

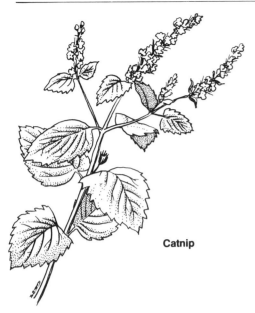

Catnip

Like other members of the mint family, catnip is an easy-to-cultivate perennial that can readily spread throughout the garden. Cats will help the gardener keep it in check, however; neighborhood felines, rolling in delight on the catnip and surrounding plants, can reduce a well-grown stand to a few wisps.

Start plants from seeds or cuttings or divide a mature planting. Catnip grows in full sun to partial shade and prefers a rich, moist soil.

Space plants 12 inches apart in the garden or one to a pot. Plants will grow several feet high and may produce white flowers dotted with purple.

Use the fresh or dried foliage to share with a favorite cat or brew a tea for people.

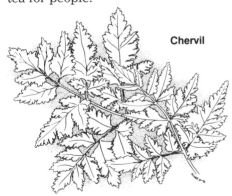

Chervil

A garden annual, chervil resembles parsley with its fernlike foliage. Its mild flavor is used in preparing bearnaise sauce and vinaigrettes. Some plants may produce thickened roots, which also can be eaten.

Sow seeds during the warm spring and fall months in the ground where they will grow or in pots for transplanting. Thin to 12 inches apart.

Pinch off flower buds to encourage leaf growth. Add fresh chervil foliage to soups, salads and marinades.

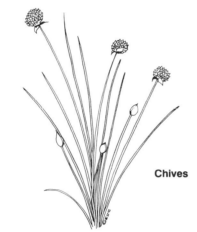

Chives

Members of the onion family, chives have purple flowers and garlic chives, white. Both are easy-to-grow perennials. Sow seeds or divide clumps to obtain new plants. Chives grow in most soils and in filtered to full-sun locations. After flowering, the plants often set seed that germinates wherever it scatters.

Cut the foliage frequently to use whenever the cook needs an onion taste. When plants become overgrown and lanky, trim the hollow, grasslike leaves to renew the plantings. Chives make an ideal potted plant and grow readily even in small containers.

Comfrey

Grown from seeds or divisions, comfrey forms towering clusters of large leaves with little pink or blue blossoms. Tolerant of cold weather, a plant can grow up to 5 feet tall. Cut it back after the New Year to encourage new growth.

Choose a location carefully; comfrey is likely to be a permanent planting. Transplanted, it is almost bound to leave some of its extensive root system to begin a new plant in the original spot.

Some organic gardeners think the roots tap minerals deep in the soil and make them available to other plants. As indicated by the common names, healing herb and knit-bone, comfrey's uses, however, have been mainly medicinal.

These days, concoctions of leaves and roots are confined to external applications as ingestion, once practiced, may be unsafe.

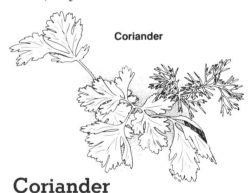

Coriander

Feathery-leaved coriander grows several feet tall. White flower clusters yield seeds with a citrus taste to flavor poultry, pastries and curry powder.

Young leaves, often sold as cilantro or Chinese parsley, also are added to soups and salads. The flavor is essential to Thai and Mexican cuisines, among others from hot climates, but it can be strong, so use it sparingly at first.

Sow this herb in the ground where it will grow, or start in small pots and transplant 12 inches apart.

Grow in full sun to partial shade. Harvest of the top few leaves can begin when plants are just 6 inches tall.

Cumin

Here is an herb for Florida's long warm seasons. Plant it during early spring in Central and North Florida and fall through spring in South Florida.

The thin-leaved plants grow only 8 to 12 inches tall, often sprawling across the soil. Start transplants or sow seeds directly in the soil, leaving 4 inches between plants.

Cumin

Gather the seeds by pulling an entire plant. Hang it in a bag to catch the seeds as they begin to scatter. The spicy seeds are used to flavor chili, spaghetti sauce, curry mixtures, soups and meat dishes.

Dill

When the weather is warm and there is no danger of frost, dill grows so easily the word weed often becomes part of its name. The seeds scatter freely and it seems that every one germinates.

Sow dill directly in the soil or raise transplants. Although feathery, plants can grow more than 4 feet tall, so space them at least 12 inches apart.

One or two plants may be enough to eat, but consider whether others, with their cool, blue-green foliage, can serve as ornamental fillers in the flower garden.

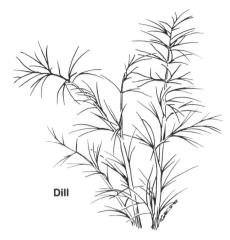
Dill

Both leaves and seeds are used in cooking and preserves. The seeds make pickles dill, while chopped fresh dill adds a clean, almost pine flavor to salads, vegetables, meats and dips. It's indispensable in Scandinavian cooking, used every way that parsley is and more.

Fennel

Fennel

With its feathery leaves and yellowish, flat-topped flower clusters, fennel greatly resembles dill. Distinguish the two by their flavors — fennel smells and tastes like licorice — and their stems — dill's are hollow while fennel's are filled with pith.

Grow sweet fennel for its seeds and foliage and use much like dill; choose a bronze version for its ornamental foliage. Braise or steam the bulbous base of Florence fennel as a vegetable.

Sow seeds of any kind of fennel during fall and early winter, spacing plants 12 inches apart. They will grow at least 2 feet tall and may need staking. Blanch bulbs of Florence fennel by pulling soil up around the base even before the flowers form.

Cut leaves from plants at any stage and harvest seeds as a cluster begins to ripen. Use with meat, in salads and for tea.

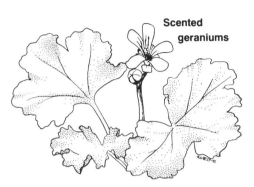
Scented geraniums

Scented geraniums

Scented geraniums, relatives of the bright, big-flowered pelargoniums, were a favorite in our grandmothers' gardens and do equally well today. New plants are easy to propagate from cuttings and seeds often are available.

Grow in perennial beds or patio pots and give them well-drained but moist soil and partial sun.

Popular scents include rose, lemon, apple, mint and several pungent varieties such as cinnamon and clove.

In their era, leaves were floated in finger bowls, and oils of geraniums were distilled for perfume and rose water. Some varieties have been made into jellies, but most people just keep scented geraniums to crush and smell a leaf from time to time.

Ginger

Edible ginger grows vigorously throughout the state. Buy pieces of fresh ginger root at grocery or specialty food stores and plant in rich, moist soil.

Space about 12 inches apart. Plants grow about 4 feet tall, with narrow leaves and infrequent but exotic flowers almost like small, greenish-yellow orchids.

The stalks die in winter in cool locations, but grow continuously in warmer regions. Each fall, the thicker tubers can be harvested.

Ginger roots can be stored fresh and whole, or dried and ground into powder. They also freeze well.

Add sugar for crystallized ginger candy. Ginger also can spice meats and vegetables — especially Oriental dishes — or flavor gingerbread. Grate only half as much fresh ginger for a recipe that calls for dried.

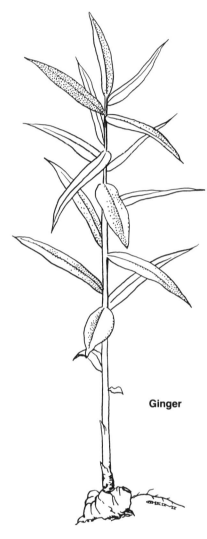

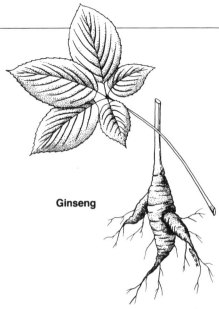

Ginseng

A native herb, ginseng will grow only in the cooler climate of North Florida. The plant grows 18 inches tall, with compound leaves of five leaflets. Plant seeds, seedlings or roots in a shady site and mature roots, 3 to 4 inches long, will be ready to harvest in five to seven years.

Ginseng roots once were considered to have almost magical properties, especially in traditional Chinese medicine where the plant is known as jen-shen, or manlike.

The more closely a root mimicked a human shape, the more effective it was thought to be. Today, the roots are used to flavor teas.

Horehound

Horehound, which derives its name from its old-time use as a remedy for dog bites, grows particularly well in Florida. Spreading, tidy-looking perennial plants grow 1 to 2 feet tall and thrive in hot, dry conditions. Some gardeners like to grow horehound among flowers for the decorative effect of its velvety, gray foliage.

Set new plants at least 12 inches apart and harvest stems and leaves as needed for candies, cold remedies and teas. The flowers are bitter.

Lavender

Traditionalists like the clean smell lavender gives to stored bed linen or a drawer of lingerie. This fragrant herb is used in sachets, potpourris, flower arrangements and exotic vinegars.

It is grown from seeds, cuttings and divisions of older clumps. Set plants in the ground or cultivate in pots, and grow in full sun in a porous, well-drained soil. Overwatering quickly rots the plants.

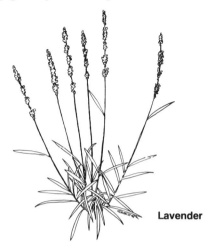

Favorite varieties of English and French lavender have purple flowers, but white-flowered kinds also can be found. All parts of the plant are fragrant, but the blooms are most aromatic.

Harvest when flowers begin to open, cutting stems around midday for maximum fragrance. Hang in bundles to dry or spread individual stems over a screen.

Lemon balm

Lemon balm is an easy-to-cultivate perennial in the mint family. Plants grow from seeds, cuttings or division of older clusters and reach a height of about 2 feet. Periodically prune or pinch back older plantings to keep them compact.

As the name suggests, leaves and stems have a pleasing lemon scent. Pick fresh young foliage to add to drinks and salads, or to substitute in recipes that call for lemon grass. Dry to use in sachets and potpourris.

Lovage

People who like celery will enjoy this look-alike, taste-alike plant that grows 6 feet tall and several feet wide. One or two plants will supply a family with enough tender stems and leaves for the year. All portions of the herb are used, even the roots.

Lovage likes cool weather and fades during the hot seasons. In many areas it must be treated as an annual.

Start seeds in pots to transplant, or sow directly in the ground. In the garden, space plants 12 inches apart.

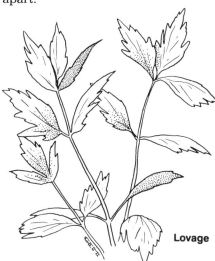
Lovage

Harvest leaves and stems, and use like celery or parsley to flavor vegetables, soups, meat dishes and salads. Roots can be made into a tea.

Marjoram

Two very similar marjorams, sweet and pot species, produce small, oblong leaves and a sweet fragrance. Sweet marjoram grows tall and pot marjoram is a creeping plant. Start either from seeds or cuttings, or by dividing older clumps.

The plants are winter-hardy and survive well in the herb garden, flower border or a container on the patio.

Keep plants bushy by frequently pinching bits to use and cutting away flower heads. Harvest leaves as needed to flavor meats, salads and egg dishes.

Marjoram

Mint

Mints are popular, but most gardens include only peppermint and spearmint. A connoisseur will want to grow apple mint, English mint, orange bergamont mint, pineapple mint and maybe woolly mint as well.

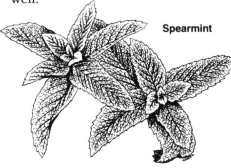
Spearmint

Give these rampant growers either full sun or partial shade. To further encourage the bushy, vine-like growth with its crisp, minty fragrance, just select a naturally moist area or plant under a dripping faucet.

Seeds are small but germinate quickly when sown in a starter mix of peat and perlite. Keep moist and seedlings slowly will grow 18 to 24 inches tall. Plantings also can be started from cuttings and by dividing older clumps.

Use young mint leaves to flavor drinks, soups, meat dishes and pastries.

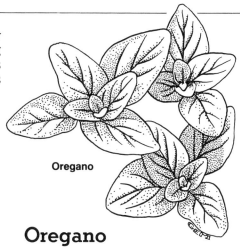
Oregano

Oregano

Often called wild marjoram, oregano is a close relative of sweet and pot marjorams, and has a similar taste but a stronger flavor. Begin a home planting by starting seeds or cuttings in pots. As they grow, plants will creep across the soil and may gain a foot or more in height.

Pick young leaves for flavoring favorite dishes. Italian cooks like oregano for sauces, and it is a staple in Greek cuisine. It's also used with vegetables and meats.

Parsley

Many gardeners consider parsley a common vegetable rather than a herb. For complete information on parsley, see the parsley profile in Appendix I, page 237.

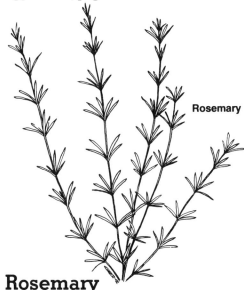
Rosemary

Rosemary

Most gardeners enjoy growing an herb with this much history. Rosemary features in Shakespeare's *Hamlet* as well as in ancient folklore. It's often associated with the Virgin Mary.

Plants grow long, twisting stems with linear, resinous leaves almost like short pine needles. Older plants bear small lavender blossoms.

Plants can be started from seed, but a cutting or division is easier and much quicker. To keep plants compact and attractive, harvest the highly scented stems and foliage frequently or prune periodically.

Use rosemary to flavor meat and fish, sauces and fruit. Rosemary is a traditional herb in Italian cooking. The spicy aroma is a welcome addition to sachets and potpourris.

Savory

Herb gardeners grow two species of savory, summer and winter. Both have linear, aromatic, peppery-tasting foliage. Summer savory is an upright annual growing more than a foot tall. In Florida, the perennial winter savory often develops weak stems and grows less than a foot tall.

Start either type from seed sown in containers. Both varieties do best in full sun. Summer savory likes a soil improved with organic matter; winter savory prefers soil to be sandy but moist. Pick as needed to flavor salads, beans, soups and meat dishes.

A healthy specimen can grow more than 2 feet tall, but a cold winter can kill foliage to the ground. On the other hand, summer heat and humidity often cause a plant's decline. All in all, it's a bit of a challenge to grow.

Cooks who aspire to classic cuisine try it anyway. Tarragon adds a delicate licorice flavor to meats, vegetables, soups and salads. Soak tender leaves and stems in white or wine vinegar to use in tartar sauce and marinades.

Mexican or Russian tarragon to grow from seeds also are marketed and look similar but have different flavors.

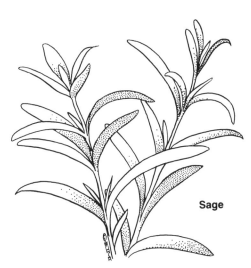

Sage

Neat, 18- to 24-inch-tall plants of garden sage make attractive additions to the landscape. The gray-green foliage has a spicy aroma when rubbed. In addition to the common species, gardeners enjoy the red flowers of pineapple sage, and varieties with golden, blue and tricolor foliage.

Sage will start from seeds or cuttings and grows readily in poor soils. Once established, it needs only a little water and fertilizer.

Periodically pinch out the new tips to cause branching and keep the plant compact.

Use the leaves anytime to season meat, vegetable, egg and cheese dishes. Sage is essential to poultry stuffings and common in sausages. It is another fragrance to add to sachets and potpourris.

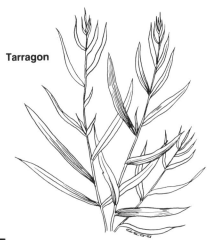

Tarragon

To grow true French tarragon, start with a plant or part of one. Because the sterile flowers produce no seeds, true tarragon can be perpetuated only through cuttings and division.

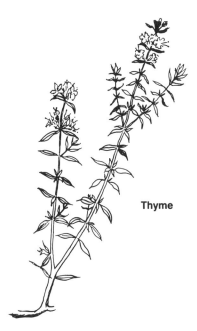

Thyme

Creeping to upright in habit but always short, thyme is a good, small-leaved herb for any garden. It is a great potted plant for the patio.

Varieties include English, French, lemon, woolly, coconut- and caraway-scented thymes; more are grown for fragrance and appearance than for cooking.

Start new plants in containers; sow seeds or stick cuttings. In the garden, space them about a foot apart.

Use common thyme to flavor soup, meat, vegetables and barbecue sauce. Cut it into bunches to hang and dry, or remove the leaves and dry on stretched cheesecloth. Brew it for tea, which is said to be very calming.

Watercress

Watercress, with its tangy taste, is a kind of nasturtium. Its native habitat is flowing streams, but it can be cultivated in containers. In fact, to grow watercress in a stream, start plants in pots first.

To grow it in the garden, dig a bed 6 inches deep and line it with polyethylene. Add 2 inches of soil that has been enriched with compost or peat moss, or use a highly organic potting mix. Adjust the pH to 7.0 or slightly above, and incorporate a small amount of fertilizer.

Lightly sow the small seeds over the soil. Keep seeds moist. When the seedlings are up and growing, usually in about five days, gradually raise the water level until the plants are standing in water. Thin them to 6 inches apart. Begin harvesting in about a month.

Use watercress in salads, soups, sandwiches and as a garnish. The established bed can supply cuttings to start a new one.

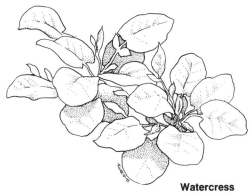
Watercress

Herbs for the Florida garden

Name	Growth cycle	Propagation	When to plant	Spacing*	Part used	When to harvest
Anise (*Pimpinella anisum*)	annual	seeds	year-round	18	seeds	when ripe
Basil (*Ocimum basilicum*)	annual	seeds	fall and spring	12	leaves	as needed
Bay laurel (*Laurus nobilis*)	perennial	cuttings	year-round	potted plant	leaves	as needed
Borage** (*Borago officinalis*)	annual	seeds	fall and spring	18	flowers, leaves	as needed
Caraway (*Carum carvi*)	biennial	seeds	fall and spring	12	seeds	slightly unripe
Cardamom (*Elettaria cardamomum*)	perennial	divisions	fall and spring	18	seeds	slightly unripe
Catnip (*Nepeta cataria*)	perennial	seeds, cuttings	year-round	12	leaves	as needed
Chervil (*Anthriscus cerefolium*)	annual	seeds	fall and spring	12	leaves	as needed
Chives (*Allium schoenoprasum*)	perennial	seeds, divisions	fall-spring	8	leaves	as needed
Comfrey (*Symphytum uplandicum*)	perennial,	seeds, root cuttings	year-round	18	leaves	as needed
Coriander (*Coriandrum sativum*)	annual	seeds	fall-spring	12	leaves, seed	leaves as needed, seed when ripe
Costmary (*Chrysanthemum balsamita*)	perennial	seeds, divisions	spring	12	leaves	as needed
Cumin (*Cuminum cyminum*)	annual	seeds	spring	4	seed	when ripe
Dill (*Anethum graveolens*)	annual	seeds	fall and spring	12	leaves, seeds	leaves as needed, seed when ripe
Fennel (*Foeniculum vulgare*)	perennial	seeds	fall and winter	12	leaves, seeds	leaves as needed, seed when ripe
Garlic (*Allium sativum*)	perennial	cloves	fall	6	bulb	when mature
Ginger (*Zingiber officinale*)	perennial	root divisions	year-round	12	rhizome	when mature
Ginseng (*Panax quinquefolius*)	perennial	seeds, seedlings	spring	12	root	when mature
Horehound (*Marrubium vulgare*)	perennial	seeds, cuttings	spring	12	leaves	before bloom
Lavender** (*Lavandula angustifolia*)	perennial	cuttings	fall and spring	12	leaves	as it blooms
Lemon balm (*Melissa officinalis*)	perennial	seeds, cuttings	fall and spring	12	leaves	as needed
Lovage (*Levisticum officinale*)	perennial	seeds, plants	fall and spring	12	leaves	as needed
Marjoram, sweet (*Origanum majorana*)	perennial	seeds, cuttings	fall and spring	12	leaves	as needed
Mint, peppermint (*Mentha piperita*); spearmint (*Mentha spicata*)	perennial	seeds, cuttings, divisions	year-round	12 12	leaves	as needed
Oregano (*Origanum vulgare*)	perennial	divisions	fall and spring	24	leaves	as needed
Parsley (*Petroselinum crispum*)	biennial	seeds	fall-spring	12	leaves	as needed
Rosemary** (*Rosmarinus officinalis*)	perennial	seeds, cuttings	fall and spring	24	leaves	as needed
Sage ** (*Salvia officinalis*)	perennial	seeds, cuttings	fall and spring	18	leaves	as needed
Savory, summer (*Satureja hortensis*); Savory, winter (*Satureja montana*)	annual, perennial	seeds	spring; spring	12 12	leaves	as needed
Tarragon** (*Artemisia dracunculus*)	perennial	cuttings, divisions	fall and spring	12	leaves	as needed
Thyme** (*Thymus vulgaris*)	perennial	seeds, cuttings	fall-spring	12	leaves, flowers	as needed
Watercress** (*Nasturtium officinale*)	perennial	seeds, cuttings	fall-spring	6	leaves	as needed

* In inches. ** Prefers near neutral or slightly alkaline soils.

13
Kindergardens

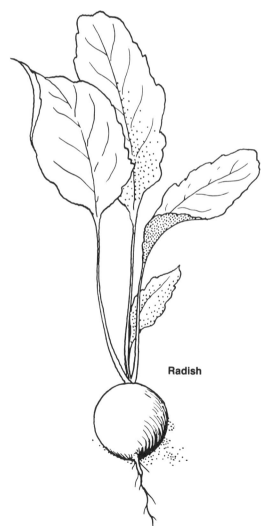
Radish

DIGGING FOR WIGGLY worms, watching seeds sprout and growing vegetables they normally never would eat — there are plenty of reasons why children like gardening. And educators are discovering that gardening projects help students learn a variety of subjects while having fun.

Although the connection between science education and gardening may be the most obvious one, there are many other benefits from children's gardening programs. The healthy outdoors activities combine science and horticultural skills to develop an understanding of the environment. Through planting and nurturing, children also make strides in personal growth, learning from successes and failures.

Children also need to know that since food comes from the earth, we must preserve it. Tilling the garden and planting the seeds or transplants offer experiences that will be remembered throughout life.

Why not designate a garden just for the children? They, too, need a place to dig in the dirt and delight in the miracles of seeing plants grow.

The one farm experience most families still can provide is that of growing plants for food. How many children think milk comes from the grocery store or that you pump the cow's tail to fill a carton? These days, few people can keep their own cow. However, even if the garden is just a big flowerpot, almost everyone can learn firsthand the pleasures of growing a tomato and starting a pineapple plant.

Children will need adult guidance, but grown-ups will enjoy these activities too. For the very young, keep sessions short. Use plants that grow rapidly. Radishes are up and growing in four to five days and ready to eat in three or four weeks. The fanciest marigolds still flower in six weeks. Like other beginning gardeners, kids are impatient, so make the first efforts the most rewarding.

When potting up the tomato transplants for the family garden, leave a few for the youngsters. Kids like to imitate; consider it a compliment. A little competition can be family fun; nothing better than a race to beat good old Dad or Mom to produce the first fruit. Kids can easily handle and enjoy assuming the responsibility for their own plants.

How about creating their own

plot, maybe at the corner of the family garden? Just a little 4-foot by 4-foot area and some leftover seeds can produce beans, corn, broccoli and tomatoes any boy or girl would love to put on the table.

In most families the rule is this: If a family member raises the crop, everybody eats it. A few families, however, also give each member an absolute veto on anyone's growing a particularly disliked vegetable.

Most gardeners can think up easy projects for the budding horticulturist. Here a few longtime favorites:

1 inch deep along the sides of the jar where they can be seen as they sprout. Moisten the soil and set the jar in a bright area of the house.

Germination usually begins in three to four days. The seeds swell and the outer coverings crack. Soon the roots head downward and the seed leaves push up above the soil.

Keep the jar in bright light and watch the young plants develop. Mist with water as needed to keep the soil moist. The seedlings can become fairly sizable before they outgrow the jar.

When the jar no longer can contain the seedlings, it is time to end the study.

2. Forest in a jar

Materials needed: Extra-wide-mouth jar; radish or other quickly germinating seeds; soil; egg carton.

Completion time: Two to three weeks.

Left to their own devices, kids usually will sow seeds too close together. Just for fun, turn a jar green and grow a forest of seedlings.

Place a large jar on its side and fill it an inch or two deep with soil. Keep the jar from rolling by resting it in the top of an egg carton. Spread seeds thinly over the surface of the soil, cover with a bit more soil, and moisten.

Seeds may germinate in less than

two days. Keep the developing plants in bright light and mist them with water. They will hit the roof before it is time to give up on this project.

3. Edible sprouts

Materials needed: Quart jar with lid; a third of a cup of mung beans; alfalfa, curly cress, buckwheat, lentils or other seeds eaten as sprouts. Inquire at a health-food store for new ideas.

Completion time: Three to five days.

Enjoy the rewards of a quick harvest: Sprouting seeds takes just a few days. The sense of accomplishment is almost instantaneous. Mung beans are the most traditional, but others add tangy, nutty flavors to a meal.

1. Seed view jars

Materials needed: Wide-mouth jar; snap bean seeds; soil.

Completion time: Two to three weeks.

Almost everyone will be interested in observing the miracle of germination and watching seeds grow. Plant seeds against the sides of a glass jar to give beginning gardeners a window on the process. Explain that inside a seed is a live plant, ready to grow when given water and air.

Fill a glass jar with soil to within a few inches of the top. Press seeds

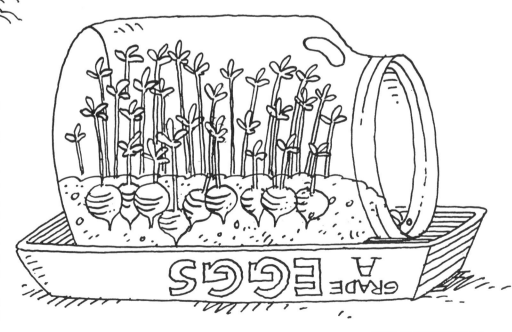

Select a clean jar to fill with a third of a cup of edible seeds. Punch several holes in the lid. Try to keep the size of the holes smaller than the size of the seeds.

Before bedtime, cover the seeds with water and cap the jar. The next morning, drain out the water (cheesecloth or a strainer may help in holding onto the seeds) and turn the jar on its side. Spread the seeds out along the now-horizontal side of the jar and watch them grow.

Twice daily, rinse the seeds with water so they won't ferment as they sprout. When they are an inch or so long — usually in about four days — they are ready to eat, either by the handful or in sandwiches and salads. Store surplus sprouts in the refrigerator.

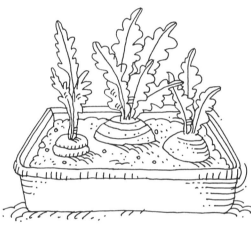

4. Root-top gardens

Materials needed: Tops (usually the discards) of carrots, beets or turnips; a shallow tray (like one for making ice cubes) or saucer; sand.

Completion time: Two to three weeks.

As a novelty, take the part of root vegetables usually tossed out by cooks and use these portions to grow new leaves. Save the tops, including the top edible half an inch of carrots, beets or turnips.

Set the tops close together in a small, shallow tray filled half an inch or so deep with sand. Moisten the sand.

Keep the vegetable tops in bright light inside, or on porch or patio. The old tops will grow new foliage, but don't expect a harvest from these plantings.

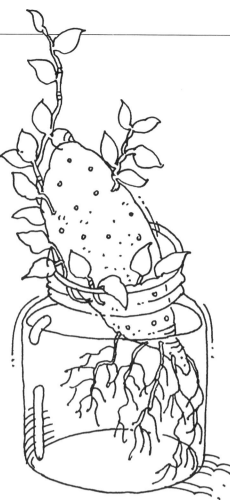

5. Sweet potato vine

Materials needed: Sweet potato; vase or jar with a narrow top.

Completion time: Two to three months.

Sweet potatoes are roots, but the first growth produced by the plant is a shoot with stems and leaves. This growth is called adventitious; biologically, it is unusual. A sweet potato that shows buds will grow the best, but any potato eventually will sprout.

Set the sweet potato with the plump end resting in the opening of a vase or jar. Fill the container with water so the potato is partially submerged.

In a few weeks shoots will sprout, forming stems and leaves. Later, roots form on the stems and potato base and grow into the water.

Let the vine grow and treat it like a houseplant, or grow transplants for the garden. When the young shoots are 6 inches long and forming roots, snap them off to be transplanted to the garden or a pot of soil. Provide a trellis for the top growth. Keep the soil moist and feed with a scattering of 6-6-6 over the surface of the soil every three to four weeks. About 120 days later, new sweet potatoes will be ready to pick.

Plan this project for the warm growing season, March through August.

6. New pineapple plant

Materials needed: A ripe pineapple; 6-inch pot; vermiculite.

Completion time: Six to eight weeks.

Young and old alike, gardeners will enjoy starting a new pineapple plant. Begin the fun by saving the top of a fruit.

Separate the leafy stem from the rest of the top. It is easy to remove what fleshy fruit remains so the stem, often with some preformed roots, becomes visible. Strip away a few lower leaves, and it is ready to plant. Allow it to dry a day or two, anyplace out of the sun, or plant it immediately.

Fill a pot with a rooting medium — vermiculite is best — and moisten. Press 1 to 2 inches of the pineapple stem into the vermiculite.

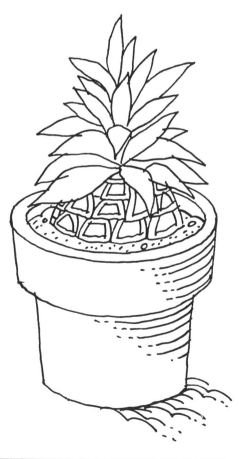

Keep the container in filtered sun and keep it moist. Rooting should occur in just a few weeks.

Once a stem is fully rooted, move it to a larger container of soil or set it in the garden to grow.

With normal care, a plant eventually will have a flower and then a fresh pineapple, but it will take about two years to bear fruit.

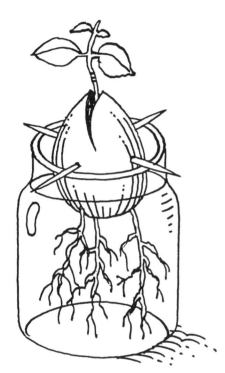

7. The avocado trick

Materials needed: Avocado; plastic cup; four toothpicks.

Completion time: Four to six weeks.

Avocados have one of the largest seeds gardeners will encounter — big enough for small hands to hold, even if it is slippery. Let youngsters help separate one from a fruit. Explain there is a plant inside the seed and that most of the seed is food for the baby plant.

Notice the seed is pointed at one end and flat at the other. The flat end is the bottom, from which a taproot will grow. Insert the toothpicks into the sides of the seed half an inch from the bottom, spacing them evenly around the sides.

Fill the cup with water and balance the seed with its toothpicks across the top of the cup. The bottom of the seed should rest in the water. Keep the cup full of water and set in a bright light. In a few weeks, roots should grow into the cup and a shoot begin to grow upward.

The avocado can grow in water for weeks, filling the cup with roots, but it is better transplanted into a pot of soil when a fist-size, loosely woven root system forms. Given bright light or full sun, avocado seedlings make good houseplants. Pinch out the top to make them bushy.

Seedling trees planted outdoors will bear a crop in five to seven years, provided they never experience a freeze. Most are sensitive to cold. They seldom make it more than a few winters without being killed back in Central Florida and rarely survive at all in Northern Florida.

8. Citrus from seed

Materials needed: Orange, grapefruit or other citrus fruit; soil; a 6-inch pot.

Completion time: Six to eight weeks.

Save some large seeds from a breakfast grapefruit or when squeezing orange juice. Wash them and let them air-dry for a day before planting several in a pot of soil.

Set the container in a bright, sunny location. Most of the seeds will sprout within a few weeks. Pinch out by hand or use scissors to cut out all but the strongest shoot. Grow it as a houseplant or patio specimen.

Seedlings can grow into fruiting trees, but expect to wait eight to nine years for a harvest.

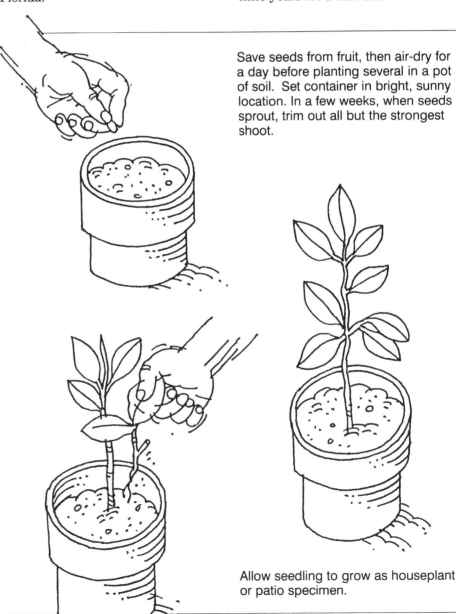

Save seeds from fruit, then air-dry for a day before planting several in a pot of soil. Set container in bright, sunny location. In a few weeks, when seeds sprout, trim out all but the strongest shoot.

Allow seedling to grow as houseplant or patio specimen.

Fill containers will soil. Sow seeds, cover with soil, then moisten.

When seedlings are 2 weeks old, transplant them to individual small pots or sections of an egg carton.

9. Starting transplants

Materials needed: Containers to plant in, including egg cartons, plastic salad trays, cottage cheese cartons or shallow pots; potting soil; tomato, broccoli or cabbage seeds.

Completion time: Six to eight weeks.

All family members can have fun starting their own garden transplants. For plants that will continue growing and produce a harvest, start tomatoes midsummer or late winter and broccoli or cabbage during the fall.

Don't waste money on pots. Use what is on hand from the fast-food shop, kitchen or garden. Punch holes in egg cartons, salad containers or other trays to provide good drainage. Do buy a sterile soil mix, or blend equal parts of peat moss and vermiculite to make your own.

Wet the soil and sow the seeds lightly; most will germinate. Cover the seeds with a sprinkling of soil and water again. Cover the container with its lid, wet newspaper or another container.

As soon as the first seed starts to sprout, remove the cover and move the container into good light. Keep the soil moist, and feed weekly with a houseplant fertilizer.

When the seedlings are 2 weeks old, transplant them to individual little pots or divisions of an egg carton. Continue to give them full sun, water and weekly fertilizer in readiness for planting in the garden.

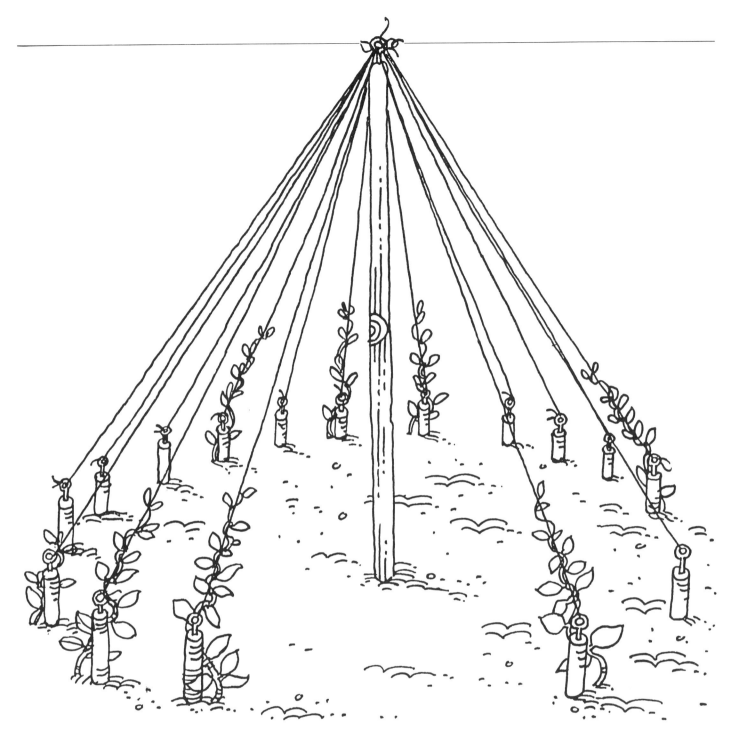

10. Bean tepee

Materials needed: One 2-inch by 2-inch treated board 8 feet long; one large and 16 small screw eyes; weatherproof string; 16 small stakes; pole bean seeds.

Completion time: Six to eight weeks.

Every kid likes a hideaway, an enclosed spot in which to sit and think or play with friends. An open back yard may be the ideal place to set up a tepee or two where kids can grow their own green walls.

Leave a way to get inside and a bean tepee makes a great place for youngsters to play as well as a space-efficient way to grow food for the family.

To begin a tepee, take an 8-foot pole of pretreated lumber and sink it at least 2 feet in the ground.

Place the large screw eye in the top of the pole. Till a circular area to about 3 feet out from the base of the pole and prepare the site for planting with a light feeding of 6-6-6.

Drive the small stakes into the soil 3 feet out from the pole. Space them equally, but leave an 18- to 24-inch gap on one side for the entrance. Place the small screw eyes in the top of each stake.

Run string from each small stake to the top of the pole to form the tepee outline. Plant two to three bean seeds at the base of each small stake. Cover the seeds an inch deep and keep the soil moist.

When the beans sprout and begin to grow, train the vines up the strings. Allow older vines to cross over from one string to another. Feed the planting lightly every two to three weeks.

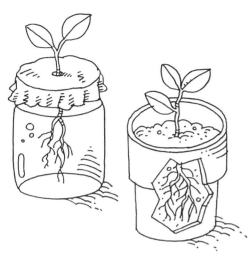

11. Rooting cuttings

Materials needed: A growing tomato plant, mint or similar succulent, easy-to-snap, green-stemmed plant; container with vermiculite; jar of water; aluminum foil.

Completion time: Six to eight weeks.

Youngsters are surprised at how a sprig from a plant will make another plant. Allow them to watch the process in a jar of water, but also show them how it works when roots have a better medium in which to grow.

Fill a shallow pot to the top with vermiculite and moisten thoroughly. Also fill a jar with water and cap with some aluminum foil. Take 4- to 6-inch tip cuttings from a tomato or a mint plant and stick one or more in the pot and jar. Set in a bright location to root.

Roots will begin to form within two to three weeks. Starting the second week, it's okay to peek: Gently lift the cutting from the vermiculite. Grow a mature plant from a cutting by transplanting it to a pot of soil when the roots are several inches long.

12. Halloween pumpkin

Materials needed: Garden space, with a sunny area at least 8 feet square for the vines to ramble over; Big Max pumpkin seeds; 6-6-6 fertilizer.

Completion time: 120 days.

Till a large garden spot. Add organic material to sandy soils. Around the middle of July, plant a group of three or four seeds. Space seeds several inches apart.

Keep the soil moist. Once the seeds begin to grow, scatter 6-6-6 fertilizer lightly over the pumpkin patch every three or four weeks.

As the plants begin to flower, watch for little pumpkins to appear. Give them time to set and begin to swell, then cut off all but two pumpkins per plant. When the plants die back after about 120 days of growth, a big pumpkin should be ready for Halloween.

For a personalized pumpkin, use a ballpoint pen or a sharp instrument to shallowly carve initials or designs into the skin of a small pumpkin. As the pumpkin matures, the scar from the carving will heal, leaving the designs behind.

Note to adults: Pumpkins are susceptible to downy mildew. If leaves develop yellow-to-brown, angular spots and a downy mold on the underside, control with a fungicide. This may be a good opportunity to teach children the importance of reading labels and taking precautions when handling garden chemicals.

13. Square-foot garden

Materials needed: Lumber and nails to make a box a foot square and 6 inches deep; soil; seeds or transplants; fertilizer.

Completion time: Eight to 10 weeks.

Every member of the family can build his or her own square-foot garden. Set the boxes together and the combined garden can be impressive. This activity shows how each individual contributes to the success of the whole garden.

Some people beg shallow wooden fruit or vegetable boxes from food stores, but most build their own, using 1-by-6 pressure-treated lumber.

Allow a loose fit between the bottom boards to ensure good drainage, or drill holes at least half an inch in diameter in the bottom of the box. Line each box with shade cloth or screening material to contain the soil.

Fill with soil to within an inch of the top; use good quality potting soil and there won't be weeds. What will grow depends in part on the season. For a single 1-foot box, good candidates are:

FALL AND SPRING
Beans — four seeds
Corn — one seed
Cucumbers — one transplant or seed
Eggplant — one transplant
Pepper — one transplant or seed
Squash — one transplant or seed
Tomato — one transplant

WINTER
Broccoli — one transplant or seed
Cabbage — one transplant or seed
Lettuce — four transplants or seeds
Onions — 20 transplants or seeds
Radishes — 50 seeds
Turnips — 20 seeds

Good care primarily consists of keeping the soil moist. Like other containers, boxes need to be watered when the soil begins to feel dry. Young plants may need water only every few days; older plants, daily. Feed weekly with a 20-20-20 fertilizer mixed at a rate of 1 tablespoon to a gallon of water.

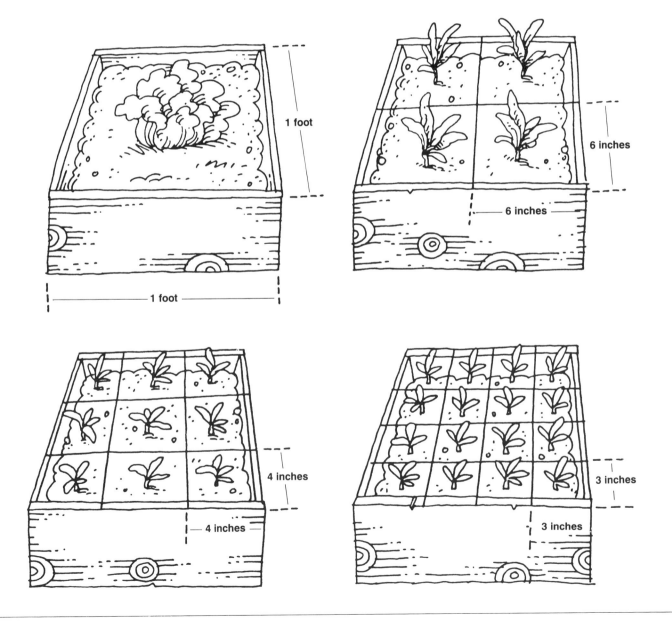

14. Child's own garden

Materials needed: Small plot of ground; seeds or transplants; fertilizer; mulch.

Completion time: One season.

A garden for a child can be just a 4-foot by 4-foot sunny spot, tilled and raked clear of weeds. It is best to start with a small plot so youngsters will stay interested and will be able to reap rewards without being overwhelmed.

Choose seeds at the store or use transplants. Perhaps the child has tried one of the earlier activities in this chapter and has a plant that needs a home. For very young children, here are vegetables that will give maximum success in the shortest time:

FALL AND SPRING
Beans — seed
Cherry tomatoes — transplant
Cucumber — transplant or seed
Eggplant — transplant
Pepper — transplant
Squash — transplant or seed

WINTER
Broccoli — transplant
Cabbage — transplant
Collards — transplant or seed
Lettuce — seed
Onions — transplant
Potatoes — seed pieces
Radishes — seed
Turnips — seed

Plant vegetables in rows or use the square-foot method. Follow the instructions on the packet of seeds or the tag of a transplant.

Mulch with compost, old hay or lawn clippings. Water the garden when the surface of the soil begins to dry. Feed every three to four weeks with a light scattering of 6-6-6.

Note to adults: Insects and diseases may affect the garden, even though these crops are relatively pest-free. Use biological controls where possible.

15. Worm farm

Materials needed: Cardboard or wooden box; plastic bag; garden soil; organic matter; manure; worms.

Time to completion: 90 days.

As they wiggle through the soil, worms help build garden soil. What child does not like to chase a worm or two through the soil?

Build a worm farm using a cardboard or wooden box lined with a plastic bag. Place a few holes in the bottom of the bag, then fill with a

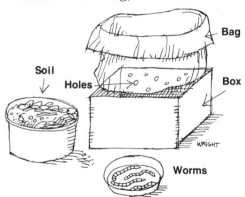

mixture of garden soil enriched with organic matter of leaves, grass clippings or compost and a few cups of manure. Turn the mixture and moisten.

Allow the prepared soil to set for a few days, then add the first worms dug from the garden or bought as red worms from a bait shop. Keep the soil moist and turn in more organic matter throughout the summer.

Periodically add some of the worms to a garden soil that has been enriched with organic matter, which will provide food for them.

113

16. Family fruit tree

Materials needed: Citrus or deciduous fruit tree; peat moss; sunny garden spot.

Completion time: A lifetime.

"My very own tree" can be a child's pride and joy. Plant the tree when the family is young and watch child and tree grow up together.

In Central and South Florida, citrus trees need little care to produce fruit, so they make the best choice. In northern sections of the state, consider planting a peach, apple or pear.

All that is needed is a sunny spot, some peat moss or compost, and a shovel. Work up a large planting site. Loosen the soil, work in the peat, and plant the tree at the same depth it was growing in the container. Wet the whole planting site well and the tree is ready to grow.

Visit the tree every few days and water well. For the first year, feed lightly with 6-6-6 every six to eight weeks during the warm months. See the chapters on fruit trees for advice on continuing care.

Even when the child is grown, it will continue to be "my tree."

17. Sky-high sunflowers

Materials needed: Garden space in full sun; seeds of sunflower variety Mammoth, Giganteus or other large-flowered type.

Time to completion: Ten to 12 weeks.

Watch the sunflowers grow higher and higher. Soon you will need a ladder to touch the top. The plants are full of vigor and can grow more than 10 feet tall when given good care. Have each family member grow a plant or two and encourage competition.

Plants grow spring through fall in northern and central areas of the state; they grow year-round farther south. Plants are best started from seeds sown directly in the ground. Make sure you have a tall-growing variety that will produce big flower heads.

Sunflowers grow in sandy soils, but are more likely to shoot sky-high when organic matter is added to the planting site. Here is a chance to experiment, leaving one planting area plain sand and the other, improved with peat moss, manure or compost. The enriched garden site will hold extra moisture and supply nutrients to help produce tall plants.

Sow seeds about half an inch deep and 12 inches apart. Keep the soil moist. In seven to 10 days the seedlings will push up through the soil. To grow tall plants, feed every two or three weeks with a handful of 6-6-6 fertilizer scattered across the surface of the soil under the plant but away from the stem.

Measure the height of plants at least weekly. When the plants are more than head-high, a flower bud will begin to emerge in the top of the plant. Many blooms are 10 to 12 inches in diameter, forming bright yellow blossoms that appear to follow the sun across the sky.

When the outer yellow petals begin to dry and the seeds are plump, it is time to harvest the head. The birds sometimes beat you to the crop, but they need to eat, too. Let the flower dry in a shady, moisture-free area for two to three weeks. The heads then can be hung out as needed to feed birds, or the seeds can be harvested.

Pick the seeds off or rub the dry flower head over wire screening that has holes a half an inch wide or larger. To roast, toast on a lightly oiled baking sheet at 350 degrees Fahrenheit for a few minutes. Sprinkle with salt, and they are ready to eat.

14

Citrus — how to grow the state crop

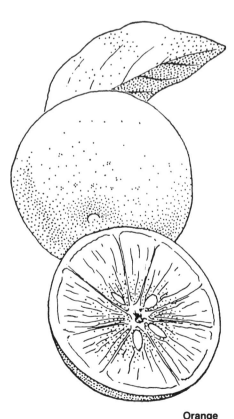

Orange

CITRUS TREES NEED NO mollycoddling to produce sweet, juicy, home-grown fruit. Although apples, peaches and pears need almost constant attention, citrus is practically carefree.

Originally from southern Asia, citrus found a home in the New World when Columbus carried seeds to Haiti in 1493. In the early 1500s, Spanish explorers and colonists carried them to Florida, where the trees flourished with minimal care.

Some citrus grew wild in North and Central Florida. Explorers and visitors often found trees naturalized along the St. Johns River, loaded with golden fruit. Formal cultivation began sometime in the early 1800s. The Don Phillippe grove in Pinellas County, planted between 1809 and 1820, is believed to be one of the state's oldest.

By the late 1800s many groves were established. During the 1893-94 season citrus production reached 5 million boxes. Production plummeted a year later when a mighty freeze reduced the crop to 147,000 boxes. The record yields of the late 1800s were not equaled until the 1909-10 season.

Freezes have played a major role in the history of Florida citrus, continually pushing production southward. Since the memorable freezes of 1983 and 1985, few commercial groves remain north of the line drawn by State Road 50 through Orlando and across the state.

Today most of the annual crop, which topped 180 million boxes in the late 1980s, comes from lower Central and South Florida.

In home culture, freezes also are the major hazard; otherwise the trees just about grow themselves. Although groves may be abandoned, individual trees survive, and a harvest may be found for the picking on street corners, at apartment complexes and in subdivisions. It's one of the things that makes Florida feel a bit like paradise.

In North Florida, only hardy citrus survives without winter protection. Good choices are satsuma, kumquat and limequat. Gardeners who are willing to provide protection or who live along the coast where the ocean moderates the temperatures may want to experiment with other varieties.

South of State Road 50, most cit-

117

rus trees appear safe from killing freezes. Only lemons and limes need special protection when grown in northern Central Florida.

Citrus trees are more resistant to cold when they are dormant. Periods of cool weather through the fall and early winter before a freeze are a great help. In the end, however, cold does the damage, and some kinds of citrus can take lower temperatures than others. Consider the temperatures at which trees are likely to be damaged when choosing what to plant:

Citrus trees	Degrees Fahrenheit
Lime and lemon	28-30
Meyer lemon	24-26
Temple	24-26
Tangerine	22-24
Orange	22-24
Grapefruit	22-24
Tangelo	20-24
Kumquat and limequat	18-20

Citrus fruit generally is less hardy than foliage and trees. Most fruit will be damaged if exposed to temperatures between 26 and 28 degrees for one to two hours.

Fruit still can be used after a freeze; usually the harvest can continue for several weeks. If it looks good and tastes good, generally it is edible. Off flavors and pungent odors are the first signs that fruit is deteriorating and should be avoided.

Site selection

Citrus trees need well-drained soil and full sun to produce good harvests. They will take naturally to these locations, growing vigorous root systems and full canopies of foliage.

The common orange, mandarin and grapefruit trees are large and need plenty of growing room. A spacing of 20 to 25 feet apart is ideal. Home growers prepared to do regular pruning can opt to crowd their trees.

Citrus can be sheared and topped to fit a crowded back yard or even a tub. Realistically, most varieties need a minimum of 12 feet in height and width to produce well.

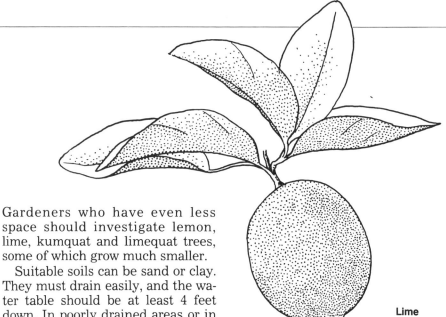

Lime

Gardeners who have even less space should investigate lemon, lime, kumquat and limequat trees, some of which grow much smaller.

Suitable soils can be sand or clay. They must drain easily, and the water table should be at least 4 feet down. In poorly drained areas or in soils that flood during the rainy season, plant trees above the normal soil level in raised beds or large containers.

A near-neutral soil pH of around 7.0 gives the best yields, so test the soil before planting. If it is too acidic, correct by adding lime. Growing trees usually tolerate soil that is too alkaline, but watch for signs of deficiencies in the minor nutrients.

Commercial growers rarely add anything else to their soils. Gardeners may find it hard to resist adding peat moss or compost. In soils that drain freely, these additions help hold moisture and supply additional nutrients. Because a tree's feeder roots will range far afield, be sure to work in any additions over a large area, not just with the fill soil when planting.

Tree selection

Quality citrus trees are available from garden centers and retail nurseries. Plants are inspected by the Florida Department of Agriculture and certified free of major citrus pests.

A tree that looks good, with a relatively straight trunk and green color, is likely to be the best buy. Avoid trees with few or yellow leaves and spindly stems. They may become good specimens in time but will need extra care.

Big trees are tempting but often turn out to be a mistake. Big trees suffer more transplant shock and often are difficult to re-establish in a new location. Trees about 3 feet tall will make vigorous growth almost from the start and quickly will catch up to the bigger ones.

Fruit on a young tree looks appealing and at least guarantees the variety. Don't expect production to continue, however. Experts recommend stripping fruit from young trees for the first few years.

Once fruit sets, branches normally stop growing, so although leaving fruit may yield a small harvest, it is likely to stunt the tree's future growth. By pulling the first fruit, in just a few years growers obtain big trees that bear good harvests.

Many trees won't bear fruit for several years after being set in the ground. They may not even flower; if they do, the blossoms often drop. Young trees are busy making roots and shoots. Don't expect a good crop for five to seven years.

Almost every tree in a nursery will have a swollen area about 6 inches above the soil line, which is the graft union. But there are some exceptions. Limes often are produced by air layering, and Meyer lemons and calamondins typically are grown from cuttings. There is new interest in growing other citrus from cuttings, but most citrus is grafted.

Grafting adds a variety of citrus that bears superior fruit to a root system that improves disease resistance, fruit quality or cold hardiness. Many rootstocks have been developed, but home growers rarely have a choice. What is available is what the growers shipped. Some rootstocks are particularly useful in Florida, however. For example, the following contribute these qualities:

• Carrizo Citrange — Produces good quality fruit of acceptable size plus good yields. Trees are large, fairly cold hardy and grow rapidly. Tolerant to foot rot and burrowing nematodes but sensitive to citrus blight.

• Swingle Citrumelo — Increasing in popularity because it gives resistance to blight and Tristeza virus. Trees are moderately vigorous, cold hardy and citrus-nematode tolerant. They produce good quality fruit.

• Rough Lemon — Produces a deep root system in sandy soils. Gives large fruit and high yields. Little used because trees are sensitive to cold, susceptible to foot rot and citrus blight; yields the poorest quality fruit.

• Cleopatra Mandarin — Cold hardy and tolerant to foot rot; a good-quality fruit producer. Used with mandarin fruit, Temples and tangelos.

• Sour Orange — Offers superior cold tolerance, resistance to foot rot and produces excellent quality fruit. Once popular, use of this rootstock is declining because trees are susceptible to Tristeza virus, which may stunt or kill trees.

• Trifoliate Orange — The most hardy rootstock used in colder areas with satsuma fruit. Trees are resistant to foot rot, and fruit quality is rated good, but in general is considered inferior to that produced on other rootstocks.

Tree planting

In general, skip the many steps traditional to planting other trees. Commercial growers plant citrus by the thousands without any special soil preparation, priding themselves on the speed with which they set trees in the ground. It takes a blink of an eye to open a hole, set the tree, pull soil around the roots and water.

These trees, usually bare-root, are best planted during late fall and winter. Container-grown plants commonly sold at garden centers have strong root systems and can be planted any time of year. If planted fall through early winter, they will spread their roots and be ready to grow by spring, but they will need protection from severe weather.

Gardeners can take a little more time and add peat moss, compost or bone meal to the soil, but it isn't necessary. Citrus trees are vigorous and with normal good care will root rapidly into the surrounding soil.

Unlike other fruit trees and ornamental plantings, citrus trees are never mulched. A disease called foot rot flourishes on wet trunks, and a mulched citrus tree is usually short-lived. It is a good idea to keep weeds and grass away and leave the soil bare around the trunk, just to prevent foot rot. If there is any question about water pooling around the trunk, plant the tree a little higher.

Grower-preferred planting of citrus

• Pick a sunny planting site 4 feet square and clear it of grass and weeds.

• Dig a hole in the middle of the site, a little bigger than the container.

• Don't add fertilizer, peat or manure to the hole or fill soil.

• Remove the tree from the container, disturbing the roots as little as possible.

• Position the root ball at its original depth, with the graft union at least 2 inches above ground level.

• Pull soil around the roots, watering as you plant.

• Build a dike or soil ring 4 to 6 inches high and 2 feet out around the trunk to aid in watering.

Planting citrus

Position container-grown plant level with top of the soil line. Deep planting often leads to trunk and root rots.

- Place the tree on a beginning maintenance program, but do not feed for a month after planting.

Care of young trees

For the first three years new plantings need special attention to water, fertilizer and weed control.

Citrus trees need moisture as well as time to dry between waterings. Soil that is damp constantly can kill a tree by causing root and trunk rots. In well-drained soils, newly planted trees can be watered every other day. Continue for the first few weeks, then cut back to once or twice a week. Just a bucket or two of water emptied into the irrigation ring around the tree is all that is needed.

Fertilizer on a regular schedule will produce maximum growth. Wait to fertilize until new growth begins, about four to six weeks after planting. Apply fertilizer every six weeks from March through September. For the first year, use half a pound of 6-6-6 fertilizer with added minor elements the first time, and a pound every time thereafter. During the next two years, apply a pound of fertilizer to each tree every six to eight weeks for every year it has been in the yard.

To further protect against nutrient deficiencies, apply a foliar spray to young trees for the first four or five springs. After a flush of new growth, use a citrus minor-nutrient fertilizer.

Clean cultivation helps reduce disease. Only 1 to 2 feet around the trunk need to be completely clear of grass and weeds. Many gardeners like to keep the area out to a tree's drip line free of vegetation, enlarging the circle as the tree grows. These growers think maintenance is reduced and their trees look better.

The cleared space then may seem a tempting spot to plant flowers, shrubs and perennials, but it's not a good idea. Plantings that reduce air movement under citrus should be avoided. Drier conditions help reduce disease problems.

As a young tree sends out new branches, leave them unless they start from below the graft union. Rub away or cut off buds that form along the short trunk of the rootstock. All other growth helps feed the growing tree. There will be plenty of time later to shape the tree as it approaches fruit-bearing age.

Most pest problems that afflict young trees are minor. Leaf spots, caterpillars and aphids can blemish the foliage or cause the leaves to curl without hurting the tree. Gardeners who can't live with the look should check the table under citrus pests for recommended controls.

Care of older trees

Once a tree has been in place for three years, maintenance becomes minimal; water as needed and feed three times a year.

Citrus is deep-rooted and can withstand some drought. When the soil really begins to dry out, water is needed.

Apply enough water to thoroughly moisten the soil, which usually means watering once or twice a week during dry, hot weather and less often during cooler months. Spring and early fall, when the weather is warm but dry, typically are the times irrigation is needed most.

Feed established trees in mid-February, June and early October.

There are many ways to determine the amount of fertilizer a tree needs, but the easiest goes by trunk circumference. Measure around the trunk 6 inches above the ground; then use half a pound of fertilizer for each inch of circumference. A maximum of 20 pounds can be applied at each feeding.

Many citrus fertilizers are available, but any 6-6-6 formula will do. Most gardeners choose one that also contains minor nutrients, which may be labeled essential nutrients.

The easiest way to apply fertilizer is to scatter it under the spread of the tree and out past the drip line. Gardeners worried about harming their lawn can divide the fertilizer among 6- to 8-inch-deep holes made 2 feet apart over the same area.

With either method, water after fertilizing to encourage roots to take up the nutrients. The watering also will minimize turf burn.

Citrus trees usually assume an at-

Fertilizing citrus

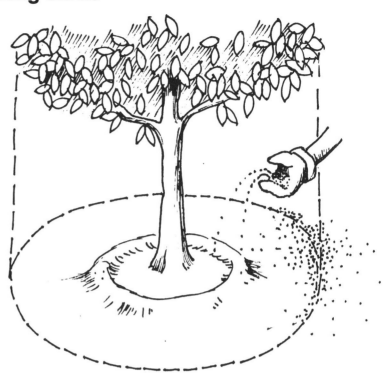

Feed the entire root system of the tree. Scatter fertilizer from the trunk out past the drip line.

tractive, rounded silhouette with minimal pruning. Eliminate criss-crossing branches within the framework of the tree. Make maintenance easier by pruning away lower limbs; at least keep the lowest part of the trunk clean. Sprouts from below the graft union may take over the tree.

Vigorous shoots, called water sprouts or suckers, can arise anywhere along the trunk and within the tree. These may be thorny and non-productive for a few years but eventually will form bearing limbs. Keep them if needed to round out the tree or to replace a declining limb; otherwise they can be pruned out or tipped back.

Older citrus trees rarely need any other care. Gardeners willing to tolerate a few pests and fruit and foliage that are not picture-perfect usually can avoid pesticides. Leaves may turn black from sooty mold and fruit may become brownish or bumpy. The fruit will taste just as good, and overall production seldom is affected.

Choosing a variety

Selecting which tree to plant is like picking a favorite ice cream; it's hard to choose when so many are good. Because only a few trees will fit in a crowded landscape, the right choice is important.

It is difficult to choose a variety of orange, mandarin or grapefruit purely on the basis of taste. A year's weather, the stage at which a fruit is picked, the age of the tree and individual taste preferences all affect a judgment. Closely related citrus varieties can be distinguished by counting seeds and looking at shape and color, but taste is quite subjective.

Probably the most satisfactory way of selecting varieties is to choose those that fruit in succession. With careful planning, citrus can be harvested from October through June.

Earliest to ripen include the K-Early tangelo, the satsuma mandarin and the Robinson tangerine. Don't be surprised if the first picking is somewhat bitter; early fruit often is low in sugar. However, it's not too bitter to taste good, and flavor tends to improve as the season advances.

Growers of juice oranges anxiously await the first Hamlins, popular because they begin to ripen in late October, to be followed by Parson Browns in November, Pineapples in December, and Valencias from February through June.

Navel oranges ripen in late October. They can be juiced but, because they are easily peeled and sectioned, usually are reserved for eating fresh.

Mandarins are popular early and midseason varieties. This relatively miscellaneous collection of citrus often is characterized by a loose, easy-to-peel skin.

Together with similar hybrids, they comprise a group of exotic and delicious citrus. Popular choices in this category include Dancy and Sunburst tangerines, Orlando and Minneola tangelos and Temple and Murcott Honey oranges.

Almost every home planting needs a grapefruit tree, if only to keep breakfast-lovers happy. Naturally ripened grapefruit are midseason varieties that start to mature in November.

Connoisseurs, however, wait late into the season to pick grapefruit at its sweetest. The original seedy Duncan still rates tops on flavor; varieties with few or no seeds include Marsh, Thompson and Red Blush.

Lemons, limes, kumquats and calamondins tend to be ever-bearing. Because the demand for fruit drinks, salads, marmalades and pies often is limited, these trees typically are grown only by gardeners with a special liking for these fruits or those who have extra space.

In the end, fruit selection comes down to personal preference, so do some taste tests before planting. The farmers' market should have a good selection of citrus as it ripens. Sampling popular varieties throughout the season will help gardeners to plan a succession of citrus for many years of eating pleasure.

Oranges

Ask a commercial grower which citrus fruit he enjoys the most, and it's likely to be an orange. Multipurpose oranges can be squeezed, sectioned or eaten fresh from the tree. Florida production of oranges reached a record high of more than 200 million 90-pound boxes in the 1979-80 season. Even in bad years it consistently is more than 100 million boxes.

Gardeners favor the navel orange, a delicious fruit that ripens around Thanksgiving. Earlier in this century, the navel was the Christmas stocking orange for many children. Though they produce less juice than other varieties and a tree yields less fruit, navels are preferred for their large size, ease of peeling and refreshing juice.

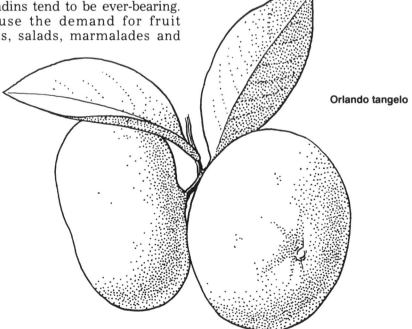

Orlando tangelo

Like a number of mandarins, some oranges and a few grapefruit, navels have a bump on the bottom of the fruit. The bump is a rudimentary fruit, often seedless because it lacks functional pollen. Some years the navel end is the fruit's downfall, harboring rot organisms or insects. The bitterness from the peel tends to get in the juice when a navel is thoroughly squeezed, so commercial processors don't like them. The trend today is for fruit with only a small navel.

Navel oranges originated in the Mediterranean area and were carried to Brazil before coming to the United States. Early arrivals were planted in Florida around 1835. In 1873 the U.S. Department of Agriculture introduced what has become the most popular variety, the Washington Navel. Other varieties available include the Barrington, Dream and Summerfield.

In Florida and around the world, the most popular juice orange is the late-season Valencia. Also an Old World fruit, possibly from Spain or Portugal, it was introduced to Florida in 1870 by E.H. Hart of Federal Point, near Palatka.

Seedless Valencias swell with so much juice, they set a standard for the industry. They ripen after February, so trees are flowering as the previous season's crop is harvested. These are the trees that wow the tourists. Lue Gim Gong and Pope Summer are selections that ripen late even for Valencias, into the summer months.

When choosing varieties, remember that trees holding fruit late into one year often produce less the following year. The late-season bearing may be partially responsible for alternate bearing, a pattern of a year of heavy production followed by a year of light production. Trees that carry their fruit into the winter months also tend to be less cold hardy.

Hamlin oranges rank next in popularity among fruit juices for the state's citrus industry. In 1879 the Hamlin was found as a seedling growing near DeLand. The crop is early, beginning to ripen in October. Hamlins are popular because they ripen before the weather turns cold. They bear heavily and they are seedless.

Compared with other varieties, however, fruit quality usually is considered poor. Other long-time favorites well-suited to home gardens are Parson Brown, Pineapple, Queen and Jaffa.

Few of the varieties introduced since the 1900s have become commercial favorites. Recent introductions, however, have made some real progress toward combining the early bearing qualities of the Hamlin with the flavor of the Valencia.

Home growers may wish to try selections developed by C.J. Hearn of the U.S. Department of Agriculture Horticultural Research Laboratory in Orlando and released to the market in 1987. Look for Midsweet, Sunstar and Gardner.

Orange

Oranges

Type/variety	Season of maturity	Hardiness	Seed per fruit	Average diameter (inches)	Comments
Gardner	January-March	hardy	6-24	2½-3	Ripens January through March. Color and quality of juice is rated better than the Hamlin. Trees are vigorous.
Hamlin	October-January	hardy	0-6	2¾-3	Early juice orange; popular because it ripens before danger of freeze.
Jaffa	December-February	hardy	0-10	2½-3	Introduced to Florida in 1883, possibly from Palestine, by H.S. Sanford. Shows good cold-resistance but bears erratically. Trees are subject to splitting.
Midsweet	January-March	hardy	6-24	2½-3	Improvement over Hamlin for juice color and quality. Fruit ripens in January and remains firm on the tree through March.
Navel	October-January	hardy	0-6	3-3½	Good fruit to juice or section. Fruit may be few but tend to be large.
Parson Brown	October-January	medium	10-20	2½-2¾	Discovered as a seedling by the Rev. N.L. Brown near Webster, Fla., in 1865. Fruit is early but juice quality is poor — acid and low in sugar.
Pineapple	December-February	susceptible	15-25	2¾-3	Chance seedling discovered by the Rev. J.B. Owens near Citra, Fla., in 1860. Fruit is seedy; juice quality and color are excellent. Fruit will not store on tree.
Queen	December-February	hardy	15-20	2½-3	Seedling tree found near Bartow, Fla., before 1900. Similar to the Pineapple orange. Previously known as King; name changed to avoid confusion with the King mandarin.
Sunstar	January-March	hardy	6-20	2½-3	Trees appear more vigorous than older selections of Hamlin and Valencia. Juice improved in color over Hamlin.
Valencia	February-June	hardy	0-6	2¾-3	Leading variety of sweet orange in Florida and throughout the world. Standard of excellence for eating and juicing.

Mandarins and hybrids *

Type/variety	Season of maturity	Hardiness	Seed per fruit	Average diameter (inches)	Comments
Ambersweet	October-December	moderate	0-15	3-3½	Easy to peel and section orange hybrid. Juice has excellent flavor and dark-orange color. Gives consistent yields yearly.
Dancy	December-January	hardy	6-20	2¼-2½	Easy-to-peel, popular tangerine for the holidays. Trees tend to be alternate bearing (heavy crop one year, light the next).
Fallglo	October-November	susceptible	30-40	3-3½	Easy-to-peel, sweet fruit resembling the Temple. Colorful juice. Resistant to scab.
Minneola	December-January	hardy	7-12	3-3½	Tangelo with such sweet taste, many call it Honeybell. Fruit often has a pronounced neck.
Murcott	January-March	hardy	10-20	2½-2¾	Very sweet, late-season fruit. Often called honey tangerine but most likely a hybrid. Trees quite susceptible to scab fungus.
Orlando	November-January	hardy	0-35	2¾-3	Tangelo, result of a cross between Duncan grapefruit and Dancy tangerine. Cup-shaped leaves. Trees are heavy feeders.
Ponkan	December-January	hardy	3-7	2¾-3½	Easy-to-peel tangerine. Fruit is delicious but will not ship. Trees tend to be alternate bearing.
Robinson	October-December	hardy	1-20	2½-2¾	Tangerine. Needs cross-pollination from tangelo or Temple to produce well. Susceptible to limb, twig dieback.
Satsuma	September-November	very hardy	0-6	2¼-2½	One of first to ripen of home-grown citrus. Often edible when green; fruit stores poorly on tree.
Sunburst	November-December	hardy	1-20	2½-3	Hybrid with bright color, sweet taste. Needs cross-pollination from tangelo or Temple to be good producer.
Temple	January-March	susceptible	15-20	2¼-3	Easy-to-peel, sweet, very juicy fruit. Grow in protected location. Susceptible to scab.

* Additional but less-popular mandarin-type fruit includes the K-Early, Seminole, Osceola, Nova and Lee hybrids.

Mandarins and related hybrids

Mandarins are specialty fruits often referred to as loose-skin oranges. Some divide easily into sections and many have an open center that helps distinguish them from oranges. Most are fruity-tasting and aromatic. They are peeled and eaten fresh, used in salads, or juiced in blends with oranges.

Probably native to southeast Asia, mandarins came to the United States via Europe. One group of mandarins is believed to have been imported from Tangier, Morocco, hence the name tangerine.

One of the most popular, the Dancy tangerine, comes from a chance seedling found in the grove of Colonel George L. Dancy at Buena Vista, Florida, in 1867. The colonel reportedly was the first to call this type of mandarin the kid-glove fruit.

The Robinson tangerine is the earliest to ripen, beginning in October, but it doesn't taste as good as others. It is also susceptible to dieback. Unless growers particularly want early fruit, it's a poorer selection for home planting. One of the

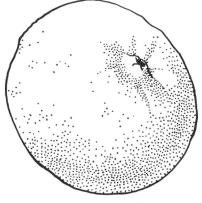

Dancy tangerine

newest tangerines, Sunburst, ripens only a little later, during November and December. Fruit is bright orange and the flavor, excellent.

Earlier than tangerines is the mandarin known as the satsuma. If grown on trifoliate rootstock, it is also extremely cold hardy. Satsumas mature in late September and October but keep for only a few weeks before becoming puffy and tasteless.

Home growers favor other mandarins. The Ponkan is an aromatic fruit with a mild flavor, but it ships poorly. The Murcott, also called honey tangerine, has a rich flavor and bright orange color. It is ready to harvest January to March. The King mandarin, of excellent quality and deep orange color, is the latest of the group, maturing between March and April.

The newest mandarin-type fruits are hybrids. Tangelos, for example, result from crossing mandarins — usually a tangerine — with grapefruit. Pollination studies began in 1892 at the USDA field station in Eustis.

The Orlando tangelo is an early success, a hybrid of the Duncan grapefruit and the Dancy tangerine from a cross made between 1908 and 1912. Gardeners like the look of the bright orange fruit. Trees begin to bear at an early age; to carry the crop they need extra fertilizer during the fall. The leaves, characteristically very cupped, help identify the variety. Other tangelos from these early crosses include the Minneola and the Seminole.

Crosses between mandarins and oranges yield hybrids known as tangors. The Temple orange, found as a chance seedling in a grove near Winter Park, apparently was a naturally occurring case. Though the trees are somewhat tender, home growers cherish their Temples, hoping to harvest each February and March the spicy, deep-orange fruit with its pebbled peel.

The Temple is one parent of the mandarin hybrid Fallglo. Fallglo's similar fruit ripens about two months earlier, however, avoiding possible cold injury. Fruit is excellent in taste and quality; juice is dark orange.

Mandarin hybrids often need to be pollinated by another variety. A planting given only one kind of pollen yields fruit that is sparse, small and often seedless.

Robinson, Temple, Lee, Orlando, Minneola and Fallglo all make effective pollinators for other varieties. Gardeners interested in growing any one of the hybrids should plan on planting another one nearby.

Grapefruit

Left to ripen naturally, all grapefruit varieties are midseason crops, with best flavor developing around February. Those who do not mind an acid taste find many varieties edible beginning in November.

Home growers need not be in a hurry to harvest, however; grapefruit keeps well on the tree. As the season progresses, it only becomes sweeter. It is not unusual to see people still picking grapefruit in May or June.

The grapefruit was born in the New World, probably as a mutation or natural hybrid of the pummelo, or shaddock. The large pummelo was known to have been growing in the West Indies at the time the grapefruit came to notice.

First mention of the grapefruit occurred in Barbados in 1750 when it was called the forbidden fruit. Later it was reported in Jamaica under a similar name; by 1814 a Jamaican who called it a grapefruit thought the fruit resembled a shaddock, with a flavor somewhat like grapes.

More likely, however, the name arose from the fact that the fruit grows in a cluster as grapes grow in a bunch.

Grapefruit entered Florida in 1823, first planted by Count Odette Phillippe near Safety Harbor on Tampa Bay.

Stock for this grove is believed to have been brought from Cuba. Real interest arose in 1885 when trial shipments of Florida grapefruit made a hit in Philadelphia and New York.

Commercial production has continued to be important, and Florida has been the scene for introducing many new kinds of grapefruit. Home growers choosing a variety face many possibilities.

The oldest variety of grapefruit grown in Florida is the Duncan. This is thought to have been a seedling originally planted by Count Phillippe and named by A.L. Duncan. Duncans are large and seedy, pale to light yellow in color. Most gardeners think the outstanding flavor and the quantity of juice more than repay time spent in picking out all the seeds.

The most widely grown grapefruit in the world is the Marsh or

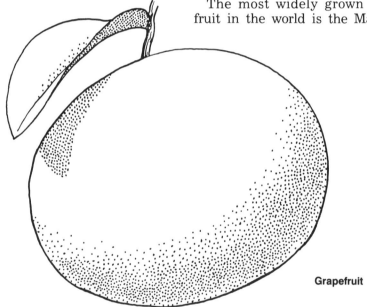
Grapefruit

Grapefruit

Type/variety	Season of maturity	Hardiness	Seed per fruit	Average diameter (inches)	Comments
Duncan	November-May	medium	30-70	3½-5	Oldest grapefruit variety. White-fleshed. Considered by many to have superior taste. Good for sectioning.
Flame	November-May	medium	0-6	3¾-4½	Red blush in the peel and dark red flesh.
Foster	November-March	medium	30-50	3½-5	Matures early. Develops a pink blush in the peel.
Marsh	November-May	medium	0-6	3½-4½	Most widely grown grapefruit throughout the world. White-fleshed. Sugar and acid content slightly lower than seedy varieties.
Pink Marsh	December-May	medium	0-6	3¾-4½	Similar to Marsh but pink-fleshed. Color fades as season progresses. Also called Thompson.
Ray Ruby	November-May	medium	0-6	3½-4	Red blush in the peel and medium red flesh.
Redblush	November-May	medium	0-6	3½-4½	Name describes pink blush on peel; flesh color is crimson. Also called Ruby Red.
Star Ruby	December-May	susceptible	0-6	3½-4	Dark pink peel and deep red flesh. Leaves may show signs of nutrient deficiencies.

Marsh Seedless, discovered as a seedling near Lakeland in 1860. Fruit quality is excellent. Similar in all respects is the pinkish version known as Pink Marsh or Thompson, from a limb mutation found in 1913 at the grove of W.B. Thompson in Oneco.

Redblush, a mutation of the Pink Marsh discovered around 1930, is popular for the deep pink color of its flesh. It is also called Ruby Red; the name Redblush appears more descriptive of the fruit as it is picked from the tree. Fruit is smaller than the Pink Marsh but quality is similar. A reliable producer, this is a favorite with home growers.

The Star Ruby, a relatively new introduction, gives home growers the option of fruit blushed pink in the peel and colored deep red inside. The flavor, too, is appealing. Trees are sensitive to cold and often show symptoms of nutritional deficiencies.

The variety New Flame was commercially released to the Florida market in 1987. Trees appear vigorous while fruit quality is good, with an external blush and internal color nearly as red as the Star Ruby. New from a Texas producer is Ray Ruby, with similar characteristics.

Acid citrus

The acid citrus grouping includes lemons, limes and other fruit with specialty uses. Most are processed to use in beverages, pies, marmalades, preserves and sauces.

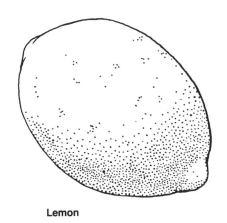

Lemon

The different fruits exhibit varying degrees of cold hardiness. Limes and lemons are very tender and restricted to the warmer southern portions of the state; the reasonably hardy limequat, kumquat and calamondin push the northernmost limits of citrus-growing.

Columbus carried the lemon, native to northwestern India, to the New World on his second voyage in 1493.

Today the most widely planted lemon in the state is Bearss, a variety discovered near Lutz. Other good varieties available for home culture include Eureka, Lisbon and Villafranca. Depending on variety, lemons can ripen throughout much of the year.

Two citrus resembling lemons also are cultivated for their acid fruit, especially to use in beverages.

Ponderosa lemon is grown as much for the ornamental value of the small trees as for the fruit, which is large, yellow, pear-shaped and has a thick peel. Fruit of the Meyer lemon resembles large oranges. The bushy, spreading plants need width in which to grow; they are more cold-tolerant than true lemons.

Of the commonly grown citrus, limes are the most sensitive to cold. Though a few trees have persisted in warmer pockets of Central Florida, in-ground culture usually is limited to South Florida. Trees are small and adapt readily to container culture.

Perhaps the most popular is the Key lime, brought to the New World by early explorers. It escaped from cultivation and naturalized in the West Indies, Central America and the Florida Keys, giving rise to the names Key, West Indian and Mexican lime. The tree is known for its blossoms, among the most fragrant of any citrus. Fruit matures year-round, with a main crop produced in the summer.

The hybrid Tahiti lime, also called the Persian lime, is important commercially in South Florida. This is believed to be a cross between a true lime and another citrus. The main crop matures in summer, but fruit often is produced year-round.

Crosses between the Key lime and the kumquat result in the cold-tolerant limequat. Varieties available for home culture include Eustis, Lakeland and Tavares. All resemble the Key lime in shape and taste.

Acid citrus

Type/variety	Season of maturity	Hardiness	Seed per fruit	Average diameter (inches)	Comments
Calamondin	year-round	very hardy	6-10	1-1½	Tree is small, upright, suitable for container growing. Heavy producer.
Key lime	year-round	susceptible	12-20	1-1½	Small tree, can be grown in containers to be protected from cold. Highly aromatic fruit, blossoms. Also called Mexican lime.
Kumquat	year-round	very hardy	6-10	¾-1	Small tree with few thorns. Recommended varieties include Marumi, Meiwa and Nagami.
Lemon	July-December	susceptible	1-6	2-2½	Can be grown in containers and moved indoors during cold weather. Numerous varieties include Bearss, Eureka, Lisbon and Villafranca.
Limequat	year-round	hardy	0-16	1-1½	A hybrid of key lime and kumquat. Resembles Key lime in size, shape.
Meyer lemon	November-March	hardy	10	2½-3	Grows as a wide-spreading bush. Fruit resemble an orange with a very smooth skin.
Ponderosa Lemon	year-round	susceptible	20-30	4-5	A lemon hybrid. Grows as a small, ornamental tree. Fruit has a thick rind.
Tahiti lime	June-September	susceptible	0	1¾-2½	A hybrid also called Persian lime, this is the commercial lime of the state. Can be grown in containers to be protected from cold.

The ornamental kumquats, from China, are extremely cold-tolerant. Species popular in Florida include Marumi, with small round fruit; Meiwa, with large, round fruit; and Nagami, with oval fruit. Fruit is eaten peel and all for a spicy, acid taste. Trees are small, reaching a maximum of 10 feet.

Also from China, the calamondin was introduced to Floridians in 1900 as an acid orange. The calamondin grows as an ornamental small tree, producing fruit year-round. Sometimes offered as a houseplant, it makes a good container plant in northern areas of the state.

When to pick citrus

Picking the first fruit of the season is exciting. Is it the right color? Has it softened? Will it have the same sweet taste as last year? What if the fruit is mealy, sour or dry. What went wrong?

As with many gardening questions, answers can be elusive. Citrus trees often come with a property, and the new owner may have no clues as to variety, past care or possible cold injury. Some gardeners are growing citrus surprises: One bite of the fruit puckers the mouth, curls the tongue and frustrates the gardener. The fruit arises from the sour and often bitter rootstock variety. This occurs when a budded, chosen variety dies off and a branch from the rootstock develops into a tree. These trees can't produce sweet fruit unless a new, desirable variety is budded onto them.

Although it won't make anyone ill, citrus tastes bitter, sour or just not ripe if picked too soon. Color only hints at ripeness because many varieties taste good before they develop the familiar shades of yellow and orange — if, in fact, they ever do. Ripeness is a taste decision, but one thing is for sure: All citrus is truly ripened on the tree. Flavor never improves once fruit is picked.

If fruit seems to be nearing maturity, taste one. Some growers leave fruit on a tree for another few weeks after they think it is ready to develop a sweeter taste. In rushing to harvest, gardeners may miss the sweetest, juiciest fruit of the season.

Dry or mealy fruit typically results from a cultural problem. The tree may be too young to bear well, but perhaps the care program should be reviewed. Too much water or fertilizer can result in poor-quality fruit.

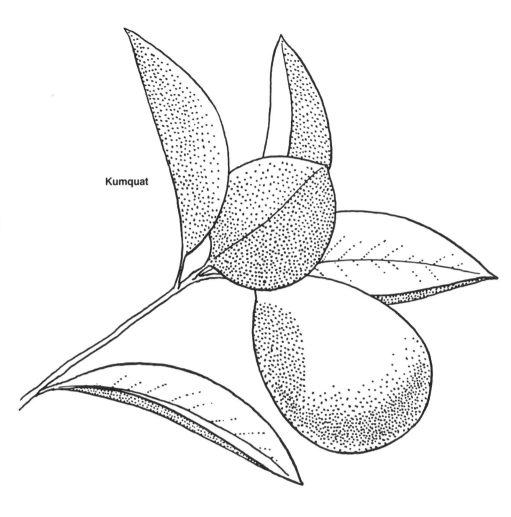
Kumquat

Pest control

Citrus plantings are likely to do well without any spraying. Healthy trees are highly resistant and a few pests will hardly affect production. In addition, gardeners content to let nature take its course find many biological controls help eliminate problem insects.

Some beneficial organisms can look quite alarming.

Red Ashersonia fungus, for example, is sure to worry first-time growers. This crusty, white to orange growth feasts on immature whiteflies. It often is called the friendly fungus. A brown whitefly fungus also is common.

The larval stages of lacewings and ladybugs may resemble little dragons. Gardeners who notice them among the aphids are fortunate because these larvae feed on large numbers of the pests and may be the only control needed.

Gardeners who spray can upset the balance of nature and are likely to kill off their allies. Unsprayed, however, fruit almost certainly will be blemished — although it will taste just fine — and leaves are likely to be curled and spotted or filmed with sooty mold.

This black coating on the surface of leaves is a fungus that grows on the droppings of sucking insects like aphids or scale. Sooty mold eventually peels off or it can be removed with an oil spray.

Gardeners who do not mind a few

fruit blemishes but who want healthy-looking limbs and foliage can spray once a year, when most pests are present. A spray combining oil, malathion and Benlate, carefully timed for mid-June to mid-July, will reduce many insect and disease problems.

Gardeners who cannot break the pest-control habit and who demand absolutely clean fruit and trees must consider spraying three times a year:

- Spring — late April to early May, a copper fungicide and malathion insecticide.
- Summer — mid-June to mid-July, a combination spray of oil, malathion and Benlate.
- Fall — during October, malathion.

These products are pesticides and must be handled carefully to avoid personal or plant injury. Read labels carefully and observe the time that must pass between last application and harvest. To minimize danger to people and trees, consult the general instructions on spraying in Chapter 18.

Before starting indiscriminate preventive spraying, find out what the problem is. Gardeners can take a particularly alarming or prevalent problem to the local garden center or extension service for advice. Chances are it will require no action at all.

Common pests of citrus

Pest	Description	Chemical controls*	Comments
Aphids	Green to red, pear-shaped insects feed on new growth. They suck juices from the foliage and usually are found on the underside of leaves or clustered around buds. Black sooty mold and white skins that have been shed also may be prevalent.	malathion, insecticidal soap	Growth of young trees is contorted, but damage often is observed only after aphids have left the trees. Leaves of affected plants curl as they grow. Before reaching for chemicals, check new growth for presence of aphids. Ladybugs often provide adequate control.
Caterpillars	The most common is the orange dog caterpillar, which is dark brown and white, and resembles a slug or small snake. Chews holes in leaves.	malathion; *Bacillus thuringiensis*	Protect small trees by handpicking caterpillars. Orange dogs are the immature stage of the black-and-yellow swallowtail butterfly.
Greasy spot	Spots on foliage are yellowish at first, gradually turn oily brown or black. Fruit may be dotted with dark specks.	oil; copper fungicide	To reduce infection, rake and remove fallen leaves. Control by spraying mid-June to mid-July.
Melanose	A fungus that produces a roughened blemish on foliage and fruit. Small rough spots are brown or purplish.	copper fungicide	Remove the source of infection by keeping trees free of dead wood. If control is needed, spray in late April.
Rust mites	Small, insectlike creatures, barely visible to the naked eye. Pierce, suck and feed on fruit, turning it brown.	oil; sulfur; insecticidal soap	Mites affect the looks of fruit, not its quality, so control is unnecessary unless clean fruit is of great importance.
Scab	A fungus that produces pointed bumps and roughened areas on foliage and fruit.	copper fungicide	Trees tolerate most infections. To control, treat when trees are in full bloom and producing new growth.
Scale	Small, white to dark-brown bumps or shields that adhere to leaves and stems. The waxy covering can be scraped off to expose the insect beneath. Sucks plant juices.	malathion; oil; malathion and oil	Often controlled by tiny parasitic wasps. Use chemical controls only if major infestation occurs.
Spider mites	Eight-legged, tiny, insectlike creatures; red to yellow in color. Pierce, suck and feed on leaves, causing them to yellow. Use hand lens to check foliage.	oil; insecticidal soap	Mainly a problem during dry season. Adequate watering reduces injury to plants and need for sprays.
Whiteflies	Small, white, mothlike adults mature in spring, summer and fall. Young are green and scalelike on the underside of leaves.	malathion; oil; malathion and oil	Heavy populations may build on trees and foster sooty mold. Seldom cause serious damage.

* Follow all label instructions when mixing and applying pesticides.

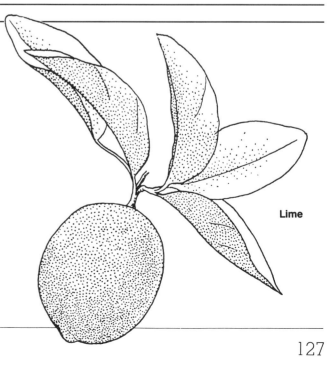

Lime

15

Deciduous fruit that can take the heat

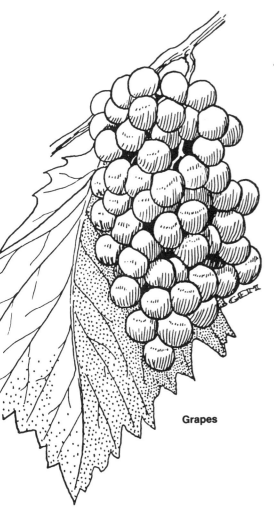

Grapes

A SUCCESSFUL VEGETABLE patch is likely to tempt a gardener into growing other edible plants. Because few can devote much space to fruit growing alone, many people use fruit-bearing trees, shrubs and vines as decorative elements in their landscapes. Grapes can be trained as a hedge. Pears, peaches and apples make good accent or background plantings, and figs or blueberries can be used wherever attractive shrubs are needed.

Don't expect the harvests to be effortless. Most fruit plantings require ongoing attention to fertilizer, pruning and pest control. Left alone, the plants will not only yield little but may end up being eyesores.

Fruit plants produce and look their best when given the right conditions — primarily, plenty of sun and lots of elbowroom. Congested plantings produce less and make picking and tending much more difficult.

First choose a fruit to suit the available space. Most fruit plants spread rapidly. Then select a variety to suit local temperatures. Although summers may burn some familiar varieties, in most cases the critical factor is the amount of cool weather a plant requires in order to break dormancy and flower.

To count as cool weather, temperatures must remain below 45 degrees on a fairly constant basis. The Panhandle area can expect more than 500 hours of cool weather a year; South Florida, as little as 50.

Plants that do not receive the hours of cold they need will be slow to bloom and develop fruit. After a few years, they lose vigor and decline. Plants that get too many hours of cold will flower prematurely. New fruit often will be damaged by freezes.

The number of chilling hours received helps divide Florida into growing regions of North (N), Central (C) and South (S). A major consideration in choosing a variety is whether it is suited to the region.

Varieties also differ in their resistance to nematodes, other insects and diseases and in overall fruit quality. The cooperative extension service tries to balance these factors in preparing recommendations. It is worth the effort to find these tested varieties at garden centers or from mail-order companies.

In order to get a good crop of some kinds of fruit, several varieties need to be planted. Some muscadine grapes, for example, bear only female flowers. To achieve good pollination, growers need to plant another variety nearby. Others that benefit from companion varieties include apples, blueberries, pears and pecans.

Use the following guidelines to choose a likely variety, meet its needs and ensure a harvest.

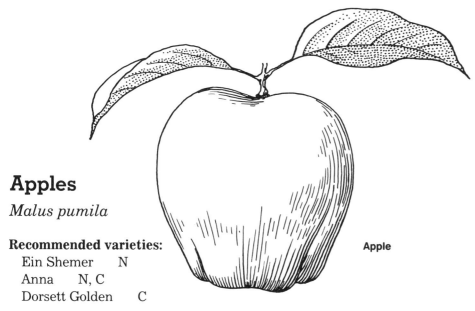
Apple

Apples

Malus pumila

Recommended varieties:
Ein Shemer   N
Anna   N, C
Dorsett Golden   C

For years, memories of fresh, crunchy apples prompted Florida gardeners to try growing them in spite of all advice. Today many gardeners enjoy Florida varieties that produce tasty, early summer fruit that rivals Northern favorites.

Try to ensure good pollination by planting two varieties together: Anna and Dorsett Golden in central parts of the state; Anna and Ein Shemer in the north. Good schemes do go wrong and often the two varieties will not bloom at the same time; they will bear fruit nevertheless.

Anna is the predominant Florida apple. Fruit is the size and color expected of an apple, with a red blush covering almost half of the greenish skin. Dorsett Golden develops a pinkish blush on a yellow skin. Fruit is small but trees are good pollinators.

Ein Shemer produces fruit up to 2¾ inches in diameter — rounded yellow apples with a sweet taste.

All Florida apples are low-chill types selected to need a relatively short period of cold in order to break bud dormancy. They require 300 to 400 hours of temperatures below 45 degrees to break bud, while Northern varieties require more than 600. Florida apples sometimes break bud too early and get caught by a frost. When this happens, the fruit is lost for the year.

Soil for apples must be well-drained. If apple roots are wet, they rot. Low, moist soils can be mounded. The only other concern about soil is acidity. Apples need a pH of near neutral, 6.5. Have the soil tested. If it is too acid, adjust with lime before planting.

Nothing else needs be done before planting. Don't add organic matter to either the land or the planting hole. Such additions may contribute to waterlogged soil and rotting roots. Simply plant a tree at the same level it was growing in its container and begin a good care program.

Compared to many Northern varieties, Florida apple trees are small, but expect growth to shoot more than 20 feet tall. Prune trees yearly to keep them to a 15-foot height. Keeping them small is much easier for gardeners who choose trees grafted onto a M106 dwarfing rootstock. Ideal for sandy soils, this rootstock keeps trees to a 12-foot height. Some nurseries may offer apple varieties on this rootstock during early spring; ask.

Although some summer grooming will be needed, plan to do major pruning in January. The newest cultural advice suggests working toward an open Christmas-tree shape so sun shines among the branches. The more light reaches the fruit, the more color it will have.

A good-looking apple tree will have a central trunk and five or six well-spaced major limbs. Use short wood braces to spread the limbs away from the trunk; a wide, 60-degree angle helps limbs carry a heavy load of fruit. Branches off the main limbs bear the fruiting spurs, short stubby growths that each year produce a few leaves and all the fruit. Don't remove these stubs if you want a crop. Do eliminate vigorous new growth that clogs the center of the tree.

Apple trees require a lot of care. Not only do they need fertilizing on a regular basis but they also must be sprayed to control both insects and diseases.

Begin pest control during the winter dormant season with an oil spray to protect against scale insects, which suck juices from the trunk and limbs. When the trees begin to bloom, and again when two-thirds of the petals fall, apply Agrimycin to control fire blight. Bees carry pollen between blossoms and without them there would be no fruit, but bees also carry this bacterial disease from pears or plums to apples. Fire blight attacks new growth and can destroy the tree.

Bitter rot, which causes brown, pungent-tasting areas in the fruit, attacks apples during humid weather. Watch for this disease beginning after bloom when fruit is small and continue until harvest. Spray trees with a Captan-Benlate mix every seven to eight days when conditions are damp. Get increased effectiveness by using a spreader-sticker — a wetting agent — in the spray tank. Spraying with insecticides containing malathion and Sevin also may be necessary, but only when pests such as aphids are a problem.

Borers enter the trunks of apple trees near the base, destroying the wood and causing a telltale ooze. Products are available at garden centers for use on fruit trees to prevent or control borers. Treatments in June and August may be necessary.

Big, plump apples require lots of feeding. Begin in January by feeding with a 10-10-10 fertilizer. Give each tree a handful, about 4 ounces. Reapply at bud break and every month through August. As apples begin to form and each month thereafter, also apply a small handful of calcium nitrate. This helps prevent the physiological watery core disease and keeps apples firm.

Apple trees need soil that is moist but not wet. A young tree requires 5 to 10 gallons of water a week; a mature tree, about 50 gallons. Irrigation depends on the weather and soil type but normally should be scheduled for once or twice a week.

Blackberries

Rubus species

Recommended varieties:

    Brazos   N, C, S
    Flordagrand   C, S
    Oklawaha   C, S

It's easy to fill a pot with plump blackberries from a backyard planting. Given a good yearly pruning to restrict the growth, blackberries are one of the easiest deciduous fruits to grow. Plants often grow rampant if left to themselves. The bushy vines send up suckers from the roots and start new roots where stems touch the ground. With this habit of growth and their thorny stems, blackberries make a great privacy fence. Just be sure to plant them where they have room to wander.

The three varieties of blackberries that grow in Florida can be divided into two groups. Plant the early fruiting Oklawaha and Flordagrand together for cross-pollination, and train them up a trellis. The semierect Brazos won't need another pollinator or a trellis. It grows with some stems sprawling and some upright.

Plants may be difficult to find. Garden centers often would rather avoid handling the prickly stems, but in most localities a few will offer plants for sale. Some of the best

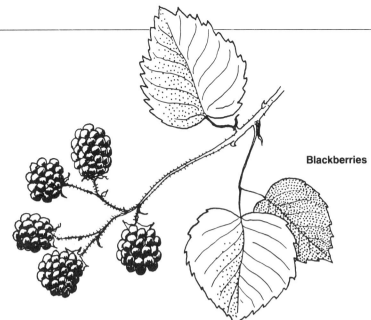

Blackberries

starts are begged from neighbors already growing blackberries. Just dig up a few rooted shoots and plant in a prepared garden site to have blackberries forever.

Blackberries adapt to a wide variety of soils and accept a pH within a range of 5.5 to 6.5. Set plants 4 to 6 feet apart in a row. Give them a thick mulch to control weeds and conserve moisture, but expect to water them once or twice a week during the dry season. Feed new plantings every eight to 10 weeks February through September with 3 ounces of 6-6-6 or 8-8-8. Give mature vines 5 ounces per plant in February, June and late August.

Pick the plump, solid fruit when the color changes from red to purple. For Oklawaha and Flordagrand varieties, harvest begins in April; for Brazos, around May 1. At first just a few will ripen, but soon picking will be an every-other-day affair for about 30 days.

Cut all plants back to the ground immediately after harvest. Seemingly devastating, this practice removes many potential insect and disease problems along with old, non-productive canes. By the fall, plants will produce new fruiting canes for the next year's crop.

Although blackberries are not immune to pest problems, most gardeners find the plants escape major infestations. If insects such as thrips, mites, stink bugs and beetles, or if diseases including leaf spot and anthracnose seem to be killing the plants, look for pesticides specifically labeled for use on blackberries.

Blueberries

Vaccinium corymbosum
Vaccinium ashei

Recommended varieties — rabbiteye:

    Beckyblue   (1)*   N
    Climax   (1)   N
    Bonita   (1)   N
    Premier   (1)   N
    Bluegem   (2)   N
    Choice   (2)   N
    Tifblue   (2)   N
    Chaucer   (2)   N, C
    Woodward   (2)   N, C
    Blue Bell   (2)   N, C
    Delite   (2)   N
    Avonblue   C

Recommended varieties — high-bush:

    Golf Coast (3)   C
    Misty   (3)   C
    Sharpblue   (3)   C

* For cross-pollination purposes, plant two or more varieties of the same number together.

Blueberry bushes get the nod from home growers who want fruit from a plant that is exceptionally ornamental. The head-high shrubs sport small, glossy leaves: blue-green in spring and summer, bright red in fall. Even the bare twigs of winter are attractive. In early spring they flower in clusters of small, cream-colored hanging bells.

Most gardeners are persuaded to plant by the thought of the sweet berries. Just four or five plants yield enough for a household. Birds will be just as interested, but they can be discouraged with netting.

Gardeners in Central Florida can enjoy an extended harvest by planting both high-bush and rabbiteye varieties. The high-bush blueberry is the most consistent producer, especially after mild winters.

Sharpblue, which grows up to 6 feet tall and wide, is recommended for home planting. Count on this variety to have the first fruit of the season, large flavorful berries ripening during May.

Plantings need the cool weather of winter to mature flower buds. Most blueberries are adapted to North Florida and a few for the central region. South Florida is too warm for available varieties.

Rabbiteye varieties grow in both central and northern areas of the state. These are giants among blueberries, growing up to 18 feet tall. Gardeners can allow maturing plants to grow about 7 feet tall and use the planting as a hedge. What do rabbits have to do with it? As the berries start to mature, they turn pinkish, the color of a rabbit's eye.

All the rabbiteye varieties recommended will produce well in North Florida because of the cool winters, which are needed by the plants. In central parts of the state, most years seem to be cold enough to guarantee an abundance of the fruit, which ripens May through June.

As with other blueberries, gardeners achieve best results by planting rabbiteye varieties in groups for cross-pollination. In Central Florida, Woodard, Bluegem and Choice are a proven combination because they receive adequate cold weather most years.

Blueberry bushes grow in either sun or partial shade, but expect top fruit production in sunny spots. Be sure to test the soil. It must be acidic, between 4.5 and 5.2 in pH, for the plants to grow.

Dig the planting site at least 6 inches down. If the soil pH is more than 5.2, incorporate a pound of sulfur for each 100 square feet at least three weeks before planting. Do not use aluminum sulfate to increase soil acidity; the aluminum could poison the plants.

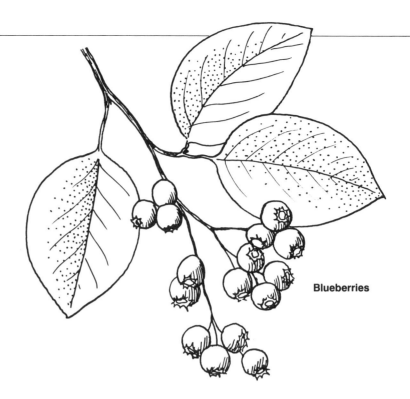

Blueberries

Sandy soils will need additions of organic matter. Mix liberal quantities of peat, leaves or compost with the soil while tilling or planting. Heavily mulch blueberries growing in sandy soils.

Most nursery blueberry bushes are container-grown and can be transplanted any time of year. Their root systems are relatively delicate. Dig holes large enough to allow roots to spread naturally without crowding. Gently fill the soil back in, making sure the plant is set in the soil at the same depth it was in the container. Water well.

To get plants established, it's essential to maintain moisture levels. To develop strong, vigorous plants, the key is to fertilize properly.

Blueberries are very sensitive to nitrogen. Too much fertilizer will kill young plants. In particular, never add fertilizer to the planting hole. When it is time to fertilize, use a camellia-azalea product. Nitrogen sources in other formulas can build up in the soil and prove toxic to the plants.

Begin fertilizing after plants have been in the ground for six to eight weeks. New plants can take an ounce of camellia-azalea product in April, June and August. Spread it evenly over the soil as far as the foliage spreads, then water.

Over the next two or three years, gradually increase the rate of application to a quarter of a pound per plant. Continue to fertilize large, mature plants at this higher rate, once in February and again after the harvest.

Watch for signs of iron chlorosis, indicated if young leaves turn yellow between veins. Most garden centers sell a soil amendment to correct for iron deficiency, but iron chlorosis also can result from a too-high pH. Check soil acidity to make sure it stays below 5.2.

Rejuvenation pruning helps keep established plantings productive. Blueberries bloom on the top 6 to 8 inches of new growth, so every year or two after harvest, cut plants back to stimulate new growth. Prune high-bush varieties to about 3 feet tall, rabbiteyes to about 7.

Once plants are about 5 years old, gardeners can produce a more natural, spreading plant by pruning one or more major branches to the ground, but do not prune more than a fourth of the plant in a year. Vigorous new branches will grow from the base. Over a four-year period, the entire plant will be renewed. Blueberries can be tipped back too, like other shrubs, to stimulate branching and the growth of more flowering stems.

Plants are relatively pest-free, but birds love the berries. Feathered friends may not wait as patiently as humans for all the red color to disappear from the fruit. During the last few days on the bush, berries double in size and grow sweet. Small plantings may require a net covering to ensure a harvest.

Figs

Ficus carica

Recommended varieties:
   Alma   N, C, S
   Brown Turkey   N, C, S
   Celeste   N, C, S
   Green Ischia   N, C, S
   Magnolia   N, C, S
   San Piero   N, C, S

A planting can supply a summer harvest of fresh figs. The small trees can blend with existing greenery, but more often make a dramatic focal point for a patio or poolside planting. The soft green foliage is deeply notched, and the trees have bold, grayish stems. The fruit is always welcome, eaten as picked or used in salads, conserves and old-fashioned jams.

An Old World plant native to the Mediterranean region, the fig has been valued for more than its abundant fruit. A few leaves, hastily grabbed in the Garden of Eden, may have served as the first clothing. To the Hebrews, the fig symbolized abundance and peace; to the Egyptians it was the tree of life.

These weren't the only civilizations to hold this plant in high esteem. For the Greeks, the appearance of new growth on the fig trees signaled the end of winter storms and the beginning of the sailing season. In general, however, conquerors, explorers and kings continue to cultivate figs for the reason gardeners do today: Figs offer a special taste treat.

Wherever the crop is grown, culture is similar. Figs like sun, moisture and rich soil. Plants have a shallow root system but can withstand adverse conditions, even drought, if the soil is enriched with organic matter. Gardeners should add lots of manure, sawdust, leaf mulch or compost to sandy soils. Then, when figs are in the ground, heap similar materials over the soil as a mulch.

As a plant grows, train it to three or four trunks. This keeps the tree open, letting in the sun that makes it more productive. Figs respond to fertilizer, but overfeeding will result in lots of growth and no fruit. About 2 cups of 6-6-6 spread under the canopy of each plant is sufficient. Apply in late winter, mid-spring and late summer. Avoid feeding too late in the season, as new growth needs to harden off before cold weather.

Figs produce a main harvest in early summer and occasional fruit for several months thereafter. Growers who have heard that figs must be pollinated by a tiny wasp should know that this applies only to California varieties.

Florida figs produce only female flowers and bear fruit without being pollinated. Be sure to obtain plants from local growers and garden centers or from Southern mail-order suppliers.

Celeste is a popular variety for home culture. The small fruit, purplish-bronze to light brown in color, ripens from mid-June to mid-August. Eaten fresh, it is considered the best of the Southern varieties. Trees will not bear fruit in seasons following severe freeze damage and tend to drop some of the crop during extremely hot weather.

Brown Turkey figs rival Celeste in popularity, perhaps partly because they will bear fruit following severe freezes. They have the longest ripening season of the recommended varieties. The bronze-colored, medium-sized fruit ripens from early July until late fall.

A few other varieties also are grown in Florida. Green Ischia produces green fruit that ripens mid-July to early August. San Piero bears very large, purplish-black to purplish-bronze fruit June through August. Magnolia produces large bronze fruit from early July to late August.

Although fig trees generally can be found at garden centers, they are easy to start from cuttings. Just take a pencil-thick shoot 8 to 10 inches long. Treat the cut end with rooting powder and insert it several inches deep in a pot of vermiculite or loose potting soil. Moisten, then enclose the cutting, pot and all, in a clear plastic bag. Set it in a shady area and leave it for eight to 10 weeks, until roots start to grow. Allow it to continue growing until the roots fill the pot, then transplant to the landscape or a permanent container.

Two problems are likely to afflict figs. Fig rust is mainly a problem during hot, humid months. It shows up first as brown spots on the fo-

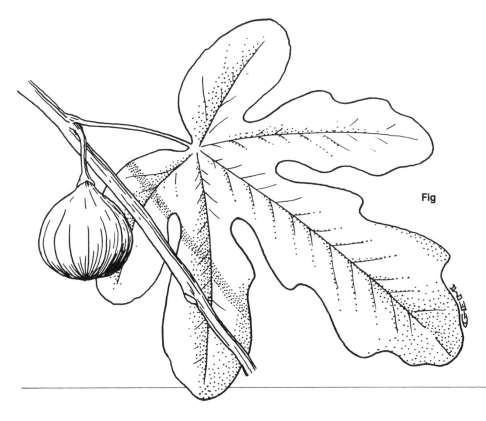
Fig

liage. In time, whole leaves decline and fall. To control this disease, spray with a fungicide that contains copper.

Nematodes can be controlled only by fumigating the soil before planting. These pests cause swollen roots, which prevent plants from absorbing water and nutrients. Plants may lack vigor and show signs of nutrient deficiencies. Even with nematodes, figs sometimes survive and continue to produce if they are well-mulched and soil is kept moist constantly.

Grapes

Bunch — *Vitis labrusca* and hybrids
Muscadine — *Vitis rotundifolia*

Recommended varieties — bunch
  Blue Lake   N, C
  Conquistador   N, C
  Lake Emerald   N, C
  Orlando Seedless   N, C
  Stover   N, C

Recommended varieties — muscadine
  Fry   *   N, C
  Welder   N, C
  Cowart   N, C, S
  Dixie   N, C, S
  Jumbo*   N, C, S
  Noble   N, C, S
  Southland   N, C, S
  Summit *   N, C, S
  Triumph   N, C, S

*Female variety; requires a self-fertile variety for pollination.

Grapes have become, second only to citrus, Florida's most foolproof fruit. The earliest settlers found grapes growing wild. Fruit from these wild vines was small, with thick skin and many seeds. At best the species were semisweet but often were downright sour.

Under cultivation the native grapes grew larger and more palatable, though most were still thick-skinned and seedy. Early producers wanted grapes with more customer appeal. Following the 1894 freeze, they planted more than 500 acres with Northern varieties of bunch grapes — Concord, Niagara and Ives. By the early 1900s, disease and hot, dry weather had wiped out the vines.

Another attempt was made in 1926 when more than 5,000 acres were planted with Munson crosses. By 1938 these, too, had failed. At the time their decline was blamed on vine degeneration; in 1953 it was found to be due to Pierce disease.

Muscadine grapes have been more successful. The first named variety was discovered in 1760 in North Carolina near the Scuppernong River. Some people still call all muscadines Scuppernongs. In nature, muscadines grow as either male or female plants. Growers had to plant some of each. A breeding program established by the U.S. Department of Agriculture in New Smyrna made a breakthrough in 1907 by producing a plant with both male and female characteristics — a self-fertile muscadine.

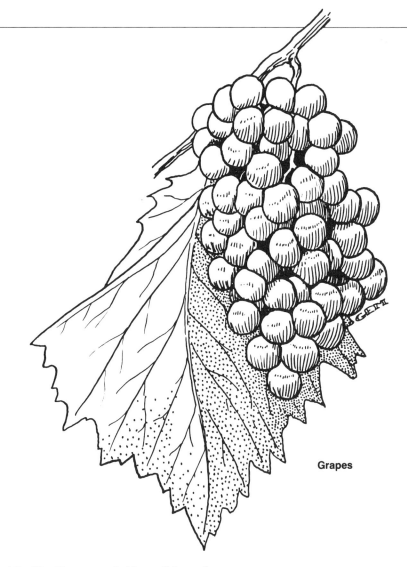
Grapes

In 1959 state research programs began to develop both bunch and muscadine types of grapes suited to Florida. The Florida Institute of Food and Agricultural Sciences program has produced many of the disease-resistant varieties available today. A seedless variety, Orlando Seedless, rivals the Thompson Seedless for desirable characteristics and is considered especially good for home production. Other much-improved grapes are just around the corner.

■ BUNCH GRAPES

Bunch grapes are the first to bud, flower and ripen. Fruit is sweet and relatively thin-skinned, ranging in color from purple to light green. Gardeners can harvest clusters from June through July. Although they will need to be sprayed, plants are vigorous and easy to grow. Popular varieties are self-fertile; no pollinator is needed.

To grow in Florida, bunch grapes

must be resistant to Pierce disease. Leaf hoppers, the bugs that spread the bacterialike organism from plant to plant, cannot be controlled. Affected vines gradually lose vigor, turn yellow and brown, then die. Lack of resistance killed vines in early experiments with Northern and seedless varieties, while the first resistant varieties — Lake Emerald, Blue Lake and Stover — still are popular today. Look for the newest developments in grapes, mostly seedless, to be among bunch types.

■ MUSCADINE GRAPES

Muscadine vines are almost carefree; spraying usually isn't necessary, but pollination is more problematic. Plants of modern varieties may be perfect-flowered, with both male and female reproductive portions present. These will produce fruit on their own.

Other plants, however, have only female flowers. Interplant these with some self-fertile vines. As a rule at least every third plant should be a perfect-flowering type for good fruit production.

Though thick-skinned, the juicy muscadine fruit is tasty. The name probably comes from the kinds that have a musky flavor. If this does not appeal, try another variety; there is a selection for just about every taste.

The crop appears in short, nearly round clusters of four to 15 grapes, which do not ripen all at once. Expect to harvest big, round individual grapes July through September.

■ CARE, FEEDING OF YOUNG VINES

Plant grapes in any open spot where a trellis or arbor will fit. Use the lush growth to screen a less-than-perfect view, for instance, and reap the double benefit of fresh summer fruit. Traditionally, grapes are planted during winter, but container-grown plants can be planted any time of year.

Any loose, well-drained soil will do; special preparation usually is not required. Gardeners who can't resist adding organic matter should improve a large area, not just the fill soil. Adjust the pH to around 6 or 6.5.

If they are to produce well, grapevines must be kept under control. Begin by planting along a trellis or arbor. Bunch grapes should go 8 to 9 feet apart. Space muscadines every 15 to 16 feet. The most popular trellis consists of No. 9 or No. 10 wire strung between poles set about 20 feet apart. Run two wires at heights of 2½ and 5 feet, or use three wires, placing one at 2 feet, 4 feet and 6 feet above the ground.

Begin by training each new vine up a 5- to 6-foot stake. Remove all weak growth. Remove all growth, in fact, except single shoots to grow each way along the wires. Then let the vine grow. Grapes are vigorous. Vines usually begin to fill the wires or arbor within two years. Given good care, they will yield a small crop in two years, with full production in three to four years.

Encourage plant vigor and fruit production with a good fertilizer program. Feed new vines monthly from March through September. Apply 2 ounces per vine of a 12-4-8 fertilizer at each feeding. Follow a similar program the second year, but use 5 ounces of fertilizer at each feeding until September, when only 2 ounces are needed.

Water frequently when the vines are first planted. The limited root systems may need water every two or three days. Soon, however, watering every three to four days is enough. Apply a mulch to stretch the time between waterings and to discourage weeds.

■ MAINTAINING MATURE VINES

Grapevines grow luxuriantly if care is good. By winter pruning time they will be a tangled mass. Summertime yields depend on winter pruning. Growers must reduce vines to just a few main canes that bear flower and foliage buds for the new year. Don't skip the pruning; it's a major part of any growing program.

All grapes produce best when trained to a single upright trunk with four to six canes left to grow sideways. Both bunch types and muscadines require specific treatments to maintain maximum yields and must be dealt with before spring growth begins.

With bunch grapes, vigorous new growth should replace the old fruiting canes each year. Trace back four to six healthy canes to near the main trunk. Shorten these to eight to 12 buds. Cut off all other growth, but leave a single short stem containing two to three buds near each main cane. These stubs will produce new canes for the next pruning time.

Muscadine grapes are grown on four to six permanent canes, called

Uses of Florida grape varieties

Variety	Fresh market	Wine	Juice, jelly	Pick your own	Home garden
Muscadine					
Cowart					X
Dixie		X			X
Fry*, **				X	
Jumbo*				X	
Noble		X	X		X
Southland	X				X
Summit	X				
Triumph				X	X
Welder**		X	X		
Bunch					
Blue Lake			X		X
Conquistador**	X	X	X	X	X
Daytona					X
Lake Emerald		X			
Stover	X	X		X	X
Suwannee**	X	X		X	X

* Female vine, requires pollinator.
** Not recommended for South Florida.

Dormant-season pruning of grapes

Bunch grapes

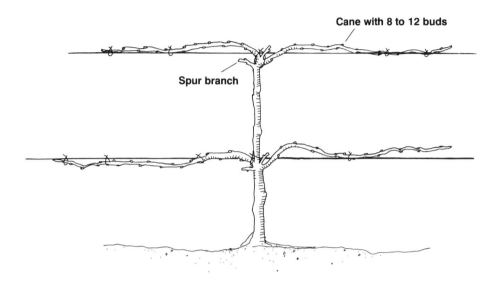

Renew the canes of bunch grapes each year. Save 1 new cane per trellis wire. Tip the ends of the canes back to 8 to 12 buds. Leave a small, 2- to 3-inch bud spur branch at the base of each major cane to begin new growth in spring.

Muscadine grapes

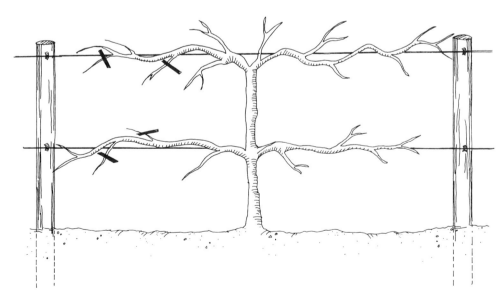

Permanent canes, or arms, are maintained on the muscadine trellis. Prune by clipping new side branches back each winter, leaving 2 or 3 buds on each.

arms, that originate from the trunk. Reduce each season's leafy growth to short stems of two or three buds arising from the arms. If necessary, thin the bud-bearing stems to leave them 4 to 6 inches apart.

After pruning, grapes ooze sap from the cuts. This bleeding doesn't hurt the plant, affect future production or require use of a pruning paint.

Fertilize regularly. Give a mature muscadine vine a pound of 12-4-8 in April, June and September. With bunch grapes, use a pound in March and half a pound in May and September. Increase these amounts a little as plants grow older.

Continue to water once or twice a week. Grapes are tolerant of drought and often develop best flavor when on a limited watering schedule. As harvest time approaches, water more frequently — as often as three or four times a week — to keep fruit from cracking.

■ CARE OF SEEDLESS GRAPES

Orlando Seedless grapes naturally grow in long clusters of small but very sweet fruit. Gardeners who want plump, Thompson-size grapes must, like commercial growers, prune the clusters and treat developing fruit with gibberellin solution, a growth regulator.

To increase fruit size, tip out the lower end of the cluster, or tail, immediately after bloom, when fruit first forms. Remove up to two-thirds of the tail. Obtain maximum size with two applications of Pro-Gibb, a commercial preparation of gibberellin available from agricultural supply houses. The gibberellin growth regulator expands the cluster, enlarges the grapes and suppresses gritty traces of seeds.

Mix a solution of 1 to 2 milliliters of Pro-Gibb to a liter of water. Apply the first spray when the young grapes are 4 to 5 millimeters in diameter and a second treatment seven to 10 days later. Mist individual fruit clusters with a hand-held spray bottle.

■ PEST CONTROL

Tough and durable, muscadine grapes usually produce acceptable yields without being sprayed. Bunch grapes are more susceptible to diseases, usually on foliage and fruit. Look for a spray labeled for home use on fruit, one that specifically lists grapes, or consult the extension service for recommendations.

Start a spray program in spring when new shoots are 3 inches long; continue every 10 days until a week before harvest. Follow instructions when using pesticides.

Nectarines

Prunus persica

Recommended varieties:

Sundollar	N
Suncoast	N
Sunraycer	C
Sunmist	C

The nectarine is a peach in disguise. Flavor and texture are similar, but the fruit lacks fuzz.

Most likely originating from chance mutations, nectarines have been known for more than 2,000 years. Even today, limbs that bear nectarines occasionally will turn up on trees in peach orchards.

Cultural practices are the same as for peaches. Trees need to be pruned to the same open-center habit of growth and require similar care. Because the same diseases and insects can be expected, most growers follow a peach spray-schedule. The smooth skins make nectarines a bit more susceptible to rots and wind burn.

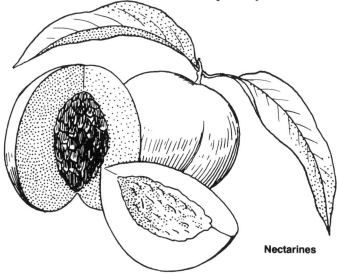

Nectarines

Select varieties with care. Like peaches, nectarines should be grafted onto a nematode-resistant rootstock. The amount of winter cold will determine which varieties to plant in specific regions.

Peaches

Prunus persica

Recommended varieties:

Flordadawn	N
Floraglobe	N
Flordaking	N
Flordacrest	N
FlordaRio	N
Flordaglo	C, S
Flordaprince	C, S
Flordabelle	C, S
Tropic Sweet	C, S
Rayon	C, S
Flordared	S
Florda Grande	S
Red Ceylon	S

Peaches require special attention, especially in terms of pest control.

Gardeners willing to take the extra trouble will enjoy juicy, ripe peaches early each summer.

Like other temperate-zone fruit, peaches require a certain amount of cool winter weather. Just how much differs with variety, so selecting the right variety can be the key to success.

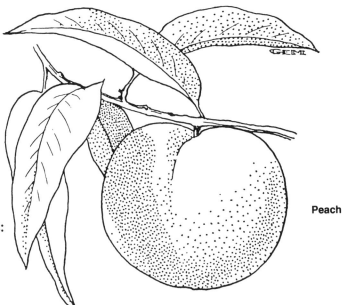

Peach

Once they have received the necessary hours of chilling, trees break dormancy and burst into bloom. Short-dormancy trees that grow and fruit well in South Florida will bloom too soon farther north and suffer freeze damage to flowers and fruit. However, a tree that doesn't get enough cool weather may never bloom properly.

Whether the soil is sandy or clay, any well-drained site suits peaches. Plant trees on raised mounds in poorly drained areas. Amending the soil rarely is necessary, but gardeners can add organic matter. Adjust soil pH to around 6.5.

Container-grown trees can be planted any time of year but plant bare-root trees in winter. Dig a hole deeper and wider than the size of the root system. The tree should be set at its original growing depth. Water well while filling in the hole with soil. Build a dike of dirt a couple of inches high and make a temporary basin around the young tree to help hold water over the next few months.

CARE OF YOUNG TREES

Train peach trees right from the start. Cut back the main stem to within 2 feet of the ground, keeping three to five side branches evenly spaced around the trunk to form the main limbs of the tree. Remove all other side shoots.

Cut the top even if a tree has little side branching. New shoots will form to create needed limbs. Encourage them, unless they sprout from below the graft union.

Because rootstocks are chosen primarily for nematode resistance, branches or suckers arising from the base of the tree will not contribute quality fruit. Remove them early.

Trees should grow out and slightly upward in a soup-bowl shape. Prune with this shape in mind. Trees grow rapidly. Two to three years of attention will result in a well-shaped tree.

Young trees need both water and fertilizer to grow properly. Keep the soil moist during the first few weeks. Add a bucket or two of water to the basin at the foot of the tree every few days. Later, as the roots spread into the surrounding soil, water once or twice a week.

Feed frequently. Use a balanced 6-6-6 or 8-8-8 analysis fertilizer in heavy soils and 12-4-8 in sand. Just a light scattering every six to eight weeks from spring through early fall will supply a young tree's needs.

During the second year, fertilize two times, possibly three. In January and again in late May, scatter a pound of fertilizer under the tree and out past the drip line. If growth slows or the foliage yellows, make an additional application during August. Use a complete fertilizer again or just nitrogen in the form of a quarter pound per tree of sodium nitrate, calcium nitrate or ammonium nitrate.

CARE OF TREES

Make sure peach trees receive enough water during the hot, dry growing season. Irrigation once or twice a week usually is adequate. Mulch with old hay, grass clippings or compost.

Continue to feed trees in January and late May. Use 1 pound of 10-10-10 or 12-4-8, or 1½ pounds of 6-6-6 for each 100 square feet of area scattered under the limbs and out past the drip line. To maintain summer growth, especially in Central Florida, feed again during August at half the above rates.

A major trimming every year keeps peaches growing in an open habit and producing well, and removes dead or diseased wood. Prune trees when they are dormant, during January, before buds begin to swell.

To keep the harvest within easy reach, increase the size of fruit and control pests, remove up to a third of the past season's growth. Continue to aim at a soup-bowl shape, with outer limbs gradually curving upward. Open the center of the tree to allow good air movement and make spraying easier. Eliminate most branches that grow straight up to keep trees wide and small to medium-sized.

After peach trees flower, thin the young fruit. When it reaches the size of a quarter, remove enough peaches to leave one every 6 inches or so along the branches. New owners often skip this step, which results in numerous but small fruit.

PEST CONTROL

Many insects and diseases affect peaches. To keep trees alive and productive for any length of time, they must be sprayed. Start before the growing season by applying a dormant spray of either lime sulfur or miscible oil immediately after pruning.

As the flower buds swell, begin to spray at regular intervals 10 to 14 days apart with a pesticide labeled for home use on peaches. Most garden centers offer convenient blends.

These usually contain the insecticides malathion and methoxyclor and a fungicide, Captan. Read labels and be sure to discontinue spraying 21 days before harvest.

If pests get out of hand closer to harvest time, use single products: malathion or Sevin for insects, Captan or Benlate on fungal diseases. Be sure to follow instructions and note the time that must elapse between last application and harvest. Resume spraying after harvest if necessary to control insects that attack leaves and limbs.

Peach trees are particularly vulnerable to borers. These white, grublike larvae girdle and kill trunks and large limbs. Keep checking for telltale signs of oozing sap or flaking bark.

If only a few, borers can be dug out from the gummy spots on a tree trunk. Otherwise, follow label instructions and use insecticides Thiodan or Lindane on tree trunks when borer damage can be expected, after harvest and throughout the summer.

How to prune a new peach tree

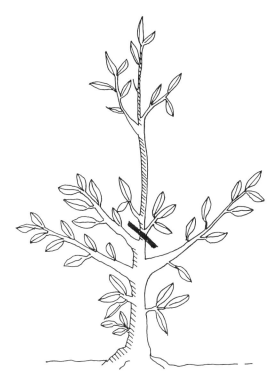

After planting, remove the top of the young peach tree. Allow 3 or more well-spaced branches to develop the basic limb structure.

Winter pruning of peach tree

After a year's growth, the tree becomes crowded with small limbs and strong, upright branches.

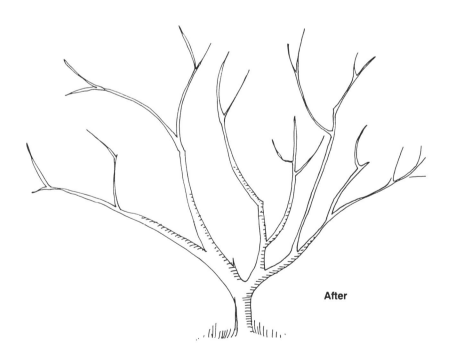

Prune during the dormant period from late December through January. Thin out at least a third of the previous year's growth and maintain an open, low-spreading habit.

Pears

Pyrus communis

Recommended varieties:
  Baldwin   N
  Carnes   N
  Flordahome N, C
  Hood   N, C
  Pineapple   N, C
  Kieffer   N
  Orient   N
  Tenn   N

Florida pears ripen during summer and early fall. Fruit is big, juicy and flavorful, but some varieties may contain quantities of gritty stone cells and usually are better canned than fresh.

Varieties Flordahome and Pineapple require cross-pollination. Plant them together or with variety Hood. Any combination of two of the three should bloom at the same time, resulting in good fruit production.

Plant bare-root trees during the winter months while they are dormant; container-grown ones can be planted any time. To plant, make a hole several inches deeper and larger than the root ball. Suspend the tree in the hole so that it will end up at its original growing depth, and water the fill soil in around the root system.

Pears grow well in both sandy and loamy soils as long as the soil is well-drained. Soil amendments usually are not necessary.

For the first year, feed young trees lightly every six to eight weeks between February and September. Scatter a little 6-6-6 or 8-8-8 under the spread of the branches.

Give older trees a lean diet to keep new growth and the disease fire blight, which attacks new growth, within control. Trees more than a year old need 1 pound of fertilizer for every year the tree is old, up to a maximum of 10 pounds. Split the total amount between two applications, one in January and another in June. Spread it under the branches and out past the drip line.

Irrigation will depend on soil type. Don't let trees wilt. Young trees may need watering as often as every two or three days. When roots

Winter pruning of pear tree

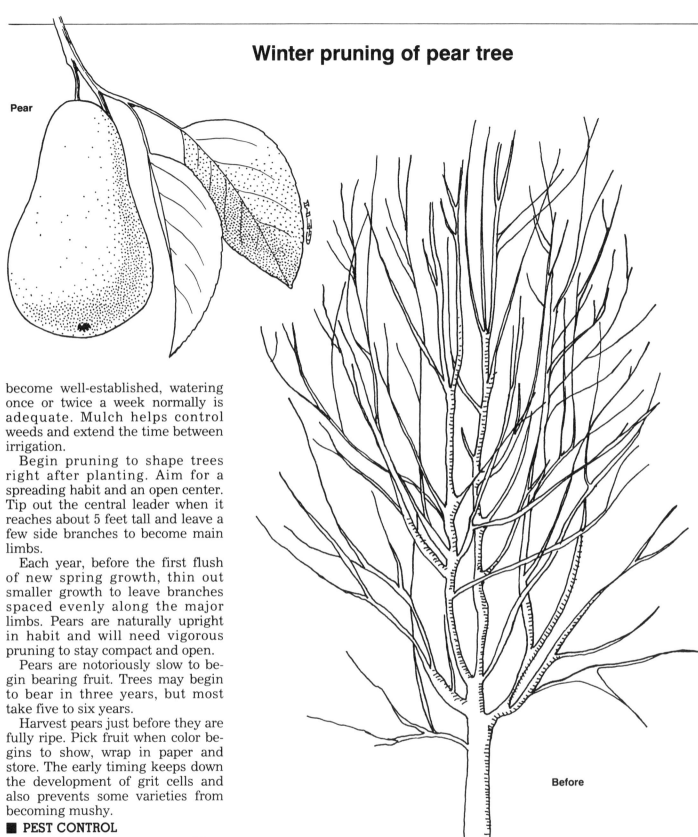

Pear tree has clusters of upright, closely spaced limbs.

become well-established, watering once or twice a week normally is adequate. Mulch helps control weeds and extend the time between irrigation.

Begin pruning to shape trees right after planting. Aim for a spreading habit and an open center. Tip out the central leader when it reaches about 5 feet tall and leave a few side branches to become main limbs.

Each year, before the first flush of new spring growth, thin out smaller growth to leave branches spaced evenly along the major limbs. Pears are naturally upright in habit and will need vigorous pruning to stay compact and open.

Pears are notoriously slow to begin bearing fruit. Trees may begin to bear in three years, but most take five to six years.

Harvest pears just before they are fully ripe. Pick fruit when color begins to show, wrap in paper and store. The early timing keeps down the development of grit cells and also prevents some varieties from becoming mushy.

■ **PEST CONTROL**

Fire blight is the worst problem of pears. This bacterial disease attacks home and commercial plantings alike, turning young growth brown and black. When it appears, prune and burn affected branches and start a spray program. Spray with streptomycin or streptomycin plus copper at early bloom, full bloom and late bloom.

Leaf spot diseases can occur any time after bloom until leaves drop in the fall. To save the foliage of a badly affected tree, use a copper fungicide spray every 10 to 14 days.

Insects, especially scales, may sap foliage, limbs and trunks. Control these insects with a miscible oil spray during the dormant season, around mid-January.

Pecans

Carya illinoinensis

Recommended varieties:
  Elliot   N
  Stuart   N
  Curtis   N, C
  Desirable N, C
  Moreland   N, C

Trying to grow pecans can be frustrating. Trees grow 60 feet tall and equally wide, too big for many small yards. Gardeners with the space to grow one may find a pecan makes a grand shade tree but doesn't deliver a good harvest of nuts. The climate of North Florida suits pecans best. Trees may produce reasonably well in Central Florida but yields are greatly reduced farther south and, therefore, aren't recommended.

Squirrels in the neighborhood will cancel out most production in any tree located near a building or overhead wires. Try to set a tree out in the open, and wrap the trunk with a metal sheet that can be adjusted as the tree grows wider. Other pests on the fruit and caterpillars on the foliage also may diminish returns. Finally, pecans are slow to begin production. Gardeners may wait seven years or more for the first crop.

Garden centers supply good grafted varieties. They may arrive container-grown, but since the root system is quite deep, the most convenient packaging is a plastic bag with moist peat or other medium around the bare roots.

To plant, dig a hole about 2 feet wide and 3 feet deep. Spread out the roots and gradually add soil, watering as the hole is filled to en-

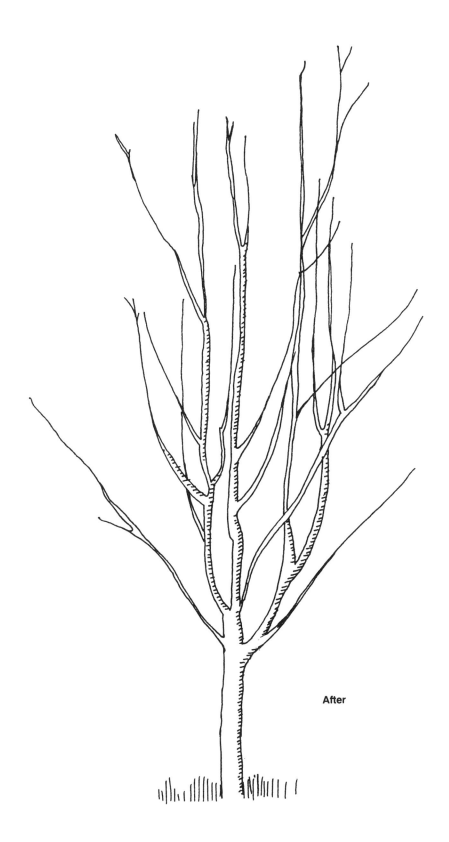

During dormant winter months, thin out entangled or closely spaced limbs. Shorten tall branches to keep fruit within convenient picking range.

sure good soil-to-root contact. After the tree is in place, shape the soil around it to make a basin to hold water. Cut back up to half the tree above the graft union to help balance the roots to the top portion of the tree.

Early pruning should train a tree to a single, straight trunk. Choose one young shoot for the purpose and shorten all competition. Keep side branches spaced evenly around and not closer than 12 inches up and down the central leader. From this point on, pecan trees should need no additional pruning.

If a pecan must be confined to a small landscape, training can be modified. To produce a more compact tree, cut back all long limbs to cause more branching lower down. The tree will spread outward rather than forming a tall, single-trunk tree.

Young trees need frequent water. In sandy, well-drained soils, fill the water basin every three to four days during hot, dry weather. Older, established trees will need thorough watering about once a week.

Give a new tree its first feeding in May. Apply a pound of 6-6-6 or 10-10-10 or look for a formula made especially for pecans. For future feedings, allow 2 pounds of fertilizer for each year the tree is old, up to 40 pounds. Apply each year in February. Broadcast evenly under the spread of the tree and out past the drip line.

Along with major nutrients, pecans need zinc. If using a fertilizer that doesn't include 1 percent zinc, make an additional application of zinc oxide. Use 2 to 4 ounces the first two years and 1 pound per tree thereafter. Broadcast evenly under the branches.

■ PEST CONTROL

Where squirrels do not beat gardeners to the crop, insects or diseases may. In a good year there usually will be enough for all, grower included, without major spraying. To guarantee a harvest, however, a grower must deal with pests.

Caterpillars that feed high in the trees are the most noticeable. In the larval stage they are mostly a nuisance by forming webs and dropping excreta, but they rarely are a

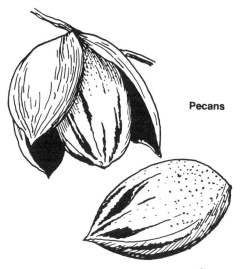

Pecans

serious threat to tree or crop. Some gardeners cut nests from trees and some spray.

Many of the more common sprays for use against caterpillars can be applied to pecans; check specific labels.

Pests that do affect harvest include scab disease and insects such as the nut casebearer, pecan weevil and hickory shuckworm. Consult an extension service agent for specific recommendations on pesticides.

Good sanitation helps control some pests. Many gardeners will find evidence of twig girdlers, in the form of small limbs clipped from the trees. Collecting and disposing of the branches, which contain eggs of these insects, will break the life cycle.

Persimmons

Diospyros kaki

Recommended varieties:

Fuya (Fuyugaki)*	N, C
Hachiya	N, C
Hanafuyu*	N, C
Hayakume	N, C
O'Gosho*	N, C
Saijo	N, C
Tamopan	N, C
Tenenashi	N, C

Persimons, which ripen during late summer, are full of dextrose sugar. Ancient Greeks named them *Diospyros,* food of the gods. Modern gardeners who find them equally delicious may wish to add a tree or two to their landscape.

* non-astringent

Native American persimmons grow from Connecticut to Florida and as far west as Kansas. The fruit was used by both Native Americans and early settlers but never has received high marks for flavor or quality. In any climate mild enough, the fruit of choice is the Oriental persimmon, brought to the United States more than 100 years ago.

Some varieties bear astringent fruit. Astringent persimmons must be completely soft and ripe before they can be eaten. Anyone who has ever bitten into an unripe fruit will remember the mouth-puckering sensation. Unlike citrus, persimmons continue to ripen once picked off the tree. Non-astringent fruit does not have the same pucker. It is sweeter-tasting and can be eaten while still somewhat firm.

Tanenashi, a longtime favorite, is an astringent variety. Trees are prolific, bearing large quantities of bright-yellow, seedless, conical fruit 2 to 4½ inches long and almost as broad.

Fuyu, with its non-astringent fruit, also is popular. Mature fruit is smooth, glossy and deep orange. Some persimmon has a squarish shape and light orange flesh. They can be eaten much like an apple. Other recommended varieties include O'Gosho, Hachiya and Tamopan.

During late summer and fall, taste local persimmons to find a favorite variety. Look for them at roadside stands, supermarkets and in gardeners' yards. Note results. Plants usually are not available until January or February.

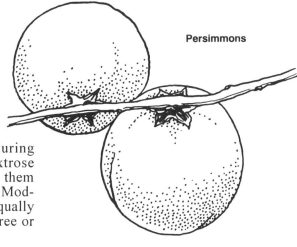

Persimmons

Like citrus, persimmons often are grafted. Even though native varieties do not produce the best-quality fruit, they often are chosen for rootstocks suited to local climate and soil conditions.

Plant new trees in well-drained soil. Give them full sunlight and room to develop. Each wide-spreading tree needs 20 feet to the nearest tree canopy. If planting in a lawn area, keep the area around the trunk free of grass and do not dig deeply when weeding, as feeder roots grow close to the surface.

A persimmon tree needs a strong, open framework or it will break under a heavy load of fruit. Immediately after planting, prune back to a height of 28 to 36 inches. Leave no more than five or six branches along the trunk to become major limbs. Keep this and future growth headed outward to keep the structure strong and fruit within easy reach.

Feed young trees frequently. Use a 6-6-6 or similar product every six to eight weeks during warm weather to establish a strong, spreading, branching habit. After three years, make the diet lean. Just the fertilizer from the lawn will do.

Bearing persimmon trees do better hungry. Given extra dollops of fertilizer or water, they may produce a display of flowers but are likely to drop their fruit. A persimmon on its own sets fruit parthenocarpically; that is, without being pollinated. Fruit produced in this way is very susceptible to stress caused by variation in tree growth. One way to improve fruit retention is to plant another variety, Gaiely, just for pollination. Pollinated fruit will have seeds, but is less affected by stress.

Water during dry months to help reduce stress. Water may be needed every three to four days in sandy soil, less often if soil is heavy or organic. A mulch over the root system also will help by slowing evaporation.

Persimmons rarely have problems with pests, which is fortunate because few pesticides are labeled for use on the trees. A dormant oil spray can be used during winter to combat scale insects on trunk and limbs.

Plums

Prunus salicina and hybrids

Recommended varieties:

Early Bruce*	N
Excelsior	N
Kelsey	N
Mariposa*	N
Methley**	N
Ozark Premier	N
Gulf Gold	C
Gulf Ruby	C

* Female variety; needs a self-fertile variety nearby for pollination.

** Western Panhandle only.

Both red and yellow plums grow wild throughout much of the state, often along fences where birds and other animals spread the seeds. Only in North Florida, however, do most varieties produce good yields.

Most of the old, familiar varieties need a considerable period of cold before breaking winter dormancy. Central Florida seldom is cold enough for long enough to permit good bud development and fruiting. New varieties Gulf Gold and Gulf Ruby require less cold and appear to produce well after a normal Central Florida winter.

Early Bruce and Mariposa plums, which have female flowers only, must be pollinated by another variety. Any other variety will bear some fruit by itself but produces much better when another variety is planted nearby.

Plums need the same care as peach trees. Trained to the same spreading, open shape, plum trees should grow up to 15 feet tall. Water and fertilize like peach trees. To keep the harvest pest-free, find a fruit-tree spray labeled for home use on plums and apply at regular intervals according to the directions.

Plums

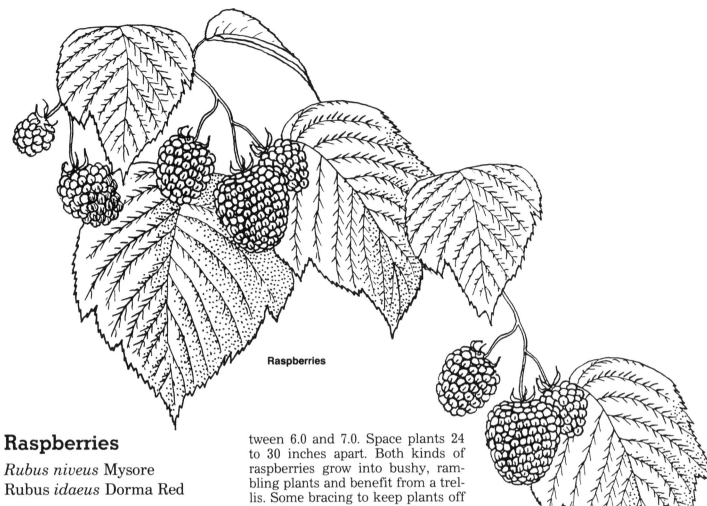
Raspberries

Raspberries

Rubus niveus Mysore
Rubus *idaeus* Dorma Red

Recommended varieties:
Dorma Red   N
Mysore   C, S

Gardeners who remember the sweet taste of Northern raspberries have trouble believing they won't do well in Florida. Old summer-ripening favorites require chilly winter weather and a significant dormant period. Only the variety Dorma Red has been a good producer in Florida and only in far northern regions of the state.

Gardeners in Central and South Florida can try the tropical Mysore raspberry. Many years they'll be frozen back in colder regions, but protected plants can bear sweet, black raspberries December through June.

Typical brambles, Dorma Red and Mysore are propagated by taking suckers from the base of mature plants or by rooting cuttings. Plant in a prepared, nematode-free garden site. Enrich the soil with compost and adjust the pH to between 6.0 and 7.0. Space plants 24 to 30 inches apart. Both kinds of raspberries grow into bushy, rambling plants and benefit from a trellis. Some bracing to keep plants off the ground and to spread the canes is all that is needed.

Feed new plantings with 3 ounces of 6-6-6 or 8-8-8 every eight to 10 weeks from February through September. Give mature vines 5 ounces per plant in February, June and late August. Keep the soil moist and apply mulch to help control weeds.

Raspberries bear fruit on the previous year's growth. In colder locations, mulch Mysore raspberries heavily to protect the fruiting stems. Even if they freeze, new spring growth may produce a small crop late in the season.

If plants grow out of bounds, tip back canes a bit to keep them more compact. Once they have produced a harvest, cut canes to the ground. They will bear no more fruit. Let new canes grow for next year's crop. This yearly pruning and removal of old canes may be enough to keep pest problems under control. If not, use a pesticide labeled for raspberries.

Florida chilling hours

For many types of deciduous fruit, the most critical factor in successful culture is the chilling hours, or amount of cool weather a plant requires in order to break dormancy and flower. To count as cool weather, temperatures must remain below 45 degrees on a fairly constant basis. The number of chilling hours received helps divide the state into growing regions of North, Central and South.

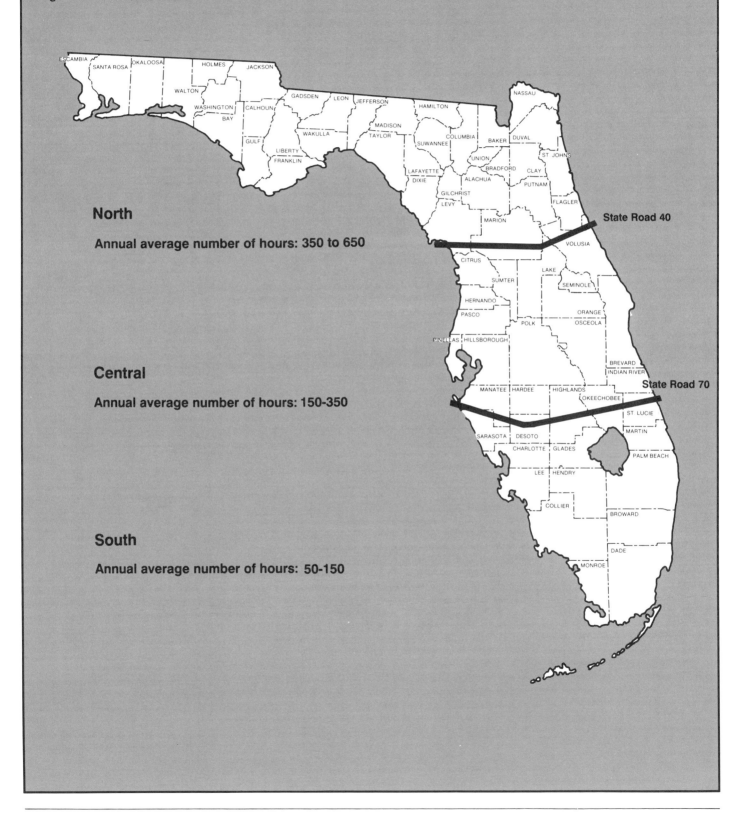

North

Annual average number of hours: 350 to 650

Central

Annual average number of hours: 150-350

South

Annual average number of hours: 50-150

16

Plant a grove of exotic flavors

Banana

AGRICULTURE MAY HAVE begun in the tropics. Certainly, tropical fruit has been cultivated for a long time. Mangoes were grown in India more than 4,000 years ago. The Mayans, Aztecs and Incas knew about growing avocados as early as 291 B.C.

One bit of Mayan folklore tells how the Indian Seriokai used avocados to track his unfaithful wife. As they fled, the runaway lovers ate their favorite fruit, discarding seeds as they went. A trail of avocado trees sprang up for Seriokai to follow.

With bright colors, odd shapes and rich, tangy flavors, tropical fruit tempts most gardeners into trying to start trees from seeds.

Unfortunately, do-it-yourself propagators are guaranteed fruit only in frost-free regions. Gardeners whose winters are cool must select hardy varieties and protect their plants from cold.

Even with 10,000 acres devoted to avocado production and another 2,500 to mangoes, Florida lies above the true tropics, which end just below the Keys.

Cold protection occasionally may be needed anywhere in the state, but gardeners in South Florida usually can grow whatever exotic fruit they choose. Tropical plantings extend up the coast to Tampa on the west and Merritt Island on the east.

Along the coasts, Gulf and ocean breezes temper the flow of cold air from the north. Frequent freezes and an occasional frost may nip the tops of trees or cause a year of poor production, but tropical fruit generally flourishes — not just common commercial varieties, but exotics people are just learning to appreciate.

In inland and northern areas, gusts of cold can be expected each winter to limit production of tropical fruit. Where temperatures often sink below freezing, stick to fruit known to survive the mid-20s. Plant the Surinam cherry to eat fresh or in jellies, the carambola, a deeply ridged dessert fruit and the bright red, ready-to-eat lychee. Each will yield harvests throughout Central Florida if given a run of two or more successive warm winters.

With avocados, varietal selection can mean the difference between productive and barren years. If crushed foliage smells pleasantly of anise, a tree has Mexican parentage and will do better in cold weather.

Varieties Young, Gainesville and

Mexicola survive temperatures into the high teens. Brogdon, Winter Mexican, Lula and Taylor can take temperatures into the 20s. During extremely cold years, gardeners may count themselves lucky if even the trees survive, but when winters are mild, they can expect small to medium-sized fruit by summer.

A cool winter will cause nubbins on mango trees. Seeds fail to develop when fruit sets while temperatures fall below 40 degrees. The fruit will be small but tasty.

Fruit too tender for north and central areas of the state can be grown in 15- to 25-gallon tubs or containers. A well-drained homemade soil mix is ideal. Use equal parts peat moss and perlite, plus a tablespoon of dolomitic lime for each gallon of soil. Position a plant at the same depth it originally was growing to prevent the root and crown rots that plague many tropical plantings.

Try growing carambolas, mangoes, lychees and other small, bushy tropicals in containers. When frost warnings are sounded, tip the plants on their sides and cover, slide them under the canopy of a tree or, for maximum protection, pull them into a garage, porch or heated enclosure.

Few fruiting plants have to be kept as tall trees. Even under grove conditions, avocados and mangoes are pruned back to about 15 feet to facilitate maintenance and harvesting. Home gardeners should prune the trees regularly to keep them broad, spreading and about 12 feet tall. Don't be afraid to nip or prune tips to promote branching or direct growth.

Just as gardeners in New England plant seeds indoors in late winter for a head start on tomatoes, Florida gardeners increase their chances of harvest by starting tropical fruit early.

To be sure of a passion fruit harvest, for instance, start seeds or cuttings a month or so before setting them out in the garden. Like grapes, grow the vines on a trellis of two lateral wires and permit only four main leaders to develop. Train them along the wires. Let the side branches hang down and there will be fruit by fall.

Papayas also need an early start to be sure of fruit in Central and North Florida. Start plants from seed in January so they are about 6 weeks old when it is time to put them in the ground in early March.

Florida varieties often grow as separate male and female plants, so set plants out in groups of three and plan to cull out most of the males when they flower. Males are easy to spot; their blossoms are produced on long stems, while female blooms are held close to the trunk. One male to every 20 female papayas is about right. If planting in rows, leave male plants on the ends.

To find more exotic tropical fruit as well as a better selection of ordinary ones, gardeners may need to travel to production areas near Homestead, Miami and Melbourne.

For fruit grown from seeds that is hard to obtain and often shared between neighbors, try the *Florida Market Bulletin*. Specialists and small growers offer plant materials for sale or exchange in the columns of this publication, which is free to state residents.

Avocados

Persea americana

Native to Mexico, Central and South America, avocados are among Florida's most popular fruit. The buttery pulp that surrounds large, single seeds contains minerals and significant quantities of vitamins A and B along with a high proportion of oil — up to 30 percent.

Florida old-timers tell stories of buttering their bread with avocado flesh during the dairy shortages of World War II. Using whole-grain bread and adding bean sprouts, health food enthusiasts do the same today.

A water bowl shaped like two back-to-back avocados found in Peru and dated to 900 A.D. suggests South American Indians have known and used the fruit for many years.

Spanish explorers to the New World tasted avocados almost upon arrival. The soldier Martin Fernandez de Enciso wrote of them in Columbia during 1510, and Cortez tried Aztec avocados in Mexico during 1519.

The Spanish are believed to have brought avocados to Florida, where they were well-established by 1835. A description of that very cold winter tells of frozen alligator pears in St. Augustine. The first recorded plantation was Henry Perrine's, near Miami in 1833.

As with other tropical fruit, commercial planting has been attempted throughout the state, but major production has been confined to South Florida and the coasts. The trees survive in North Florida only with lots of winter protection; fruit is an occasional thing.

Modern avocado varieties often combine ancestry from the three main groups:

• Mexican. Trees often are identified by the anise odor of crushed foliage. This is the hardiest, often surviving temperatures to 18 degrees, and is planted as far north as Gainesville. Fruit is small, weighing up to a pound; thin-skinned; and green to purple. It ripens June to October.

• Guatemalan. Trees exhibit medium hardiness, surviving temperatures in the 21-25 degree range. Fruit is thick-skinned, green to reddish and weighs up to 5 pounds. Ready to pick September to January.

• West Indian. The least hardy. Trees succumb when temperatures fall below 25 degrees. Fruit is large — up to 5 pounds, green to reddish, and has a medium-thick, leathery skin. Harvest May to September.

For the best fruit, plant named varieties. Seeds are tempting because they're so easy to grow. The fruit that eventually results may resemble that of the parent tree, but factors such as hardiness and length of time to first harvest are unpredictable.

Because avocados don't grow well

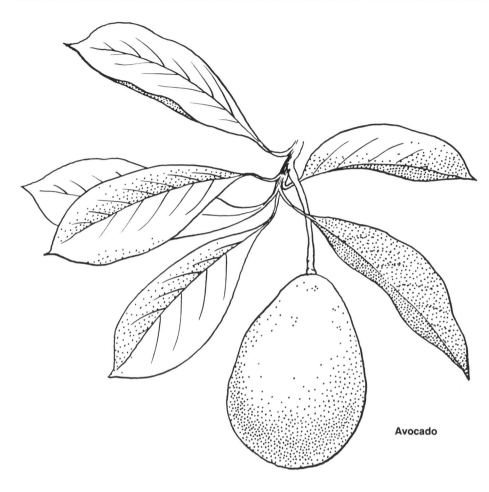

Avocado

Recommended avocado varieties

Variety	Parentage	Season of maturity	Fruit size	Fruit color	Cold tolerance	Scab resistance
Booth 7	Guatemalan X West Indian	Oct.-Dec.	10-20 oz.	green	medium	moderate
Booth 8	Guatemalan X West Indian	Oct.-Dec.	9-28 oz.	green	medium	moderate
Brogdon	Mexican X West Indian	July-Sept.	8-12 oz.	purple	high	moderate
Choquette	Guatemalan X West Indian	Nov.-Feb.	24-40 oz.	green	medium	high
Gainesville	Mexican	July-Aug.	6-8 oz.	green	high	moderate
Hall	Guatemalan X West Indian	Nov.-Feb.	20-30 oz.	green	medium	moderate
Lula	Guatemalan X West Indian	Nov.-Feb.	14-24 oz.	green	high	low
Mexicola	Mexican	July-Aug.	4-6 oz.	purple	high	moderate
Monroe	Guatemalan X West Indian	Nov.-Jan.	24-40 oz.	green	medium	moderate
Pollock	West Indian	July-Sept.	18-40 oz.	green	low	high
Ruehle	West Indian	Aug.-Sept.	10-20 oz.	green	low	high
Simmonds	West Indian	July-Sept.	16-34 oz.	green	low	high
Taylor	Guatemalan	Nov.-Feb.	12-18 oz.	green	high	moderate
Tonnage	Guatemalan	Sept.-Nov.	14-24 oz.	green	high	moderate
Waldin	West Indian	Sept.-Nov.	14-28 oz.	green	low	high
Winter Mexican	Mexican	Aug.-Sept.	10-12 oz.	green	high	moderate

from cuttings, a tree must be grafted to come true to type; most gardeners select container-grown favorites from a garden center.

For the best yields, plant more than one variety. Although most varieties will produce some fruit if planted alone, almost all produce more if cross-pollinated.

Avocados will grow in almost any soil, from deep sand to chunky limestone, as long as it is well-drained. Improve sandy soil by adding liberal quantities of organic material over a wide area. Follow good planting procedures and set a tree at its original growing depth. Add a mulch, not only to conserve moisture and prevent weeds but also to protect the shallow feeder roots.

Keep new trees moist, watering every two or three days during hot weather. As root systems become established, water once or twice a week.

Feed new trees every two months during warm weather. Start with a quarter of a pound of 6-6-6 or avocado-special fertilizer, and gradually increase the rate to a pound. Distribute it under the spread of the tree and out past the drip line.

In succeeding years, use 1 to 2 pounds of fertilizer for every year the tree is old, and divide the total amount between three or four evenly spaced applications. Don't apply more than 10 pounds of fertilizer in any one feeding. Feed in late winter, midspring, summer and early fall.

Gardeners will need to add minor nutrients to alkaline soils. Use sprays containing copper, manganese and zinc for the first few years, then just manganese and zinc as the tree matures. Iron deficiencies also may occur; use iron chelates made for use with alkaline soils as needed.

Left alone, trees may grow 40 feet tall. Keep them short and wide-spreading for easy picking and management. Cut out the top of young trees, leaving only those young shoots that grow outward, and maintain a 12- to 15-foot height by periodic pruning. Trees can be topped occasionally after harvest, but expect reduced production the following year.

Few pests significantly affect avocados. Apply insecticides only when mites, scales, borers or thrips appear to be hurting production. Diseases can cause more damage to fruit and foliage. Where leaf spots and scab are a problem, spray regularly with copper fungicide.

Avocados never really ripen on the tree. As they reach maximum maturity, they crack at the stem end and drop to the ground. Pick them any time after they reach the expected size and let them soften, which may take three to eight days. Because avocados mature over a period of several months, they can be stored on the tree until needed.

Bananas

Musa species and crosses

Recommended varieties: Apple, Dwarf Cavendish, Florida Sweet, Grand Nain, Ice Cream, Lady Finger, Orinoco, Rajapuri

Native to India and China, bananas have traveled far. Early Indonesian and Arab traders carried them to Africa. In the 16th century, the Spanish distributed bananas to the farthest warm reaches of a global empire.

Today, most of the world's commercial production comes from formerly Spanish territory. Climates in Central America and the Philippines suit plants that thrive on long stretches of 90- to 100-degree sunny days and rainy nights.

Another once-Spanish outpost, Florida is comparatively cool and dry. Although they are tropical plants and sensitive to cold, bananas produce edible fruit throughout the state because they grow so quickly. They thrive during the hot, humid summers. All it takes is one warmish winter or good protection from the cold and a banana plant usually will flower and fruit during the months that follow.

Unprotected plants freeze to the ground when temperatures drop below 32 degrees. With many varieties, however, roots and basal shoots will survive short spells of temperatures between 25 and 28 degrees and send up new growth when warm weather returns.

Under these circumstances, bananas in northern parts of the state are grown more as foliage plants; gardeners in South Florida can count on fruit almost year-round.

A banana plant is not a true tree; in fact, it grows more like giant grass. The long, broad leaves push through the ground wrapped tightly around one another, forming the so-called trunk. They unfurl toward the top, to end as a plant anywhere from 5 to 25 feet tall, depending on variety. As they age, the leaves tatter artistically in the wind.

After 10 to 15 months, a central stalk pushes up through the center of the leaves and starts to flower. Until they open, the relatively unimpressive flowers are covered by purplish bracts. The end of the stalk looks like one huge, heavy purple-maroon bud.

Banana

Flowers bloom and fruit develops in groups, called hands, of 10 to 20. The stem of fruit bends over toward the ground. With many varieties only the first few hands mature into plump, harvestable fruit.

Home plantings are started from shoots that sprout vigorously around established banana clumps. Use a spade to split off suckers when they are just a few feet tall. Strip off the outer leaves, leaving just a skinny shoot to continue growth.

The plants are tough and can be moved almost any time, but plenty of rain and near-tropical temperatures make spring and summertime ideal. Dig planting holes several feet wide and deep. Mix in liberal amounts of compost or peat with the fill, and mulch the planting.

Pour on the good care. Growth during the first few months will determine the size and number of fruit produced. Bananas like an improved growing site with consistently moist soil.

Fertilize plantings monthly from spring through early fall. Select a product high in nitrogen especially formulated for bananas, or use a 6-6-6 analysis. For 100 square feet of soil surface, start with half a pound for young plants and gradually increase to a pound by flowering and fruiting time, about a year later. Sprinkle the fertilizer over the whole spread of the planting.

Water during dry seasons to keep the soil moist but not wet. A mulch around the base of the plants will conserve moisture and restrict weed growth.

To harvest, wait until the first hand starts to yellow, then cut the whole stem from the plant. Remove the still-blooming lower buds and hang the stem of bananas in a cool, shady spot. Gather hands daily as they proceed to mature down the stalk.

A banana plant produces only one stem of fruit. Once harvested, the central stalk will die back, but the banana patch will be cleaner and healthier if an old plant is cut to the ground. Suckers will grow from the base of an old plant. Leave three to five well-spaced suckers to develop into strong, new plants.

Good winter cold protection increases the likelihood of a good harvest. Growers in cold areas can protect young shoots and trunks for several feet above the ground by enclosing plants with wire mesh 4 feet high and about 36 inches around, then surrounding them with leaves and other organic matter. Even when upper foliage and trunks turn brown and mushy, plants get a head start on the season to come. In spring, remove the wire and spread the leaves around as mulch.

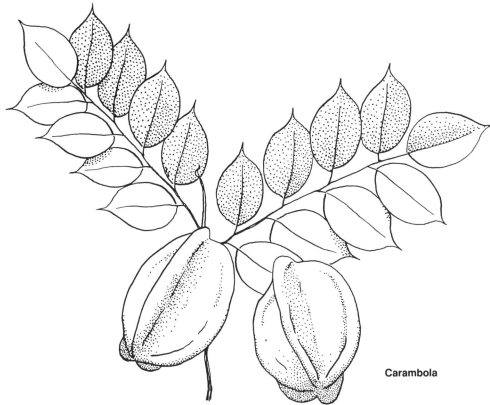
Carambola

Carambolas
Averrhoa carambola

Recommended varieties: Golden Star, Newcomb, Pei Sy Tao, Starking, Thayer, White

Juicy carambola fruit can be squeezed for a refreshing drink, sliced into a salad or consumed straight from the tree. The bright yellow color and unusual waxy appearance attract immediate attention. Star-shaped slices make an eye-catching garnish.

The trees, which grow 25 feet tall and have light to dark green foliage, make attractive features in and of themselves. Added attractions are the several flushes of pink to lavender clusters of flowers and the ornamental fruit, which matures September through April.

Established trees will survive temperatures of 26 degrees for short periods. If damaged by cold, one often will grow back to form a bushy but productive plant.

Trees do best in the warmest parts of Florida but have fruited in the Central Florida area after a succession of mild winters. Microclimates such as those found on the south side of lakes may make sporadic production possible even farther north.

The ridged fruit can be small and sour, but good selections are about 5 inches long and have a sweet, acidic flavor reminiscent of orange pineapple. Plantings can be started from seed, but the best varieties are propagated by grafting.

Carambola trees thrive in well-drained soils. They like a slightly acid pH but will do well in alkaline soils if given attention to minor nutrient needs. Follow good planting practices, then mulch. In northern locations, choose a protected area shielded from winter winds.

Keep the soil moist, watering once or twice a week. Trees kept too dry during fruit development will drop a large proportion of the fruit.

Feed young trees every other month with 6-6-6 or fruit-tree fertilizer. Scatter light applications of a quarter of a pound to half a pound under the spread of a tree from spring through fall. For mature trees, increase the rate to 1 pound for each inch of estimated tree diameter measured 4 feet above the ground, to a maximum of 10 pounds. Feed in March, May and early October.

Trees grown in alkaline soils will need a minor nutrient spray of zinc and manganese and a soil drench of chelated iron once or twice a year.

Carambolas need little pruning. Trees naturally assume a rounded shape that is resistant to wind.

Guavas
Psidium guajava

Recommended varieties: Blitch, Miami Red, Miami White, Patillo, Supreme, Red Indian, Ruby

Guavas are native to tropical America. Growing 20 feet tall, sometimes with multiple trunks, and with beautiful mottled bark, they make good landscape trees.

Though found in cooler areas, they are considered hardy only in South Florida, along Central Florida's coasts, and in a few warm interior areas. Trees are damaged when temperatures fall to 27 degrees.

After a damaging winter, plants often sprout from the base to make a bushy shrub. Two or three years later they may be producing a harvest. Reliable production, however, is restricted to the lower third of the state.

Like many tropical fruits, guavas grow readily from seed, but these plants often bear inferior fruit. Named varieties are grafted or air-layered, and most growers buy them at a nursery.

Select a well-drained site. Improve sandy soils with organic matter and set new plants at their original growing depth. Mulch to conserve moisture and control weeds.

Feed new plantings with a quarter of a pound of 6-6-6 every two months during good growing weather. The second year, increase the rate to 1 pound per application. As trees begin to mature, reduce feeding to three times a year — March, June and August.

For each application, measure a pound of fertilizer per inch of estimated tree diameter, up to a maximum of 5 pounds. Sprinkle it under the entire spread of the tree and out past the drip line.

Guavas benefit from foliar sprays, especially when grown in alkaline soils. Use a product that contains manganese and zinc once or twice a year. If iron is needed, treat the soil with chelated iron.

Keep the soil moist. As new trees establish root systems, water frequently. Water mature trees once or twice a week throughout most of the growing season. Trees may need extra watering during blossom and fruit set, when they are extremely susceptible to stress.

For good fruit production on an easy-to-manage tree, keep the tree 12 to 15 feet tall. Prune to a single short trunk with three to five main limbs and encourage outward-growing branches. Periodically thin or top a tree to encourage new branching, more flowers and better fruiting.

Guavas flower in two main flushes, April through May and September through October. Fruit ripens 90 to 120 days later. Fruit is round and white to yellow, sometimes with a pink blush.

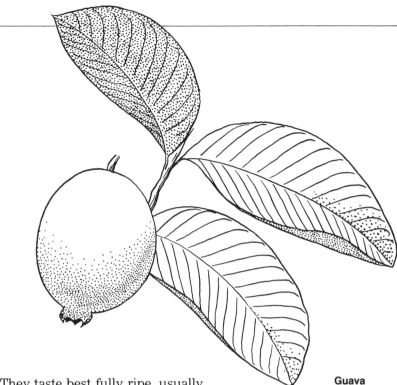
Guava

They taste best fully ripe, usually about the time they are ready to fall from the tree. Cut one in half to reveal white, yellow or pink flesh that people eat with a spoon, add to a salad or make into jam. Some people find the smell offensive; to others, it is the epitome of tropical scents.

Few pests affect guavas, but growers should be alert for infestations of scales, whiteflies or caterpillars and apply controls if needed.

Unfortunately, growers who find larvae burrowing through the ripening fruit will find that no control exists for the Caribbean fruit fly, which has been a problem in South Florida and, during warm years, in Central Florida.

Kiwis
Actinidia chinensis

Recommended varieties: Abbott, Allison, Bruno, Greensill, Hayward, Matua, Monty, Tomuri

Native to China, kiwis have adapted to regions with a mild and uniform climate, including sections of California, Australia and New Zealand. Vines were introduced into the United States around the turn of the century. Recently the fruit has become quite popular.

Sweet and slightly acid with a strawberry texture, the fuzzy, khaki-colored, egg-shaped fruit is a familiar sight in supermarkets, a staple of nouvelle cuisine and a challenge to Florida gardeners.

The vines grow well throughout the state but rarely bear much fruit. Growers looking for more than attractive foliage and a few small, fragrant flowers are apt to be disappointed.

One of several problems is the amount of winter cold kiwis require in order to break dormancy and flower. Varieties need 400 hours of temperatures below 45 degrees, more chilling than can be found in most parts of the state.

Kiwi plants grow best where summer days are warm but nights are cool, conditions almost unobtainable in Florida. The vines are hardy; when dormant, they survive cold temperatures better than citrus. However, in warmer parts of the state that cool down gradually in the fall, kiwis may fail to go dormant and be susceptible to sudden freezes.

Kiwis are another exotic fruit easy to grow from seeds. The tiny black seeds embedded in the lime-green flesh germinate readily. Seedlings lack uniformity, however, and popular varieties are grown from cuttings or are grafted.

The vining plants need lots of room to grow. A grape arbor or trellis, with kiwis spaced 10 to 15 feet apart, is ideal. Male and female flowers are borne on separate plants; place one male plant for every six to eight females. Expect one vine to grow more than 25 feet in a year. Flowers and fruit, if any, will be on the previous year's growth. Plants flower in the spring and fruit ripens in the fall.

Kiwis grow rapidly in well-drained, sandy soils. Keep the soil moist and mulched, and the vines will fill the trellis in a year or two.

Feed vines with 6-6-6 each February, May and August. Apply 1 to 2 pounds for each 100 square feet of soil surface under and near the arbor or trellis.

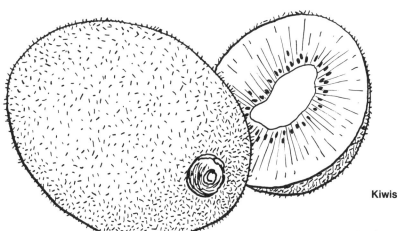

An annual pruning restrains the abundant growth and encourages fruiting. Allow the vines to fill the trellis or arbor through the summer, removing only enough extra growth to keep a plant in bounds. Each winter, while the plants are dormant, cut back growing tips and remove older canes to keep up the supply of new and potentially fruiting stems.

Pests and diseases have not been a problem in Florida.

Loquats

Eriobotrya japonica

Recommended varieties: Oliver, Tanaka, Wolf

Large, dark green leaves and cream-colored clusters of flowers on a tree that may grow 25 feet high make the loquat a good source of shade and a popular accent in landscapes throughout Florida and north into Georgia.

Many homeowners overlook the additional benefit of the fruit, which can be sweet, slightly acid and tasty. It can be eaten fresh or used in jelly, jam or preserves.

Kiwis

Loquats flower during fall and early winter. Fruit follows, ripening during the late winter and early spring. The timing makes flowers and fruit vulnerable to winter cold. They are damaged by temperatures that dip into the mid-20s, although trees are hardy into the teens. Gardeners can expect fruit consistently in South Florida, most years in central regions and only occasionally farther north.

With the harvest a chancier thing, sellers in North and Central Florida rarely distinguish loquat trees by variety. They simply sell loquat trees, easy to start from seed. Farther south, named varieties are chosen for the quality of fruit and are propagated from air-layers or grafting. Because fruit varies in flavor from poor and tasteless to excellent and spicy, search out named varieties.

Choose a full-sun location for a new tree, and follow usual planting procedures. Most soils suit loquats — they even do well near the beach because they are moderately salt tolerant, which permits their use when protected from spray by buildings or other more salt-tolerant trees.

Do avoid planting in areas prone to flooding. Adding organic material over a wide area is beneficial but not necessary. Mulch to conserve moisture.

Water young trees frequently for the first few weeks, then reduce to once or twice a week. For the first few years, encourage new growth with a light scattering of 6-6-6 every six to eight weeks during warm months.

Feed mature trees in February, June and early October. Estimate a tree's diameter 4 feet above the ground and use half a pound of balanced fertilizer per inch of diameter, up to a maximum of 5 pounds. Apply the fertilizer under the spread of the tree and beyond the drip line.

Loquat trees do well left to themselves, but gardeners can help a little by pruning for a straight trunk and cutting out crisscrossing branches. Fruit can be thinned, too. To grow big, plump loquats, remove up to a third of the fruit in each cluster after it sets. Well-tended trees will set heavy crops and produce large fruit.

A 5-year-old tree may begin to produce fruit. Fruit ripens in about 120 days when, depending on variety, it turns yellow or golden. Leave it on the tree until the peak of ripeness to develop the best flavors. Fruit is ready to harvest when slightly soft.

Few pests affect loquat trees, but fire blight, a bacterial disease, can cause severe damage. The disease is likely to appear after a moist spring when rain washes the bacteria among new, susceptible growth. Young branches die rapidly, turn-

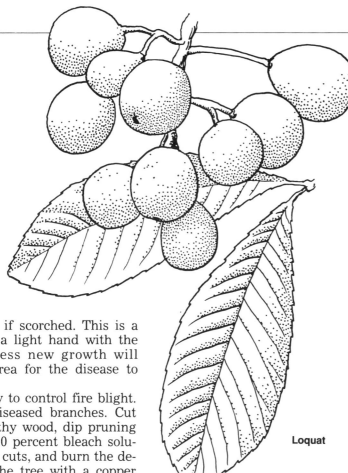
Loquat

ing black as if scorched. This is a time to use a light hand with the fertilizer. Less new growth will mean less area for the disease to take hold.

Act quickly to control fire blight. Prune out diseased branches. Cut back to healthy wood, dip pruning shears in a 10 percent bleach solution between cuts, and burn the debris. Spray the tree with a copper fungicide to help reduce spread of disease. Several sprays will be needed at two-week intervals.

dark green foliage that sweeps down toward the ground as the tree ages. Young leaves are reddish in color but turn green and shiny when mature. Given protection from chilly winds when young, they make superb landscape trees.

Lychees are native to China, but adapt well to the warm climate of South Florida. Southern and coastal areas of Central Florida are about as far north as reliable harvests can be expected. Mature trees will survive short spells of temperatures as low as 24 degrees, but fruit production suffers.

Given a succession of warm years, lychee trees do bear fruit in Central Florida's interior, but because lychee trees produce sporadically even under the best conditions, a good harvest can be expected only once or twice in 25 years.

The trees grow best in sandy soils improved with organic matter. Add liberal quantities over a large area around the planting hole. Acid soils are best, but lychees will grow and fruit in alkaline soils if given additional minor nutrients. Follow good planting procedures and add mulch.

Lychees like a moist soil and can withstand short periods of flooding. Water young trees frequently. Mature trees will need to be watered once or twice a week.

Feed new trees every other month from spring through fall with a quarter of a pound to half a pound of 6-6-6 or fruit tree fertilizer. Fertilize older trees in March, May and early October. Apply 1 pound of fertilizer per inch of estimated tree diameter measured 4 feet above the

Lychees
Litchi chinensis

Recommended varieties: Bengal, Brewster, Hak Ip, Hanging Green, Kwai Mi, Mauritius, No Mai, Sweet Cliff, Yellow Red

Gardeners may have to grow their own to find out how wonderful fresh lychee fruit can taste. The red or rust-colored skin peels away to reveal white pulp that resembles gelatin surrounding a single brown seed. The flavor, sweet and slightly acid, is a tropical sensation.

Lychee trees grow 40 feet tall with a dense rounded canopy of

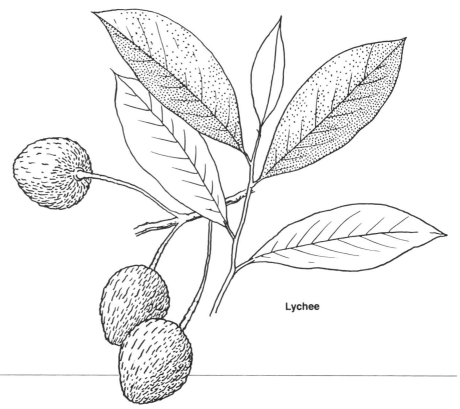
Lychee

ground, up to a maximum of 10 pounds. Sprinkle it under the spread of the tree and out past the drip line.

In alkaline soils, lychees will need two or three evenly spaced applications of minor nutrients. Drench the soil with an iron chelate solution and apply zinc and manganese in the form of a foliar spray.

New trees usually are started from air layers and will begin to produce in three to four years. Flowers are borne in large clusters of small greenish blossoms from March through April. Fruit matures mid-May to early July. Consume fresh or freeze for later use. Expect a good harvest about once every three or four years in good production areas of South Florida.

Mangoes

Mangifera indica

Recommended varieties: Adams, Carrie, Early Gold, Fascell, Florigon, Haden, Irwin, Keitt, Kent, Palmer, Ruby, Saigon, Sensation, Smith, Tommy Atkins

People usually refer to a whole range of fruit when trying to describe the taste of mangoes. They may be the quintessential tropical fruit, as important around the world as apples are in temperate climates.

Inventive cooks use mangoes in compotes, jams, chutneys, ice cream, sherbets, pies, puddings and cobblers.

Related plants give us pistachios, cashews and lacquer, but pests such as Brazilian pepper, poison oak and poison ivy are in the same family. Some people will break out in a rash after picking or peeling mangoes; however, almost everyone can enjoy eating the fruit with no ill effects.

Mangoes have been cultivated for more than 4,000 years. Probably originating in India and Southeast Asia, mangoes gradually spread through the tropics, arriving in the Americas during the 1700s. The first plantings in the United States were made in Florida in 1833 with mangoes shipped from Mexico. Cold weather and disease plagued these early plantings.

Winter temperatures still keep most mango plantings in the warmest parts of the state, especially along the coasts of South Florida.

During warm years, gardeners try growing mangoes as far north as

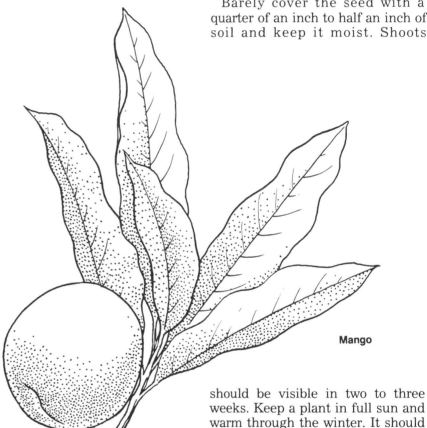

Ocala, but production is not dependable. Trees are damaged as soon as temperatures fall below freezing. Mature trees can withstand a few hours of 25-degree weather, but leaves and small branches are killed.

Mangoes should taste luscious, something like a peach, with a smooth, melting texture. Popular kinds may weigh between half a pound and 3 pounds when ready to be picked.

Supermarkets find their customers choose fruit with lots of color, so they tend to offer only varieties that have at least a red or purplish blush. Some of the prettiest are almost entirely red. Varieties that ripen green to yellow may be even more flavorful; home gardeners should consider them.

It is tempting — and easy — to save a mango pit and start a tree from seed. Clip an edge of the husk and peel it away from the seed. Use a loose potting mix and plant the seed on edge, tilted a little so the convex side points down. From this position, the roots, which appear first, will grow straight down.

Barely cover the seed with a quarter of an inch to half an inch of soil and keep it moist. Shoots should be visible in two to three weeks. Keep a plant in full sun and warm through the winter. It should bear fruit in four to five years.

Unfortunately, few mango trees grown from seed will produce trees exactly like the parent. Most Florida mangoes are hybrids, so seedling offspring rarely yield fruit much like the ones they came from. Fruit from seedlings usually is extremely fibrous; fair-tasting at best, and sometimes with a strong flavor of turpentine.

It is fun to experiment with growing seedling trees, and a seed with the right genes can yield a tree well worth the effort. However, mangoes grown for fruit are almost all obtained by grafting.

Mangoes tolerate a range of conditions. Trees produce well in both sand and limestone soils. Plantings can tolerate some flooding, but they grow and produce better when soils are well-drained. Adding organic materials to the planting site will encourage vigorous root growth, but it is not required.

Besides weather, the major factor in developing a productive tree is good care. Use 6-6-6 or a fertilizer formulated for mangoes and feed young trees every two months from late winter through early fall, applying a quarter of a pound at first and gradually increasing to a pound by year's end.

For older trees use 2 pounds for every year a tree has been in the ground, up to a maximum of 15 pounds, and divide between three feedings in February, June and October. Trees grown in alkaline soils will need extra copper, zinc and manganese during the first four or five years and zinc and manganese from then on. Apply these minor nutrients once each spring in the form of a foliar spray.

Mango trees grow tall, wide and handsome. They can reach 50 to 60 feet high and almost as broad, with clumps of large, evergreen leaves weighting young branches toward the ground. New foliage comes in shiny coppery reds and purples.

Even if most don't quite reach maximum size, mangoes make handsome shade trees when left to themselves. Gardeners interested in fruit production usually let a tree reach fruiting age and produce several harvests, then prune tops and sides after harvest to keep it broad and 15 to 25 feet tall.

Mangoes flower December through April, depending on variety. The fragrant but not very showy flowers appear in large clusters, but only a few set fruit. Most stems bear a single mango. How heavy the crop is varies from year to year.

Mangoes mature in 100 to 150 days, with most ripening between May and September. Pick them as their green color fades into the color they will be when mature. Bring them indoors to soften to an edible stage when, like peaches, they yield slightly to the touch.

Mango anthracnose, a fungus disease, is most likely to limit fruit production. Sunken black lesions may appear anywhere on an infected plant, especially in moist weather. Keep the ground under the tree clean of dropped leaves and fruit and prune off diseased and dead branches.

Where anthracnose control is needed, spray with a copper fungicide when the flowers first appear and several times more as the fruit begins to form, through late spring.

Papayas
Carica papaya

Recommended varieties: Cariflora, Solo

Lurking among the citrus and the ornamentals, the huge handlike shapes of papaya leaves are a familiar sight in many landscapes. Although they may grow 30 feet tall, papayas aren't really trees at all, but giant herbaceous plants. How perennial they are depends on temperature.

Given ideal conditions, a papaya plant in South Florida might produce fruit for 20 years. A run of mild winters in Central Florida might give a grower two or three years of fruit. In North Florida, every winter predictably will reduce papaya plants to mush.

With papayas, however, gardeners who can't count on mild winters can grow their own crop insurance. Start seeds during fall and overwinter young plants in a greenhouse or sunny room. Transplant outdoors when warm spring weather arrives. Papayas grow fast. By the following fall the transplants can be producing fruit.

A collection of papaya fruit shows great variability. It can range from nearly round to long, thin and oblong in shape and can resemble anything from gourds to mangoes. It can weigh as little as half a pound or as much as 12 pounds. Some are ripe when golden yellow while others soften and are ready to eat when the skin is green; the flesh may be golden, orange or pink.

The plants hybridize freely. Growers who save their own seeds and who buy or trade seed with other growers can develop papayas with different characteristics.

Papaya plants may be male, female or bisexual. Male flowers are borne on long stalks and are early to bloom. Female flowers bloom close to the trunk, where fruit usually forms. Bisexual plants exhibit a mixture of flower types and perfect blooms, flowers with both pistils and stamens. Only plants with female or perfect flowers will produce fruit.

Most papayas are pollinated by sphinx moths. Gardeners who would like to try their own hand can predict reliable results from particular crosses:

• Moving pollen from male-only flowers to female-only flowers will produce fruit with seeds that when planted give an equal number of male and female offspring.

• Transferring the male pollen from a bisexual flower to a female-only flower will produce fruit with seeds that when planted give an equal number of female and bisexual offspring.

• Self-pollinated bisexual flowers or pollen moved from the male flower portion of one bisexual flower to the female portion of another will produce fruit with seeds that when planted results in twice as many bisexual plants as female plants.

• Moving pollen from a male-only flower to the female portion of a bisexual flower will produce fruit with seeds that when planted give an equal number of male, female and bisexual offspring.

Although ratios can be estimated, the actual sex of a specific plant cannot be determined until it flowers. To make the sex life of a papaya even more complicated, some plants seem to change their sex while adjusting to growing conditions.

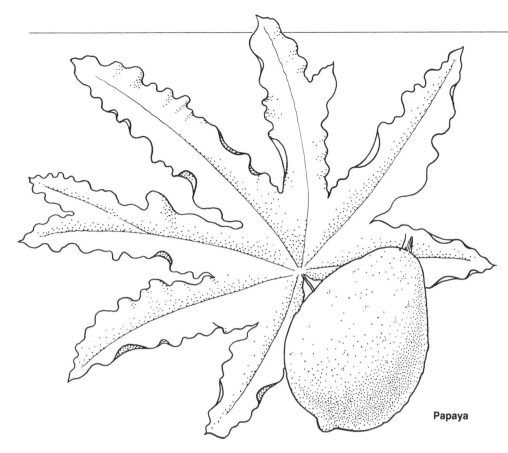
Papaya

Only female and bisexual plants are of real value for fruit production, of course. If a great many male plants occur in a planting, eliminate most to make room for plants that will bear fruit. Keep a few males to ensure pollination.

When the fruit is ripe, papaya seeds are ready to germinate, although they may remain viable for several years if kept cool and dry. Remove the gelatinous coating, air-dry the seeds, and sow them two or three to a container.

Given bright light and moisture, the seeds are quick to respond. If more than one sprout appears in a pot, choose one to keep or let them all grow and thin them later in the garden.

Set young plants in the garden at a 6- to 8-foot spacing whenever the weather is warm; the sooner the better once spring arrives in central and northern areas in order to have fruit by fall. Leave the soil unimproved, or add liberal quantities of peat moss or compost. Papayas in an improved soil will need less ongoing care.

They will need frequent watering but cannot stand soggy soil. Water as the surface dries — frequently for young plants and about twice a week for older papayas. Mulches help stretch the time between irrigation.

A vigorous plant that reaches heights of 20 to 30 feet needs frequent feeding. Start with a balanced fertilizer, either 6-6-6 or 10-10-10, at the rate of a quarter of a pound every two weeks. Gradually increase the rate to half a pound until the plants are about 8 months old, then reduce the frequency to once a month. Gardeners who improve their soils and use a mulch can reduce the amount of fertilizer by half.

Trees may freeze to the ground during severe winters. Papayas are cold-sensitive and the foliage and trunks turn to mush. If heavily mulched, the lower trunk often survives and new shoots grow from the base. Prune a plant back to maintain two new shoots. The still-healthy root system speeds growth; by August, a plant will once again be bearing fruit.

As the stem lengthens, a plant drops its leaves from the bottom up. A tuft of huge leaves, 2 feet wide with 2-foot-long stems, will be left as an umbrella over the year's cluster of fruit.

Papayas are ready to eat when they soften. If gathered too soon, the fruit will be bland. Growers often find that smaller varieties and ones that turn deep orange are the sweetest tasting.

Many pests attack papayas. They are susceptible to nematodes, which can at least be postponed, if not prevented, by fumigating the soil before planting. Other hostile insects include the papaya fruit fly, papaya webworm and papaya whitefly.

To date, few pesticides are labeled for use on papayas; contact the extension service for the latest recommendations.

Fungus diseases, which affect fruit and foliage, are easier to control. Use maneb or Daconil if anthracnose rots the fruit, and sulfur if powdery mildew covers leaves with a whitish film.

Viruses mottle leaves, cause greasy rings and spots on fruit, and distort and weaken plants. Until now, a grower's only recourse has been to destroy affected plants before a virus spreads to other plants.

The Tropical Research and Education Unit of the University of Florida may represent the wave of the future, however, by developing a variety called Cariflora. Its rounded fruit appear to be quite resistant to ringspot.

Passion fruit

Passiflora edulis — purple

Passiflora edulis flavicarpa — yellow

Passiflora quadrangularis — giant granadilla

Recommended varieties: none selected

Most people enjoy the slightly acid to sour taste of passion fruit. The vines are cultivated in the

157

warmer regions for their rounded, egg-shaped fruit. Three types — purple, yellow and giant granadilla — commonly are grown.

To end up with good fruit, it's important to start with the right kind of plant. Related ornamental passion vines appear throughout much of South and Central Florida. These are grown mainly for their red or blue flowers and seldom produce fruit. The wild species, maypop, grows from Central Florida north and produces a small edible fruit, but most gardeners consider it a pesky weed.

Sensitivity to cold keeps plantings of the giant granadilla and yellow passion fruit confined to South Florida and warm spots in Central Florida. The purple passion fruit will grow farther north in areas that receive only light frosts.

Start a new vine from seed or cuttings. Stick cuttings in vermiculite, keep them in the shade and mist frequently. Seeds germinate in 10 to 20 days and the new plants grow rapidly. When the plants are 10 to 16 inches tall, they are ready for a permanent location. Plants grown from cuttings may flower and fruit the first summer or fall, while plants from seed will take a year or two.

The vines grow vigorously and need an arbor or trellis for support. Space plants 10 to 15 feet apart. Direct shoots up wires or wooden lathes, and do not prune from spring through fall. During winter, when plants are dormant, prune out all dead and weak growth. Cut main shoots back to strong, vigorous stems filled with new buds.

Passion fruit vines are short-lived. They may live for more than a decade, but expect three to five years of productivity. When a plant develops considerable amounts of dead wood and vigor diminishes, it is time to remove it.

Plant vines in a well-drained garden site. They like an acid soil, although the yellow passion fruit will tolerate alkaline soils if supplied with minor nutrients. Feel free to add liberal quantities of organic matter to sandy soils. Keep plantings moist and apply a mulch.

Passion fruit thrives with light but frequent feedings. Use a formula such as a 6-6-6 with minor nutrients, and give each vine 4 to 6 ounces every four to six weeks during warm months. Spread fertilizer under the length of the vine to cover the root zone. From time to time throughout the year, plants in alkaline soils also will need soil drenches of chelated iron and foliar sprays that contain minor nutrients.

Most vines flower from spring through summer. The purple and yellow species have white flowers with dark blue centers. Flowers of the giant granadilla are white with a maroon inner portion. All types of fruit are harvested summer through early winter.

Both purple and yellow passion fruit undergo rapid color changes as they ripen. From green, they turn to deep purple, almost black, or deep yellow. To avoid a woody taste, leave them on the vine until they drop. Collect fruit frequently so it doesn't deteriorate or attract animals. Both kinds are grown for the juicy pulp that surrounds the seeds and are used fresh, in beverages or in jellies.

Giant granadillas are eaten whole. Pick them when the skin is an intense golden color. The fruit is served as a cooked vegetable or the pulp and fleshy seed covering can

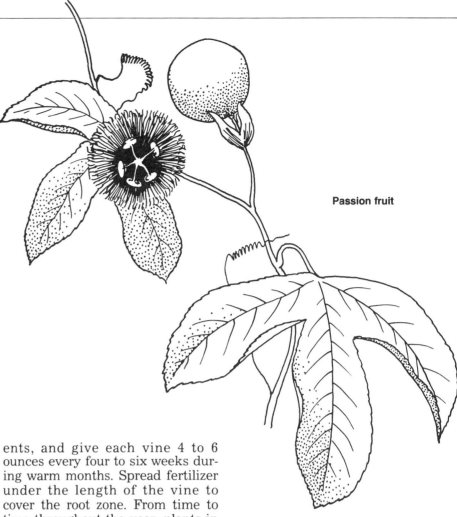

Passion fruit

be used in desserts and beverages.

Passion fruit is relatively pest-free. Nematodes and fungi that attack roots are the most common problems; the best controls are to grow plants in nematode-free soils and to maintain good drainage. Purple passion vines often are so sensitive to nematodes, they must be grafted onto the yellow variety.

Pineapples
Ananas comosus

Recommended varieties: Abakka, Natal Queen, Pernambuco, Red Spanish, Smooth Cayenne

Perpetuate a Florida tradition by planting a pineapple patch. All it takes is a well-drained garden spot, a pH test and adjustment to around 6.5 if necessary, and the addition of plenty of organic material.

In the mid-1800s, field-ripe, Florida pineapples brought a dollar a dozen in New York, Baltimore and Philadelphia. Pineapples were a major crop for pioneers living on the St. Johns River and in the Keys. "By 1876 there was hardly a settler from New Smyrna to Jupiter, but had his pineapple patch," wrote H.R. Saunder, an early shipper.

At the turn of the century more than 5,000 acres of pineapples were cultivated and 1 million crates were heading to market. Production dropped drastically around 1910 as an equal supply of Cuban pineapples combined to glut the market. The once-prosperous state industry declined completely when faced with additional problems of nematodes, freezes and droughts.

Today pineapple production prospers in backyard gardens. After a mild winter, residents harvest fruit that costs as much as $2 each at a grocery store. It's an easy fruit to grow, requiring little care.

Cold weather is the biggest problem faced by home growers. Exposure to temperatures below 40 degrees turns pineapple leaves yellow, although it may also encourage fruiting. Freezing temperatures cause severe damage. Plantings can be covered when freezing temperatures are predicted, but even then, pineapples can be frozen to the ground. Few die, however, and new shoots appear from the main bud, or base, to renew growth. Harvest will be reduced to only a few pineapples the first season after a freeze, and it will be a year or more before production is back to normal.

An easy way to start a new plant is to save the crown of foliage from the top of a fruit. Cut it off, leaving just a bit of flesh. Strip off a few lower leaves, stick the fleshy bit several inches into soil and it will root quickly. Or, let the top air-dry for a day or two and remove the flesh to expose the stem. Roots, ready to grow, often will be visible.

Other portions of a pineapple plant can be used. Shoots, called slips, develop below the fruit; ratoons, which are clusters of foliage, form from below-ground stems; and suckers grow between the leaves. Each is a small, new plant; cut it off at its base and give it a good growing medium.

Vermiculite or a loose potting mix is ideal, but many gardeners skip the bit of extra bother. Stick the new plants 12 to 18 inches apart and a few inches deep into a prepared garden soil, keep them moist, and away they grow.

Soil won't need much preparation unless nematodes are a problem. Nematodes can be attacked only before planting by fumigating with Vapam or performing soil solarization.

Pineapple

For gardeners in cooler parts of the state or with ongoing nematode problems, containers are the answer. A 3-gallon pot holds an individual pineapple plant and a soilless mix of equal parts perlite, vermiculite and peat moss. To provide some nutrition, incorporate a cup of bone meal and a cup of cottonseed meal with every 5 gallons of prepared mix.

Plants tolerate drought and usually get by with just the moisture from rainfall. Hower, the plants need adequate water and fertilizer to grow big and produce large fruit. Keep the soil moist. Plants in pots may need watering every day during hot, dry months and several times a week in cooler weather. In the garden, mulch plants to help keep soil moist and weeds under control.

During warm weather, drench plants in pots with a liquid 20-20-20 solution every three to four weeks. Give plants in the ground some 6-6-6 every four to six weeks. A light scattering per plant or half a pound for each 100 square feet will supply the necessary nutrients.

Pineapple plants can take up to three years to flower, although most begin within 15 to 30 months. Cool temperatures stimulate flowering, but if the weather doesn't cooperate, try forcing them: Place several apples or bananas among the pineapple's foliage. Cover the plant with a clear plastic bag to seal in the ethylene gas produced by the ripening fruit. Protect the plant from direct sun, then wait three days before removing the bag and fruit.

The attractive pinkish-purple flower should appear shortly, followed by a small fruit that slowly grows to maturity. When it's ready to harvest, fruit should turn from green to yellowish-orange and should have the familiar pineapple smell. In the real pioneer tradition, trim the crown with a sharp knife to form a handle and then, with a firm grip, peel and eat.

Remove the pineapple but leave the plant. Although a stem yields only a single fruit, suckers will develop from the original plant to produce subsequent crops. Mature plants will fruit for several years before production declines.

Pomegranates

Punica granatum

Recommended varieties: Purple Seed, Spanish Ruby, Wonderful

A well-packaged fruit, the pomegranate is wrapped in a leathery skin, with each of many seeds covered with an edible, sweet to slightly acidic gelatinous pulp. It can be a challenge to peel.

Pomegranate juice is used to make drinks, sherbets, jelly, grenadine and marinades. The seeds are added to salads and desserts.

Pomegranates grow throughout the state. Reaching a height of about 15 feet, they make ornamental, multistemmed shrubs or small trees. In spring they are covered with beautiful orange bell-shaped flowers. Big, round fruit follows June through October in central and northern areas; year-round in southern locations. Because best production follows a cool winter — and plants have survived a temperature of 10 degrees — this exotic fruit does better in central and northern regions of the state.

Pomegranates prefer acid soils; growth and production are poor where they grow on alkaline sites.

Plants can be grown from seed, but the best varieties usually are propagated from cuttings or air layers. Most gardeners will be dealing with container-grown plants. Prepare a planting site with liberal additions of organic matter. Dig a hole deeper and wider than the root ball and plant the new shrub.

Keep the soil moist until the roots become established. Pomegranates are drought-resistant but produce well when watered once or twice a week. Add a mulch over the roots to stretch the time between waterings.

When plants are young, give them frequent light scatterings of fertilizer from spring through fall. After the first year, follow a regular shrub feeding program, fertilizing in February, May, July and October. Use a pound of 6-6-6 to 100 square feet of soil, and spread it under the limbs and out past the drip line.

Pomegranates fruit on new wood, so it can't hurt to prune out older, unproductive growth. Trim suckers that arise from the base as well as any crisscrossing branches to reveal a clean silhouette when the plants lose their leaves for the winter.

The light-green, narrow leaves usually add to the plant's beauty but may host one of the few pests to affect pomegranates: leaf spot, a fungus disease. Use a copper fungicide if needed to prevent premature leaf drop, which tends to be a problem in South Florida.

The flowers bloom for several weeks during the spring, then develop into fruit several inches across. Yellow at first, then changing to pink, pomegranates finally turn red when ripe. It won't hurt to leave some on the tree a little longer. They decorate bare branches and only get sweeter with time.

Pomegranate

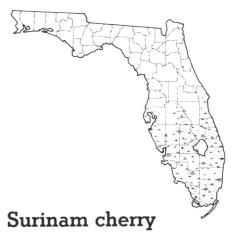

Surinam cherry

Eugenia uniflora

Recommended varieties: none

Shiny evergreen leaves make the Surinam cherry attractive year-round. Plant it as an informal hedge or shear it to a formal shape. Keep it as a container plant or let one grow 15 feet tall as a small, multistemmed tree.

Surinam cherry

However it is used, the Surinam cherry yields a harvest of globular fruit an inch across, ridged like tiny pumpkins and coming in colors mostly red but sometimes orange or pink and ripening to maroon or almost black.

Immature fruit tastes resinous and unpleasant; ripe, it develops a tart-sweet flavor. Fruit varies in quality because most plants are grown from seed. Producers have begun to make selections of the best-tasting varieties, and these selections are propagated by cuttings or grafting. Common named varieties have yet to emerge.

While the Surinam cherry grows best in South Florida, it has been successful into Central Florida. Plants are quite hardy, surviving temperature dips into the 20s. Even if they freeze, plants often sprout up from the crown, and growers in southern and central parts can expect renewed production in three to four years.

Surinam cherry grows in most soils. Plants survive in poor soils and take lots of abuse. For good fruit production, however, growers should follow good planting practices. If possible, add lots of organic matter to the site. Surinam cherry prefers slightly acid conditions, but plants tolerate alkaline soil when supplied with minor nutrients.

Keep the soil moist by watering once or twice a week, especially while the fruit develops. Feed new plantings every six to eight weeks with a scattering of a quarter of a pound to half a pound of 6-6-6 over 100 square feet of soil. Use 1 pound once in spring, summer and fall to fertilize older shrubs. Plants in alkaline soils will need iron chelates applied as a soil drench and minor nutrients in a foliar spray once or twice a year.

The plants take well to being clipped and continue to bear fruit, though less, of course. Wait until after harvest to prune.

Small flowers open spring through early summer, and fruit matures in 35 to 50 days. The crop is ready to pick when the fruit is deeply colored and slightly soft. Eat it fresh, or split and pit it to use in fruit salads, pies, jellies, jams and wine.

More exotic, tropical fruit

Name	Plant type	Hardiness zone	Season	Fruit description	Use	Varieties
Atemoya *Annona hybrid*	small tree	S	fall	large, smooth to segmented, white pulp, creamy sweet	fresh, drinks, ice cream	African Pride, Page
Barbados cherry *Malpighia glabra*	shrub	S	April-Oct.	small, lobed, bright red, high vitamin C	fresh, juice, jelly, ice cream	Florida Sweet, B-17
Black sapote *Diospyros digyna*	medium tree	S	winter	medium, dark green to black, sweet	fresh, desserts	Bell
Carrisa *Carissa grandiflora*	shrub	C, S	year-round	small, red, milky juice	fresh, salads, sauce, juice	
Cattley guava *Psidium littorale*	shrub	C, S	July-Aug.	small, round, red or yellow	fresh, juice, jelly	
Cherimoya *Annona cherimola*	small tree	S	summer	large, green, sweet white flesh	fresh, juice	
Coconut *Cocos nucifera*	palm tree	S	year-round	large spherical nut covered with fibrous husk	fresh, drink, ice cream, oil	Malayan Dwarf
Feijoa *Feijoa sellowiana*	shrub	N, C, S	summer-fall	medium, gray-green, many small seeds	fresh, jelly, preserves	Choiceana, Coolidge, Superba
Jaboticaba *Myrciaria cauliflora*	small tree	C, S	all year	small, maroon to black, white gelatinous pulp	fresh, jelly, jam, wine	
Jujube *Zizyphus jujuba*	small tree	N, C, S	fall	small, oval, yellow to brown	fresh, dried, preserved	Leon Burk, Tigertooth
Longan *Euphoria longana*	medium tree	S	July-Aug.	small, spherical to ovoid, light brown, gelatinous	fresh, dried	Kohala
Macadamia *Macadamia intergrifolia*	medium tree	C, S	July-Nov.	small, nut enclosed in a hard shell	fresh, processed nuts	
Mamey sapota *Calocarpum sapota*	large tree	S	summer	large, ovoid to ellipsoid with brown skin; flesh red to brown	fresh, ice cream, jelly, conserves	Copan, Magana, Mayapan, Pantin, Tazumal
Miracle fruit *Synsepalum dulcificum*	small tree	S	year-round	small, oval, red, sweet	fresh	
Monstera *Monstera deliciosa*	foliage plant	C, S	Aug.-Oct.	long, green, sweet, aromatic	fresh, salads	
Prickly pear *Opuntia ficus-indica*	cactus shrub	N, C, S	Aug.-Sept.	small, pear-shaped, yellow, red pulp	fresh	
Sapodilla *Manilkara zapotilla*	large tree	S	summer	small, round or egg-shaped, brown skin and flesh, sweet	fresh, juice, jelly	Brown Sugar, Mondello, Prolific, Russell
Sea grape *Coccoloba uvifera*	medium tree	C, S	summer	small, globose to pear-shaped, white or dark purple skin	fresh, jelly, jam, wine	
Tamarind *Tamarindus indica*	large tree	S	April-June	pod; brown, acid pulp around seeds	drinks, sauce, preserves, chutney	
White sapote *Casimiroa edulis*	medium tree	S	spring-summer	medium, custardlike, sweet, yellowish pulp	fresh, marmalade	Blumenthal, Coleman, Dade, Maltby

17
Gardens for special places

BOUNTIFUL HARVESTS CAN be produced in unlikely places. A window box, patio container or bag of soil can be used to grow food. Why waste the space on purely decorative plants? Leaves of lettuce, spinach and chard can be very attractive. Some pretty flowers are edible and most edible fruits are ornamental.

Gardeners cramped for space grow herbs on a bathroom windowsill, tomato plants in bags of soil on a concrete patio and a blueberry bush in a tub beside the door. Find a way to put edible plants in a bright, sunny area and they will yield leaves, flowers and fruit.

Most vegetables and many types of fruit don't mind a bit of crowding. Varieties have been developed for small spaces. Trees sometimes can be dwarfed by pruning. Where there is room for a vine to meander, let it seek its own light — just remember there needs to be a way to get the harvest.

Windows

Many popular herbs and vegetables can be grown on a windowsill. Leafy crops usually will survive with only half a day of sun, but edible fruit and flowers, including broccoli, cauliflower and open squash blossoms, require full sun. Based on light available, here are some suggestions for the first-time windowsill gardener. Choose dwarf varieties when possible.

Use pots, planter boxes or impro-

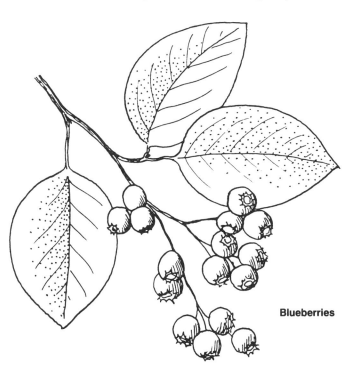
Blueberries

Sun requirements of vegetables, herbs

Vegetables		
Half-day sun	**Full sun**	
Collards	Broccoli	Onions
Lettuce	Carrots	Peppers
Mustards	Collards	Radishes
Onions	Cucumbers	Spinach
Spinach	Eggplant	Squash
Turnips	Lettuce	Tomatoes
	Mustards	Turnips

Herbs	
Half-day sun	**Full sun**
Basil	Basil
Chives	Chives
Marjoram	Dill
Mints	Marjoram
Oregano	Mints
Parsley	Oregano
Thyme	Parsley
	Thyme

vise containers. Especially when operating on such a limited scale, avoid problems by buying or making a potting mix. To make, combine equal parts of peat moss and perlite with half a tablespoon of dolomitic lime added to each gallon.

The prepared mix gives plants a loose, porous medium in which to sink their roots. It is moisture-retentive, pH-adjusted to about 6.5 and, at least to start with, free of soil-borne insects and diseases.

Make sure containers have drainage holes and place a tray of pebbles beneath. This lets water drain but keeps it off the woodwork. The plants appreciate the extra humidity as water evaporates from the pebbles up among the leaves.

Don't forget that windows provide not only flat surfaces but also air space. Tomatoes and cucumbers have been developed especially to be grown in hanging baskets. Many herbs also are suitable.

Start with seeds, sets or transplants. Adventurous gardeners consider seeds to be the only way to obtain many herbs and vegetables. Onion sets quickly provide ready-to-eat scallions and, provided they choose the right varieties, container gardeners can get a head start on tomatoes, peppers and eggplants by using transplants.

Once seeds or plants are set in soil, don't be stingy with water, but do wait until it is needed. Young plants can go a few days between waterings while large vegetables and herbs may need moisture once or twice a day. Soak plants each time until moisture seeps from containers, then wait to water again until the soil feels slightly dry.

Gardeners with just a few crops to tend can add a quarter of a teaspoon of 20-20-20 or other high-analysis fertilizer to a gallon of water and simplify feeding by using this solution every time they water.

Light comes in windows from only one direction, while to be productive, plants need light from all sides. Develop a schedule for turning plants once or twice a week. Once they start to wander, vines may need gentle guidance to keep them in the best light.

Harvests from window gardens are likely to be small and soon over. Don't allow the space to sit idle. As one crop finishes, start another. Expect some pests. Most can be hand-picked or washed away with soapy water. Only in rare instances will pesticides be needed. When they are, take plants outdoors for spraying. Don't bring them back until chemicals have dried and odors have subsided.

Patios

Patios give growers more scope. Pyramid gardens, raised beds and containers on wheels are possibilities. Available light is a limiting factor, but it is always likely to be brighter outside than indoors.

Where every inch counts, gardeners don't have space to waste on the

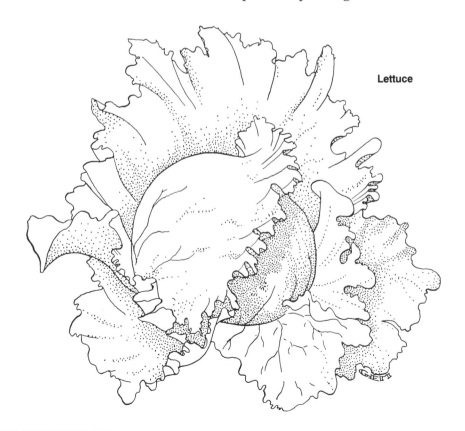

Lettuce

Windowsill garden

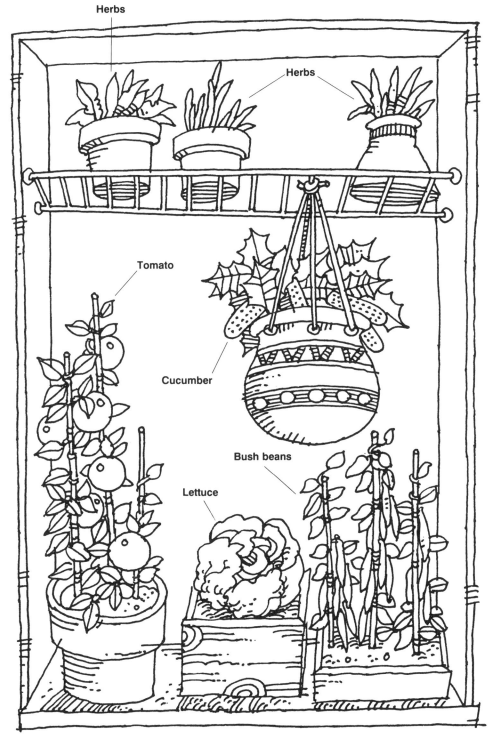

Bright windows can become good production areas for herbs and vegetables. Add extra shelves and hang plants to get full use of available light. Turn crops periodically for better sun exposure.

pests and weeds that come with ordinary garden soil. Make or buy a soilless potting mix. It's usually cheaper in large amounts, but growers who can't afford as much potting medium as they need can combine relatively clean soil with plain peat moss.

The bigger the container, the better. A 12-inch pot holds more than twice the few carrots or radishes that fit a 6-inch pot. Growing beans becomes a possibility. Small varieties of tomatoes grow in 1-gallon buckets, but 5-gallon planters permit the large types.

Most vegetables and herbs have shallow root systems, so containers do not have to be deep. A depth of 8 to 12 inches usually is adequate.

Because space is at a premium, be imaginative. Replace purely ornamental plants with ones that are dual-purpose. Instead of ligustrum, try a lime, fig or blueberry. For overhead shade and fruit to boot, choose a mango, avocado or loquat and keep it trimmed to size.

Because they are close to buildings, patio gardens may provide just enough extra protection for marginally hardy plants to succeed. Even in northern sections of the state, patio gardeners can sneak cold-sensitive trees through winter by using innovative plant covers and a little heat.

Big plants need big containers. Wooden boxes 2 feet square and 18 inches deep, half-barrels, clay pots and large nursery tubs all work. Consider setting them on rollers so plants can be moved against the house for shelter from a freeze or into a better patch of sun.

Good drainage is essential. Don't be fooled into thinking a layer of rocks in the bottom of a pot can substitute for drainage holes. Make sure water drains from the base of containers or into bare ground from raised beds. Set tubs on pebbles or wedges of wood so they don't sit in puddles.

Container gardening is intensive gardening. Patio gardens can't look after themselves. Their No. 1 requirement is water. Water thoroughly every time the soil surface begins to dry. A drip system and a timer can tend this chore when watering by hand is not feasible. Just check frequently to ensure that plants are getting enough moisture and that none of the emitters are clogged.

Potted plants need frequent feeding. Herbs and vegetables do best fed twice a week with a half-strength solution of 20-20-20. Mix half a tablespoon to a gallon of water and drench the soil at each application. Most trees and shrubs do fine given 20-20-20 mixed at usual strength once a week during warm months.

Time-release fertilizers make the job easier and more economical. Read the label, choose a product that contains only fertilizer and apply as instructed to take care of the next several months. Anything labeled for use on foliage and other container-grown plants is fine.

Gardeners with drip irrigation systems can feed as they water. Fertilizer injectors and regulators add measured amounts of nutrients to the system; follow manufacturers' instructions.

To take most advantage of space and to keep them looking their best, patio plants need extra attention. Think of it as large-scale bonsai. Vegetables and fruiting woody plants can be pinched back, pruned, tied and trained. Grow as many crops as possible skyward, along a trellis, fence or wall. Try an espaliered apple or pear — or weave several together to form a living screen.

Even large plants will conform. Citrus, mangoes and avocados can be kept to 12 feet tall and still provide a harvest. Prune regularly to restrict growth. When new shoots have grown a foot or two, cut out a

Patio garden

Fruit and vegetables can take the place of ornamentals on the patio. Use trees, shrubs and vines for permanent plantings and fill in with herbs and vegetables grown in pots and planters.

few inches to cause branching. Use heavy wire or a length of wood to temporarily reinforce angles and direction.

Pests will be the same but may be easier to control than in a full-size garden or orchard. Be vigilant against invaders. Many can be handpicked or washed away. See Chapter 18 for specific recommendations on insects and diseases.

Greenhouses

When the weather is fine, few gardeners see the need for a greenhouse. However, an enclosed habitat provides security — a haven from the elements for both plant and grower. It also is a good place to extend the season, allowing production of warm-season crops when the weather outside is nippy.

Temperatures don't have to freeze for crops to stop producing. Temperatures consistently below 60 degrees keep many warm-season vegetables and types of tropical fruit from maturing. Most tomatoes won't set buds once temperatures fall below 55 degrees. Young transplants may turn yellow, unable to use available nutrients. Peppers, eggplant, cucumbers and melons are affected similarly.

A gardener with a greenhouse can be sure of bringing cold-sensitive trees and shrubs through the winter. Pineapple and banana plants in pots, even limes, avocados and mangoes if they're kept to minimal heights, can be ushered inside before temperatures plummet.

Damage is more likely when plants are young and small. A greenhouse can provide protection during the first year or two, until stems toughen enough to resist the cold.

Gardeners with a place to start transplants get a head start on the season. Seeds germinate better and transplants make maximum growth when protected from rain and wind. Grown under cover and heated at night, vegetable seedlings can be ready for the garden in six to eight weeks even in the middle of winter.

A start in a greenhouse also can be useful with some tropical plants. To be sure of fruit by fall in Central and North Florida, plant papaya seeds in November or December so transplants are ready for the garden by March.

Passion fruit vines grown from cuttings over the winter also can give a harvest by fall.

With all their season-extending advantages, greenhouses typically are built just for fun — because gardeners enjoy green smells and playing in the soil. The bill can be staggering. Strong, long-lasting metal and glass structures can cost thousands of dollars; even more if they include amenities such as stainless steel benches, air conditioning and retractable shades.

Most gardeners go a more moderate route and rely on wood, fiberglass and polyethylene. All of these materials are more or less perishable. Moist greenhouse conditions, for example, will quickly rot most natural lumber. Wood used in a greenhouse should be pressure-treated. Gardeners who grow plants such as bromeliads — including pineapples — which are sensitive to the copper used in treated lumber, will need to substitute native cypress.

Fiberglass and polyethylene are shorter-lived but cheaper than glass. Fiberglass for greenhouses is extra heavyweight; grower supply companies carry it in 4-foot-wide sheets. Polyethylene for a greenhouse needs to be resistant to ultraviolet light so it doesn't degrade rapidly in the sun.

Whatever material is chosen, it should transmit near-white light. Clear glass, fiberglass or plastic can be given a temporary cover of shade cloth or paint if light levels are too intense.

The purpose of a greenhouse is to help plants survive the most adverse conditions. For most plants, the hardest time is winter, when the sun's arc is low in the sky.

There are fewer hours of winter light. Because it travels through more atmosphere, it is not as strong. Plants need maximum light exposure during winter months. The sun's rays arrive at a slant, so it is important that the sides of a greenhouse as well as the roof let in as much light as possible.

Situate a greenhouse where it will receive full sun, and try to balance other considerations. A north-south orientation gives individual plants optimum exposure. If it is attached to a building, however, put a greenhouse on the south side.

Look out for shadows from nearby trees or buildings — shadows

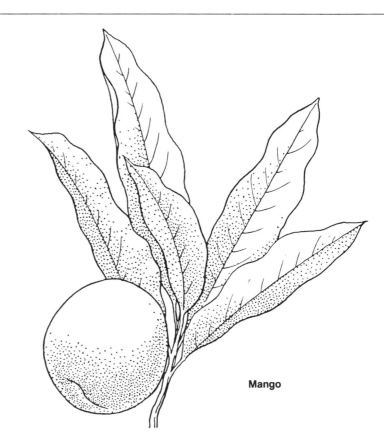

Mango

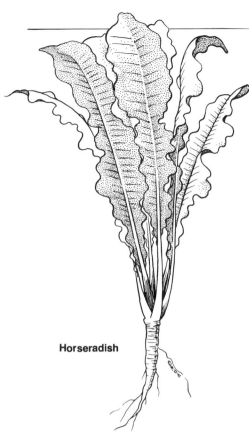
Horseradish

will be at their longest from late fall through early spring. Try to provide a location that gives some protection from winter's harsh northerly and northwesterly winds.

Greenhouse ventilation is extremely important. Summer temperatures in an enclosed greenhouse quickly reach over 120 degrees. Even on a cold winter day heat will build up to nearly 100 degrees.

Vents in the roof or sides are essential. Push them open for cooling and to reduce the humidity that fosters many diseases. An easy way to ventilate a hobby greenhouse is to hinge the sides. Prop them open in winter and remove them entirely in summer.

Even a small greenhouse needs a fan to move the air, reduce humidity and regulate the temperature. In winter, fans distribute sun-warmed air. They help cool the place in summer. Special greenhouse fans are available, but many gardeners use portable home units.

Clear glass, plastic or fiberglass doesn't hold much warmth on a cold winter's night. Depending on what they grow, most gardeners will want to add some form of heat. In general, tropical plants are injured when temperatures dip below 55 degrees. Warm-season crops take temperatures down to 45, and very hardy crops, to 35. Many gardeners will spend $40 to $50 in a winter to heat a small greenhouse.

If positioned away from damp locations, electric heaters provide safe, clean heat for small greenhouses. Kerosene and gas heaters usually are reserved for larger structures. Be sure to operate heaters according to instructions and ventilate properly.

A gardener with a greenhouse can enjoy edible and ornamental plants year-round:

● **Fall**

Germinate seeds of cool-season vegetables and flowers.

Grow transplants for the garden.

Cultivate vegetables for winter production.

● **Winter**

Shelter cold-sensitive fruit, vegetable and foliage plants.

Start transplants for tropical fruit that need long growing seasons.

Germinate cool- and warm-season fruit and vegetables.

Grow and harvest vegetables, fruit and herbs — a garden in containers.

Garlic

Revive winter-weary windowsill herbs and vegetables.

● **Spring**

Germinate warm-season vegetables, fruit and herbs.

Start new plants from cuttings.

Grow pots of vegetables and herbs as replacements for the garden.

● **Summer**

Germinate warm-season vegetables and herbs.

Grow replacement plants for the garden.

Greenhouse culture is another variation on container gardening. Plants grow in pots or beds filled with prepared medium. Soil substitutes can be purchased or made from equal parts peat and perlite with half a tablespoon of dolomitic lime added to each gallon of mix.

Any improved soil can be used, but in a hothouse atmosphere where plant problems can develop quickly, the growing medium must be relatively pest-free.

Follow normal procedures for starting new plants from seeds or cuttings. A greenhouse merely provides a sheltered place for gardeners to do whatever they ordinarily would do outdoors. Shade cuttings and seeds at first. Give them full sun when they begin to grow.

In the warmth and light of a greenhouse, plants can use surprising amounts of water. Check daily. Small seedlings may stay damp for a day or two, but vigorous transplants and full-grown plants may need water twice a day.

Greenhouse seedlings and plants quickly outgrow containers. Leave seedlings and plants too long in their pots and growth will stall. Root-bound plants will be slow to start growing again.

Pot plants into larger containers or be ready to move them outdoors to the garden. Growers who have a garden ready and waiting for their transplants can be proud of their timing.

Rapid growth calls for liberal use of fertilizer. Liquid fertilizers are convenient. Apply them in solution to moist soil, watering plants thoroughly.

For gardeners whose needs outgrow a watering can, garden centers

Garden in the greenhouse

Extend gardening fun with a greenhouse filled with fruit and vegetables. Best planted during the cooler months, the greenhouse provides shelter from wind and cold and extends the season for warm-weather crops into winter. Seedlings and transplants also can be started here, then moved to the garden or landscape.

sell a siphoning device that connects a bucket to a hose. Do safeguard the water supply by installing a backflow preventer at the faucet. This is especially important when applying fertilizer and pesticides through siphons and hose-end sprays.

For rapid growth of seedlings, transplants and container crops, feed twice weekly using a half-strength solution of half a tablespoon of 20-20-20 to a gallon of water. Once a week will do for crops approaching harvest, but mix the fertilizer full-strength, using 1 tablespoon per gallon.

Slow-release fertilizers are even easier. Find them at garden centers and wholesale supply companies and follow label instructions. In general, the encapsulated nutrients are sprinkled over the soil surface. They release food to the plant during the next three to four months when the plant is watered.

Plants wintering in the greenhouse may need less attention. Short days and cooler weather often induce a semidormant state. Plants that are barely growing need less water and fertilizer, and some days the chore can be skipped altogether. Water when the surface soil begins to dry. Begin to fertilize when plants begin to grow again, usually in late winter.

Expect pests to thrive in the greenhouse. See Chapter 18 for the kinds of problems to expect. When plants grow in such proximity, insects and diseases can spread rapidly. Keep alert for infestations and be prepared to act quickly. Sometimes prompt action — picking off just a few leaves or getting rid of one plant — will eliminate the need to spray. Biological controls also can be successful in the greenhouse.

Read labels carefully before selecting and applying a pesticide. Some products are approved for outdoor use but are not labeled for use in a greenhouse, where confined spaces and reduced ventilation concentrate the exposure and the risks. If insecticides or fungicides must be applied, this is the time to don protective clothing and a respirator.

Hydroponics

Growers who are ready to abandon their gardens to the nematodes and weeds can dump that bug-infested soil for a fresh start with hydroponic plant culture. Eliminate the problems that plague home plantings by trading backyard soil for a nutrient-enriched solution.

There are 16 essential nutrients, including hydrogen, oxygen and carbon from water and air, needed to make plants grow in liquids as well as they do in soil. Plants grown hydroponically often are healthier, and yields often are higher. It is easier to keep production techniques relatively sterile, maintain a high level of nutrition and avoid a number of pests.

Some people can't believe that hydroponic crops have as much nutritional value as fruit and vegetables grown in soil. Nutritionists say there is no significant difference. Does the taste change? Differences in varieties grown and climate, not cultural techniques, account for different flavors.

Hydroponic plant culture is rewarding because it gets results. For growers who stick to high-value crops like cucumbers, tomatoes and

Hydroponic garden

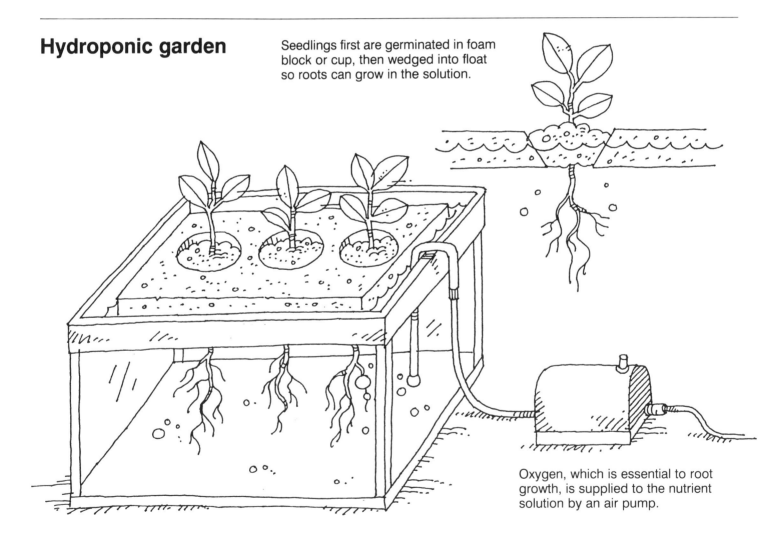

Seedlings first are germinated in foam block or cup, then wedged into float so roots can grow in the solution.

Oxygen, which is essential to root growth, is supplied to the nutrient solution by an air pump.

Grow vegetables without soil hydroponically. A Styrofoam float holds leaves and stems above water while roots feed in nutrient-rich tank of solution.

Hoagland solution

Salt	Grade	Nutrients	Per 25 gallons water	
			ounces	tablespoons
Potassium phosphate (monobasic)	technical	potassium, phosphorus	½	1
Potassium nitrate	fertilizer	potassium, nitrogen	2	4
Calcium nitrate	fertilizer	calcium, nitrogen	3	7
Magnesium sulfate	technical	magnesium, sulfur	1½	4

Trace element formulas

Salt (chemical grade)	Nutrients	Amount of water*	Amount to use**
Boric acid, powdered	boron	½ gallon	½ pint
Manganese chloride	manganese, chlorine	1½ gallons	½ pint
Zinc sulfate	zinc, sulfur	2½ quarts	½ teaspoon
Copper sulfate	copper, sulfur	1 gallon	1/5 teaspoon
Iron tartrate	iron	1 quart	½ cup
Molybdenum trioxide	molybdenum	1 quart	1 ounce

* Mix with 1 teaspoon salt for stock solution. ** Mix with 25 gallons of Hoagland solution.

lettuce, it can be profitable as well. Hydroponic gardens can be expensive. To set up less than 100 square feet of growing space can cost several hundred dollars.

Start small and test the waters. To experiment with a practical, purely hydroponic system, make a floating garden. Use a dishpan, aquarium or plastic-lined trough to hold a nutrient solution. Tanks need only be 6 to 8 inches deep. Paint transparent containers a dark color on the outside to discourage algae growth and to keep light from causing chemical changes in the solution.

Find rectangular panels of Styrofoam three-quarters of an inch to 1 inch thick at building supply stores. Cut a block to fit the tank, and suspend crops through small holes cut in the Styrofoam. Let roots dangle and grow in the nutrient solution.

Oxygen will be in short supply. For a small hydroponic unit, a gardener will need the kind of aerator used for a small aquarium or to keep fish bait alive.

Many nutrient solutions are available. A number are for sale, with all the chemicals ready to mix in water. Many gardeners like to experiment with making up their own, finding individual fertilizer salts locally or through mail-order supply houses.

Most start by making a general-purpose solution of the most important nutrients, then add small amounts of separate solutions of minor nutrients. After preparing and mixing all solutions, the resulting liquid is used to fill the growing tank. Turn on the aerator and it is ready to plant.

If the dishpan garden proves successful, the hydroponic approach can be expanded greatly. Many other techniques of hydroponic culture have been developed, along with the floating garden. For one of the simplest, fill a large bushel basket with mulch, insert transplants, and drench daily with a weak fertilizer solution.

More complicated schemes involve filling troughs with coarse aggregates and flowing nutrient solutions, but the basic principles are the same. Libraries and the cooperative extension service can provide more information.

For plant nutrients, first-timers should start with a recipe already proved successful. One of the oldest is the Hoagland solution, which supplies the most necessary nutrients of nitrogen, phosphorus, potassium, calcium and magnesium.

The accompanying tables provide information for preparing 25 gallons of basic solution and formulas for adding trace elements to the solution.

Gardeners working with chemicals — including fertilizer — should wear gloves. Also keep the ingredients and solutions out of the children's reach. It is best to store the

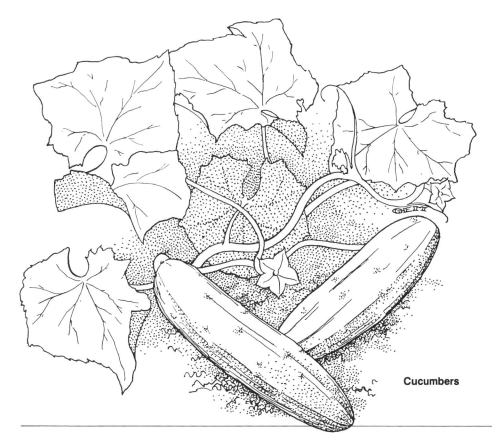
Cucumbers

Peppers

chemicals in a cool, dry, dark and secured room or storage area.

Prepare young plants for hydroponic culture by sowing seeds in a porous but supportive medium. Gray-colored Oasis blocks, available at floral design shops and gardening supply stores, are ideal. Cut the rectangular blocks into 1-inch cubes.

Make a shallow depression in each cube to hold a seed. Keep seeds moist by covering the cubes with newspaper until they germinate. Water like any other seedlings with a weak nutrient solution.

When roots grow out of the cubes, it is time to plant. Gently wedge the cubes into holes cut through the floating foam panel to secure the plants.

Alternatively, start seeds in Styrofoam coffee cups filled with perlite or vermiculite. Use a pencil to poke holes in the lower half and bottom of each cup. Sow seeds and keep moist.

When roots begin to grow through the pencil holes, take the float and cut holes smaller than the top circumference of the coffee cups. Gently wedge each cup into the float so the roots dangle in the nutrient solution.

Plants deplete nutrients from the solution as they grow. Plan to drain a tank and replenish the solution on a regular basis. Change the solution weekly during the first few weeks; twice a week as plants grow older. If the liquid level drops between changes, add water.

Use indicator paper, available at some garden centers, to monitor the acidity of the hydroponic solution. If the pH doesn't stay in the 6.5 to 7.0 range, nutrients may drop out of solution. If necessary, adjust the pH by adding acid or basic solutions.

Once they get the hang of making a nutrient solution, gardeners have only to train their plants and watch out for pests. Climbing plants, and plants that grow tall and might tip over, will need some sort of trellis. Control pests using the cultural and chemical techniques in Chapter 18.

Bags of soil

Have the most fun and the least fuss by growing plants in bags using a technique that is a cousin to hydroponic culture. Buy sterile potting soil, and let the bag it comes in be the container. Or mix your own potting medium in a thick plastic garbage bag.

Put a bag on a balcony, patio or vacant lot. It's portable, so the location can be temporary. Once a crop is finished, grab the sack and run. Many gardeners won't settle for just one bag but will plant several, each with a different crop.

Any flat surface in a sunny place can be the growing area. If the surface is soil, keep down competition from weeds and reduce contamination by stretching out a sheet of plastic before placing the bags flat on the ground.

Cut two slits about an inch long near the bottom of each bag for drainage. Slit the top of the bag, or make an X in the middle of the top, for planting.

Crops such as tomatoes, peppers, cucumbers and melons usually are installed as transplants; lettuce, beans, carrots and corn often are sown directly in the bags of soil.

Water and fertilizer tell most of the rest of the story. Gardeners who water by hand should check daily to see if the growing medium needs moisture.

However, bag culture lends itself to the more carefree system of drip irrigation. Kits, available from garden centers, are quick and easy to install. Place an emitter at each bag and the watering is accomplished by turning on the faucet. Better yet, set a computerized timer on the faucet and escape for the weekend, worry-free.

During the less stressful months, plan to water about twice a week for 20 minutes at a stretch. When plants are large, and during hot, dry weather, set the system to turn on every day or two. Monitor results and fine-tune the schedule as needed.

Sack garden with drip irrigation system

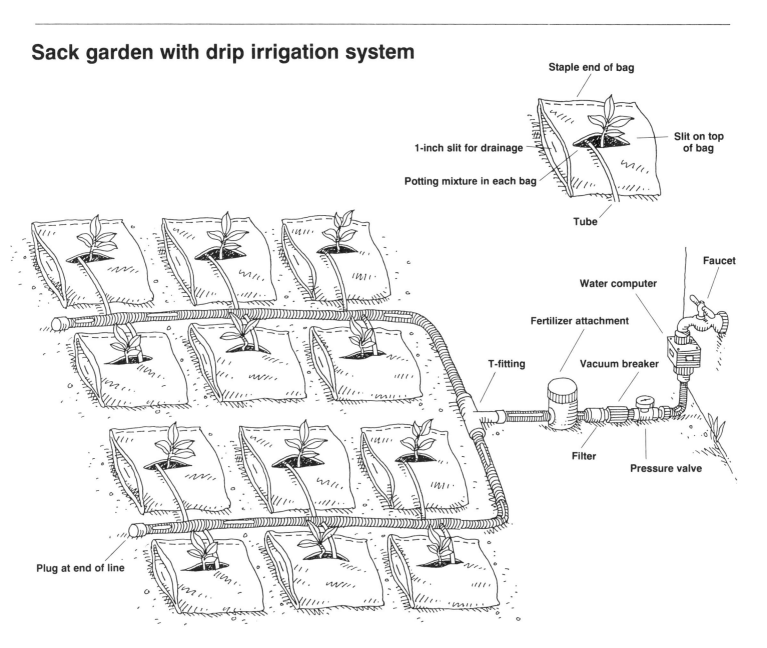

Sacks of soil become food production sites on patios, balconies or paved lots. Water the planted, soil-filled sacks by hand or add a drip irrigation system. A water computer controls the drippers at the bags. Fertilizer can be added during waterings to make the garden almost carefree.

To keep them growing vigorously, plants in bags will need regular doses of fertilizer. Check to see that soil is moist, then soak individual sacks twice a week with a half-strength solution of 20-20-20. Make maintenance easier by supplying fertilizer through the drip irrigation system.

Fertilizer tablets and other concentrated products made for this purpose can be found at garden centers. Follow manufacturers' instructions.

Vigorous plants may need vertical support. Maximize use of space by finding ways to hold cucumbers, tomatoes and other vining crops up off the ground. Bag culture is so easy that this may be the most time-consuming task connected with it.

Expect the usual pests, except that nematodes and other soil-borne organisms should not be a problem. To reduce threatening infestations, follow pest control suggestions in Chapter 18.

When one crop finishes, be ready with the next. Bags of soil can be used again. Sift out old stems and roots and replant. A clean bag of soil can produce several harvests before the soil becomes contaminated and it is time to add it to the in-ground garden or the compost pile.

18

How to control pests and diseases

SCARECROWS AND WHIRLIgigs won't keep harmful insects or plant diseases away, but pesticides may do more harm than good. It takes a balancing act to protect a particular crop while safeguarding the neighborhood.

"The only good bug is a dead bug" was the motto of growers who once poured on powerful new chemical controls as they became available.

Ironically, the effort to produce totally clean crops has contaminated soil and water, destroyed wildlife and injured growers and consumers. Even beyond environmental costs, the ongoing outlay turns out to be extremely expensive.

Now there is movement to use safe, natural pest controls, and it exerts a major influence at university research centers, in home gardens and on farms around the world.

Today, plant growers practice integrated pest management. It's a wait-and-see approach. When pests are anticipated, gardeners often are able to head them off by employing non-chemical techniques known to reduce pest problems.

Only when harmful insects and diseases reach threatening levels do growers apply controls. Today, they first try biological and natural controls.

Once found only in the pages of obscure gardening catalogs, these now appear on the shelves at many garden centers. Combined with good growing techniques, natural controls may do the job. With inte-

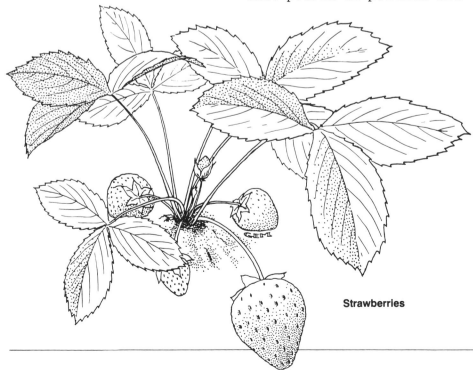
Strawberries

grated pest management, chemical controls are a last resort.

Know the enemy

Deciding what solution or combination approach to apply begins with properly identifying the problem. Knowing what insect is involved can help a gardener choose between options that can include handpicking, traps or low-toxicity pesticides.

Pests may not be visible when the sun is shining brightly. Stand and look — then stare a little. They may appear. Among other considerations, jumping for a pesticide without an enemy in sight may mean waiting a week or more before using the crop. It can take skill to find the culprits. Here are a few hints to help check for insects:

- Use a hand lens to look for small pests.
- Inspect under leaves and next to stems.
- Changes in stem and leaf color may be caused by insect gatherings — put the hand lens on the subject.
- Insects may fold over leaves to make a home — look inside.
- Some pests hit and run. Dig down in the soil near the stem.
- Cut open affected fruit. Pests may be lurking inside.
- Check at night with a flashlight — insects often feed while gardeners sleep.

Determine whether the insects found are responsible for the damage. Some insect invasions are secondary. The only bugs to be seen may merely be taking advantage of an existing situation. A few beetles in a fruit may have entered a hole made by a caterpillar or a crack caused by water damage. It's easy to jump to the wrong conclusion.

Some insects are on the gardener's side. Finding them may be a sign that the bad guys already are under attack.

A gardener may find ladybugs high in the orange tree among curled and damaged leaves. As adult bugs, orange-red with black dots, they are easy to identify. In the larval stage they resemble little dragons. At any stage they are beneficial, feeding on the unobtrusive little green, black or red aphids that cause damage.

Try to tolerate a few pests if the beneficial insects are at hand. They can provide sufficient control if plant producers and gardeners learn to live with a certain amount of damage. Only when the total crop is threatened should anyone reach for a pesticide.

If the following are on the scene, a problem may be under control without further intervention:

- Praying mantids, also called mantises.
- Lady beetles, also called ladybird beetles or ladybugs.
- Assassin bugs.
- Parasitic wasps (braconid wasps), which cocoon on surface of caterpillars.
- Lacewings.
- Wasps.

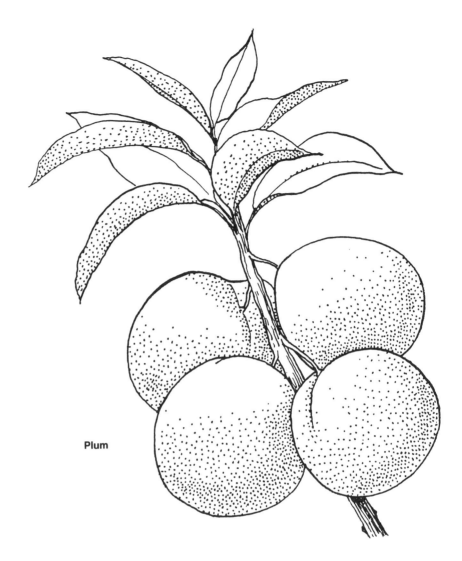
Plum

Non-chemical controls

■ BY HAND

Handpicking insects from plants is an age-old pest control that still works fine today. It seems silly to spray a whole plant trying to kill a small caterpillar. Even a cluster of the pests on one plant out of five hardly warrants the effort of priming the sprayer. Handpicking also is a good way to get to know the bugs.

It used to be the kids' job. Rewards may have been a penny for 12 caterpillars, or just room and board. The price of labor has gone up and dropping the bugs into a container of alcohol is a safer idea than the can of kerosene gardeners used to use, but youngsters still can be persuaded to pick the garden clean of bugs.

Be prepared to sacrifice a leaf or two. If a colony of aphids clusters on a growing tip, it may be best to cut it away. Leaves infested with leaf miners can be plucked away. Most healthy plants have leaves to spare, and it is worth cutting away a few leaves to discourage a developing infestation.

When there are just a few borers in the trunks of trees or stems of squash vines, they can be located and destroyed. Run a wire through the holes made in fruit trees to puncture the insects, or slit open a squash stem and pluck out the pest and destroy. Cover the cut squash stem with soil and the plant should continue to grow.

■ ENTRAPMENT

Some insects and related pests, especially slugs and snails, can be captured where they hide. Give them a false sense of security by providing places. Leave a board or pot in the garden path — they like the moist, cozy darkness found underneath. Then take an early morning stroll to collect the catch and do them in.

Other pests get stuck on sticky boards. A bright yellow shade is enticing to many bugs, and when they land on a properly gummy surface, they cannot fly away. Garden centers offer fancy and perhaps slightly higher-quality sticky boards, but many gardeners like to make their own.

To make one, use a 4-inch by 12-inch rectangle of bright yellow plastic. Coat one or both sides with petroleum jelly. Screw to a post or hang in the garden. Place several in the vicinity of susceptible plants to capture whiteflies, leaf miners and other flying pests.

■ MECHANICAL BARRIERS

Simple but effective barriers fool cutworms every time. Cutworms, the larval stage of a moth, usually leave volunteer seedlings alone but encircle and gnaw through the stem of transplants. They can't or won't climb a paper, cardboard or plastic-foam collar placed around the transplant's stem, however.

To make a barrier effective, press it into the soil and surround the first few inches of the stem above the ground. Install collars while setting transplants in the ground so as not to lose a single plant.

■ PREDACIOUS ORGANISMS

This is where pest control becomes more art than science. To start with, pest populations must build up enough to lure in the good bugs, so gardeners must learn to tolerate some bugs and plant damage in order to use these controls wherein one organism attacks another.

Beginner organic growers buy ladybugs and praying mantis egg cases to try to establish a local presence. Too often, however, these mobile insects move on to greener pastures. Researchers suggest gardeners opt for other good bugs, ones more likely to stick around.

Other allies against aphids are available; green lacewings, for example. Allow aphids to suck juices from plants and they will secrete honeydew, which attracts lacewings. Soon the voracious young, which resemble miniature alligators, can be observed feeding on the aphids.

Tiny braconid wasps lay eggs not among but inside the aphids. Their young devour their hosts from within, each leaving a mummified aphid body with a hole at the back showing where a young wasp has made an exit.

To avoid problems with mites, stop using pesticides. In landscapes that have not been treated, long-

Lady beetle

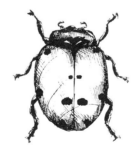

Lady beetles that are solid orange with black dots are common, but many forms live among garden and fruit plantings. Also called ladybird beetles and lady bugs, the immature stage resembles a miniature dragon. Both feed heavily on aphids.

Praying mantid

Brown and green forms of the praying mantid use their strong front legs to capture plant pests.

Lacewing

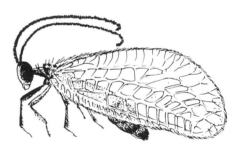

Lacewings and larvae, called trash bugs, are predators of aphids, mites and other plant pests.

legged predatory mites are quite prevalent and are a successful control.

A parasitic nematode termed a steinernematid eliminates a number of ground-dwelling insects, including caterpillars, mole crickets, root weevils, grubs and fungus gnats. This nematode seeks out immature stages and infests the pests with bacteria.

Usually the victims die within 48 hours and the nematode reproduces on the decomposing pest. Buy the nematodes, available from some mail-order companies, and apply to moist soil; they have a short life under dry conditions.

Ichneumon

The ichneumon, which resembles a wasp, will not sting but does parasitize insects that feed on crops.

Braconid wasps

Small, black braconid wasps parasitize caterpillars by laying eggs through the skin. Cocoons are spun on the surface as the young wasps near maturity.

Assassin bug

Usually inconspicuous in the landscape, assassin bugs have a long, curved piercing mouthpart for feeding on garden pests.

Nature controls caterpillars with the help of bacteria; now gardeners can too. Most garden centers sell commercial solutions of *Bacillus thuringiensis* bacteria to apply as a spray. Sensitive caterpillars consume treated plants and stop feeding; in a few days, they die. Like many natural controls, this one doesn't work overnight.

Biological controls can be as close as the garden center or may require a mail-order catalog. Garden centers stock products that store on the shelf, including *Bacillus thuringiensis* solutions, which is sold under several brand names, including Biotrol, Dipel and Thuricide.

Beneficial insects usually must be ordered from companies that grow and can quickly ship predators for release in gardens. Check Appendix III under organic gardening supplies, garden magazines or the local extension office for addresses.

■ NATURAL CHEMICALS

Plants yield a number of relatively non-toxic insecticides. Their effects can be tough on six-legged but mild on human consumers. Most have existed for years and are now being rediscovered by gardeners.

Even natural chemicals can harm the person applying them. Use them cautiously. Read the label and follow instructions. The label will state that pyrethrins, for example, kill fish and amphibians. Especially, take note of the time that must lapse between last use and harvest.

Practice the biological and non-chemical controls already discussed and hold these natural chemicals in reserve.

Gardeners who apply any insecticide run the risk of destroying beneficial insects. Killing local bees, for instance, can spell doom for much of a harvest. Try to avoid spraying during the early part of the day. For times when pests do

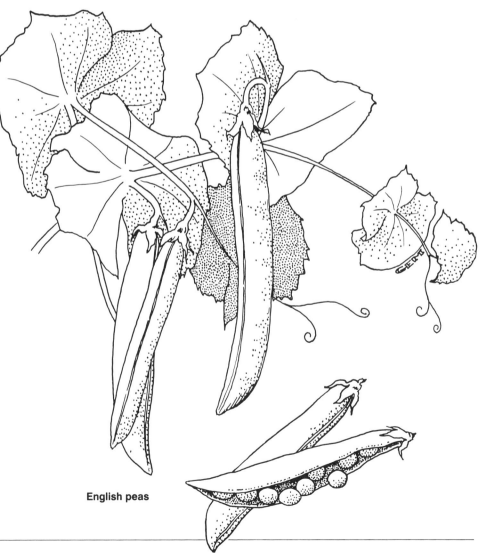

English peas

get out of hand, look for products considered to be among the safest.

■ SYNTHETIC INSECTICIDES

Usually the most toxic, petroleum-based and similar man-made pesticides are safe only in the hands of the most responsible gardeners. A careful reading of the label often scares gardeners out of their first spray. Many decide to stick to crops that don't call for such measures.

Some synthetic pesticides can be applied near harvest time, but most impose a substantial waiting period before the crop can be harvested. The time between last spray and harvest can help determine whether to use a particular pesticide. If the crop overripens while the pesticide residue wears off, it's too late to use this form of control.

Synthetic insecticides may save a harvest when all other methods have failed. It's probably good that labels cannot be lackadaisical. Too many gardeners have been affected by misused pesticides.

Agricultural workers have been contaminated by materials drifting down the cuffs of loosely fastened gloves. Wear gloves, coveralls, boots and goggles; to be especially safe, add a respirator. Such heavy protection may not always be necessary but is a good precaution in the face of increasing information about long-term effects.

Protective clothing and equipment used to apply pesticides should be stored separately, and gardeners must take care to avoid cleaning up anywhere where residues end up down the drain or otherwise contaminating ground water.

Rates of application are especially important with the more toxic chemicals. Gardeners always can use less, but never should add more pesticide to the tank than the label suggests.

Spray each plant so as to leave appropriate amounts of pesticide to control insects and diseases. Use of a spreader-sticker often helps the same amount of spray cover much more area.

Many synthetic pesticides are approved for home use. Read labels carefully to determine what to use on a problem.

Chemical controls for common insect pests

Natural	
Insecticide*	Pests
Azadirachtin	aphids, beetles, caterpillars, leafminer, vine borers, whiteflies
Bacillus thuringiensis	caterpillars
Insecticidal soap	aphids, mealybugs, whiteflies, spider mites, grasshoppers, scales
Oil	scales, mites, whiteflies
Pyrethrin	aphids, beetles, caterpillars, fruit flies, mites, thrips, weevils
Rotenone	aphids, beetles, caterpillars, fruit flies, mites, thrips, weevils
Synthetic	
Insecticide*	Pests
Diazinon	aphids, cutworms, mole crickets, thrips, leaf rollers, mealybugs, caterpillars, leafhoppers, beetles, grasshoppers
Dimethoate	leaf miners, mites, aphids, mealybugs, leafhoppers
Malathion	aphids, beetles, caterpillars, thrips, leaf rollers, whiteflies, leafhoppers
Sevin	caterpillars, beetles, leafhoppers, stink bugs, thrips

* Use pesticides only for crops listed on the label. Note time between last spray and harvest.

Common insect pests

■ APHIDS

Description: Pear-shaped. Various colors; may have wings. Cluster in new growth and under succulent leaves.

Damage: Cause new growth to curl and become distorted. Sooty mold often builds up on leaf surfaces.

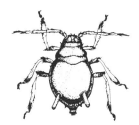

Controls: In small numbers, aphids can be tolerated or washed from plants with a mild soapy solution. Biological controls that may be released or found working in the garden include braconid wasps, lacewings and ladybugs.

In some vegetables, such as lettuce, aphids are a nuisance and apt to be an unwanted addition to a salad. Effective chemical controls range in toxicity from insecticidal soap, rotenone and pyrethrin to malathion and diazinon.

■ BEETLES

Description: Many kinds. May be striped, spotted or solid-colored. Usually less than half an inch in size. Common garden pests include

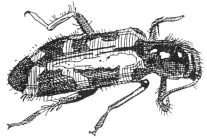

Colorado potato beetle, Mexican bean beetle, flea beetle and cucumber beetle.

Damage: Chew holes in leaves, stems, flowers and fruits.

Controls: Beetles may cluster on a plant or make several stops while feeding. Some can be tolerated, but large populations can destroy a crop. One of the easiest methods of control is handpicking into a container of alcohol and destroying the pests. Chemical controls include rotenone, Sevin and diazinon.

■ CATERPILLARS

Description: Many green or brown, but colors vary. May be striped along side or back. Less than an inch to several inches long.

Common garden pests include armyworms, cutworms, loopers, hornworms, bean leaf rollers and tomato pinworms.

Damage: Chew holes in stems, leaves, buds and fruit.

Controls: The ideal control is to handpick and destroy caterpillars when young. Some can be identified at the egg stage and rubbed from stems and foliage. Nests and webs can be cut from trees.

Stiff 3-inch collars of paper, cardboard or plastic foam around the stems of transplants prevent cutworm damage.

Spraying with the biological control *Bacillus thuringiensis* is effective against many species of caterpillars, and parasitic nematodes may be released to control caterpillars in the soil.

Chemical controls include rotenone, pyrethrin, Sevin and diazinon.

■ FLEA HOPPERS

Description: Black, one-eighth inch long with long legs. Skip quickly across leaf surfaces. Excrete black dots across the foliage where they feed.

Damage: Suck juices from foliage. Produce yellow-dotted leaf surface. Affected plants decline in vigor; if severely infested, they die.

Controls: These insects can be tolerated in small numbers but quickly build large populations. Chemical controls include a mixture of rotenone and pyrethrin; malathion; and diazinon.

■ LEAF MINERS

Description: Flylike adults rarely linger to be noticed by gardeners. Yellow maggots make tunnels beneath leaf surfaces; signs of their presence are white squiggly tracings and blotches on leaves.

Damage: Mostly cosmetic, but chewed leaves suffer reduced efficiency. Severely affected leaves turn brown and die.

Controls: Gardeners generally learn to put up with some leaf miner damage and control by picking and discarding affected leaves. Sticky boards will trap and help control the adults.

Although many chemicals are labeled for use on leaf miners, the insects quickly develop resistance. Products still found useful on some crops include Di-Syston, a soil treatment, and dimethoate, a foliar spray.

■ MEALYBUGS

Description: Soft-bodied. Covered with white, waxy powder, some with long waxy filaments from rear of body.

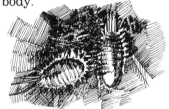

Damage: Suck juices. Leaves frequently wilt or drop. Plants weaken and decline rapidly.

Controls: Cut away and destroy portions of plants with heavy infestations. Daubing mealybugs with alcohol or washing them off plants with soap works well. Effective predators include the lacewing and the mealybug destroyer.

Chemical controls include insecticidal soap, malathion and diazinon.

■ MOLE CRICKETS

Description: Light brown, about 2 inches long when mature. Front legs are short, with shovellike feet for digging. Back legs are long, typical of crickets. Life cycle begins in the spring with numerous very small young hatching from eggs laid in the ground.

Damage: Mole crickets live mainly underground but come to the surface to feed. Tunnels raised about half an inch above the ground often disturb plant roots. Active crickets also can cut young plants off at ground level and pull them to a tunnel entrance.

Controls: Though many mole crickets in a garden can damage plants, a few should not cause concern. They are rarely a major prob-

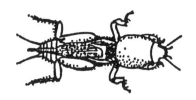

lem. Soil fumigation before planting may help if they are particularly prevalent.

Check the label of diazinon; for some crops, treating the soil before planting may be suitable.

■ SCALES

Description: Almost any color. Small, often less than a quarter of an inch, insects are covered by a waxy coating or shell that may be circular, oval, oblong or pear-shaped.

Damage: Suck juices. Cause leaves to yellow and die. Growth of stems and trunks is restricted; entire plant declines.

Controls: Pick or brush infected plants clean. Branches with major infestations can be cut and destroyed. Miscible oil sprays are ex-

tremely effective. Other chemical controls include insecticidal soap, malathion and malathion plus oil.

■ SLUGS AND SNAILS

Description: Not really insects at all, these are mollusks, with slimy, extremely soft, long bodies. A snail will pull into its spiral shell when disturbed. Eyes on stalks resemble horns. Brownish or gray in color. Leave slime trails.

Damage: Chew large, ragged holes in leaves and flowers.

Controls: Slugs and snails seek shelter during daylight hours; put out a moist board or pot for them to hide under. They like beer and will gather at a shallow dish of beer set in the garden.

Or, make a bait using one can stale beer, 1 pound brown sugar and 1 teaspoon 50 percent Sevin wettable powder. Mix until pasty, smear on the underside of a board and prop the board just above the soil.

A commercially available bait uses methaldehyde. Do not use poison baits around children or pets.

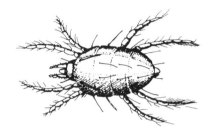

■ SPIDER MITES

Description: Very small; may be visible only under hand lens. Often eight-legged. Various colors. Often found on underside of leaves. When numerous, may form filmy webs.

Damage: Suck juices. Leaves turn silvery and curl, sometimes developing yellow dots. Plants rapidly deteriorate and die.

Controls: Mites quickly build large populations; numbers can double in just days. Many predatory mites exist; release more to aid in control.

Chemicals that help reduce mite infestations — but also will kill predatory mites — include insecticidal soap, oil sprays and sulfur.

■ STINK BUGS

Description: Large piercing-sucking insects half an inch to more than 1 inch long when mature. Identifiable by a shield-shaped back. Color ranges from green to brown and black in adults. All have an offensive odor when disturbed.

Common garden types include the green stink bug, brown stink bug, leaf-footed plant bug and big-legged plant bug.

Damage: Piercing-sucking feeding habits damage pods and fruit causing contortions and hardened

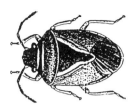

areas. Affected foliage and stems often wilt and turn brown.

Controls: A few stink bugs appear to be regular residents of any garden, and some are predacious instects. Controls are needed only when a large population or damage develops. Handpicking usually will suffice.

Chemical controls include insecticidal soap, pyrethrin, malathion, Sevin and diazinon.

■ THRIPS

Description: Small, linear black or yellow insects.

Damage: Rasp leaves and flowers, then suck the juices. Plant portions curl and brown.

Controls: The tiny insects often are overlooked until major damage occurs. Chemicals giving control in-

clude a combination of rotenone and pyrethrin, malathion and diazinon.

■ WEEVILS

Description: Adult insects have snoutlike mouthparts and are about an eighth of an inch long. The juvenile is grublike and white. Common types include the cowpea curculio and pepper weevil.

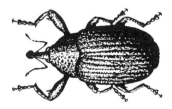

Damage: Weevils frequently feed inside fruit or vegetable pods. Females lay eggs in the flowers or fruit. The eggs grow into the grub-

like larvae that damage and discolor edible portions.

Controls: Prevention appears to be the only control. If expecting damage, begin spraying with malathion, Sevin or diazinon when plants bloom. Once infestations occur, handpick affected plant portions.

■ WHITEFLIES

Description: Light-colored adults resembling tiny moths swarm in a cloud when an infested plant is disturbed. Young are pale green and found on underside of leaves.

Damage: Suck juices. Generally weaken plant, leaving it susceptible to disease. Often responsible for buildup of sooty mold on leaves.

Controls: Give sticky boards a try to capture many of the adults before they lay their eggs. The whitefly parasitic wasp, whether released or living in the landscape, will help. Chemical controls include insecticidal soap, oil sprays, pyrethrin, malathion and diazinon.

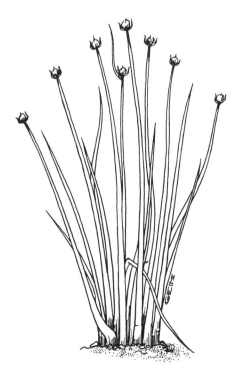

Bunching onions

181

Diseases

When foliage, stems or roots look blotched, spotted or blighted and insect culprits cannot be found, chances are a disease is to blame. The term disease tends to lump problems due to nematodes, nutritional and other cultural deficiencies together with problems caused by microorganisms, the ones considered here.

Fungus, bacteria and virus organisms range from barely visible to microscopic. Easiest to identify are the common fungi, often called molds. Plant problems such as leaf spots, blights, rots, mildews, scabs and galls often are caused by fungi. Many harbor in plant debris or in the soil and survive for long periods without a live plant to live off. They may need particular conditions before they start to grow and damage crops. Gardeners need to take care not to contribute to favorable conditions by supplying too much water or fertilizer.

A fungus reproduces by splitting off growing tips or by producing units known as spores. The reproductive bits are blown, washed or splashed, or carried by insects and animals, then await circumstances and openings for another round.

Like fungi, bacteria usually enter plants through wounds or natural openings. Once inside, they divide and multiply to cause fruit rots, wilts, galls and leaf spots. Mostly one-celled and very small, bacteria are washed easily about by rains or irrigation.

Viruses usually are transmitted by insects, sometimes by nematodes or humans and occasionally by contaminated seeds. Damage shows up as stunting, yellowing — which includes mottling and mosaics — and malformations such as twisted, puckered or unnaturally narrow leaves. The microscopic viruses consist of particles of nucleic acid with a protein coating. In a living host, the genetic material causes infected cells to produce more viruses. A virus may lie dormant in dead plant material for as long as 50 years.

Microorganisms lurk everywhere, and plants under stress are more susceptible. To keep disease from getting a start, maintain good growing conditions. Above all, use compost. Decomposing organic matter supports organisms that feed on pathogens; it substitutes for some fungicides. The more humus, the more beneficial nematodes — ones that attack the nematodes that injure plants. To help plants stay healthy:

Peach

- Plant in sunny locations where leaves dry rapidly.
- Make sure soil is well-drained.
- Remove old plant debris.
- Till soil before planting.
- Adjust soil pH to suit the crop.
- Choose disease-resistant plant varieties.
- Buy healthy-looking specimens; don't install sickly plants in the landscape.
- Keep growing areas weeded.
- Use mulches to conserve moisture, reduce weeds and control spore movement.
- Water thoroughly but no more often than needed.
- Too much fertilizer leads to weak, sappy growth that is susceptible to disease; do not exceed recommended amounts.
- Prune weak branches and diseased or dead wood from shrubs and trees.
- Rotate crops in the vegetable plot.

Gardeners are more efficient than insects in spreading disease. Don't handle plants when leaves are damp. After handling a diseased plant, wash hands, tools and bottoms of shoes and cleanly dispose of the debris.

Plants may succumb despite all precautions, especially if weather favors the disease. Almost always, plants infected with a virus must be discarded. No chemical treatments exist. A few pesticides work against bacterial diseases, and there are a good number of fungicides.

Some chemicals must be applied weeks before planting a crop. See Chapter 4 on soil preparation for instructions on using the fumigant Vapam, as well a description of soil solarization. Both procedures control many soil-related problems, including diseases.

Gardeners apply most fungicides in the form of sprays or drenches during the growing season. Products may be classified as natural or synthetic products. Consider all of them toxic and follow label instructions to the letter.

Common diseases

◼ POWDERY MILDEW

Most plants are susceptible to this white fungus. White circles usually appear first under older leaves. The spots grow larger, grow together and eventually cover both surfaces and stems of most leaves. Leaves turn pale, then shrivel and brown. Flowering and photosynthesis are inhibited.

Warm, humid weather favors development. Encourage good air movement among plantings. Gardeners usually can wait until the organism begins growth before applying controls.

Keep plants widely spaced to encourage air circulation. Wait until the disease appears to apply a fungicide.

◼ RUST

These fungi stunt and sometimes kill plants as they cover leaves with pustules of reddish brown spores. Rub them and they leave a finger streaked rusty brown. High humidity encourages their growth.

Planting resistant varieties is the best control. Space plants to provide good air movement. Fungicides offer some control when applied early.

◼ DOWNY MILDEW

This fungus disease often attacks squash, cucumbers and melons, covering leaves with yellow to brown angular spots about a quarter of an inch across. Especially in wet conditions, the spots quickly develop a grayish mold on the underside of the leaves. Leaves droop, turn brown and die. Other diseases often join the party.

For the best control, plant resistant varieties. If none is available, do preventive spraying with fungicide during moist, humid weather.

◼ SEEDLING BLIGHTS

Even sterile planting mediums aren't free for long of the many fungal organisms that rot soft, young plants at ground level. Often called damping off, it is a common problem for seedlings started indoors where conditions are less than ideal. Seedlings in the garden may have trouble too, especially if the ground is soggy, the air doesn't circulate or the weather is cloudy, cold or wet.

Seed treatments and preplant fungicides are available for the most susceptible crops. Soil fumigation may help. The best solution is to provide the best possible growing conditions, giving well-spaced seedlings bright light, good air movement and well-drained soil.

◼ FIRE BLIGHT

Fire blight is a bacterial disease of plants in the rose family including apples, pears and loquats; main-

Powdery mildew

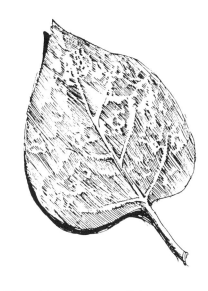

The white powdery mildew fungus grows across the surface of squash, melons, beans and other vegetables as well as some fruit trees. Plant vigor and production usually are reduced.

Rust

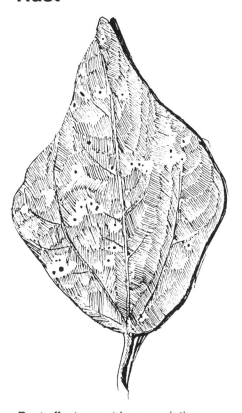

Rust affects most bean varieties. Pustules of brown spores are surrounded by yellow halos of infected leaf tissue.

Chemical controls for common diseases

Natural	
Chemical	Diseases controlled
Bordeaux mixture	blights, leaf spot, fruit rots, scab
Coppers	leaf spot, blights
Garden sulfur	powdery mildew, rusts, scab, brown rot

Synthetic	
Chemical	Diseases controlled
Captan	fruit rots, blights, leaf spot, downy mildew, scab
Chlorothalonil	leaf spot, downy mildew, blights, powdery mildew, scab, fruit rots, rust
Copper formulations	leaf spot, blights
Mancozeb	leaf spot, downy mildew, scab, blights, fruit rots
Maneb	leaf spot, downy mildew, blights, scab
Zineb	rust, leaf spot, downy mildew, leaf blight

ly a problem of spring and early summer.

Fire blight attacks new growth, rapidly turning it brown or black and leaving it looking scorched. Not only leaves and flowers but entire limbs may die.

Prune affected portions back into healthy growth. Forestall the disease by spraying at regular intervals during flowering and through spring.

■ FUSARIUM WILT

Fungi that cause wilt clog the tissues that conduct water in vegetables including tomatoes, sweet potatoes, watermelons, cabbages, Southern peas and beans.

As they approach maturity, affected plants wilt, turn yellow and die. Cut lower stems lengthwise to find signs of the characteristic brown streaking.

Choose resistant varieties whenever possible. Stressed plants are more vulnerable: tomatoes grown in dried-out soil under winter sun, peas in soggy soils, plants sapped by nematodes.

Affected plants cannot be saved. Remove and destroy them. Avoid replanting a crop in an infected site — spores remain viable for years — or fumigate the soil.

■ LEAF SPOTS

Most plants are susceptible to one or more bacterial as well as fungal organisms that cause spots on leaves. First yellow, then brown, the center may drop out of a spot, leaving it looking as though an insect did the damage. Leaf spots flourish when the weather is warm and wet or rainy; even dew will make things worse.

Use resistant varieties when possible and keep the leaves as dry as possible by directing water to the soil surface and irrigating during sunny hours. Never work among wet plants. Some gardeners spray at the first sight of infection; fungicides usually control leaf spot.

■ FRUIT ROTS

Most fruit is susceptible to disease from the moment it forms until harvest.

Starting with brown or black spots, often an entire fruit turns mushy and bad-smelling. Excessive moisture or unfavorable weather

Downy mildew

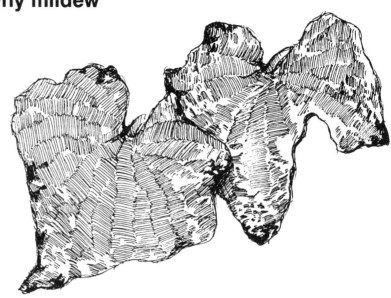

Downy mildew produces yellow to brown, often angular, spots on the foliage of squash, cucumber and melon crops. Spots on the lower leaf surface may be covered with a downy mold.

Seedling blights

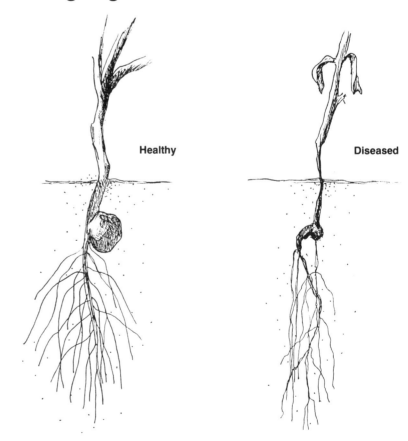

Seedling blights rapidly cause young plants to shrivel and dry. Avoid overwatering and plant in clean soil to prevent this fungal disease.

hastens the process.

Depending on the crop, fungicide sprays may begin with fruit formation and intensify as harvest nears.

Carefully select products to use on each particular fruit, noting time between last spray and harvest.

■ BLIGHTS

A catchall term for diseases that quickly turn foliage and stems black or brown. Many fungi and some bacteria produce symptoms in many vegetables.

Well-grown plants in good soil will be the most resilient. Crop rotation also helps.

Gardeners with persistent problems resort to soil fumigation and fungicide treatments.

■ GALLS

Fungi and bacteria may enter wounds or bruises and cause plant cells to multiply abnormally at the site. Then puffy, enlarged galls, sometimes with a leathery exterior, show up on stems, leaves or roots. Plant vigor is reduced; secondary infections can cause decay.

Avoid potential problems; carefully check plants before buying and insist on pest-free specimens.

On a plant with home-grown gall, prune away affected portions if possible, then sterilize the shears with rubbing alcohol to avoid spreading the disease.

Fumigating the soil before replanting may take care of previous infestations.

■ USE PESTICIDES SAFELY

Read the label when selecting a pesticide. Make sure the crop it will be used on is listed. It is a misuse of the product to use it on any plant not specifically mentioned. Improper application could be harmful.

The person using a pesticide should be the only one to handle it. Keep children, pets and other adults away from mixing and spraying. Don't leave pesticides accessible; secure them in a cabinet when not in use.

Let family members know when spraying will take place and keep them informed of when it will be safe to harvest a planting.

Consider wearing protective clothing, gloves and boots, a respirator and a mask. Feeling silly is a

Fire blight

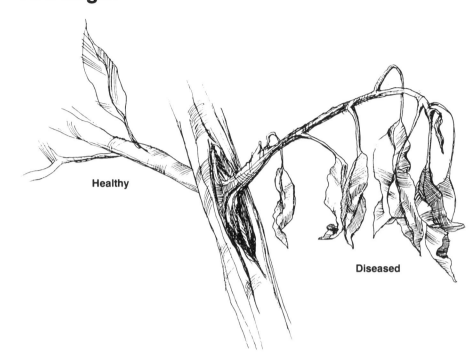

Fire blight affects members of the rose family, including apples and pears. The rapidly browning flowers, fruit and limbs should be pruned from the tree.

Fusarium wilt

Fusarium wilt is a disease in which the water-conducting tissues of the plant are plugged by bacterial or fungal organisms. The best controls are to use clean soil and plant resistant varieties.

Leaf spots

Leaf spots have many shapes and colors. Most will need to be controlled to prevent reduced plant growth and production.

Brown rot

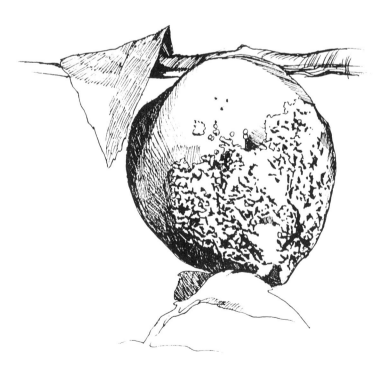

Brown rot affects peaches, nectarines and plums. As with most fruit diseases, preventive control must begin before damage is noticed.

Blight

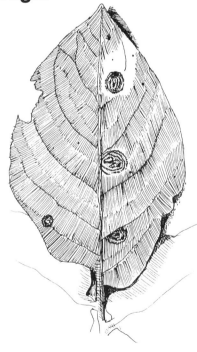

Blights cause the rapid decline of landscape plantings. Leaves may become spotted and brown, or entire limbs may decline.

Crown gall

Crown gall is first noticed as a proliferation of plant tissue near the soil line. It is caused by bacteria. Good grafting techniques and sanitation practices are the best forms of prevention.

small price to pay for protection from spills and accidental drift.

Make applications thorough; wet all portions of a plant. Doing the job thoroughly may reduce the need for repeat applications. A sticker-spreader can help in the task, effectively wetting waxy bits of plant as well as pests. Products that do not benefit from the use of a sticker-spreader will mention the fact on the labels.

Pesticides can be used in a responsible manner. Use the following as guidelines:

• Read the label.

• Choose the safest pesticide for the problem.

• Consider wildlife when making a selection.

• Apply pesticides on calm days.

• Mix pesticides in a well-ventilated area.

• Make careful measurements and completely use pesticides once mixed; don't store leftovers.

• Clean spills immediately.

• Thoroughly clean equipment.

• Triple rinse and wrap empty bottles in newspaper for disposal with trash.

• Properly dispose of unused pesticide concentrates, not in the garbage but at a hazardous waste collection point.

• Maintain records of what pesticides were applied and when.

• Use the pesticide completely or share with someone who can.

• Small quantities of pesticide solutions can be applied to other landscape pests as labeled.

Cover up for best protection from pesticides

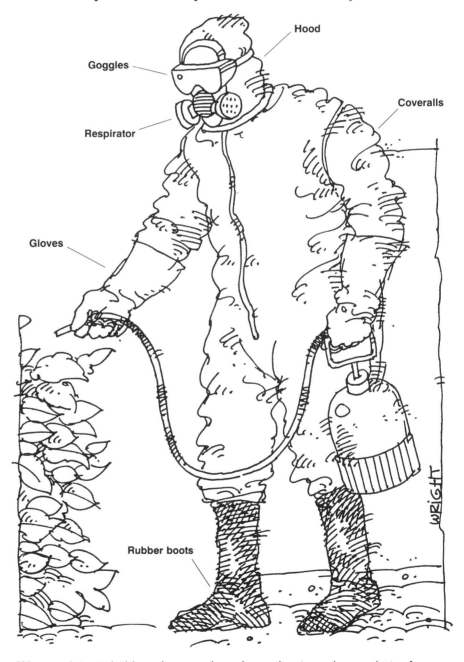

Wear resistant clothing plus goggles, gloves, boots and a respirator for maximum protection from pesticide drift. Clean pesticide residues from protective gear after use. Do not launder coveralls with other clothing.

Appendix I

Vegetable profiles

Key to vegetable profiles

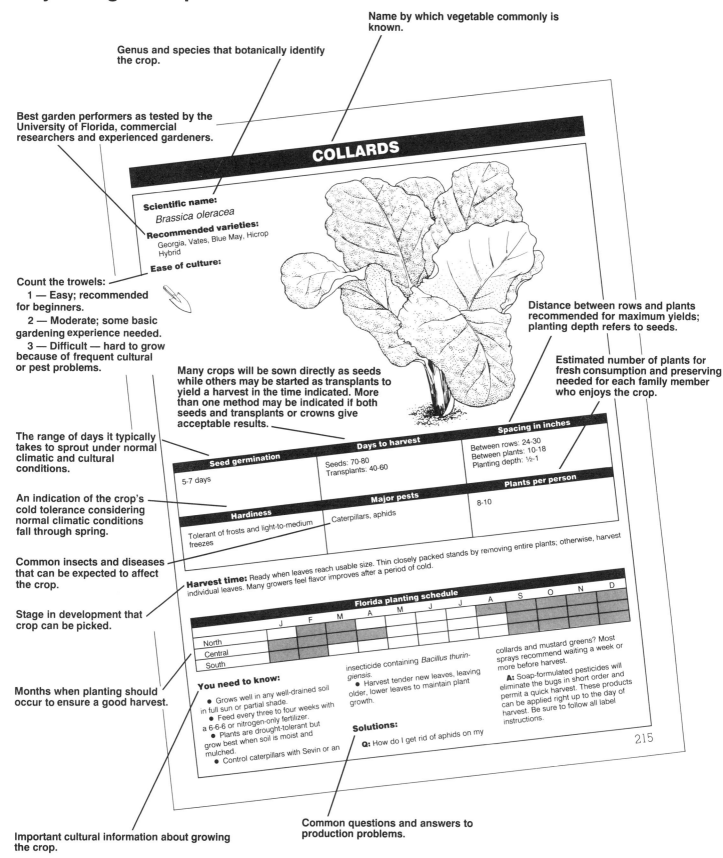

- **Name by which vegetable commonly is known.**
- **Genus and species that botanically identify the crop.**
- **Best garden performers as tested by the University of Florida, commercial researchers and experienced gardeners.**
- **Count the trowels:**
  1 — Easy; recommended for beginners.
  2 — Moderate; some basic gardening experience needed.
  3 — Difficult — hard to grow because of frequent cultural or pest problems.
- **Many crops will be sown directly as seeds while others may be started as transplants to yield a harvest in the time indicated. More than one method may be indicated if both seeds and transplants or crowns give acceptable results.**
- **Distance between rows and plants recommended for maximum yields; planting depth refers to seeds.**
- **Estimated number of plants for fresh consumption and preserving needed for each family member who enjoys the crop.**
- **The range of days it typically takes to sprout under normal climatic and cultural conditions.**
- **An indication of the crop's cold tolerance considering normal climatic conditions fall through spring.**
- **Common insects and diseases that can be expected to affect the crop.**
- **Stage in development that crop can be picked.**
- **Months when planting should occur to ensure a good harvest.**
- **Important cultural information about growing the crop.**
- **Common questions and answers to production problems.**

ASPARAGUS

Scientific name:
Asparagus officinalis

Recommended varieties:
Mary Washington (may be purchased as crowns ready to plant or grown from seed)

Ease of culture:

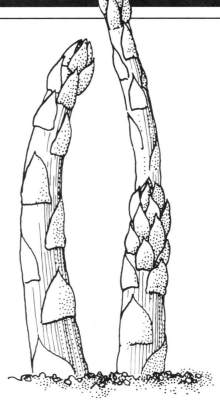

Seed germination	Days to harvest	Spacing in inches
14-21 days	Crowns: 2 years Seedlings: 1-3 years	Between rows: 36-48 Between plants: 12-18 Planting depth: 6
Hardiness	**Major pests**	**Plants per person**
Tolerant of frosts and freezes	Caterpillars	10-15

Harvest time: Once plants are established, cut or snap off at ground level the first spears to appear in March and April. Harvest when 7 to 10 inches long for a period of four to six weeks.

Florida planting schedule												
	J	F	M	A	M	J	J	A	S	O	N	D
North												
Central												
South					Not recommended							

You need to know:

- Asparagus is a garden perennial that may last for 10 years; soil should be well-prepared.
- Enrich planting site with peat moss, compost or manure.
- Fumigate soil to deter nematodes and weeds.
- Plant crowns or transplants in a trench 6 to 8 inches deep, spreading out the roots. May be double-cropped in a 5-foot-wide bed with rows 1 foot from each edge.
- Cover crown with 2 inches of soil. Gradually add more soil to fill the trench as plants begin to grow.
- Apply a heavy mulch of old hay, straw, manure or compost to conserve moisture and control weeds. Replenish as needed.
- Water to keep soil moist and encourage growth. Reduce watering during dormant winter season.

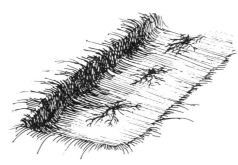

ASPARAGUS

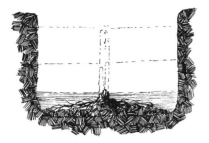

- Feed with 6-6-6 or similar product every four to six weeks, spring through fall.
- After the four- to six-week harvest, allow future top growth to develop bushy, tall plants spring through early winter. Plant tops should die back with the return of cool weather. If they never go dormant, mow to the ground in early to mid-February.
- Begin harvesting after two full years of growth from crowns or three years from seedlings. Harvest only a few shoots the first two years. Serious cropping over a four- to six-week period can begin the next year.

Solutions:

Q: Asparagus seed often is listed in catalogs, but I notice most gardeners plant their crops from roots. Can plants successfully be grown from seed? When and how should the seeds be planted?

A: Growing the crop from roots saves time, but asparagus also can be successfully started from seed. Variety Mary Washington generally can be found in seed packets from garden centers and mail-order companies. One packet will produce about 60 roots. From seed to first light harvest takes about three years.

Sow seeds in a large container or garden row. Space the seeds 4 inches apart and cover with a half-inch of soil. Keep soil moist; germination will begin in two weeks. Container-grown seedlings can be transplanted to the garden or larger containers when the fernlike stems are 6 to 8 inches tall. After one year of growth, move the plants to a permanent garden site, spacing the plants 12 to 18 inches apart.

Q: Tall, ferny asparagus stems are shading neighboring plants in my small garden. Must I allow the tops to grow so high?

A: Lots of top growth is needed to produce plump roots filled with stored food to nourish new shoots. The tall tops, which can grow 6 feet high, will have to be tolerated if you want an abundant harvest. Remove the foliage only when canes decline or when winter dormancy is to be induced around February.

Perhaps the plants can be moved to another part of the garden or landscape where the foliage won't interfere with the growth of other plants. Asparagus makes a great-looking ornamental during the warm seasons; allow it to grow as a light, airy hedge or in a border area between houses. Just be certain the new location receives plenty of sunlight.

Transplant during the winter, while the roots are dormant. Do not harvest for at least one year after transplanting.

Notes

BEANS, LIMA

Scientific name:
Phaseolus limensis

Recommended varieties:
Bush — Fordhook 242, Henderson, Jackson Wonder, Dixie Butterpea

Pole — Christmas, Florida Butter, Sieva, King of the Garden

Ease of culture:

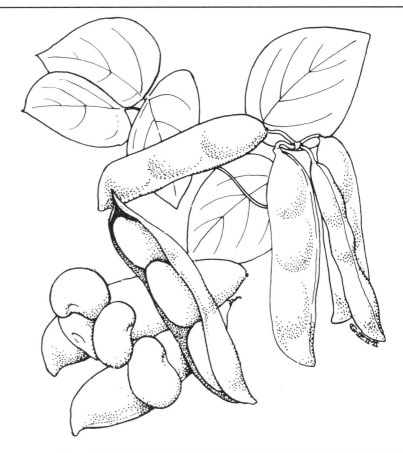

Seed germination	Days to harvest	Spacing in inches
7-10 days	65-75	Between rows: 24-36 Between plants: 3-4 Planting depth: 1-2
Hardiness	**Major pests**	**Plants per person**
Tender, damaged by frost	Caterpillars, mites, beetles	Bush: 40 Pole: 20

Harvest time: Pick fresh lima beans when the seeds fill the pods and before the pods begin to yellow. For dried lima beans, gather pods when they have turned brown and the seeds rattle inside.

Florida planting schedule												
	J	F	M	A	M	J	J	A	S	O	N	D
North			▨	▨	▨			▨				
Central			▨	▨	▨				▨			
South	▨	▨	▨	▨	▨	▨	▨	▨	▨	▨	▨	▨

You need to know:

- Lima beans like warm weather. Schedule plantings a few weeks after snap beans.
- Easy to grow in a well-prepared garden site. Many gardeners inoculate the seeds with a nitrogen-fixing bacteria that will supply nitrogen to the plant. However, in Florida sufficient bacteria exist in the soil and treatments generally are not needed.
- Keep soil moist during germination. Water frequently — plants dislike drought.
- Mulch to maintain moisture.
- Only one or two feedings of complete-analysis fertilizer are necessary. Beans get nitrogen from bacteria living in the soil. Plantings will need extra phosphorus and potassium during the second and fifth weeks of growth; use 2-12-12 or a similar product.

BEANS, LIMA

Solutions:

Q: We have beautiful lima bean bushes with plenty of flowers but no fruit. The plants have been blooming for weeks, but the beans drop off. Why?

A: Your beans like luxurious living. Most likely, the plants are being fed too much nitrogen, which encourages foliage rather than fruit. Withhold fertilizer to help the fruit get started.

If feedings are needed while plants are producing, as indicated by yelllowing or browning of the foliage, use a low-nitrogen product — a 5-10-10 or 2-12-12 analysis — at the recommended rate.

Q: We pulled up our bean plants and found little fleshy balls attached to the roots. Does this mean we have nematodes?

A: The swellings along your roots are produced by nitrogen-fixing bacteria, not nematodes. The round growths pull easily from the roots, and most are left in the soil when plants are pulled to make room for the next crop.

In contrast, nematode damage causes roots to swell. A whole segment of the root enlarges. The results of nematode damage cannot be removed without breaking or cutting the root apart.

Notes

BEANS, SNAP

Scientific name:
Phaseolus vulgaris

Recommended varieties:
Bush — Bush Blue Lake, Contender, Roma, Harvester, Provider, Cherokee Wax, Venture, Tendercrop

Pole — Dade, McCaslan, Kentucky Wonder 191, Blue Lake

Ease of culture:

Seed germination	Days to harvest	Spacing in inches
7-10 days	55-70	Bush: Between rows, 18-30; plants: 2-3 Pole: Between rows, 40-48; plants: 3-6 Planting depth: 1-2
Hardiness	**Major pests**	**Plants per person**
Tender, damaged by frost	Bean leaf tearer, rust, rhizoctonia stem rot, nematodes	Bush: 50 Pole: 20

Harvest time: Pick when the seeds begin to swell in the pods. Small beans are very tender; harvest before they become tough and stringy. Pick every three to five days.

Florida planting schedule												
	J	F	M	A	M	J	J	A	S	O	N	D
North			■	■				■	■			
Central			■	■	■				■	■		
South	■	■	■	■					■	■	■	■

BEANS, SNAP

You need to know:

- Beans will grow in any prepared garden soil.
- Many gardeners like to inoculate bean seed with a nitrogen-fixing bacteria. This treatment usually is not necessary in Florida because the bacteria is present in the soil.
- Seed germination is good, so plant seeds at desired final spacing. Very young plants can be transplanted if they are too close together.
- Water to keep soil consistently moist until seeds germinate, then water when soil surface begins to dry.
- Mulch to keep soil from splashing onto crop.
- Because soil bacteria supply bean plants with nitrogen, use additional fertilizer during the second and fifth weeks of growth. Pick beans frequently to prolong production.
- Grow pole beans on a tepee made with poles or strings radiating from a central post. Set poles or stake strings in the ground 1 to 2 feet apart. Plant two or three seeds at the base of each pole or string. Train vines up strings or poles.

Solutions:

Q: Our beans germinate quickly and sprout healthy looking stems and leaves. However, after the first few leaves appear, the plants develop brown spots on the stems and fall over. How can we save the crop?

A: A fungus organism called rhizoctonia spreads through the stems of young bean plants, especially when they are planted in soil where beans previously have been grown.

The disease must be controlled before planting new crops. Treat soil with the fungicide Terraclor and follow label instructions to guarantee the next bean crop.

Q: Our pole beans have grown tall and are beginning to bear. The lower leaves are turning rust-colored, and the color is creeping up the stems. What do the plants need?

A: Try a low-nitrogen fertilizer to cure what is probably a deficiency of phosphorus or potassium. Select a fertilizer sold as a bloom special, usually a 5-10-10 or 2-12-12 analysis, and apply at the rate suggested on the label.

Q: Our bean plants are starting to produce, but the leaves have brown dots. Will this hurt the plants?

A: Your spotted leaves are showing rust disease. If you run your fingers over the dots you will notice brown spores that resemble rust on a steel pipe. This disease is prevalent during moist, warm weather.

Because your plants are almost ready to harvest, no control is needed; they will bear a good crop.

If the disease begins while plants are beginning to grow, leaves should be sprayed with a sulfur fungicide or Maneb. Follow label instructions carefully and make note of the date of last application. Be sure to wait the recommended interval before harvesting.

Next season, avoid the problem by planting a rust-resistant variety. The snap bean Harvester has been most resistant in home garden trials.

Notes

BEETS

Scientific name:
Beta vulgaris

Recommended varieties:
Early Wonder, Detroit Dark Red

Ease of culture:

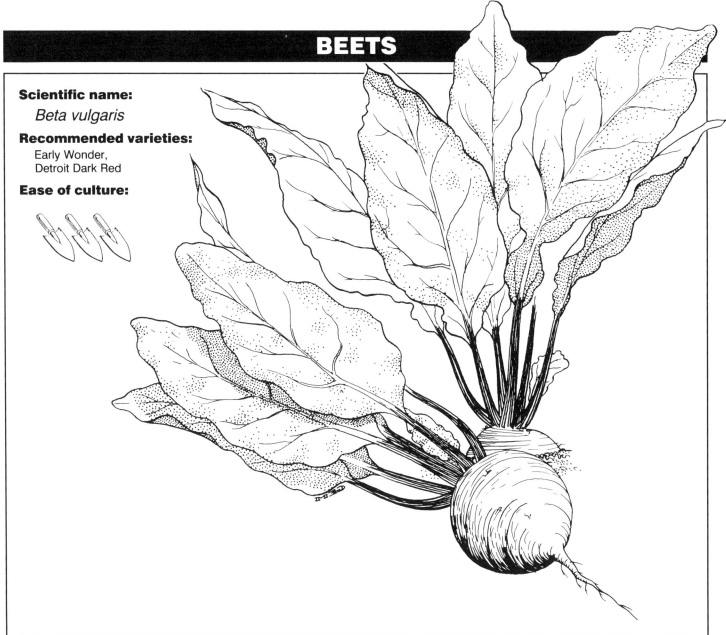

Seed germination	Days to harvest	Spacing in inches
7-10 days	50-65	Between rows: 14-24 Between plants: 3-5 Planting depth: ½-1
Hardiness	**Major pests**	**Plants per person**
Tolerant of frosts but damaged by freezes	Caterpillars, stem rot	20-30

Harvest time: Beet enthusiasts find both tops and roots delicious. For an early crop, some plants can be harvested when the roots begin to swell, but most are left to grow until 1 to 2 inches in diameter.

Florida planting schedule												
	J	F	M	A	M	J	J	A	S	O	N	D
North	■	■	■						■	■	■	■
Central	■	■	■							■	■	■
South		■								■	■	■

BEETS

You need to know:

- Wait for cool fall weather to begin sowing. For a continuous harvest, stagger plantings by sowing a few short rows every few weeks throughout the winter.
- Sandy soil is best, but any porous, well-drained site will produce a good crop.
- Improve germination by making a shallow row and moistening the soil before sowing seeds.
- Space seeds carefully. With the exception of some recently developed varieties, each beet seed is really a cluster from which several plants will grow.
- If spaced too closely, young beets can be transplanted.
- To speed growth and prevent roots from becoming woody in texture, keep soil moist. A mulch will help.
- Cover plants with loose hay, leaves or newspaper when freezes are expected.
- Feed every three to four weeks with a 6-6-6 or low-nitrogen 5-10-10 fertilizer. A scattering down the row is all that is needed to keep the crop growing.
- Beet leaves can be prepared and eaten like spinach. Control caterpillars by handpicking or spraying with an insecticide containing *Bacillus thuringiensis*.

Solutions:

Q: Why am I having trouble with my beets? I plant the seeds, they start to grow, then they wither. What is the secret in Florida?

A: Don't try to plant beets until the fall weather turns cool. When there is a lot of humidity, young seedlings are susceptible to organisms that cause rot and almost every sprout will wither.

By starting in November you will beat the heat problem and still give yourself at least three good months to harvest bright green tops and blood-red roots.

Notes

BROCCOLI

Scientific name:
 Brassica oleracea

Recommended varieties:
 Early Green Sprouting, Waltham 29, Atlantic, Green Comet, Green Duke, Early Emerald Hybrid

Ease of culture:

Seed germination	Days to harvest	Spacing in inches
5-7 days	Seeds: 75-90 Transplants: 55-70	Between rows: 30-36 Between plants: 12-18 Planting depth: ½-1
Hardiness	**Major pests**	**Plants per person**
Tolerant of cold weather but not severe freezes	Caterpillars	3-5

Harvest time: Cut large flower heads from the tops of plants before green buds open into yellow blooms. Heads in bloom can be eaten but may be tough and have a strong flavor. Allow plants to continue growing and side shoots will develop small heads, extending the harvest for several months.

Florida planting schedule												
	J	F	M	A	M	J	J	A	S	O	N	D
North	▓	▓						▓	▓	▓	▓	▓
Central	▓							▓	▓	▓	▓	▓
South	▓								▓	▓	▓	▓

BROCCOLI

You need to know:

- Broccoli may be grown from seeds sown directly in a prepared garden site or can be transplanted when seedlings show three or four leaves.
- Mulch to keep soil moist. Water early in the day so developing heads do not remain wet overnight, which could lead to rotting.
- Fertilize lightly every two to three weeks to keep plants growing after the main heads are harvested. Smaller side shoots will develop for another harvest.
- Caterpillars feed on the foliage and hide in developing heads. Sevin or insecticides containing *Bacillus thuringiensis* give good control.
- Broccoli matures rapidly. Cut side shoots several times a week to continue production.
- Large plants may need staking to protect against wind damage.

Solutions:

Q: How do we grow big heads of broccoli? Ours are much smaller than those at the store.

A: Keep your plants moist and well-fertilized to produce big plants that form large flower heads. Feed young plants every two or three weeks, using up to 1 pound of 6-6-6 per 100 feet of row. As production time nears and the heads begin to form, feed every three to four weeks.

Broccoli plants set out in early fall often take longer to grow but produce large heads. Variety also affects size. Quick-growing varieties often will produce smaller heads.

Q: We would like to grow our own broccoli transplants. Why do our attempts produce only tall, lanky plants? They receive full sun in our window.

A: Light and temperature together determine the quality of broccoli seedlings. If the growing conditions are too hot or there is not enough light, plants will become lanky. When transplants for fall are started during hot weather, they may be second-rate regardless of the care they receive.

Produce the best possible transplants by giving germinating seeds full sun. Keep the seedlings at temperatures of 70 to 80 degrees during the day. A table on the patio or bench in the greenhouse is the best location.

Windows are not as good because plants receive only a few hours of sun and sun from just one direction. Also, the higher temperatures coming through the glass window may cause the seedlings to stretch.

Notes

BRUSSELS SPROUTS

Scientific name:
Brassica oleracea

Recommended varieties:
Jade Cross, Long Island Improved

Ease of culture:

Seed germination	Days to harvest	Spacing in inches
5 days	Seeds: 90 Transplants: 75	Between rows: 24-36 Between plants: 18-24 Planting depth: ½
Hardiness	**Major pests**	**Plants per person**
Tolerant of frosts and light freezes	Aphids and caterpillars	2-5

Harvest time: Buds form at the base of the leaves. Start harvesting from the bottom of the plant by picking solid buds 1 to 1½ inches in diameter. Twist and gently tug to remove the buds or cut from plants.

Florida planting schedule												
	J	F	M	A	M	J	J	A	S	O	N	D
North									▓	▓	▓	▓
Central										▓	▓	▓
South											▓	▓

You need to know:

- Start plantings in early fall when the weather begins to cool at night.
- Plants grow well in sandy soil or garden sites enriched with organic matter.
- Seeds can be sown directly in the garden 4 to 6 inches apart and thinned later. The plants also can be sown in containers and later transplanted to the garden.
- Incorporate fertilizer into the planting area before sowing seeds. Use a 6-6-6 or similar product at the rate of 1 pound per 100-foot row.
- Keep soil moist; mulch to maintain uniform soil temperature.
- Feed established plantings monthly with 6-6-6 at the rate of 1 pound per 100-foot row.
- When plants grow 1 foot tall, cut off a few of the lower leaves to begin forcing bud growth. Continue removing additional leaves as the crop is harvested.
- Tall plants may need to be staked.
- Harvest frequently to encourage formation of new buds.

BRUSSELS SPROUTS

Solutions:

Q: We planted brussels sprouts during the winter but harvested only puffy buds. The plants grew well and were full of leaves. How can we produce the firm buds found in grocery stores?

A: Temperature has a lot to do with crop quality. Best growth and crop production is made when temperatures average 50 to 60 degrees.

Cultural practices can help compensate for the warmer weather often experienced in Florida.

Start the planting in early fall so the plants are ready to bear when cool winter weather arrives. Feed at least once a month; if growth slows or plants yellow, give additional feedings.

When plants are more than a foot tall, remove some of the bottom leaves. This treatment appears to encourage bud development and the shoots become large and firm.

Another technique to hasten bud development is to wait until the first buds are a half-inch in diameter, then cut the top out of the plant. This treatment terminates growth but encourages a good crop.

Q: Our sprouts were crawling with little green bugs. Can these be eliminated from future crops before harvest?

A: Aphids hide in the buds and suck juices from the tender tissue. Insecticidal soaps applied a few days before harvest can control these pests. When the crop is harvested, soak the buds in salty water to chase away remaining pests.

When needed, chemical sprays can be used to control the insects. Apply malathion as labeled, but wait at least seven days after treatment before harvesting the crop.

Q: Our transplants grew poorly. When we dug up a plant, the roots were in a tight ball. Why didn't the roots grow out into the soil?

A: The young plants remained in the containers too long before being moved to the garden. Next time, make sure the garden is ready when the plants are or buy plants that are just beginning to fill out the root balls.

If plants with tightly knit root balls are all that is available, try gently fluffing the roots apart before planting. Initial plant growth may be slow, but roots usually will spread out into the surrounding soil. Keep soil extra moist and feed plants every two weeks with a weak solution of liquid fertilizer for a month to stimulate additional root growth.

Notes

CABBAGE

Scientific name:
Brassica oleracea

Recommended varieties:
Green — Gourmet, Marion Market, King Cole, Market Prize, Rio Verde

Red — Red Acre, Ruby Perfection

Savoy — Savoy Ace, Spivoy Hybrid, Savoy Kind, Chieftain Savoy

Ease of culture:

Seed germination	Days to harvest	Spacing in inches
7 days	Seeds: 90-110 Transplants: 70-90	Between rows: 24-36 Between plants: 12-24 Planting depth: ½
Hardiness	**Major pests**	**Plants per person**
Survives frosts and light freezes	Caterpillars, cutworms	3-4

Harvest time: Cut small or large heads when firm. Leave basal foliage and a few small heads may form.

Florida planting schedule												
	J	F	M	A	M	J	J	A	S	O	N	D
North	▓	▓							▓	▓	▓	▓
Central	▓	▓							▓	▓	▓	▓
South	▓								▓	▓	▓	▓

You need to know:

- Plants have shallow root systems; cultivate lightly.
- Mulch to control moisture and weeds.
- Feed lightly every three to four weeks to maintain leafy growth.

Solutions:

Q: My spring cabbages grow big and round but often split open. Why?

A: An uneven water supply may cause cabbages near maturity to split. Keep the plants mulched and water two or three times a week during dry weather. It is difficult to keep large heads going on plants. Cut and store mature cabbages in the refrigerator.

CABBAGE

Notes

CANTALOUPE

Scientific name:
Cucumis Melo

Recommended varieties:
Smith's Perfect, Ambrosia, Edisto 47, Planters Jumbo, Summet, Super Market

Ease of culture:

Seed germination	Days to harvest	Spacing in inches
4-7 days	Seeds: 75-90 Transplants: 65-75	Between rows: 60-72 Between plants: 24-36 Planting depth: 1-2

Hardiness	Major pests	Plants per person
Tender, damaged by frost	Pickleworms, caterpillars, powdery mildew, leaf spot, downy mildew	6

Harvest time: Cantaloupes are ready when stem ends crack and melons slip easily from the vine. Orange color shows through the skin, and the fruit is fragrant.

Florida planting schedule

	J	F	M	A	M	J	J	A	S	O	N	D
North			▓	▓								
Central			▓	▓								
South		▓	▓					▓	▓			

You need to know:

- May be started in small pots as transplants or sown directly in a prepared garden site.
- Mulch to keep moisture supply constant.
- Spray to protect against insects and diseases when signs of injury first appear.
- To discourage insects, keep melons off soil with mulch or plastic.
- As melons reach maturity, water when surface soil becomes dry to the touch or when plants begin to wilt.
- Pick immediately when ripe.
- Other, more exotic melons are best left to experienced gardeners.

Usually grown in drier climates, they often are late in maturing, making the plants susceptible to disease during the rainy season. Stems do not slip, or separate easily from the fruit, so it is harder to tell when melons are ripe.

Varieties include:

Casaba — A white-fleshed, gumdrop-shaped melon. Surface turns deep orange, and fruit becomes aromatic when ripe.

Crenshaw — Oval-shaped, with greenish to salmon-colored flesh. Ready to harvest when rind turns yellowish-green and melon has a fruity fragrance.

Honeydew — The most successful exotic melon in Florida. The honeydew is a fair-to-good producer in home gar-

CANTALOUPE

dens. Flesh is white and very sweet when ripe. Ready to pick when fragrant; rind will turn ivory-green.

Persian — A roundish, yellow-fleshed melon. Fruit becomes fragrant and rind turns gray-green when ripe.

Solutions:

Q: Something is making holes in our cantaloupes. How can we put a stop to this?

A: Your melon pest is the pickleworm, cantaloupe's worst enemy. Pickleworms lay eggs on the foliage and fruit. When the young hatch, they feed a little, then head for the melons.

Control should begin as soon as melons form. Insecticides *Bacillus thuringiensis*, Sevin and Thiodan are labeled for use on fruit worms, including the pickleworm.

Weekly sprays may be needed to keep plants pest-free. Insecticides wash off during the hot rainy season, making it impossible to control the pickleworm. Plant crops early so they mature before the rains arrive.

Q: We grew great-looking cantaloupes, but their flavor was poor. This is puzzling because the plants had great care. What can I do to get sweet melons?

A: Flavor depends in part on variety, but environment determines the rest. If plants get too much moisture or too little sun, the melons will not taste as sweet.

The best flavor develops when cantaloupes are grown with little moisture and plenty of sun as the fruit forms.

Be sure to plant varieties recommended for Florida. Too much water near harvest time will diminish sweet flavor. Plant early and mulch to keep the soil moist. Vines can wilt a little between waterings.

Notes

CARROTS

Scientific name:
Daucus Carota sativus

Recommended varieties:
Imperator, Chantenay, Nantes, Gold Pak, Waltham Hicolor, Orlando Gold, Kundulus, Lady Finger, Little Finger, Short 'n Sweet

Ease of culture:

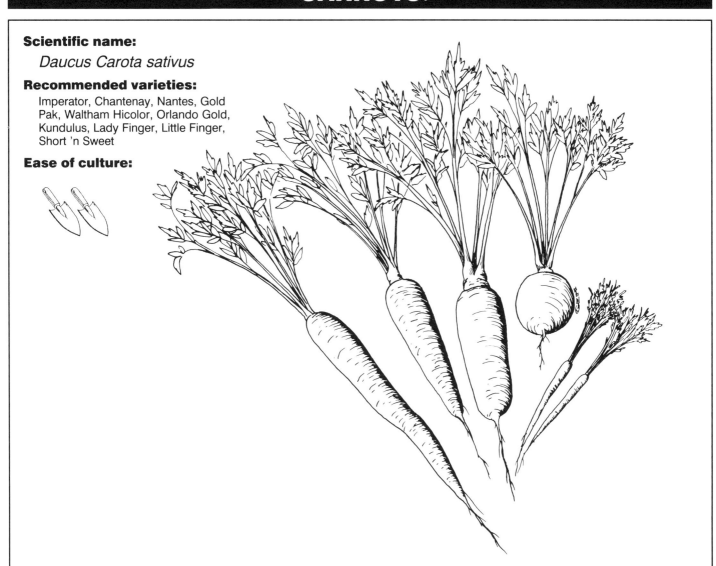

Seed germination	Days to harvest	Spacing in inches
7-10 days	65-80	Between rows: 16-24 Between plants: 1-3 Planting depth: ½
Hardiness	**Major pests**	**Plants per person**
Survives frosts and light freezes	Caterpillars, leaf hoppers	60-70

Harvest time: It is okay to sneak a peek at the growing plants, pushing the topsoil away to check the size of forming roots. When finger-size, baby carrots can be thinned and eaten. Harvest remaining crop when roots are less than 1½ inches in diameter. Larger carrots tend to be tough.

Florida planting schedule												
	J	F	M	A	M	J	J	A	S	O	N	D
North	▓	▓	▓						▓	▓	▓	▓
Central	▓	▓	▓							▓	▓	▓
South	▓	▓								▓	▓	▓

CARROTS

You need to know:

- Grow long-tapering varieties in sandy or well-drained organically enriched soil; plant shorter, stubby-to-rounded varieties in clay or rocky soil.
- Cover seeds with half an inch of loose soil or vermiculite. Vermiculite helps mark rows. Carrots can be so slow to germinate that many people plant radishes in the same row. The radishes are harvested before the carrots need the space.
- Keep the planting site moist to speed germination and keep seedlings from drying out.
- A mulch prolongs the time between waterings, keeps the soil uniformly moist and prevents maturing roots from cracking.
- Feed lightly every three to four weeks. To promote root development, use 6-6-6 fertilizer or a product lower in nitrogen such as 5-10-10 or 2-12-12.
- To guarantee a constant supply of carrots, plant 5- to 10-foot rows every three to four weeks, fall through late winter.
- Carrots are available in a variety of sizes, shapes and growth habits. Select the variety best suited for your soil conditions and cooking purposes.
- Long-tapering varieties gradually decrease in size from top to tip of root. Varieties include Gold Pak, Danvers, Imperator, Orlando Gold and Waltham Hi-color.
- Tapered, blunt-root varieties have roots that gradually decrease to blunt tips. This shape is characteristic of the Chantenay carrots.
- Cylindrical varieties are uniform in size, with just a slight taper to a blunt or rounded tip. The Nantes variety produces cylindrical, blunt roots.
- Fingerling or small carrots usually have a slender, tapering shape. Varieties include Lady Finger and Little Finger.
- Rounded types have ball-shaped roots. They grow well in compacted, dense soils. The Kundulus variety produces a rounded carrot.

Solutions:

Q: I am a failure at getting tiny carrot seeds to come up in the garden. Large seeds usually do fine but the little ones give me trouble. What do you suggest?

A: Get the seedlings up and growing with this technique: Make a shallow row and thoroughly wet the soil. Sow the seeds and cover with a half-inch of sand or vermiculite. Water the row again.

Place a board over the row to retain moisture needed for seed germination. Check under the board daily until the seedlings emerge from the soil, then prop up the board a few inches, exposing the seedlings to light. In a day or two, when most seedlings have emerged, remove the board and keep the row moist.

Another solution is to use carrot seed tape. The paper tapes, which dissolve after planting, contain seeds at properly spaced intervals. Many gardeners have found the tapes minimize germination and spacing problems common with difficult-to-handle seeds.

Q: We produce the funniest-looking carrots. Most grow several roots that look like fingers on a hand. Could there be a problem with the soil?

A: Anything that disturbs development of the main root will cause branching. Rocky Northern soils often force carrots into this form, but nematodes are usually the culprit in Florida. Rock impedes soil penetration and nematodes destroy the root tips. Control the soil pests and normal-looking carrots should appear.

Transplanted carrots also develop strange-looking roots. Carrots normally are sown directly into prepared ground. Transplanting may damage the roots, causing them to branch. Strangely shaped carrots are edible but hard to peel.

Notes

CAULIFLOWER

Scientific name:
Brassica oleracea

Recommended varieties:
Snowball Strains, Snowdrift, Imperial 10-6, Snow Crown, White Rock

Ease of culture:

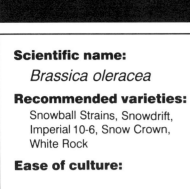

Seed germination	Days to harvest	Spacing in inches
5-7 days	Seeds: 75-90 Transplants: 55-70	Between rows: 24-30 Between plants: 18-24 Planting depth: ½-1
Hardiness	**Major pests**	**Plants per person**
Tolerant of frosts	Caterpillars, cutworms	4-6

Harvest time: Cauliflower forms a head in the center of the plant. Cut when compact and pure white. Expanding heads are old and grainy.

Florida planting schedule												
	J	F	M	A	M	J	J	A	S	O	N	D
North	■	■						■	■	■		
Central	■									■	■	■
South	■									■	■	■

CAULIFLOWER

You need to know:

- Grows best in porous soil. Add organic material to sandy soil.
- Feed frequently to grow large plants before heads develop.
- Protect when temperatures dip below 30 degrees. Cauliflower is the least cold-tolerant member of the cole, or cabbage, family.
- Keep soil moist. Plants will benefit from a layer of mulch.
- Produce pure white cauliflower by blanching the developing flower head or "curd."

When the curd is about the size of a quarter, protect it from direct sun by pulling several leaves over it and fastening them together with rubber bands, string, or twist ties. Self-blanching varieties do not need this treatment.

- Heads that have discolored are edible but may have a stronger flavor.
- Cauliflower plants produce just one head. After the harvest, remove the plants and begin another crop.

Solutions:

Q: Our fall cauliflower crop produced tiny heads. The plants stopped growing normally right after we transplanted them, and soon began producing heads. How can we get better production?

A: Your transplants probably were too old for good production. Cauliflower plants must be young and vigorous when they are set in the ground.

Blanching cauliflower

Plants that have stayed at the store or in the greenhouse too long develop hard, wiry stems. Root balls will be intertwined heavily.

Be selective when choosing transplants or grow your own and set them in the garden quickly.

Notes

CELERY

Scientific name:
Apium graveolens

Recommended varieties:
Utah strains, Florida strains, Summer Pascal

Ease of culture:

Seed germination	Days to harvest	Spacing in inches
7-10 days	Seeds: 115-125 Transplants: 80-105	Between rows: 24-36 Between plants: 6-10 Planting depth: ¼-½
Hardiness	**Major pests**	**Plants per person**
Tolerant of frosts and light freezes	Caterpillars, leaf hoppers	8-10

Harvest time: Ready to eat when stalks reach usable size. Cut individual stalks or gather entire plants.

Florida planting schedule												
	J	F	M	A	M	J	J	A	S	O	N	D
North	▓	▓	▓									
Central	▓	▓							▓	▓	▓	▓
South	▓									▓	▓	▓

CELERY

You need to know:

- Grows best in heavy soil such as muck or sandy loam. Improve sandy soil by adding organic matter. If soil has poor drainage, grow in raised beds.
- Start seeds eight to 10 weeks before transplants are needed.
- Soak seeds overnight to speed germination.
- Feed every two or three weeks with about 1 pound of 6-6-6 or similar product per 100 feet of row.
- Keep soil moist; water before surface dries out completely. Use a mulch to retain moisture.
- Many varieties are self-blanching, producing inner stems of a yellow-green to cream color.

If plants do not look pale enough to suit you, cover with a basket for a few days or stand a board on either side of the row to exclude light. Pile soil next to the board to hold it in place.

Solutions:

Q: We tried growing celery but were disappointed. The plants remained small and never turned an attractive green. What could have gone wrong?

A: Reserve your best soil for celery; plantings like a rich, moist site.

Provide extra moisture when transplants are added to the garden and continue until root growth begins.

Throughout the growing season, water when the surface soil begins to dry; mulch to ensure an even moisture supply.

Plantings also need frequent feedings with a 6-6-6 or 5-10-10 fertilizer; apply at two or three week intervals until harvest.

Q: What is root celery, and how does it differ from regular celery? Will it grow in my garden?

A: Root celery — better known as celeriac — resembles normal celery, but it has dwarf stalks and a large root portion that is eaten. Both plants are of the same species but are different varieties.

When vegetables could not be preserved easily, celeriac was a root crop grown primarily to be stored and eaten during the winter. Leaves and stalks are hollow and generally are not used.

Plant during the fall and early winter months to avoid bolting, which occurs when warm weather returns.

Like celery, celeriac needs abundant water and fertilizer. Popular varieties include Prague and Delicacy. Harvest when roots are about 3 inches in diameter. Roots typically are peeled to remove the stringy outer layer.

Notes

CHINESE CABBAGE

Scientific name:
Brassica Rapa

Recommended varieties:
Michihli, Wong Bok, Bok Choy

Ease of culture:

Seed germination	Days to harvest	Spacing in inches
5-7 days	Seeds: 70-90 Transplants: 60-70	Between rows: 24-36 Between plants: 8-12 Planting depth: ½-1
Hardiness	**Major pests**	**Plants per person**
Tolerant of frosts and light freezes	Caterpillars	6-10

Harvest time: Harvest head-forming types when firm and of useful size. Pick a few when small because the crop matures rapidly. Non-heading types can be harvested and eaten at any stage. Gather individual leaves or cut the entire plant.

Florida planting schedule												
	J	F	M	A	M	J	J	A	S	O	N	D
North	▓									▓	▓	▓
Central	▓									▓	▓	▓
South	▓											

CHINESE CABBAGE

You need to know:

- Grows well in most soils and in full sun or partial shade.
- Water frequently and mulch to keep soil moist and prolong time between waterings.
- Control caterpillars with an insecticide containing *Bacillus thuringiensis.*
- In sandy soil, feed frequently with a 6-6-6 or nitrogen-only fertilizer.

Solutions:

Q: Our Chinese cabbage crop was a failure this year. Just when we thought the plants were forming heads, they shot up seed stalks. What went wrong?

A: Weather conditions are to blame. The plants like short days and coolish weather. When temperatures consistently fall below 60 degrees during the winter, seed stalks often are the result.

When spring arrives, the longer days may trigger the flower response. The warm weather that accompanies the longer days also produces a bitter taste in the heads.

Prevent these problems by planting the cabbage during the moderate months of fall. The best growing conditions typically are found from October through December.

Q: Should Chinese cabbage seeds be sown directly in the garden, or should they be started in containers as transplants? Which technique works best for a small garden?

A: Either technique works well. When planting directly in the garden, sow the seeds a little closer than the desired final spacing. After the seedlings are up and growing, the planting can be thinned so cabbages are 8 to 12 inches apart.

Transplants often save time and garden space. A plant can be set in any available space or held in its container until there is room in the garden.

Start transplants about four weeks before they will be needed in the garden. Transfer to the garden with a ball of soil attached to the roots; bare-root transplants tend to develop seed heads.

Notes

COLLARDS

Scientific name:
Brassica oleracea

Recommended varieties:
Georgia Vates, Blue Max, Hicrop Hybrid

Ease of culture:

Seed germination	Days to harvest	Spacing in inches
5-7 days	Seeds: 70-80 Transplants: 40-60	Between rows: 24-30 Between plants: 10-18 Planting depth: ½-1
Hardiness	**Major pests**	**Plants per person**
Tolerant of frosts and light-to-medium freezes	Caterpillars, aphids	8-10

Harvest time: Ready when leaves reach usable size. Thin closely packed stands by removing entire plants; otherwise, harvest individual leaves. Many growers feel flavor improves after a period of cold.

Florida planting schedule												
	J	F	M	A	M	J	J	A	S	O	N	D
North		▨	▨					▨	▨	▨	▨	▨
Central	▨	▨	▨						▨	▨	▨	▨
South	▨	▨								▨	▨	▨

You need to know:

- Grows well in any well-drained soil in full sun or partial shade.
- Feed every three to four weeks with a 6-6-6 or nitrogen-only fertilizer.
- Plants are drought-tolerant but grow best when soil is moist and mulched.
- Control caterpillars with Sevin or an insecticide containing *Bacillus thuringiensis*.
- Harvest tender new leaves, leaving older, lower leaves to maintain plant growth.

Solutions:

Q: How do I get rid of aphids on my collards and mustard greens? Most sprays recommend waiting a week or more before harvest.

A: Soap-formulated pesticides will eliminate the bugs in short order and permit a quick harvest. These products can be applied right up to the day of harvest. Be sure to follow all label instructions.

COLLARDS

Notes

CORN, SWEET

Scientific name:
Zea Mays

Recommended varieties:
Silver Queen, Gold Cup, Guardian, Bonanza, Florida Staysweet, How Sweet It Is, Honey 'N Pearl, Illini Xtra-Sweet

Ease of culture:

Seed germination	Days to harvest	Spacing in inches
7-10 days	60-95	Between rows: 24-36 Between plants: 12-18 Planting depth: 1-2
Hardiness	**Major pests**	**Plants per person**
Tender, damaged by frost	Caterpillars, leaf spot	15-20

Harvest time: Feel, even take a peek, to see whether kernels are filling the husk. When the kernels are plump to the tip of the ear, begin to harvest. Use while the kernels are juicy. If they are pasty, the corn is past its prime.

Florida planting schedule												
	J	F	M	A	M	J	J	A	S	O	N	D
North			■	■				■				
Central		■	■	■				■	■			
South	■	■						■	■	■	■	

CORN, SWEET

You need to know:

- Corn needs rich, moist soil for best production. Add organic matter and fertilizer before planting.
- Plant seed in rows, individually or in clusters of two or three seeds, spaced 12 to 18 inches apart.
- Plant a block of several rows to ensure pollination.
- When young, corn can be transplanted to fill blank spaces in rows.
- Harvest when ripe and eat immediately. Corn doesn't store well. Even on the plant, it becomes overripe in a few days.

Solutions:

Q: We have been trying to grow corn, but our plants end up as dwarfs. How can we get them to grow tall?

A: Short plants usually result from insufficient fertilizer. Corn growing in sandy soil should be fed every two or three weeks with either a complete or a high-nitrogen fertilizer.

Plants that grow tall but have small, partially filled ears may be deficient in phosphorus. Use a balanced fertilizer, like a 12-12-12, or one with a greater percentage of phosphorus, like a 5-10-10. Follow label directions and water thoroughly.

Corn plants do poorly if they are overcrowded, short of water, or poorly pollinated. To avoid these problems, plant in blocks, thin plants to the proper spacing and keep soil moist.

Q: How can we keep our corn from being attacked by caterpillars?

A: Caterpillars feed on the stalks, foliage and ears of corn plants. During daylight hours, they often hide among unfurling leaves. They are less likely to be a major problem in the spring than in the fall.

If there are only a few, trying removing them by hand. *Bacillus thuringiensis*, a biological control, helps reduce large populations. As they ingest the spray, the caterpillars stop feeding; they may take a few days to disappear, however. Several brand-name products are available at local garden centers.

Sevin also gives good control. With heavy infestation, spray every five to seven days. Some growers combine Sevin with a *Bacillus thuringiensis* spray for better control.

Notes

CUCUMBERS

Scientific name:
 Cucumis sativus

Recommended varieties:
 Slicers — Poinsett, Ashley, Sprint, Sweet Success

 Bush type — Salad Bush Hybrid, Bush Whopper, Spacemaster, Bush Champion

 Picklers — Galaxy, SMR 18, Explorer

Ease of culture:

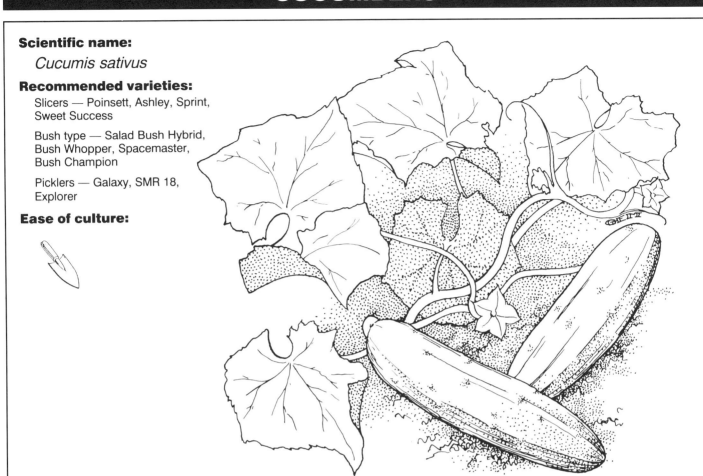

Seed germination	Days to harvest	Spacing in inches
5-7 days	Seeds: 50-70 Transplants: 40-50	Between rows: 36-60 Between plants: 12-24 Planting depth: 1-2
Hardiness	**Major pests**	**Plants per person**
Tender, damaged by frost	Caterpillars, pickleworms, angular leaf spot, downy mildew	3-4

Harvest time: Cucumbers can be picked young when fruit is first noticed or very ripe just before it starts to lose the green color.

Florida planting schedule												
	J	F	M	A	M	J	J	A	S	O	N	D
North		▓	▓	▓				▓	▓			
Central		▓	▓					▓	▓	▓		
South	▓	▓	▓					▓	▓	▓	▓	▓

You need to know:

- Choose varieties resistant to powdery mildew, downy mildew, angular leaf spot, anthracnose and scab.
- Sow seeds in a prepared garden site in groups of three or four, or spaced individually down rows.
- Mulch to conserve moisture and keep fruit clean for harvest.
- Water frequently and keep soil moist.
- Control pickleworms with a spray labeled for caterpillar control.
- Many cucumber plants bear male

CUCUMBERS

and female flowers on the same vine. Bees and other insects must move pollen from the male to the female flowers for noticeable fruit to develop.

Some new hybrids, gynoecious types, mainly produce female flowers and, potentially, much more fruit per plant.

To ensure pollination, a few seeds of another variety that produces male flowers in quantity usually are included in the seed packet.

Some new varieties, parthenocarpic types such as Sweet Success, produce only female flowers and need no pollination. Cucumbers from these varieties will be almost seedless.

Solutions:

Q: We were getting good production from our cucumbers, but distorted fruit suddenly appeared. It is narrow near the stem but almost fully developed at the flower end. What happened?

A: Fruit production probably occurred during a dry spell, and the vine did not have enough water to swell the cucumbers during early development. Water evidently arrived in time to plump out the flower end.

To avoid this problem, keep vines mulched and water frequently, especially during hot, dry weather.

Q: Our burpless cucumbers are growing long and plump, but are full of holes. What can we do?

A: Pickleworms have riddled your cucumbers. They also damage squash and cantaloupe. Yellowish waste outside small holes — about 1/16 inch in diameter — may be the first sign of the pests.

Counterattack by spraying when cucumbers begin to form or after the first sign of damage. Inexperienced gardeners may wish to spray weekly with the insecticide Sevin.

Gardeners confident of their ability to spot the pesky caterpillars can wait and treat only as needed.

Even damaged cucumbers are usable if the affected portions are cut out.

Notes

EGGPLANT

Scientific name:
Solanum Melongena

Recommended varieties:
Florida Market, Black Beauty, Dusky, Long Tom, Ichiban

Ease of culture:

Seed germination	Days to harvest	Spacing in inches
7-10 days	Seeds: 90-110 Transplants: 75-90	Between rows: 36-42 Between plants: 24-36 Planting depth: ½
Hardiness	**Major pests**	**Plants per person**
Tender, damaged by frost	Caterpillars, spider mites	2-3

Harvest time: Cut from the stalk when fruit is to 3 to 4 inches in diameter and 5 to 7 inches long. The skin should be shiny and not spring back when touched.

Florida planting schedule												
	J	F	M	A	M	J	J	A	S	O	N	D
North		▒	▒	▒	▒	▒	▒					
Central		▒	▒					▒	▒			
South	▒	▒						▒	▒			▒

You need to know:

- Eggplant may be grown from seeds or from transplants set out in a prepared garden site.
- Feed every two to three weeks to encourage growth when young. Feed every three to four weeks as plants begin to flower.
- Plants established during the spring may continue production into the fall. Stake to support several seasons' growth.
- Water at least once or twice a week.
- Check for mites during hot, dry weather. Control with an insecticidal soap.
- Pick the fruit before it is fully mature to prevent bitter flavor and to keep plants productive.

Solutions:

Q: Our eggplant is producing strange fruit. Normal purple vegetables grew last spring, but now many are brown. What caused this color change?

A: Brown skin is in the eggplant's genetic background. Breeders are able to keep this color suppressed except when aging plants grow under stressful conditions.

The partial or almost total change from purple to brown fruit is normal in plants carried over for more than one season. The summer environment is difficult for the plants and encourages the change. With this change comes a bitter taste.

The alkaloid solanine found in plants of the nightshade family, which includes potatoes and tomatoes, builds up in the

EGGPLANT

fruit, giving it an off flavor. While the vegetables may not be as palatable, they are edible.

Q: All eggplant seeds and transplants I find on the market produce purple fruit. I used to see white eggplant. What happened? Are the white varieties edible?

A: Eggplant varieties can be found in shades of purple, yellow, cream, white and combinations of these colors.

Eggplant also has many shapes, including round, oblong and cylindrical. However, the most popular varieties bear purple, oval fruit.

Two species produce white eggplants. One that resembles hen eggs is ornamental; the fruit is edible but has a bitter flavor.

Another species contains white, rounded or oval culinary eggplant. Popular varieties include Albino, Dourge and White Beauty. The flavor is mild to sweet.

Seeds are available through mail-order companies; grow like purple varieties.

Notes

ENDIVE/ESCAROLE

Scientific name:
Cichorium Endivia

Recommended varieties:
Florida Deep Heart, Full Heart, Ruffec

Ease of culture:

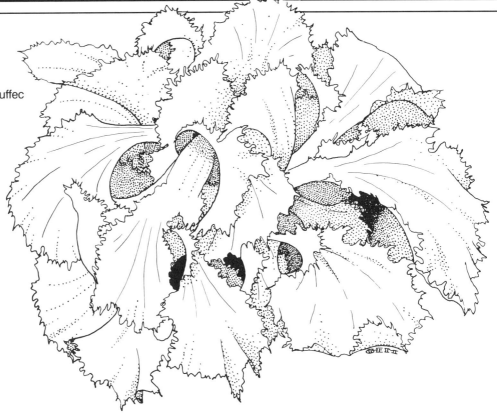

Seed germination	Days to harvest	Spacing in inches
5-7 days	80-95	Between rows: 18-24 Between plants: 8-12 Planting depth: ½
Hardiness	**Major pests**	**Plants per person**
Tolerant of frosts and light freezes	Slugs, snails, aphids	8-10

Harvest time: Cut entire plant when full of tightly packed leaves and center foliage has turned cream-colored. To produce a milder flavor, blanch by tying leaves up over inner foliage two to three weeks before harvest.

Florida planting schedule												
	J	F	M	A	M	J	J	A	S	O	N	D
North		▒	▒						▒			
Central	▒	▒							▒	▒		
South	▒	▒							▒	▒	▒	▒

You need to know:

● Grows well in moist, porous soil; needs full sun to partial shade.
● A good candidate for wide-bed culture — grow two rows, 18 inches apart.
● To encourage leafy growth in sandy soil, feed every two to three weeks.
● Frequent watering and a layer of mulch will speed growth.
● Plants grown during hot weather may be bitter. Cool-season culture produces leaves with a milder flavor.

Solutions:

Q: What is the difference between endive and escarole? We see similar plants referred to by the same name.

A: Both belong to the same genus and species; however, the flavors and the shapes of the leaves differ. Endive has curled leaves and a slightly bitter flavor. Escarole is a type of endive that has plain, broad, mild-flavored leaves. Both add a unique texture and flavor to salads.

Q: The endive was growing and form-

ENDIVE/ESCAROLE

ing heads when it split open and developed flowering shoots. We started the plants during the winter. How can we produce good heads?

A: Climate controls the flowering, or bolting, of endive. It seldom is a problem when the weather remains cool. Bolting is likely to occur when a period of cool weather is followed by warm.

Once the bolting begins, another cold spell will not stop the process. Harvest the heads at the first sign of flowering.

Cool temperatures also control the bitter taste in the plant. The leaves will have a mild flavor as long as the weather remains cool. As temperatures rise, the taste becomes strong and often undesirable. Plantings made during late fall or winter are less likely to have bolting and flavor problems.

Q: We tried starting endive seedlings indoors. The plants were placed in a bright window and grew into spindly but suitable transplants. When moved to the garden, they frequently burned. How can we prevent what appears to be sun damage?

A: Help the plants adjust to outdoor weather conditions by following a process called hardening off: Give them a few hours of full sun each day for several weeks, then move them to the garden. Seedlings grown indoors never receive the full effects of sunlight. The plants may burn or bronze a little when moved outside, but they will become tough and stocky before it is time to set them in the garden.

Notes

KALE

Scientific name:
Brassica oleracea

Recommended varieties:
Dwarf Blue Curled Vates,
Dwarf Siberian

Ease of culture:

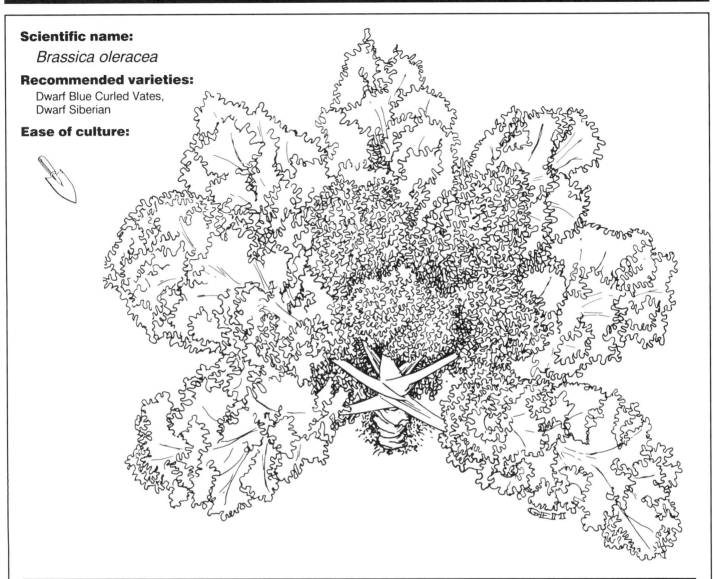

Seed germination	Days to harvest	Spacing in inches
5-7 days	50-60	Between rows: 18-30 Between plants: 8-16 Planting depth: ¼-½ |//
Hardiness	**Major pests**	**Plants per person**
Tolerant of frosts and light-to-medium freezes	Caterpillars, cutworms	10-12

Harvest time: Ready to harvest when leaves reach usable size. Use thinnings for first crop and gather individual leaves from maturing plants.

Florida planting schedule

	J	F	M	A	M	J	J	A	S	O	N	D
North	▨	▨								▨	▨	▨
Central	▨	▨								▨	▨	▨
South	▨										▨	▨

KALE

You need to know:

- Sow in prepared planting site when cool weather arrives. Seed closely to produce an early harvest of thinnings.
- A good crop for intensive techniques — scatter seeds across a wide row and cover with soil. Or, double crop by planting several closely spaced rows.
- Mulch to conserve moisture and keep soil off plants.
- To maintain tender, vigorous growth, feed every two to three weeks with a light scattering of 6-6-6.
- Control caterpillars with an insecticide containing *Bacillus thuringiensis*.

Solutions:

Q: Up North we grew kale into the summer. Why isn't it recommended as a warm-season planting in Florida?

A: Kale, like many members of the mustard family, develops its best flavor during cool weather. The plants also are more compact and produce the desirable curled leaves during winter.

Kale grown during late spring and summer often is bitter. When the rainy season arrives, the plants become susceptible to leaf spot and rot diseases.

Q: Seed packets usually recommend sowing kale directly in the garden. We have a small plot, and the few weeks of garden space saved by starting plants in containers are valuable to us. Is there a reason why we should not start the seeds as transplants?

A: Most gardeners sow the crop in the soil to save time, but kale will do just as well when started in containers.

Plant the seeds in used market packs or the sections of an egg carton. Make sure the containers have adequate drainage, then sow one or two seeds per section.

Keep the soil moist and feed the seedlings weekly to have transplants ready for the garden in three to four weeks.

Notes

KOHLRABI

Scientific name:
Brassica oleracea

Recommended varieties:
Early White Vienna, Grand Duke Hybrid

Ease of culture:

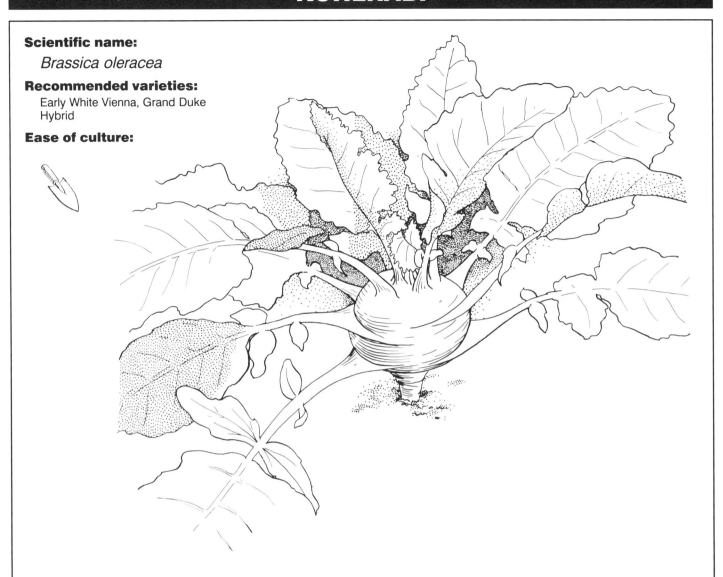

Seed germination	Days to harvest	Spacing in inches
5-7 days	70-80	Between rows: 24-30 Between plants: 3-5 Planting depth: ½-1
Hardiness	**Major pests**	**Plants per person**
Tolerant of frosts and light-to-medium freezes	Caterpillars, cutworms	10-15

Harvest time: Pull fleshy, tender stems when 1 to 4 inches in diameter. If left too long, stems grow tough and fibrous.

Florida planting schedule												
	J	F	M	A	M	J	J	A	S	O	N	D
North			▨	▨						▨	▨	
Central		▨	▨							▨	▨	
South	▨	▨									▨	▨

KOHLRABI

You need to know:

- Seed directly into prepared garden soil. This is a good crop for double rows or raised bed plantings.
- Seeds can be sown closely and thinnings harvested for an early crop.
- Encourage rapid, tender growth with frequent watering and by feeding with 6-6-6 or similar fertilizer every two or three weeks.
- Control caterpillars with insecticides containing *Bacillus thuringiensis*.

Solutions:

Q: We were disappointed with our winter kohlrabi crop. The plants developed big, swollen roots that were fibrous when cooked. How can I ensure a tender crop?

A: Some varieties are likely to produce stringy stem portions, but all plantings can become fibrous if grown under stressful conditions. Keep the crop growing rapidly to produce the best harvest. Maintain adequate nutrients, and never allow the soil to dry. A mulch will help keep the soil uniformly moist.

Q: Does kohlrabi need full sun? We would like to plant it in an area that receives morning sun but is bright the rest of the day.

A: Crops that produce leaves and stems only often yield a harvest in less-than-ideal conditions. Your site should be satisfactory for many plants in the mustard family, including kohlrabi, kale, cabbage, collards and mustard greens.

Notes

LETTUCE

Scientific name:
Lactuca sativa

Recommended varieties:
Crisp — Minetto, Great Lakes, Fulton, Floricrisp

Butterhead — Bibb, White Boston, Buttercrunch, Cindy

Romaine — Parris Island Cos, Valmaine, Floricos

Leaf — Prize Head, Ruby, Salad Bowl, Black-Seeded Simpson, Red Sails

Ease of culture:

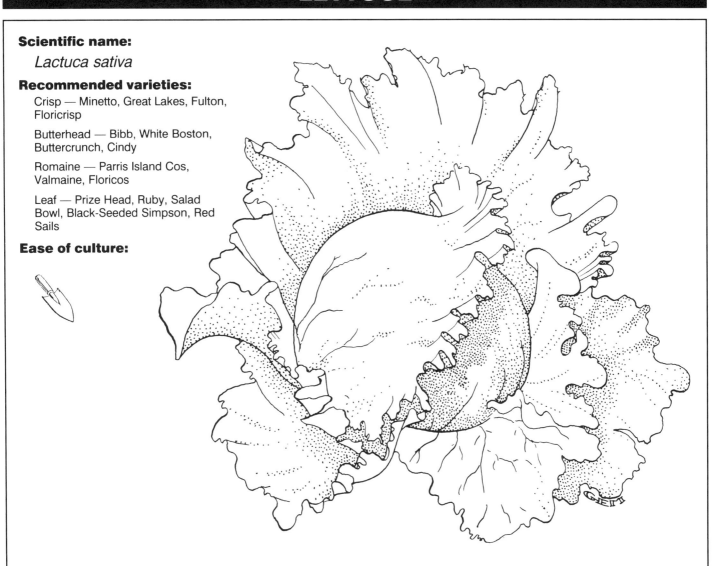

Seed germination	Days to harvest	Spacing in inches
5-7 days	Seeds: 50-90 Transplants: 40-70	Between rows: 12-24 Between plants: 8-12 Planting depth: ½
Hardiness	**Major pests**	**Plants per person**
Tolerant of frosts and light freezes	Aphids, slugs	10-12

Harvest time: Harvest leaf lettuce when leaves reach usable size. With butterhead and romaine, cut individual leaves or the entire loose head. Harvest crisp varieties as the head becomes firm.

Florida planting schedule												
	J	F	M	A	M	J	J	A	S	O	N	D
North		▓	▓						▓			
Central	▓	▓	▓						▓	▓	▓	▓
South		▓							▓	▓	▓	

LETTUCE

You need to know:

- For tender, mild-flavored leaves, begin planting when the weather cools.
- Lettuce may be seeded directly and thinned to recommended spacing, but most gardeners prefer to buy or raise transplants because the plants can be more evenly spaced in the garden.
- Plant short rows every few weeks for a continuous supply.
- A blend of types makes a good salad. Plant varieties from each category.
- Encourage rapid, tender growth with frequent, light feedings of 6-6-6 or a nitrogen-only fertilizer.
- Maintain moist soil. Water when the surface's top inch begins to dry.
- Mulch to stretch the time between waterings and to keep the foliage clean.
- Aphids hide and feed in the developing heads. Control with an insecticidal soap spray.
- Slugs curl up and feed within the leaves. A few can be tolerated and picked out at harvest time; otherwise, control with slug and snail bait labeled for vegetable gardens.
- Expect to cut bunches of leaf lettuce in 50 days, clusters of butterhead and romaine in 70 days and heads of crisp lettuce in 90 days.

Solutions:

Q: Our lettuce plants are flowering. The sap in the stems looks milky. Can we still eat the leaves?

A: Warm weather and old age often cause plants to bolt, developing the tall flower stalk. Blossoming plants are edible, but the leaves can be tough and bitter. The milky sap is normal. Cool weather and frequent, light feedings develop sweet, tender foliage.

Q: We prepared the planting site for lettuce and used tranplants to grow the crop. The heads were small and yellowish, and the leaves had brown edges. What does it take to produce big heads like those found in grocery stores?

A: Good soil preparation is only the first step in growing large heads of lettuce. Water and fertilizer encourage further plant development. Keep the soil moist; water every few days if necessary. A mulch will help retain soil moisture. Lettuce plants lacking water will develop burned foliage and remain small.

Frequent feedings encourage rapid growth and the formation of large heads. Plantings in sandy soil can be fed every two or three weeks with light applications of a 6-6-6 or nitrogen-only fertilizer. Plants growing in organic-rich soil will not need these extra nutrients to produce big heads.

Notes

MUSTARD GREENS

Scientific name:
Brassica juncea

Recommended varieties:
Southern Giant Curled, Florida Broad Leaf

Ease of culture:

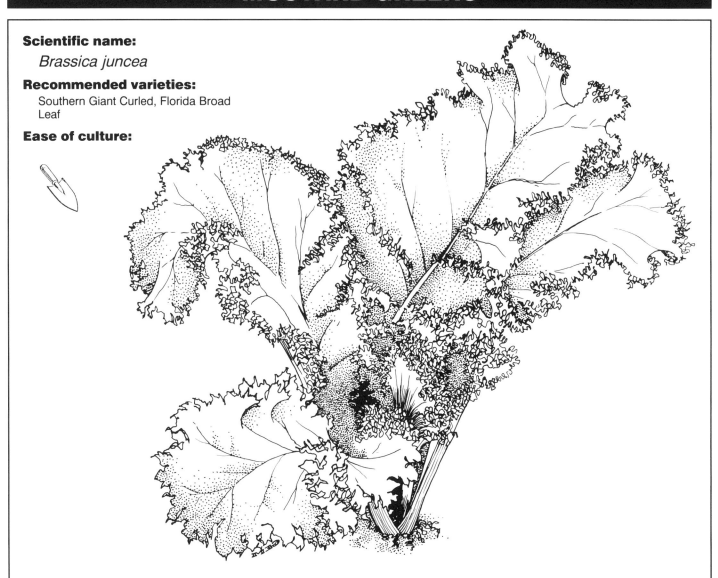

Seed germination	Days to harvest	Spacing in inches
5-7 days	40-60	Between rows: 14-24 Between plants: 1-6 Planting depth: ½-1
Hardiness	**Major pests**	**Plants per person**
Tolerant of frosts and light freezes	Aphids and caterpillars	15-20

Harvest time: Best when young and tender. Thin and use young plants when leaves are 6 to 8 inches long. Harvest individual leaves of older plants or use entire plant.

Florida planting schedule												
	J	F	M	A	M	J	J	A	S	O	N	D
North	▓	▓	▓						▓	▓	▓	▓
Central	▓	▓	▓						▓	▓	▓	▓
South	▓	▓	▓						▓	▓	▓	▓

MUSTARD GREENS

You need to know:

- Easy to grow in well-drained garden soil.
- May be seeded directly into prepared soil or transplanted when 3 to 4 inches tall.
- Ideal for wide-bed or double-cropping techniques.
- Seed or transplant closely to produce an early harvest of thinnings.
- Keep soil moist and mulched.
- Feed every two to three weeks to continue a crop of tender, mild-flavored leaves.
- May be damaged by cold and should be protected from all but light frosts.

Solutions:

Q: Just when harvest time approaches, the mustard greens become covered with bugs. Hundreds of little green insects cling to the bottoms of the leaves. How can I eliminate these pests?

A: Aphids have attacked your plants. These small, pear-shaped insects multiply rapidly. While it's doubtful it would harm you to eat a few, they do make the crop less palatable.

Many gardeners harvest the greens and wash the aphids away before eating them. This usually is successful when the numbers are small. When leaves are covered with aphids, a better control is needed. Soapy water or an insecticidal soap often is effective at removing the pests, but it must hit the aphids to be effective. The insects usually disappear a few days after spraying.

Traditional pesticides are also effective, but harvest must be timed carefully to the spray application. Malathion requries a seven-day wait after treatment and dimethoate, a 14-day wait before plants can be eaten.

Notes

OKRA

Scientific name:
Abelmoschus esculentus

Recommended varieties:
Clemson Spineless, Perkins Long Green, Emerald, Blondy

Ease of culture:

Seed germination	Days to harvest	Spacing in inches
7-14 days	50-75	Between rows: 24-40 Between plants: 6-12 Planting depth: 1-2

Hardiness	Major pests	Plants per person
Tender, damaged by frost	Stinkbugs, mites, caterpillars, nematodes	8-12

Harvest time: Cut pods when young; they quickly become fibrous. Most varieties are ready to harvest when 3 to 4 inches long, usually four or five days after the bloom opens.

Florida planting schedule												
	J	F	M	A	M	J	J	A	S	O	N	D
North			▒	▒	▒	▒	▒	▒				
Central			▒	▒	▒	▒	▒	▒	▒			
South		▒	▒	▒	▒			▒	▒			

OKRA

You need to know:

- Wait until the soil warms to plant seeds. Okra must have warm weather to grow.
- Soak seeds in water overnight to hasten germination.
- Plant in rows or groups in well-prepared soil.
- Plants may survive for several seasons, growing extremely tall. Prune lanky or non-productive plants to within a few feet of the ground to allow new shoots to form.
- Feed every three to four weeks during warm growing seasons.
- Harvest every two to three days for tender pods and to keep plants productive.
- Remove old fibrous pods overlooked during the harvest to encourage additional production.

Solutions:

Q: Our okra has just begun producing, but the pods are deformed. Many have bumps. What caused the damage?

A: The condition resulted from stink bugs eating the tender pods. The insects are flat, oval and greenish brown. They produce a pungent odor when touched. Stink bugs suck juices from the plants, leaving small wounds that interrupt growth and distort the pods.

Control is not easy because damage is not noticeable until harvest time. It's best to realize the stink bug's potential damage and use a malathion spray before the plant flowers if you spot stinkbugs anywhere in your garden.

Q: When we pulled up our okra, the roots were swollen. Do we need to treat the soil?

A: Okra is a real nematode bait. Nematodes are roundworms that live in soil. Populations of them grow rapidly on okra roots, causing knotted, swollen growths. When prevalent in the soil, nematodes hinder production and damage plants.

When removing old plants, check the roots for nematode damage. If present, use the fumigant Vapam or soil solarization techniques to reduce their population to a level that permits plant growth.

Notes

ONIONS

Scientific name:
Allium Cepa

Recommended varieties:
Bulbing — Excel, Texas Grano, Granex, White Granex, Tropicana Red

Ease of culture:

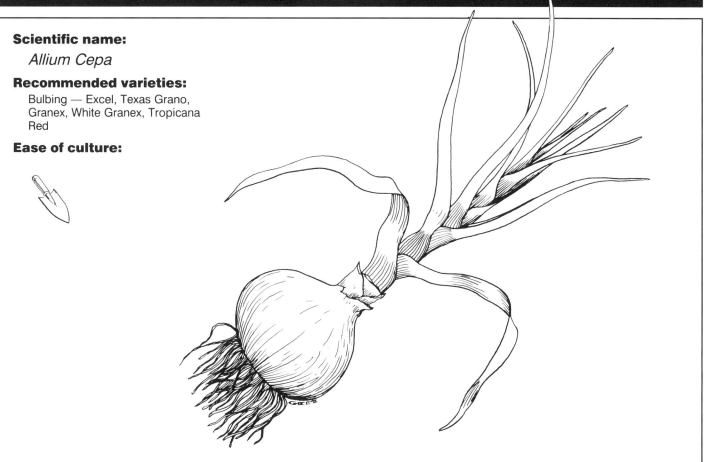

Seed germination	Days to harvest	Spacing in inches
7-10 days	Seeds: 120-160 Transplants: 110-120	Between rows: 12-14 Between plants: 4-6 Planting depth: ½
Hardiness	**Major pests**	**Plants per person**
Tolerant of frosts and light freezes	Thrips, leaf spot	For eating fresh: 15 For storing: 60

Harvest time: Onions can be eaten at any stage. Harvest young green stems as scallions when the bases begin to bulge. Gather mature bulbs in late spring after the tops fall over. Florida varieties don't store well. Keep them in a spot with low humidity to extend shelf life.

Florida planting schedule												
	J	F	M	A	M	J	J	A	S	O	N	D
North									▓	▓	▓	▓
Central									▓	▓	▓	▓
South									▓	▓	▓	

You need to know:

- Choose varieties selected for Florida that will produce bulbs during the short days of early spring.
- Grow in sandy soil enriched with organic matter.
- Feed every three to four weeks with a 6-6-6 fertilizer.
- Many gardeners pull soil away from the tops of growing bulbs, but this is not necessary.
- Onion bulbs are ready for harvest when leaves on more than half of the plants fall over.
- To harvest, gently loosen bulbs from the soil and spread out in an airy location away from direct sun.

ONIONS

- Several onion relatives also flourish in Florida gardens. They include:

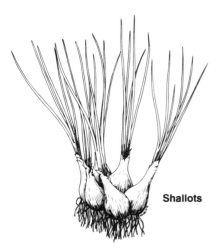
Shallots

Shallots and multiplier onions — These produce clusters of bulbs to be divided like garlic cloves. Scallions and bulbs, sometimes strong-flavored, are used mainly for cooking or making pickles.

Save extra bulbs to plant in the cool fall season. Space 6 to 8 inches apart in prepared soil. Because it is difficult to find bulbs at garden centers or mail-order companies, they frequently are shared among neighbors.

Bunching onions

Bunching onions — These types are grown to eat fresh. They produce quickly, with many varieties yielding a harvest within 50 to 75 days.

Plant seeds or divide clumps and space 2 inches apart. They will grow in clusters; harvest when pencil-size or larger. Popular varieties for Florida include White Portugal, Evergreen, Beltsville Bunching and Perfecto Blanco.

Leeks — Mild-flavored onion relatives, leeks typically are used in soups, stews and salads. They resemble scallions, with long, white bases attached to their stems. Plant the slow-growing seeds 1 to 2 inches apart in October and harvest stems during late winter and spring. They should be pencil-size to an inch in

Leek

diameter. Popular varieties include Titan and American Flag, also known as Broad London.

Garlic — Although it can be eaten fresh, garlic usually is used in cooking.

Divide a bulb into individual cloves and push into loose, fertile soil. Space about 6 inches apart. To produce well-defined cloves, feed plants frequently and, in February, remove seed heads. Harvest in May when the leaves start to yellow and collapse.

Garlic

Starts are widely available from garden centers, mail-order companies and food stores.

Solutions:

Q: We love sweet Vidalia onions. How can we grow them in Florida?

A: Florida gardeners can grow big, beautiful onions, but they will not have the sweet taste of the famed Vidalia. Varieties Texas Grano and Granex are the same, but our soil is different. Some growers speculate that the lack of sulfur in Georgia soil causes the difference; others think it is because of a combination of climatic conditions.

Q: I tried to grow onions from sets but ended up with only a few bulbs. What did I do wrong?

A: Onions grown from sets rarely produce big bulbs in Florida gardens. The little bulbs you planted probably were Northern varieties that need the long days of late spring and summer to swell to mature size. Florida is too hot for them. They will make great scallions, however.

Sets are sold fall through spring. Prepare the soil, make a furrow 1 to 2 inches deep and plant the small bulbs 2 inches apart with the root end down. Cover the sets with enough soil to hide the tops of the bulbs. Harvest developing onions when new leaves form and the basal bulb is tender.

Notes

PARSLEY

Scientific name:
Petroselinum crispum

Recommended varieties:
Moss Curled, Perfection, Italian Dark Green Plain Leaf

Ease of culture:

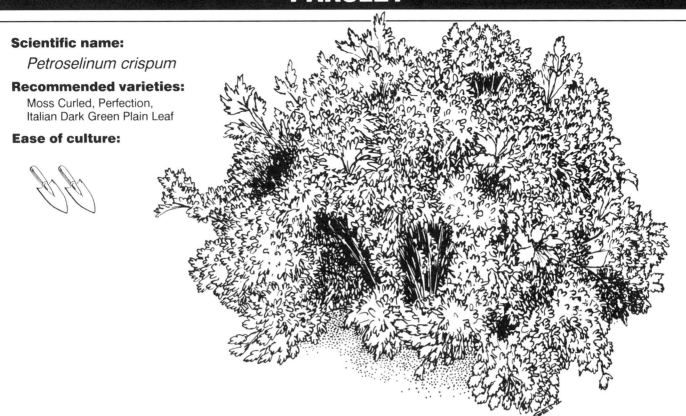

Seed germination	Days to harvest	Spacing in inches
12-14 days	70-90	Between rows: 12-20 Between plants: 8-12 Planting depth: ¼
Hardiness	**Major pests**	**Plants per person**
Tolerant of frosts and light freezes	Caterpillars	2-3

Harvest time: Ready as soon as leaves reach a usable size. Cut or pick individual leaves as needed.

Florida planting schedule												
	J	F	M	A	M	J	J	A	S	O	N	D
North		▨	▨									
Central	▨									▨	▨	▨
South	▨								▨	▨	▨	▨

You need to know:

- Seeds germinate slowly. Soak overnight before planting.
- Plant in a permanent location; plants often will grow for several seasons.
- Parsley makes a good plant for pots or hanging baskets.
- Feed sparingly every three to four weeks.
- Keep soil moist; mulch to stretch the time between waterings and to keep soil off the leaves.

Solutions:

Q: I have difficulty keeping parsley alive during the summer. Is there a secret to keeping plants growing year-round?

A: Heat and rain take a toll on parsley, which is a cool-season plant. When the rainy season arrives in summer, the root system often rots and causes the decline.

Try moving the parsley to a filtered-sun location and shelter it from rain. It still may lose leaves but will survive until cool weather returns.

Q: Caterpillars are feeding on my

PARSLEY

parsley. What's a good control?

A: Several types of caterpillars find parsley a tasty treat. If only a few plants are involved, remove the pests by hand.

When the population is large, apply Sevin or an insecticide containing *Bacillus thuringiensis*. Follow label instructions for application rates and time that must elapse between last spray and harvest.

Q: Parsley takes so long to start from seed. Is there any way to speed germination?

A: According to plant lore, "parsley must go to the devil and back seven times before it will come up." No matter what technique is used, germination usually takes about three weeks.

Some gardeners soak seeds overnight before planting to speed the process. After soaking, plant in a potting mix and keep soil moist. A plastic or newspaper cover over the soil seals in moisture. Keep the seeded container in a warm location to encourage growth.

Notes

PEANUTS

Scientific name:
Arachis hypogaea

Recommended varieties:
Tennessee Red, New Mexico A, Florigiant, NC 7, Early Bunch, Altika, Jenkins Jumbo, Florunner, Sunrunner, Pronto

Ease of culture:

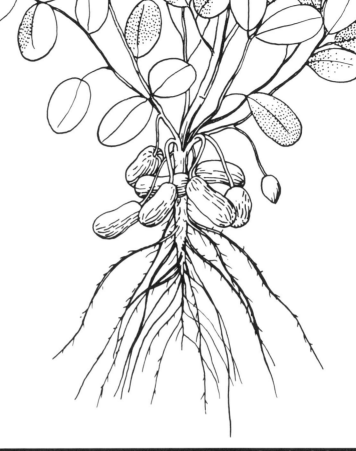

Seed germination	Days to harvest	Spacing in inches
10-14 days	Boiling peanuts: 75-80 Roasting peanuts: 125-150 days	Between rows: 24-30 Between plants: 24-48 Planting depth: 2-3
Hardiness	**Major pests**	**Plants per person**
Tender, damaged by frost	Nematodes, Southern blight, leaf spot, caterpillars	5-10

Harvest time: Check several pods because peanuts do not mature all at once. For boiling, dig when the seeds fill most of the pods. Harvest peanuts for roasting when three-quarters of the hulls have a dark interior surface.

Florida planting schedule												
	J	F	M	A	M	J	J	A	S	O	N	D
North			▓	▓	▓							
Central			▓	▓								
South		▓	▓									

You need to know:

- Peanuts have a unique growth habit. They begin flowering six to eight weeks after planting. Each yellowish blossom pollinates itself in a day.

After the blossom withers, a growth called a "peg" develops and grows downward into the soil. The peg penetrates 1 to 3 inches and swells to form the pod containing the seeds — the peanuts.

- Grow in loose, well-drained soil. Make sure the pH is around 6.0.

- Rotate the crop. Avoid planting peanuts in the same spot for at least another two years.

- Apply fertilizer to soil before planting. Incorporate 2 to 3 pounds of 6-6-6 per 100 square feet during soil preparation.

PEANUTS

- It is not necessary to inoculate seeds with a nitrogen-fixing bacteria. With the help of bacteria in the soil, plants pick up the nitrogen they need from the air.
- Ensure fully filled pods by supplying plenty of calcium. Apply 2½ pounds of gypsum to 100 feet of row when plants begin to flower.
- Do not cultivate near plants once flowering begins.
- Keep moist. Water when the top inch of soil begins to dry.
- When ready to harvest, turn the vines upward with a spading fork. Process boiling peanuts immediately.

Allow peanuts for roasting to dry in the sun for a few days; then, to keep the crop off the ground, drape vines on crosspieces nailed to poles. When thoroughly dry, pick off the peanuts and store in a dry location.

Solutions:

Q: What portion of the peanut is planted? Can we plant the entire pod, or must we extract the individual seeds?

Q: Open the pod and remove the individual seeds for planting. Seeds eventually may germinate if the pods are planted, but it would be a waste of seeds.

Try not to damage the brownish covering around the seeds as the peanuts are taken from the pods. The thin covering helps prevent rot from affecting the seeds.

Q: Last season our peanut foliage developed dark spots. The affected leaves dropped from the plants and we had a poor crop. What should we do next year to prevent damage?

A: This devastating disease commonly is called peanut leaf spot. At least two fungal organisms may be at fault.

Minimize chances of infection by turning the soil deeply and planting the crop in a different area of the garden each year.

Early plantings tend to develop the disease after much of the plant growth has occurred, so fewer sprayings are needed to protect the crop.

Early detection is important in controlling leaf spot. Begin checking for the first symptoms of the disease about a month after planting. Should they appear, begin applying preventive fungicide sprays of Bravo, Dithane M-45 or products containing copper. Repeat at 10-day to 14-day intervals. Follow label instructions for time that must elapse between last spray and harvest.

Q: We would like to roast our peanut harvest. What's the best method?

A: First, dig up the vines and allow the peanuts to air-dry, then pick off the peanuts. Roast by placing the unshelled nuts in a colander or wire basket, which will allow air to circulate around them, and place in a 300-degree oven for an hour. Stir frequently.

Notes

PEAS, ENGLISH

Scientific name:
Pisum sativum

Recommended varieties:
Garden peas — Wando, Green Arrow, Laxton's Progress

Edible-pod peas — Sugar Ann, Sugar Bon, Sugar Snap, Sugar Daddy

Ease of culture:

Seed germination	Days to harvest	Spacing in inches
7-10 days	50-70	Between rows: 24-36 Between plants: 2-3 Planting depth: 1-2
Hardiness	**Major pests**	**Plants per person**
Tolerant of frosts and light freezes	Aphids	60-70

Harvest time: Harvest and shell garden peas when pods bulge to one-quarter inch in diameter. Harvest edible-pod peas when pods begin to swell to a plump, full-seed stage. Many varieties must be snapped to remove stringy tissue along the edge of the pod.

Florida planting schedule												
	J	F	M	A	M	J	J	A	S	O	N	D
North	▓	▓	▓							▓	▓	▓
Central	▓	▓								▓	▓	▓
South	▓	▓										

You need to know:

- Wait for cool weather to begin planting.
- Sow seeds in single or double rows spaced 2 to 3 inches apart.
- Support with a fence or trellis. If planting double rows, place support between rows.
- Tall-growing varieties may need extra tying to keep plants confined to the fence or trellis.
- Fertilize only one or twice after planting.
- Keep soil moist, especially when plants begin to flower and set fruit.
- Harvest several times a week to keep production going.

Solutions:

Q: Our spring crop of peas was a failure. Just as the plants were up and growing, the whole row yellowed and died. We thought the growing conditions were ideal — warm days and plenty of sun. What happened?

A: Peas are a cool-season crop and grow best when temperatures are in the 70s. To ensure a harvest, plant peas about 90 days before hot weather is expected. Be sure to use heat-tolerant varieties recommended for Florida.

PEAS, ENGLISH

Notes

PEAS, SOUTHERN

Scientific name:
Vigna unguiculata

Recommended varieties:
Blackeye, Mississippi Silver, Texas Cream 40, Snapea, Zipper Cream, Sadandy, Purple Hull

Ease of culture:

Seed germination	Days to harvest	Spacing in inches
7-10 days	60-90	Between rows: 30-36 Between plants: 2-3 Planting depth: 1-2
Hardiness	**Major pests**	**Plants per person**
Tender, damaged by frost	Cowpea curculio, cutworm, stinkbug	15-20

Harvest time: Pods are edible in all stages. Snap young pods and cook like string beans or allow to mature and harvest when plump but before the seeds inside harden.

Florida planting schedule												
	J	F	M	A	M	J	J	A	S	O	N	D
North			▓	▓	▓	▓	▓	▓				
Central			▓	▓	▓	▓	▓	▓	▓			
South	▓	▓	▓	▓				▓	▓	▓	▓	▓

You need to know:

• Plant in a prepared garden site when the soil warms.
• Many gardeners inoculate seeds of peas and beans with nitrogen-fixing bacteria. This is not necessary in Florida because the bacteria exists in the soil.
• Peas, like other legumes, obtain nitrogen with the help of a soil bacteria; therefore, plants do not need fertilizer once they are established.
• Peas survive drought but produce better if plants are watered when the soil begins to dry. A mulch helps.
• Harvest frequently to encourage continuous flowering and pod production.

Solutions:

Q: Many of our pea pods were infested with white insects. How can we prevent this damage in future crops?

A: The cowpea curculio is a common pest of Southern peas. The adult develops a hole in a forming pod and lays an egg that grows into a white grublike

PEAS, SOUTHERN

insect that feeds on the seeds within the pod.

Control the egg-laying adults by spraying with insecticides Sevin or Thiodan during blossoming and fruit set.

Q: Although the seed packet indicated the plants were a bush variety, our peas produced vining portions. Should we trellis the plants?

A: Many varieties produce short runners but still are called bush types. Generally they need no support but may spread a bit in the garden. Some gardeners plant sprawling varieties among corn, using the stalks as support for the vines, or grow the crop near a fence.

Notes

PEPPERS

Scientific name:
Capsicum annuum

Recommended varieties:
Sweet — Early Calwonder, Yolo Wonder, Big Bertha, Sweet Banana

Hot — Hungarian Wax, Jalapeno, Mexi Bell Hybrid, Super Chili Hybrid

Ease of culture:

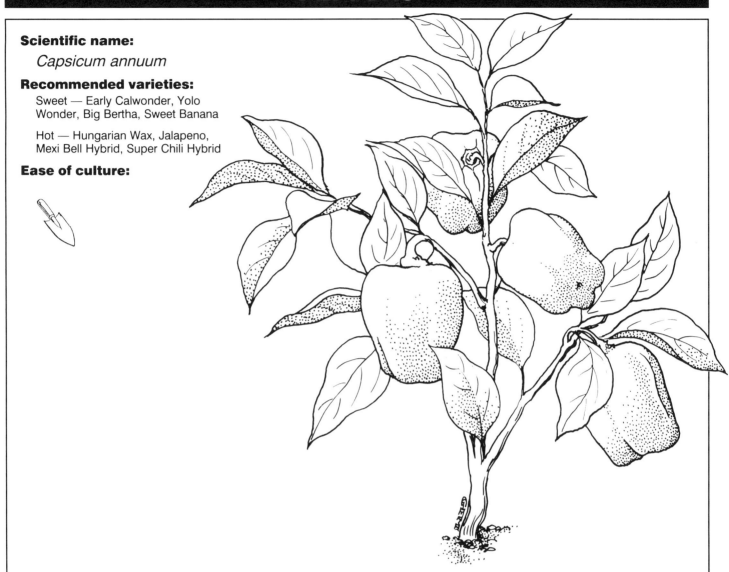

Seed germination	Days to harvest	Spacing in inches
10-14 days	Seeds: 80-100 Transplants: 60-80	Between rows: 20-36 Between plants: 12-24 Planting depth: ½

Hardiness	Major pests	Plants per person
Tender; damaged by frost	Pepper weevil, frog-eye leaf spot, caterpillars, aphids	3-5

Harvest time: Snap from plants as needed. Most are left to develop to a firm, large size. If left on the plant until fully mature, peppers often turn red.

Florida planting schedule												
	J	F	M	A	M	J	J	A	S	O	N	D
North			■	■			■	■				
Central			■	■				■	■			
South	■	■	■	■				■	■	■	■	■

PEPPERS

You need to know:

- Start seeds six to eight weeks before transplants are needed. Seeds germinate slowly during cool months.
- Plant in an improved garden soil; enrich sandy soil with organic matter.
- Feed every two to three weeks during early stages of growth and every three to four weeks thereafter. If plants produce stems and foliage but little fruit, try a low-nitrogen fertilizer.
- Branches are brittle and break easily; stake tall plants.
- Keep soil moist. Mulch to stretch the time between waterings and to keep fruit clean.
- Harvest by lifting fruit and snapping it from the plant with a twisting motion. A portion of stem usually remains attached.
- Plants may grow and produce for several seasons. Continue care while productive.

Solutions:

Q: Our pepper foliage is covered with brown oval spots. The leaves gradually drop and the plants are beginning to look bare. Will the plants ever bear peppers?

A: Warm, humid weather encourages leaf spots. Your plants are infected with frog-eye leaf spot, a fungal disease. The disease can spread rapidly among the plants. When major leaf loss occurs, the plants will not be productive and often decline totally.

Fight this disease with maneb or a copper fungicide. Make sure the leaves are covered completely with the fungicide in order to protect all the unaffected foliage.

Q: We left peppers on the plants too long and many have turned red. Are they edible?

A: Mature peppers are edible and quite tasty. In fact, the colored varieties demand the highest prices in some markets. Pick the peppers immediately and use or store.

Gardeners may allow a few peppers to mature fully, but doing so creates work for the plant. The earlier the fruit is picked, the less time the plant spends developing seeds. The plant will produce more if the peppers are picked when full size but not completely mature.

Notes

POTATOES

Scientific name:
Solanum tuberosum

Recommended varieties:
Sebago, Red Pontiac, Atlantic, Red LaSoda, LaRouge, Superior

Ease of culture:

Seed germination	Days to harvest	Spacing in inches
Rarely grown from seed	85-110	Between rows: 36-42 Between plants: 8-12 Planting depth: 3-4
Hardiness	**Major pests**	**Plants per person**
Tolerant of frosts and light freezes	Caterpillars, leaf-footed plant bug, nematodes	20-30

Harvest time: A few young potatoes may be dug early. Harvest the main crop when plants turn yellow and decline.

Florida planting schedule												
	J	F	M	A	M	J	J	A	S	O	N	D
North	▓	▓	▓									
Central		▓							▓	▓		
South	▓	▓								▓	▓	▓

POTATOES

You need to know:

- Potatoes rarely are grown from seed. Planted pieces of seed potatoes produce above-ground growth in three to four weeks.
- The potato is really a swollen stem that matures below the ground. Small depressions in the skin mark places where buds develop.

Quite often, plump sprouting buds will be evident on seed potatoes. Make seed pieces by cutting large potatoes into segments that contain one or more buds each. Most potatoes will yield four to six seed pieces. Air-dry the pieces before planting.

- In loose garden soil, plant seed pieces with the eye, or sprouting bud, pointing up. In North and Central regions, wait for freezes to end before planting.

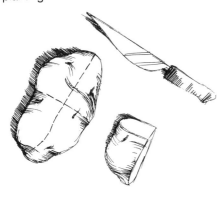

- Keep the soil moist and mulch the planting site.
- Force plants to grow extra potatoes by mounding soil or mulch around emerging stems.
- Every three to four weeks, fertilize growing plants with 6-6-6, 5-10-10 or a similar product.
- Sneak a peek — dig down around the plants as they flower or if the soil cracks. Harvest a few tender young potatoes before the main crop matures.
- Air-dry harvested potatoes. Store in a dark, cool, dry, well-ventilated area.

Solutions:

Q: Our freshly dug potatoes are covered with bumps. Can we eat the crop?

A: Root-knot nematodes have infested the crop and are living in the outer skin layer. Most people just peel the potatoes before cooking them.

Take the bumps as a serious warning, however. Unless the soil is treated, future crops also will be affected.

Gardeners can bake out nematodes by placing a clear plastic sheet over the soil for four to six weeks during the summer.

Nematodes also can be controlled by fumigating with Vapam about a month before replanting. Your cooperative extension service offers a bulletin with the full story on how to treat soil before replanting.

Q: I found a plant with a cluster of fruit resembling cherry tomatoes in our potato patch. The fruit remained hard and did not ripen like a tomato. Is it edible?

A: No, the fruit of the potato is poisonous. In fact, very little of the potato plant is edible. The only parts that can be cooked and eaten are the large swellings on the stems underground. Even these develop toxins if exposed to sunlight. They turn green and are considered poisonous.

The fruit you picked gradually will shrivel and dry out without ever softening. It may contain seeds that can be planted, but it should not be eaten.

Q: Our potato plants look good and green but some of the ends are wilting. Is there a disease at work?

A: Look out for the leaf-footed plant bug. It hides when disturbed, so be persistent. Groups of these insects surround a terminal stem and suck out the juices. This mass feeding causes considerable stem injury, which makes the end portions wither and die.

The bugs, less than an inch long, are brown with light bands across their backs. For positive identification, check their hind legs for the leaflike growths that give them their name.

If there are only a few, pick them from the plants and destroy. If the bugs are numerous or the row is long, spray with diazinon, malathion or Sevin for effective control.

Notes

POTATOES, SWEET

Scientific name:
Ipomoea Batatas

Recommended varieties:
Porto Rico, Georgia Red, Jewel, Centennial, Coastal Sweet, Boniato

Ease of culture:

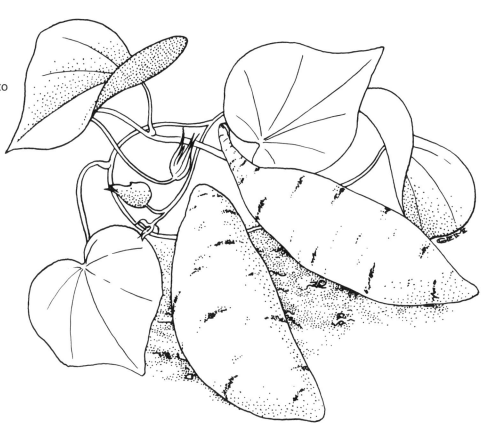

Seed germination	Days to harvest	Spacing in inches
Grown from transplants	Transplants: 120-140	Between rows: 48-54 Between plants: 12-14

Hardiness	Major pests	Plants per person
Tender, damaged by frost	Sweet potato weevil, garden fleahopper, caterpillars	5-10

Harvest time: Dig down and take a look four months after planting. The ground may start to crack when the potatoes are ready. Let roots air-dry and store in a cool location.

Florida planting schedule												
	J	F	M	A	M	J	J	A	S	O	N	D
North			▓	▓	▓	▓						
Central			▓	▓	▓	▓						
South		▓	▓	▓	▓	▓						

You need to know:

- Start with transplant slips. Grow your own from a store-bought potato or buy them from a garden center or mail-order company.

To start your own, wait until warm weather, then plant a whole potato in a secluded part of the garden. Barely cover the top with soil.

If kept moist, shoots called slips will grow and root in the soil. When they are 6 to 8 inches tall, break these growths from the potato and plant at 1-foot intervals in rows spaced 4 feet apart.

Another technique is to sprout potatoes in a dish of water. Set a third of the potato into the water, on end or side-

POTATOES, SWEET

ways, and wait for top growth to begin. The shoots will begin to produce roots that can be snapped from the potato to plant in the ground.

- Sweet potatoes grow best in sand or sandy loam. Add organic material to heavier soil.
- Plant an early crop when the weather warms in the spring. As the plants begin to vine in a month or so, cut 6- to 8-inch sections with noticeable roots from the tips of runners to start another bed.
- Feed with a low-nitrogen fertilizer every three or four weeks. Use up to a pound of a 5-10-10, 2-12-12 or similar product per 100 feet of row.
- Mulch to control weeds and maintain moisture.
- Vines will grow until there is a killing frost or freeze. Until then, dig a few potatoes and let production continue. Secondary potatoes will be produced wherever vines root down in the garden.
- Cure harvested potatoes in a well-ventilated and warm area for 10 days. (Keep air moving with a fan.) Store in a cool, dark area and use damaged or bruised potatoes first.

Solutions:

Q: The potatoes we dug are full of tunnels. Inside one we found a dark beetle with a long snout. How can we control this pest?

A: Your riddled potatoes have been feeding the sweet potato weevil. You found an adult. With reddish snouts and dark bodies, adult weevils cause little harm. White larva tunnel through the potatoes and also damage vines.

Weevils do not hibernate, so they must survive on stored potatoes or on plant pieces left in the field.

One method of control is to rotate the planting to another field. The new site, however, must be a considerable distance away. You also should destroy old plant debris and affected stored potatoes.

Once the crop is infested, no chemical control is possible. Before planting, gardeners can reduce weevil populations by fumigating soil with Vapam. Be sure the potatoes or transplants you buy are weevil-free.

Q: I just dug my sweet potatoes and found that many had split. What happened? Are they safe to eat?

A: Blame splitting on the weather or erratic watering. Most likely they developed a hard, mature skin during dry periods between rains or waterings. When moisture returned, the roots swelled with rapid new growth and ruptured in the lengthwise cracks you observed.

By encouraging rapid growth, excessive fertilizing also could have contributed to the cracking. Even though the skin is cracked, the potatoes are edible.

Prevent damage with a steady supply of moisture. Mulch your plantings, and when they go without rain for three to four days, water them.

Fertilize sparingly every four to six weeks with 6-6-6 or a similar formula at a rate of a pound per 100 square feet of garden.

Notes

PUMPKIN

Scientific name:
Cucurbita maxima, Cucurbita Pepo

Recommended varieties:
Big Max, Funny Face, Connecticut Field, Spirit, Calabaza

Ease of culture:

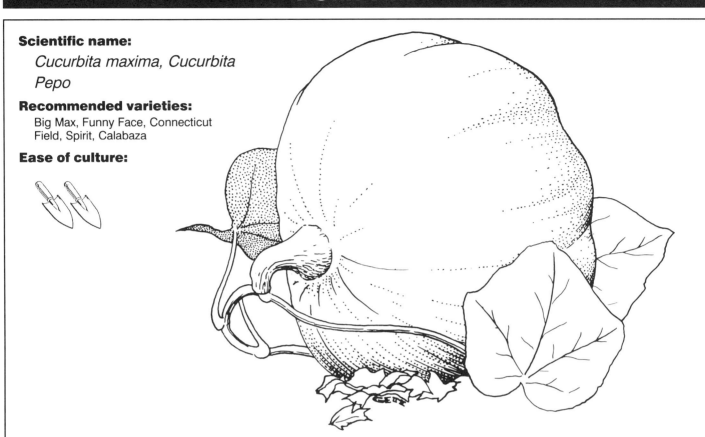

Seed germination	Days to harvest	Spacing in inches
7-10 days	Seeds: 90-120 Transplants: 80-110	Between rows: 60-84 Between plants: 36-60 Planting depth: 1-2

Hardiness	Major pests	Plants per person
Tender; damaged by frost	Caterpillars, downy mildew, powdery mildew, squash bug, vine borer	2-4

Harvest time: Leave fruit in the garden until vines begin to die.

Florida planting schedule												
	J	F	M	A	M	J	J	A	S	O	N	D
North			▓	▓			▓	▓				
Central			▓	▓			▓	▓				
South		▓					▓	▓				

You need to know:

- For pumpkins, the best soil is sand enriched with compost or similar organic matter.
- Fertilize lightly every three to four weeks with 6-6-6.
- Never allow plants to wilt. Water before the soil dries and keep plants mulched.
- Grow big pumpkins by limiting the number of fruit to one per plant. Wait until two or three pumpkins form; choose the best, and pull off the rest.

Solutions:

Q: How can I grow a big pumpkin for Halloween?

A: Go for the biggest jack-o'-lantern in town by planting Big Max pumpkins. In Florida tests, this variety produces the largest fruit, with an average weight of 25 pounds. Whoppers of more than 100 pounds have been reported elsewhere.

The crop grows faster in Florida than in most Northern states. Plant seeds in early July to harvest by October.

PUMPKIN

Notes

RADISHES

Scientific name:
Raphanus sativus

Recommended varieties:
Cherry Belle, Comet, Early Scarlet Globe, White Icicle, Sparkler, Red Prince, Champion

Ease of culture:

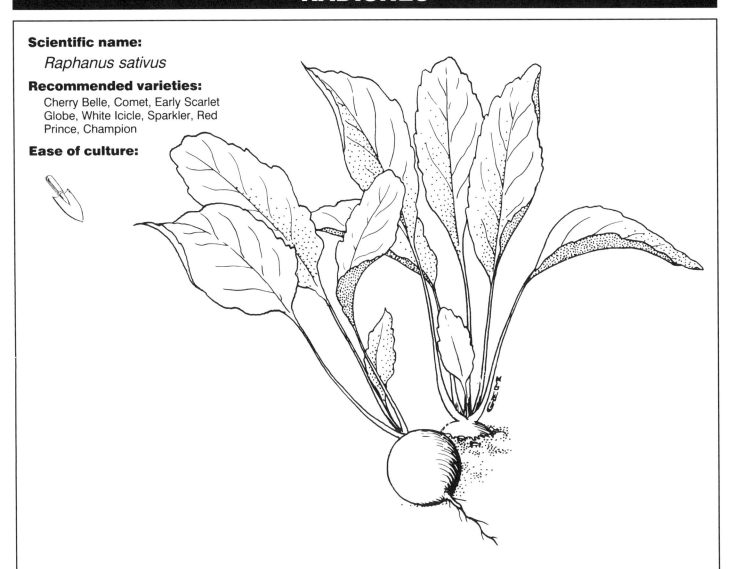

Seed germination	Days to harvest	Spacing in inches
3-7 days	25-30	Between rows: 12-18 Between plants: 1-2 Planting depth: ¾
Hardiness	**Major pests**	**Plants per person**
Tolerant of frosts and light freezes	Aphids	35-50

Harvest time: Pull when roots have swollen to a usable size and continue until they grow pithy. Radishes mature quickly.

Florida planting schedule

	J	F	M	A	M	J	J	A	S	O	N	D
North	■	■	■						■	■	■	■
Central	■	■	■						■	■	■	■
South	■	■	■								■	■

RADISHES

You need to know:

- Quick-growing and almost always successful; an ideal crop for kids.
- Wait for cool weather to begin planting.
- Sow seeds in prepared garden soil a little closer than you want plants to end up; use thinnings for early harvest.
- For a continuous harvest, plant a small amount of seed every two to three weeks.
- Seeds germinate rapidly. Keep soil moist to produce good growth.
- Additional fertilizer rarely is needed.
- When roots begin to swell, harvest the first small radishes while thinning the stand.

Solutions:

Q: We planted radishes in the spring and were disappointed. Our plants produced great tops but few roots. How can we grow better roots?

A: In a subtropical climate, a spring planting often produces a poor harvest. The warm days and mild nights encourage quick top growth but long, thready roots. Gardeners who begin planting early in the fall often observe similar growth. Radishes are a crop that must be timed for the coolest weather — usually November through February.

Some radishes produce poor roots even when the weather is cool because the plants have been grown in shade or given too much fertilizer. Radishes need full sun. A preplant application of fertilizer usually is enough to grow plump roots.

Notes

RADISHES, WINTER

Scientific name:
Raphanus sativus

Recommended varieties:
Chinese Rose, Chinese White, Celestial, Round Black Spanish

Ease of culture:

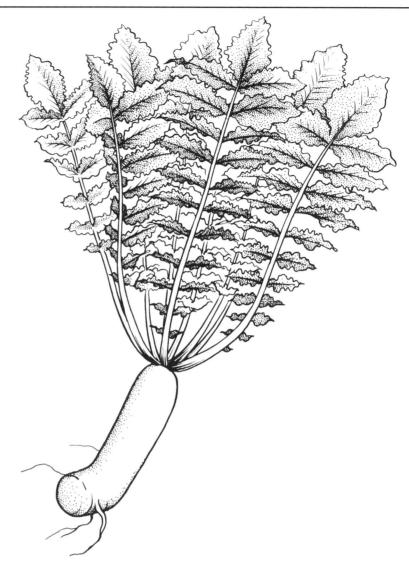

Seed germination	Days to harvest	Spacing in inches
5-7 days	60-70	Between rows: 24-36 Between plants: 4-6 Planting depth: ¾
Hardiness	**Major pests**	**Plants per person**
Tolerant of frosts and light freezes	Aphids and root maggot	15-20

Harvest time: Pull when roots have swollen to a usable size. Some varieties grow more than a foot long and can weigh more than 20 pounds. Older roots remain tender but become pithy and pungent.

Florida planting schedule												
	J	F	M	A	M	J	J	A	S	O	N	D
North									▓	▓		
Central									▓	▓	▓	
South									▓	▓	▓	▓

RADISHES, WINTER

You need to know:

- Sow during fall so roots mature when weather is cool.
- Sow seeds a little closer than desired final spacing; thin by harvesting when roots reach a usable size.
- Plant in mounded rows of soil that have been enriched with organic matter.
- Push soil up around top of developing root as the plant grows.
- Keep soil moist to produce good growth. Mulches are recommended.
- Feed lightly every three to four weeks with a low-nitrogen 2-12-12 or 5-10-10 fertilizer.

Solutions:

Q: We made a spring planting of Chinese radishes, but the crop was a failure. The roots had a sharp taste and the plants bloomed quickly. Won't the crop grow in Florida?

A: Try a fall planting. Start the seeds when the days become shorter and begin to cool. Foliage and young roots will form during the warm weather but mature when days turn cold. Moderate temperatures delay flower production and ensure a better-tasting root.

Notes

RHUBARB

Scientific name:
Rheum Rhabarbarum

Recommended varieties:
Victoria, Cherry Red

Ease of culture:

Seed germination	Days to harvest	Spacing in inches
10-14 days	Varies by region of state (See "You need to know")	Between rows: 42-54 Between plants: 24-30

Hardiness	Major pests	Plants per person
Tolerant of frosts and freezes	Nematodes	2-3

Harvest time: Use only the stalks and discard the foliage, which is toxic. Use a twisting, pulling motion to snap stalks off plant from the base when thick and about 10 inches long. Leaves should be just starting to unfurl.

Florida planting schedule												
	J	F	M	A	M	J	J	A	S	O	N	D
North	■	■	■	■	■	■	■	■	■	■	■	
Central								■	■	■		
South								■	■	■		

RHUBARB

You need to know:

- In North Florida, rhubarb is a perennial. Buy divisions of established clumps to begin a planting. Position sections of crowns and roots with buds 2 to 3 inches below soil surface.

  Harvest lightly the second spring after planting. During the third spring begin full harvesting for eight to 10 weeks.

  Plants should be dug and divided every five to eight years.

- In Central and South Florida, treat as an annual. Sow seeds in late summer to grow transplants to set in the garden during October or November.

  Harvest begins 150 days after sowing seeds and lasts eight to 10 weeks.

- Plant in soil improved with compost, peat or manure.

- Eliminate nematodes before planting, especially when growing as a perennial.

- Work a 6-6-6 fertilizer into the soil before planting. Continue to feed the developing plants; every three to four weeks in sandy soil, every six to eight weeks in areas where the soil is heavy or to encourage seasonal growth in Northern regions.

- Mulch to retain moisture. Plants are deep-rooted and need watering only when the upper few inches of soil begin to dry.

Solutions:

Q: We planted rhubarb roots obtained from a Northern company. The growth was poor during the summer and only a few sprouts developed the second year. What went wrong?

A: In many Florida gardens, the growth of rhubarb is limited by hot summers and lack of substantial cold. Only in North Florida are the winters cool enough to break plant dormancy, which encourages good growth.

Long, hot summers and frequent rains also encourage lanky growth and rot problems.

If you want to order plants from the North, have the crowns shipped during fall. Place them in the freezer for six weeks to simulate winter cold before planting in the garden.

Another approach is to get crowns that have passed through the winter in the North and are shipped in time for an early spring planting.

Either method should yield a good spring harvest, but the rhubarb still will have heat and moisture problems during the summer.

Q: Our plants grew slowly. We have well-drained sandy soil that gives good yields from other crops. What should we add to the soil for the rhubarb?

A: The key to good growth is organic matter that holds moisture and ensures a constant supply of nutrients. Add plenty of compost, clippings and manure plus bedding.

Use the raised-bed technique in poorly drained areas to ensure proper soil aeration. During rainy seasons this minimizes root rot, which could prevent good growth. Rhubarb needs adequate moisture but not standing water because that will rot the crowns.

Notes

SPINACH

Scientific name:
Spinacia oleracea

Recommended varieties:
Virginia Savoy, Dixie Market, Hybrid 7, Bloomsdale Longstanding

Ease of culture:

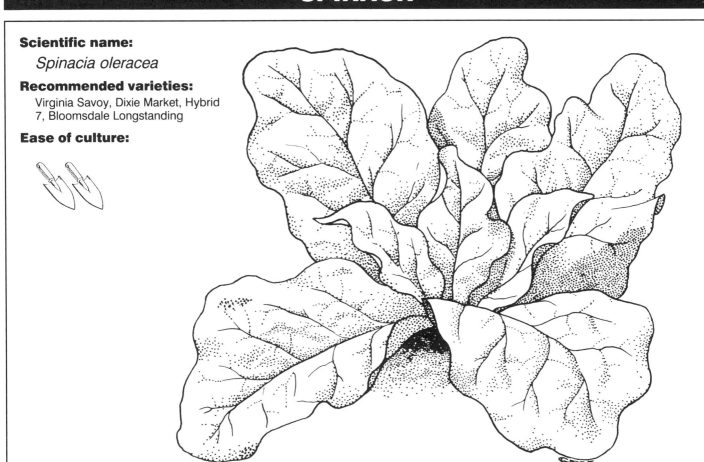

Seed germination	Days to harvest	Spacing in inches
10-14 days	45-60	Between rows: 14-18 Between plants: 3-5 Planting depth: ¾
Hardiness	**Major pests**	**Plants per person**
Tolerant of frosts and light freezes	Caterpillars	30-40

Harvest time: Begin to harvest when leaves are 3 to 4 inches tall. Cut individual leaves or the entire plant.

Florida planting schedule												
	J	F	M	A	M	J	J	A	S	O	N	D
North										▓	▓	
Central										▓	▓	▓
South	▓									▓	▓	▓

You need to know:

- Sow during cool weather in a prepared garden site.
- May be grown in single rows, but adapts well to double-cropping and wide-row techniques.
- Keep soil moist to speed germination and encourage quick growth.
- Fertilize lightly every two to three weeks with 6-6-6 or nitrogen-only fertilizer.
- Use a mulch to stretch the intervals between waterings and to keep foliage clean.
- Plants can be harvested for two to three weeks. When a seed stalk appears, cut and use the entire plant.
- To ensure a continuing supply, make monthly sowings while the weather is cool.

SPINACH

Solutions:

Q: We would like to grow a warm-weather spinach crop. Our seed catalog lists two varieties that take the heat. Will they grow in Florida?

A: Both Malabar and New Zealand species flourish spring through summer in Florida gardens.

The Malabar species, also called Ceylon and climbing spinach, must be trellised. Start plantings from seeds or cuttings. Two vines should provide sufficient harvests for a family. Prune the plants to restrict growth. Use the tender leaves and stems as a substitute for true spinach.

New Zealand grows as a bushy herb and is planted from seeds. Tip the vigorous branches as needed to cause branching; the cuttings can be eaten.

Q: I have difficulty growing spinach during the fall. The plants begin to form stems and leaves, then rot. What's wrong?

A: Plant during cool weather; seedlings are susceptible to rots when the weather is warm.

When plantings repeatedly fail, consider fumigating the soil with Vapam or following soil solarization techniques before replanting.

Rotating the crop each year to another portion of the garden also will help.

Notes

SQUASH, SUMMER

Scientific name:
Cucurbita Pepo

Recommended varieties:
Early Prolific Straightneck, Dixie, Summer Crookneck, Cocozelle, Gold Bar, Zucchini, Peter Pan, Scallopini, Sunburst

Ease of culture:

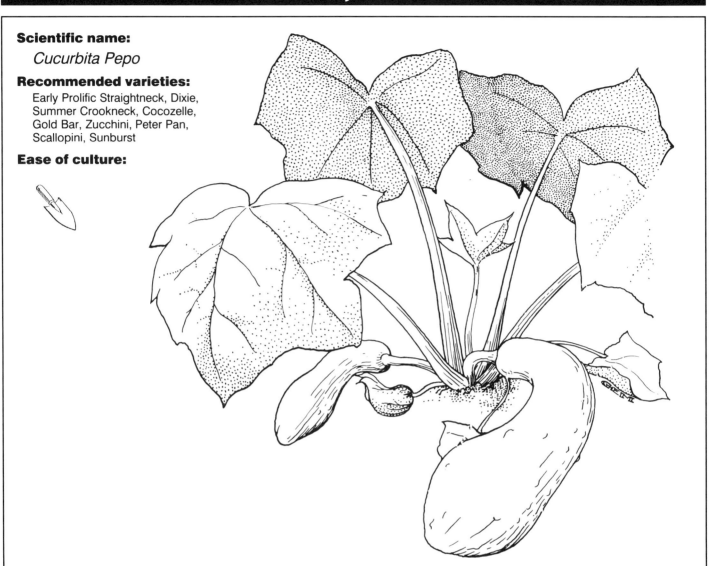

Seed germination	Days to harvest	Spacing in inches
5-7 days	Seeds: 40-55 Transplants: 35-40	Between rows: 36-48 Between plants: 24-36 Planting depth: 1-2
Hardiness	**Major pests**	**Plants per person**
Tender, damaged by frost	Caterpillars, powdery mildew, vine borers, pickleworms	4-6

Harvest time: Best picked when young. Can be harvested as soon as fruit forms, but most are left to grow until 3 to 6 inches in diameter. Be sure to pick before skin toughens and seeds grow large.

Florida planting schedule												
	J	F	M	A	M	J	J	A	S	O	N	D
North			▓	▓				▓	▓			
Central			▓	▓				▓	▓			
South	▓	▓	▓					▓	▓	▓		

SQUASH, SUMMER

You need to know:

- Squash grows best in sandy soil. The addition of a little organic matter improves water retention.
- Sow seeds or set transplants in prepared garden soil. Plant in rows or in clusters of three or four seeds.
- Feed frequently to grow large, productive plants: every two to three weeks in sandy soil, every three to four weeks in heavy clay or loamy soil.
- Mulch to conserve moisture and keep fruit clean.
- Check frequently for vine borers and pickleworms. Control by handpicking or spraying.
- To protect bees, which are needed to pollinate the crop, use pesticides only in the evening.
- Harvest frequently to keep productive.

Solutions:

Q: Our squash plants are producing plenty of flowers but no edible squash. The little fruit that does appear falls off or rots. How can we make our plants productive?

A: Gardeners anticipating their first harvest must be patient. Early in the season, new hybrid varieties may produce an abundance of female flowers but no male flowers to pollinate them. Rudimentary fruit may form, but without pollination it will remain small and appear to rot from the end.

Nothing is wrong with the plants. Male flowers soon will appear and, with the help of bees, the vines will become productive.

Q: Some of our yellow summer squash turned green with yellow spots. What caused this?

A: A few of your plants have a mosaic virus disease. The virus lives in the plant and may affect the color of both the leaves and the fruit.

The squash still is edible, but often unappealing in appearance. The only control is to remove infected plants and try to eliminate insects that carry the virus.

Q: Just when we are ready to pick a squash, we find it full of worms. They make small holes in the skin and tunnel inside. Is there a way to beat these creatures?

A: Squash is a favorite food of the pickleworm. With tough-skinned winter squash, caterpillars may not penetrate far and the wounds may heal. Summer squash is more vulnerable.

Eggs laid on foliage, flowers and fruit hatch into destructive caterpillars. They immediately begin feeding and make holes in all parts of the plant, but at harvest are most noticeable in the fruit.

The hole on the skin is just a token of the big cavity they probably have formed inside. Harvest the fruit as soon as you notice damage and try to salvage unaffected portions.

Control pickleworms early. Check plants for signs of caterpillars even before the fruit forms. Use Sevin to eliminate them. If pickleworms are prevalent, a weekly spraying may be needed.

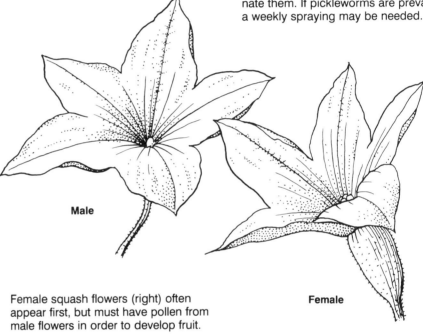

Female squash flowers (right) often appear first, but must have pollen from male flowers in order to develop fruit.

Notes

SQUASH, WINTER

Scientific name:
Cucurbita maxima, Cucurbita Pepo

Recommended varieties:
Sweet Mama, Table Queen, Butternut, Spaghetti, Jersey Golden Acorn, Table Ace, Blue Hubbard

Ease of culture:

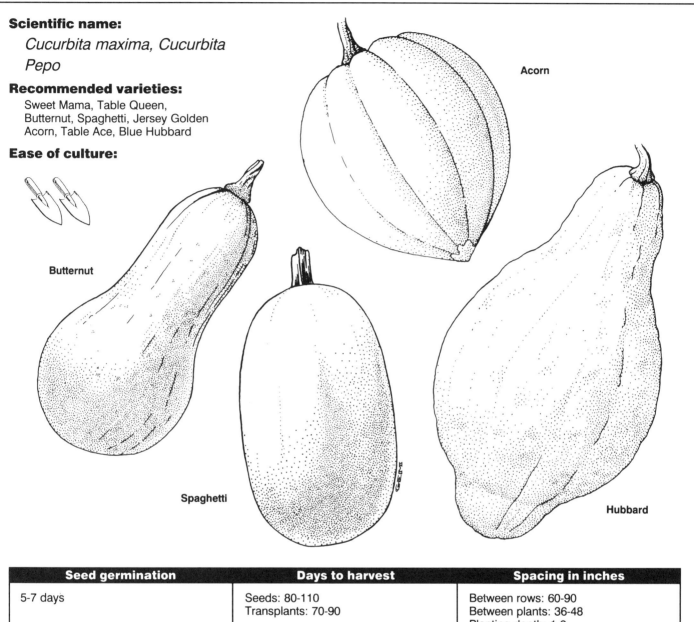

Seed germination	Days to harvest	Spacing in inches
5-7 days	Seeds: 80-110 Transplants: 70-90	Between rows: 60-90 Between plants: 36-48 Planting depth: 1-2
Hardiness	**Major pests**	**Plants per person**
Tender, damaged by frost	Caterpillars, downy mildew, powdery mildew, vine borers, pickleworms	4-6

Harvest time: Gather when fruit is fully mature. Many turn a deep green or develop some orange coloring. Leave a short piece of stem attached to the fruit when picking. Brush off soil, but do not wash before storing.

Florida planting schedule												
	J	F	M	A	M	J	J	A	S	O	N	D
North			■									
Central			■					■				
South	■	■	■									

SQUASH, WINTER

You need to know:

- Grows best in sandy soil or sand enriched with organic matter.
- Set transplants or sow seeds in groups or rows.
- Conserve space by planting bush varieties or growing vines up a trellis.
- Fertilize frequently to encourage young growth; every two to three weeks in sandy soil, every three to four weeks in clay or loam.
- Mulch to conserve moisture and keep fruit clean.
- Check frequently for vine borers and pickleworms. Eliminate by hand-picking or spraying.
- Leave fruit to mature on the vine. Store in a cool, dry space until ready to use. Winter squash's name reflects its excellent storage characteristics.

Solutions:

Q: A strange, squashlike plant grew from our compost pile. We can't decide if it's a squash or a pumpkin. How can we tell? Is it edible?

A: Some of the strangest squash grow in the compost. Their arrival may be a mystery, but the vines almost always produce big, green or yellowish-orange fruit that some call squash and others, pumpkin.

Yours could have started from discarded seeds scooped out of a squash you ate. Most volunteer plants spring from hybrid parents; their unusual fruit may resemble a distant ancestor once used in a breeding program.

No need to fret over its name, however. These large fruit generally fall under one of the three cucurbit genera, so it is always correct to call them squash. The name pumpkin, originally "pumpion," came to be applied to fruit with jack-o'-lantern potential. Neither term has real botanical significance, so a scientist will hardly ever argue with your choice. The fruit won't hurt you, but will it taste good? Try it and see.

Q: Our squash plants are big and beautiful, but suddenly the leaves are turning white. I hope this will not hurt the developing fruit. Should I try a control?

A: For squash, cucumbers and related vegetables, powdery mildew will arrive with the heat and humidity of late spring. Light cases are fairly harmless, but a thick, grayish-white coating of the leaves will cause plants to decline. Be ready with a fungicide spray during late spring. At the first sign of white coating, apply Benlate, chlorothalonil or sulfur. Repeat as recommended on the label.

Because plant breeders have not been able to select plants resistant to this fungus, your harvest will depend on your watchfulness.

Notes

STRAWBERRIES

Scientific name:
Fragaria X Ananassa

Recommended varieties:
Florida 90, Chandler, Dover, Florida Belle, Oso Grande, Sweet Charlie, Selva

Ease of culture:

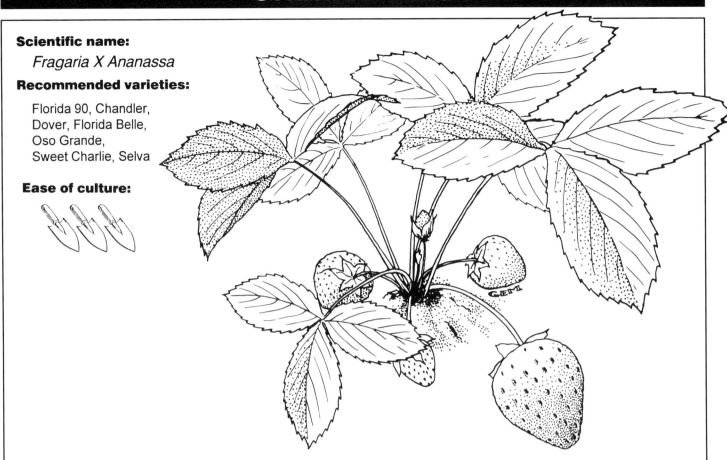

Seed germination	Days to harvest	Spacing in inches
Typically grown from transplants	Transplants: 90-110	Between rows: 36-40 Between plants: 10-14
Hardiness	**Major pests**	**Plants per person**
Plants tolerate frosts and freezes; flowers and fruit escape damage only in light frosts.	Caterpillars, slugs, thrips, mites, snails, leaf spot, fruit rot	20-25

Harvest time: Pick fruit when red. Pick every day during peak production times to beat birds and insects to the crop.

Florida planting schedule												
	J	F	M	A	M	J	J	A	S	O	N	D
North									▒	▒		
Central									▒	▒	▒	
South										▒	▒	

You need to know:

- Plant transplants. Young strawberry plants arrive at garden centers from Northern producers during early fall months.

- Grow at ground level or in raised beds. Raised beds allow concentrated production and provide extra drainage for plants that are susceptible to rot. Make beds 2 feet wide and 2 feet apart. For raised beds, mound soil 6 inches high along the edge and 8 inches high in the middle.

- Incorporate 2½ pounds of 6-6-6 fertilizer for each 100 square feet of prepared site. Place an additional band of fertilizer 6 inches deep along the center

STRAWBERRIES

of the beds — 2½ pounds to 100 running feet. This is ample fertilizer for strawberries raised as annuals.

- Moisten soil and mulch. Straw or compost are good organic materials; black plastic also can be used.
- Set plants in double rows. Start a row 6 inches from the edge of the bed and space plants 12 inches apart.
- Fan out roots; be careful not to double or crumple them. Try to set plants at the original growing depth. Cover roots but leave crown fully exposed.
- Keep soil moist. Water new plants as needed to prevent wilting; water established plants every two to three days.
- Anticipate insect, leaf spot and fruit rot problems. Apply chemical controls early to avoid harvesting pesticide-treated fruit.
- Because pests are prevalent, most growers remove plants after fruiting and replant beds in the fall.

Solutions:

Q: How do we care for strawberry plants after the harvest? In the North we allowed the beds to continue growing and used the young shoots for transplants.

A: In Florida, commercial growers and most gardeners consider strawberries an annual crop. The plants are plowed under when the season ends. Summer weather is rough on the plants, often encouraging crown rot and other problems. The plants also are susceptible to viruses and nematodes.

Still, some gardeners grow the plants through the hot, humid months to produce crops for another year. The plants are left in the bed and runners are permitted to develop into the next year's berry-producing stand, or the runners are transplanted after they root to create new plantings.

Plantings carried over will need additional feedings at six- to eight-week intervals. Use a 6-6-6 or similar product at the rate of 1 pound per 100 square feet of garden. Watch for leaf spot, rot and insect problems that may need control during summer and early fall.

Q: I dislike using pesticides during harvest time, but every year I lose many berries to bugs. Is there a way to eliminate the insects without using harsh sprays?

A: Try using natural pesticides to control the pests. Insecticidal soaps destroy many insects upon contact, and sprays containing *Bacillus thuringiensis* control many types of caterpillars. Slugs often can be coaxed to a container of stale beer set near the plantings.

If these alternatives fail to provide the necessary control, try spraying early in the season to prevent insect populations before harvest. Use synthetic pesticides when the pests are first noticed and up to the time of harvest, then stop the sprays and enjoy the crop without having to apply treatments when the berries are ripening.

Q: Seed catalogs feature strawberries that can be grown from seeds. How well do they produce in Florida?

A: Florida gardeners have had limited success with strawberries grown from seeds. The problem is with scheduling the transplants to produce a crop. For production the first year, seeds must be sown in early fall so the plants will fruit by spring. From the sowing of seeds to the first fruit is about 120 days. Most gardeners skip this fuss and buy transplants of known varieties with good production records.

Q: Will ever-bearing strawberries grow locally?

A: Most will bear some fruit, but the most successful results are from Florida varieties. By growing the recommended strawberry plants, production can extend from early winter through spring — and that is almost ever-bearing. Summer is tough on all types of strawberries, even the ever-bearing types.

Notes

SWISS CHARD

Scientific name:
Beta vulgaris

Recommended varieties:
Lucullus, Fordhook Giant, Rhubarb Swiss Chard

Ease of culture:

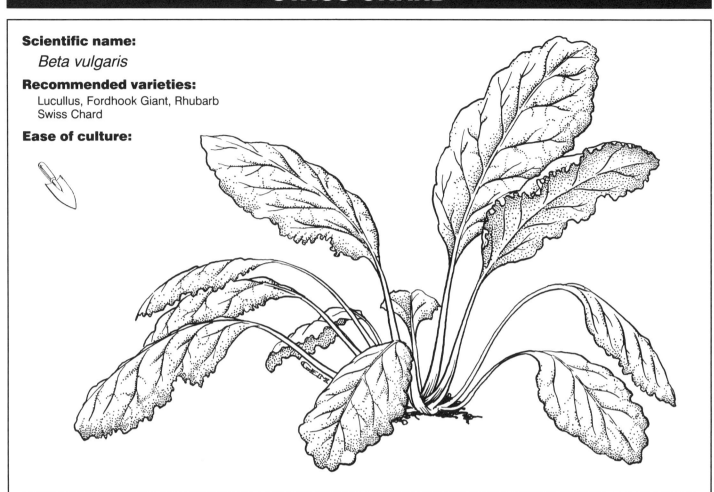

Seed germination	Days to harvest	Spacing in inches
5-10 days	Seeds: 50-60 Transplants: 40-50	Between rows: 18-24 Between plants: 8-10 Planting depth: ½
Hardiness	**Major pests**	**Plants per person**
Tolerates frosts and light freezes	Caterpillars	6-8

Harvest time: Chard can be eaten at any stage of growth. Pulling individual leaves while they are young and tender, usually 10 to 12 inches long, prolongs the growing season. Large stalks may be used like celery or asparagus. Entire plants may be harvested.

Florida planting schedule												
	J	F	M	A	M	J	J	A	S	O	N	D
North	▓	▓	▓						▓	▓	▓	▓
Central	▓	▓	▓						▓	▓	▓	▓
South	▓	▓	▓						▓	▓	▓	▓

You need to know:

- Grows well in sandy or sandy loam soil. Improve sandy soil with organic matter.
- Grow from seeds sown directly or as transplants. Sow thinly. Each seed is actually a cluster, often producing several plants.
- Thin out newly emerging plants. Extras can be transplanted to fill in blank spots in a row.
- Keep soil moist and mulch to encourage tender growth.
- Feed every three to four weeks with up to a pound of 6-6-6 or nitrogen-only fertilizer for every 100 feet of row.
- Plants eventually will flower, usually

SWISS CHARD

in the spring. At that point, pull and discard or add to compost heap.

Solutions:

Q: What happens to Swiss chard when summer arrives? Our plants have done well during the spring.

A: Swiss chard is heat tolerant and can live into the summer. When extremely hot weather arrives and daily rains begin, the plants often succumb to crown rots. Enjoy the crop until plant quality declines. Sow again in fall.

Q: Is there a difference between red and green varieties?

A: The taste is about the same, but the red variety adds color to the garden and often is used as an ornamental that can be eaten.

Notes

TOMATOES

Scientific name:

Lycopersicon Lycopersicum

Recommended varieties:

Standard — Celebrity, Floramerica, Sun Coast, Walter, Better Boy, Better Bush, Champion, Whopper, Quick Pick

Beefsteak — Beefsteak, Beefmaster, Super Beefsteak, Bragger

Small fruited — Cherry Grande, Sweet 100, Tiny Tim, Sugar Lump

Container — Florida Basket, Florida Petite, Florida Lanai, Patio Cherry

Yellow- and white-fruited — Golden Boy, Lemon Boy, Jubilee, Snowball

Pear — La Roma, Roma

Ease of culture:

Seed germination	Days to harvest	Spacing in inches
7 days	Seeds: 90-110 Transplants: 75-90	Between rows: 36-48 Between plants: 18-24
Hardiness	**Major pests**	**Plants per person**
Tender, damaged by frost	Caterpillars, leaf miner, mites, leaf spot, wilts	For eating fresh: 3-5 For processing: 5-10

Harvest time: For best flavor, pick when color has fully developed. If harvested green or pink, mature color will develop but flavor will not. Green tomatoes can be harvested then fried, preserved or pickled.

Florida planting schedule												
	J	F	M	A	M	J	J	A	S	O	N	D
North			▓	▓				▓				
Central			▓					▓	▓			
South	▓	▓	▓					▓	▓	▓	▓	

You need to know:

• There are three types of tomato plants: determinate, indeterminate and indeterminate short-internode. Determinate plants grow as small bushes and the crop ripens all at once. Indeterminate plants set and mature fruit over a period of several months. They usually are tall. Indeterminate short-internode plants are similar to indeterminate plants but are more compact. The leaves and branches grow close together.

• Look for disease resistance when buying seeds and transplants. The following symbols denote resistance:

V — Verticillium wilt
F — Fusarium wilt
FF — Race 1 and 2 fusarium wilt
T — Tobacco mosaic

The more letters on the package, the

TOMATOES

more resistant the variety.
- To avoid cold in the fall and excessive heat in late spring, follow the appropriate Florida planting schedule.
- Feed every two to three weeks when plants are young; every three to four weeks when flowering begins.

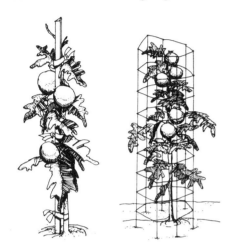

- Grow plants upright, staked or in cages so it will be easier to find pests, spray plants and harvest fruit.
- Keep soil moist but not wet.

Solutions:

Q: Our tomato plants produced a great harvest. Now they continue to grow, but the flowers open and, in a few days, drop to the ground. Can we expect any more fruit?

A: Probably not; the weather is either too hot or too cool. Tomato plants set fruit only in temperatures between 55 and 85 degrees. It's disappointing to growers, but only cherry tomatoes can take the intense summer heat. No variety will produce well during cool winter months.

It may help a little to spray the flowers with a plant hormone sold as Blossom-set, but the only real solution is to adjust your growing schedule to the weather tomatoes prefer.

Q: We are looking for a tomato that is less acid than normal varieties. Would yellow or white ones be best?

A: All tomatoes fall in a pH range of 4.0 to 4.5, considered very acidic. Overall, there is little difference between varieties. The flavor of lighter-colored tomatoes may be less intense, but there is no relationship between color and acidity.

Q: Our tomatoes have big brown spots on the bottom. They seem to ripen at first but then end up unusable. Is this a blight?

A: Your leathery, not-very-tasty tomatoes are afflicted with blossom-end rot. This is a nutritional deficiency; the plants lack calcium.

Quite often, the calcium is missing from the soil. A pH test taken before planting helps determine if the soil needs lime, which supplies calcium.

Erratic watering may keep calcium from traveling up the stems of the plants and into the fruit, so keep soil moist and water when the surface begins to dry. A mulch helps keep the roots cool and extends the time between waterings.

Too much fertilizer, too much shade, too-cool nights or injury to roots by nematodes also can contribute to this disorder.

A quick remedy is to supply calcium in a spray. Mix calcium chloride at a rate of 4 tablespoons to 3 gallons of water. Use a quart per plant and apply the solution twice weekly as a foliar feed. A commercial preparation, Stop Blossom-End Rot, is sold by garden centers.

Notes

TURNIPS

Scientific name:
Brassica Rapa

Recommended varieties:
Foliage — Shogoin, All Top Hybrid

Foliage and roots — Purple Top White Globe, Just Right, Royal Crown, Tokyo Cross, Tokyo Top Hybrid

Ease of culture:

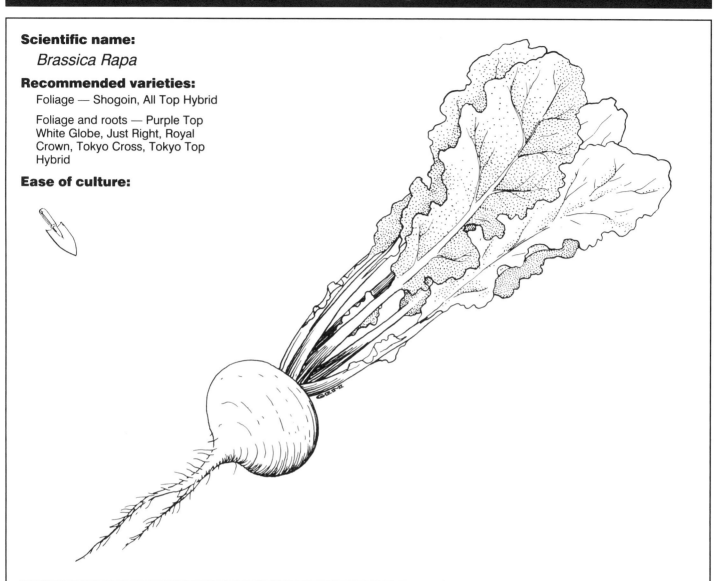

Seed germination	Days to harvest	Spacing in inches
5 days	40-60	Between rows: 12-20 Between plants: 4-6 Planting depth: ½-1
Hardiness	**Major pests**	**Plants per person**
Tolerant of frosts and light freezes	Aphids, caterpillars	5-10 feet of row

Harvest time: Thin young plants to use fresh tops, leaving room for the remaining roots to mature. Tops may be harvested at any stage but are best cut when 4 to 12 inches tall. Harvest roots 2 to 3 inches in diameter, before texture grows pithy and flavor becomes strong.

Florida planting schedule												
	J	F	M	A	M	J	J	A	S	O	N	D
North	▓	▓	▓	▓				▓	▓	▓		
Central	▓	▓	▓					▓	▓	▓	▓	
South	▓	▓							▓	▓	▓	▓

TURNIPS

You need to know:

- Turnips grow in any prepared garden soil.
- Before planting, fertilize with a complete, balanced fertilizer such as 6-6-6.
- Sow seeds 1 to 2 inches apart. Conserve space by sowing turnips in wide bands of 12 inches or more. Thin seedlings to a 4-inch spacing. Use thinnings as a first leafy harvest.
- Keep soil moist to speed germination and plant growth.
- Fertilize every two to three weeks. Use a 6-6-6 or a product high in phosphorus like a 5-10-10.
- Rutabaga, a turnip relative, needs cool winter weather to develop large roots with a robust flavor. Culture is similar to turnips, except tops rarely are eaten. Roots are ready to harvest in about 90 days, when 3 to 6 inches in diameter. American Purple Top Yellow is the most commonly planted variety.

Solutions:

Q: Our turnips were beginning to grow, then suddenly appeared to be nibbled off near the ground. At first, only a portion of the row was damaged; days later, most of the planting was gone. We found no insects. What could have happened?

A: A population of cutworms appears to be the problem. These pests live in the soil during the day and feast on tender seedlings at night. Large sections of a row or most of the crop can be consumed by these larval stages of moths.

Check closely within the row where the plants had grown. If small holes are present, dig into the soil where the insects are hiding and destroy the pests.

If the insects cannot be found or if the population is too large, an insecticide may be needed. A biological control containing *Bacillus thuringiensis* may be of help when sprayed on young plants. Chemical sprays commonly used for cutworms also will give control when used as directed.

Q: We had a great turnip crop but left many plants in the garden until the roots could be used in the kitchen. When they finally were pulled, many were cracked or infested with insects. How could we have prevented this damage?

A: Root crops left in the ground too long may crack if excessive water is absorbed by the plants. This often occurs when gardens are overwatered.

It is best to harvest root crops as they mature. Dig the turnips, then place in a plastic bag and refrigerate.

Keeping soil a bit on the dry side will help extend storage life for plants in the ground. When water is plentiful, cracking will occur and insects enter to feed.

Q: Our turnips grew great tops but small roots. We wanted both portions but had to settle on having greens. How can usable tops and roots be produced?

A: A few turnip varieties produce more tops than roots. These will grow tender, ready-to-eat leaves in 40 to 50 days. When you want a turnip for both foliage and roots, select a multipurpose variety. Seed packets should include a complete description of the variety. When the quality of the root is not mentioned, the variety probably is grown for leaves only.

Q: Colonies of green insects made our first turnip greens most unappetizing. The insects were small and primarily crawled on the underside of the leaves. How do we grow pest-free plants?

A: A few aphids may have to be tolerated and washed off the foliage during meal preparation. The insects feed by sucking juices from tender leaves. Large populations develop as harvest nears.

Anticipate aphids and monitor the plants for pest invasions. Insecticidal soaps can reduce populations but must hit the aphids directly. Soap sprays can be applied up to the day of harvest.

Chemical sprays also are available to control aphids on turnips. These may be needed when the insects appear to be resisting biological controls. The products work quickly, but the crop cannot be eaten until a week or two has passed. Follow label instructions carefully.

Notes

WATERMELON

Scientific name:
Citrullus lanatus

Recommended varieties:
Large — Charleston Gray, Jubilee, Crimson Sweet, Dixielee

Small — Sugar Baby, Minilee, Mickylee

Seedless — Tri-X-317

Ease of culture:

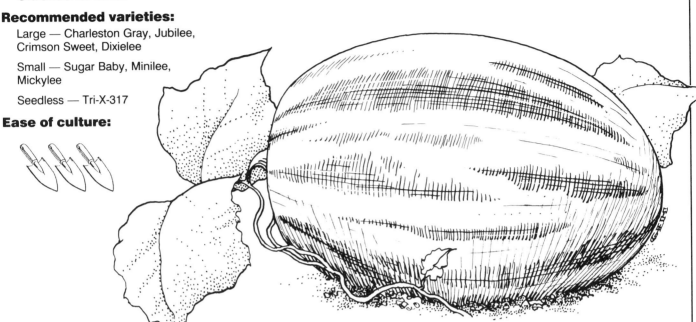

Seed germination	Days to harvest	Spacing in inches
7-10 days	85-95	Between rows: 48-108 Between plants: 15-60 Planting depth: 1-2

Hardiness	Major pests	Plants per person
Tender, damaged by frost	Caterpillars, fusarium wilt, anthracnose, downy mildew	2-4

Harvest time: Ripe melons, when rapped, echo with a dull thud. Bellies change from smooth and white to rough and yellow. The stringlike tendril on the vine nearest the melon turns brown.

Florida planting schedule												
	J	F	M	A	M	J	J	A	S	O	N	D
North			▓	▓			▓	▓				
Central		▓	▓					▓				
South	▓	▓	▓									

You need to know:

• Plant seeds in rows, individually or in groups of two to four.

• Spacing recommendations vary with varieties. For large varieties, allow 84 to 108 inches between rows and 48 to 60 inches between plants. For both small and seedless varieties, allow 48 to 60 inches between rows and 15 to 30 inches between plants.

• The best melons grow in sandy, well-drained soil liberally enriched with organic matter.

• Plant early in the spring to produce a harvest before rainy summer weather or in late summer for a fall crop.

• Grow with a moderate amount of water. Water once or twice a week once established.

• Apply a 6-6-6 or similar product seven to 10 days after seedlings emerge. Apply again when the vines begin to run and once again when flowering begins.

• Grow resistant varieties and apply fungicides as needed.

• Avoid disease problems by planting in new sites each year. Fumigate small garden sites with Vapam or follow soil solarization procedures.

WATERMELON

Solutions:

Q: Our watermelons had little flavor. Our neighbor said they may have crossed with nearby cucumbers. Could this be the reason?

A: The cucumbers did not affect your melons. The two crops do not cross. Even if they did, a change in taste would not show up until the next generation.

Poor flavor generally is caused by the weather or the gardener. Heavy rains or too much watering close to harvest can cause bland fruit because the sugars are diluted by the extra moisture. Cloudy days or too-early picking also may be to blame.

Keep plants on the dry side as harvest time nears.

Q: It's been six weeks since my plants began to flower and there's still no sign of fruit. How long do I have to wait for little watermelons?

A: Watermelon plants produce male and female flowers. Male flowers usually appear first while female flowers, which have a small fruit immediately behind the opening buds, lag several weeks behind.

Be patient. The separate sexes will get their act together and fruit will develop if bees visit the plants. Otherwise, to grow this crop you will have to move pollen from male to female flowers. This can be accomplished by using a small brush.

Notes

Appendix II

A month-by-month edible landscape gardening guide

January

✔ Plant cool-season vegetables, including beets, broccoli, cabbage, carrots, cauliflower, celery, collards, lettuce, mustards, peas, potatoes, radishes and turnips.

✔ Plant herbs for the winter garden, including anise, cardamom, catnip, chives, comfrey, coriander, fennel, horehound, mint, parsley, rosemary, sage and thyme.

✔ At midmonth, sow cucumber, eggplant, pepper, squash and tomato seeds indoors to have transplants ready by March.

✔ Fertilize cool-weather vegetables every three to four weeks.

✔ Till and fumigate soil now for a spring vegetable garden.

✔ Plant cold-tolerant fruit trees, shrubs and vines as they become available at garden centers.

✔ If weather is cool and plants are dormant, relocate fruiting trees, shrubs and vines.

✔ Perform major pruning on dormant apples, figs, grapes, peaches and pears to ensure next season's crop.

✔ Apply dormant sprays before apple and peach trees flower.

✔ Caterpillars are the major winter-season pest. Use sprays containing *Bacillus thuringiensis*, an effective and biologically safe control.

✔ Winter rains are infrequent — water when the surface soil begins to dry, normally once or twice a week.

✔ Florida's spring begins in February. Study seed catalogs and place orders early.

✔ In the greenhouse: Heat during cold nights; sow seeds for vegetable transplants; and maintain plants in containers.

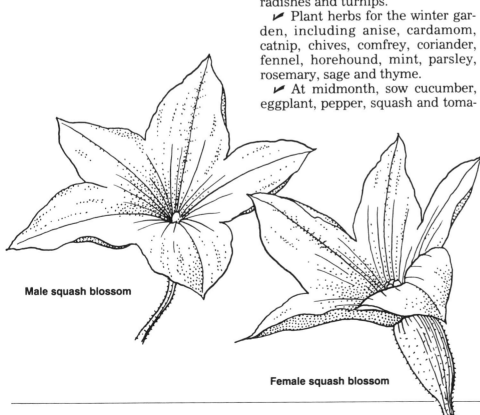

Male squash blossom

Female squash blossom

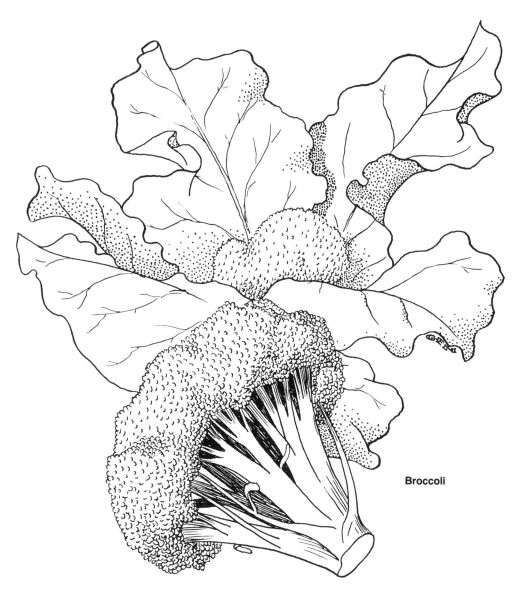
Broccoli

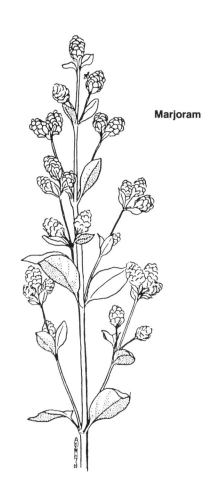
Marjoram

- Add a 2- to 3-inch layer of mulch to spring gardens.
- Rainfall is infrequent; water as needed.
- In the greenhouse: Heat during cold nights; tend warm-season crops; and sow seeds for transplants.

March

- Plan for a long, productive season by making early plantings of corn, peppers, tomatoes and watermelons. Warm-season crops to plant through the month include beans, cantaloupes, cucumbers, eggplant, okra, Southern peas and squash.
- Fertilize young vegetable plants every two to three weeks and crops near harvest, every three to four weeks.
- Sprout sweet potatoes to serve as transplants later in the spring.
- Herbs to plant include anise, basil, chives, comfrey, coriander, dill, fennel, sweet marjoram, mint, sage and thyme.

February

- Make final plantings of cool-season beets, broccoli, collards, lettuce, peas, potatoes, radishes and turnips early in the month. By the end of the month, begin planting warm-season crops, including beans, cantaloupes, corn, cucumbers, peppers, squash, tomatoes and watermelons.
- Cut back asparagus plantings early in the month to encourage a new harvest.
- Fill in gaps in the herb garden by planting anise, basil, comfrey, chives, dill, fennel, sweet marjoram, mint, sage and thyme.
- Start seeds of tomatoes, eggplant and peppers indoors or in the greenhouse to have transplants ready in six to eight weeks.
- This is the last chance to till the soil and fumigate for a spring warm-season garden.
- Make the landscape bear fruit. Find new places and plant apples, blackberries, blueberries, figs, grapes, peaches and pears.
- While there is still a chill in the air, finish transplanting bare-root trees, shrubs and vines.
- Prune low-reaching, head-knocking branches. Reduce height and remove all unwanted growth on fruit trees.
- As new growth begins, do grafting of citrus.
- After midmonth, begin feeding all trees, shrubs and vines for the new year.
- If deciduous fruit trees have flowered, begin regular spraying.
- Compost fallen leaves.

✔ Set into the ground papayas started over the winter.

✔ Finish fertilizing trees, shrubs and vines.

✔ Stake top-heavy plants and begin training vines on trellises.

✔ Compost leaves, prunings and lawn clippings.

✔ Renew mulch in all plantings except around citrus.

✔ Check frequently for garden pests. Handpick or spray as needed.

✔ Hang sticky boards to control leaf miners and whiteflies.

✔ Spray to control citrus scab as new growth begins.

✔ Continue to spray to control insects and diseases on apples, grapes, peaches and pears.

✔ As the weather warms, plants need more frequent watering. Look out for signs of nutritional deficiencies.

✔ In the greenhouse: Start transplants as needed. Move ready-to-plant vegetables, herbs and fruit trees into the landscape. Root softwood cuttings.

April

✔ Plant spring vegetables, including beans, cantaloupes, cherry tomatoes, cucumbers, eggplant, okra, peppers, squash, Southern peas, sweet potatoes, calabazas, chayotes, yard-long beans and other tropical crops.

✔ Herbs for spring planting include anise, basil, chives, dill, borage, oregano, mint, rosemary, sage, savory, sweet marjoram and thyme.

✔ Trim yellowed banana foliage, keep the soil moist and feed monthly. Good care now helps produce a bountiful crop later.

✔ Trees, shrubs and vines planted earlier in the spring need a first scattering of 6-6-6 fertilizer.

✔ Transplant container-grown trees and shrubs.

✔ Tie and stake tall and vining vegetables.

✔ Feed container gardens weekly to keep them growing vigorously.

✔ Leaf rollers, aphids, mites and caterpillars are major insect pests; leaf spot and blights are common diseases this time of year. Stand ready to control any pest that gets out of hand.

✔ Continue spray programs for deciduous fruit trees and vines.

✔ Replenish mulches to conserve moisture.

✔ It's a warm, dry month. When there is not enough rain, be prepared to water two or three times a week.

✔ Cantaloupes, cucumbers, squash and watermelons may be slow to set and hold the first fruit. Be patient; they will become good producers.

✔ In the greenhouse: Root softwood cuttings; clean pots and benches before future plantings.

Cantaloupe

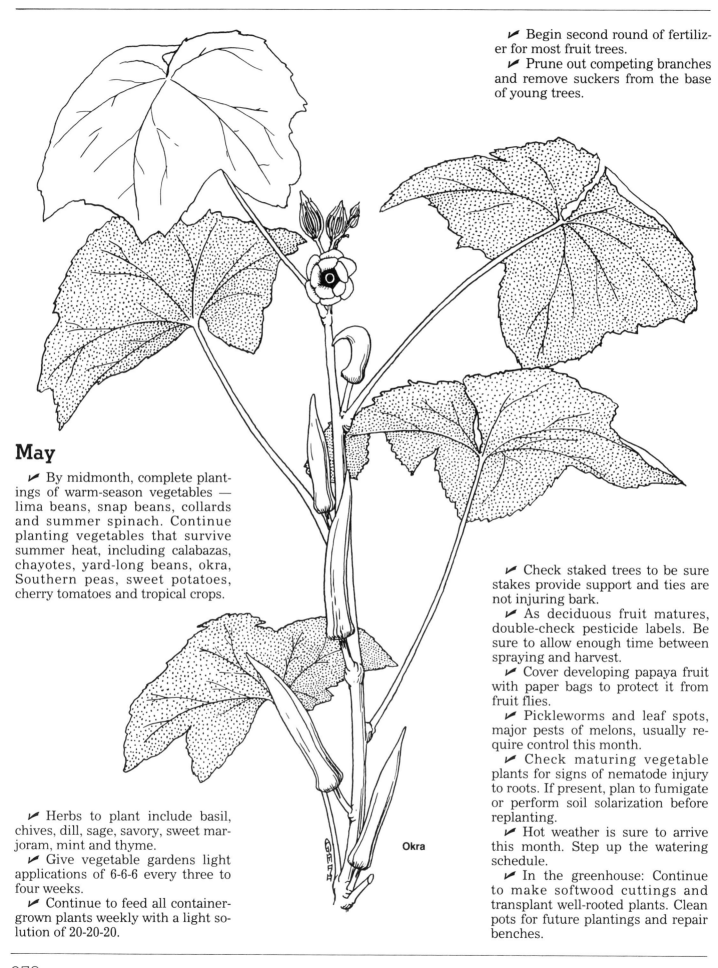

Okra

May

✔ By midmonth, complete plantings of warm-season vegetables — lima beans, snap beans, collards and summer spinach. Continue planting vegetables that survive summer heat, including calabazas, chayotes, yard-long beans, okra, Southern peas, sweet potatoes, cherry tomatoes and tropical crops.

✔ Herbs to plant include basil, chives, dill, sage, savory, sweet marjoram, mint and thyme.
✔ Give vegetable gardens light applications of 6-6-6 every three to four weeks.
✔ Continue to feed all container-grown plants weekly with a light solution of 20-20-20.

✔ Begin second round of fertilizer for most fruit trees.
✔ Prune out competing branches and remove suckers from the base of young trees.

✔ Check staked trees to be sure stakes provide support and ties are not injuring bark.
✔ As deciduous fruit matures, double-check pesticide labels. Be sure to allow enough time between spraying and harvest.
✔ Cover developing papaya fruit with paper bags to protect it from fruit flies.
✔ Pickleworms and leaf spots, major pests of melons, usually require control this month.
✔ Check maturing vegetable plants for signs of nematode injury to roots. If present, plan to fumigate or perform soil solarization before replanting.
✔ Hot weather is sure to arrive this month. Step up the watering schedule.
✔ In the greenhouse: Continue to make softwood cuttings and transplant well-rooted plants. Clean pots for future plantings and repair benches.

June

✔ Plant traditional summer vegetables, including okra, Southern peas, sweet potatoes and cherry tomatoes. Tropical crops that can take the heat include boniatos, calabazas, dasheens, roselle, sweet casavas, yard-long beans and yautias.

✔ Herbs for summer include basil, chives, dill, oregano, mint and sweet marjoram.

✔ Continue to fertilize vegetables every three to four weeks.

✔ Complete second round of fertilizer for established fruiting trees, shrubs and vines.

✔ Begin preparations for new gardens. Add organic matter to poor soils. Practice soil solarization to bake out nematodes; cover bare ground with clear plastic for four to six weeks.

✔ Keep an eye on bananas; harvest an entire stem when the first hands just begin to yellow.

✔ Reshape blueberry shrubs and hedges. Prune blackberries to the ground after fruiting.

✔ Give fruit trees a minor pruning to direct summertime growth.

✔ Examine and adjust tree ties and supports before the stormy season begins.

✔ Resume spraying of deciduous fruit trees after harvest.

✔ Rains usually provide adequate moisture for landscape plantings, but be prepared to water during dry periods.

✔ In the greenhouse: Pot rooted cuttings and feed weekly with a liquid fertilizer. Mix soil for future plantings. Clean pots, trays and cell packets for summer seedings.

July

✔ Plant only the most heat-resistant vegetables: calabazas, cherry tomatoes, okra, pumpkins, Southern peas, sweet potatoes and yard-long beans.

✔ Herbs for midsummer include basil, chives, dill, mint, oregano and sweet marjoram.

✔ By midmonth, sow eggplant, pepper and tomato seeds to have transplants available for late August.

✔ Spade, till and, where necessary, fumigate the vegetable garden in preparation for a mid-August planting.

✔ Prepare container gardens for new plantings; add soil where needed.

✔ Feed new trees, shrubs and vines every six to eight weeks during the summer.

✔ Harvest early ripening avocados and midseason mangoes.

✔ Continue to spray deciduous fruit trees after harvest.

✔ Apply a citrus spray if needed to control mites, scale and whiteflies.

✔ Control summer weeds by mowing and mulching. Use chemical treatments if necessary.

✔ Container-grown trees, shrubs and vines transplant well during the rainy season.

✔ Summer rains normally are adequate; water during dry spells.

✔ In the greenhouse: Sow seeds for fall transplants. Root cuttings from lingering garden tomato plants.

Sweet potatoes

August

✔ Sow watermelon seeds by the 10th. Wait until midmonth to plant beans, broccoli, celery, collards, corn, cucumbers, eggplant, onions, peppers, squash and tomatoes.

✔ Herbs for late summer include basil, chives, dill, mint, oregano and sweet marjoram.

✔ Place leftover seeds in a tight container and store in the refrigerator for future use.

✔ Begin the new gardening year by testing the soil. Take a 1-pint sample to the county extension office or a garden center.

✔ Soil fumigation eliminates many soil-borne pests, including nematodes, weeds, insects and diseases. However, gardeners who plan to fumigate must remember to leave a three-week gap during which nothing can be planted.

✔ Continue to give newly planted trees and shrubs a light scattering of fertilizer every six to eight weeks while the weather is warm.

✔ Fertilize grapevines as the harvest ends.

✔ Continue to spray and fertilize apples and peaches.

✔ Pears are ripening. Pick them early to avoid rots and internal browning.

✔ If plants were chilled last winter, pineapples should ripen this month. Harvest when yellow to orange.

✔ Expect caterpillars, leaf miners and beetles to be major garden pests; control as needed.

✔ Renew mulch layers around all plantings except citrus.

✔ Groom trees and shrubs; remove lanky and unsightly summer growth.

✔ Don't let plantings wilt when rains fail. Between storms, check the soil. If it's dry, water thoroughly enough to wet it about an inch deep.

✔ In the greenhouse: Sow vegetable and herb seeds for fall transplants.

September

✔ By midmonth, complete plantings of warm-season beans, cucumbers, eggplant, peppers, squash and tomatoes. Save cool-season crops of broccoli, cabbage, celery, collards, onions and turnips until the end of the month.

✔ Start seeds for cool-season transplants — Brussels sprouts, cauliflower, celery, lettuce and onion.

✔ Herbs to plant include anise, borage, coriander, fennel, lavender, mint, rosemary, sage, sweet marjoram and thyme.

✔ Prepare strawberry beds, barrels and pyramids for future planting.

✔ Continue to give hanging baskets and potted patio plants a weekly dose of liquid fertilizer.

✔ Trellis or stake tall and vining vegetables.

✔ Sneak a peek at underground sweet potatoes. Fat, plump tubers should be ready to harvest.

✔ Persimmons are ripening. Wait to eat astringent varieties until they are soft and juicy.

✔ Caterpillars are heavy fall feeders. Handpick or spray to control.

✔ Prepare now to move trees and shrubs during winter months; begin root pruning.

✔ Renew mulch layers to con-

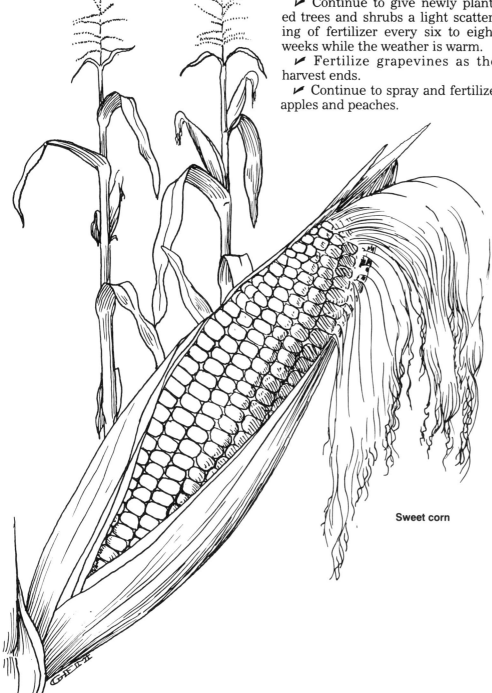

Sweet corn

serve moisture during dry fall and winter.

✔ Rainfall may decline; water to keep the soil moist. Citrus may need watering twice a week to prevent fruit from dropping or cracking.

✔ In the greenhouse: Start seeds for cool-season vegetable transplants. Prepare in-ground beds and containers for planting cold-sensitive vegetables in the greenhouse.

October

✔ Plant cool-season vegetables, including beets, broccoli, cabbage, carrots, cauliflower, collards, kohlrabi, lettuce, mustards, onions, peas, radishes, spinach and turnips.

✔ Start transplants of cool-season vegetables, including broccoli, Brussels sprouts, cabbage, cauliflower, celery, collards, lettuce and onions.

✔ Prepare and plant strawberry beds.

✔ Herbs for fall include anise, borage, chives, coriander, fennel, garlic, lavender, mint, rosemary, sage, sweet marjoram and thyme.

✔ Feed citrus, tropical fruit and grapes before midmonth with 6-6-6 or products specifically formulated for the crops.

✔ Feed container gardens weekly.

✔ Continue to plant container-grown trees and shrubs, taking advantage of cooler, less-stressful fall weather.

✔ Harvest papayas when fruit begins to yellow and soften. Start seedlings to carry over winter in colder regions.

✔ Harvest maturing sweet potatoes plus tropical chayotes, cocoyams and dasheens.

✔ Root prune trees and shrubs in preparation for winter transplanting.

✔ Pecans are ready to harvest when the husks begin to open.

✔ Renew mulches to conserve moisture during drier fall months.

✔ Water less frequently during the cooler days and nights.

✔ In the greenhouse: Plant greenhouse gardens to grow warm-season vegetables during cooler weather; sow seeds of vegetables and herbs for transplants.

Collards

November

✔ As warm-season vegetables finish producing, quickly sow or transplant crops that can take winter weather. Cool-season vegetables include beets, broccoli, cabbage, carrots, cauliflower, collards, kohlrabi, lettuce, mustards, onions, peas, radishes, rutabagas, spinach, Swiss chard and turnips.

✔ Feed vegetables every three to four weeks to keep them growing.

✔ Winter herbs include anise, chives, coriander, dill, fennel, garlic, lavender, rosemary, sage, sweet marjoram and thyme.

✔ Harvest maturing sweet potatoes plus tropical chayotes, cocoyams and dasheens.

✔ Get a jump on spring: Fall is a good time to plant most trees, shrubs and vines.

✔ Citrus begins to ripen. Pick what is needed, and leave the rest stored on the tree.

✔ Remove dead and dying branches, but postpone major pruning until late winter.

✔ Caterpillars are voracious feeders. Handpick or apply a biological control.

✔ Keep pesticides in locked cabinet. Apply only as labeled, using older products first.

✔ Renew mulch layers to conserve moisture and prevent winter injury.

✔ Plants now use less moisture; watering once or twice a week should be sufficient.

✔ Root prune trees and shrubs in preparation for winter transplanting.

✔ In the greenhouse: Sow cool-season vegetable seeds; gather cold-sensitive plants; tend warm-season vegetables; and plant papaya seeds in containers for late-winter transplants.

December

- Keep the vegetable patch going with beets, broccoli, cabbage, carrots, cauliflower, collards, lettuce, mustard, onions, peas, radishes, spinach and turnips.
- Herbs for winter planting include anise, chives, comfrey, coriander, dill, fennel, garlic, parsley, mint, thyme and sage.
- Except for vegetables, the time has passed for applying fall fertilizer. Store unused products in a cool, dry area.
- Use cooler winter days as an opportunity to move plants with less stress. Transplant trees and shrubs that were root pruned earlier in the fall. Root prune any other candidates to move in 10 weeks.
- Plan cold-protection strategy. Locate covers and erect shelters for plants.
- Handpick or spray to control caterpillars munching their way through vegetable gardens.
- Many citrus varieties are ripe. Taste to determine the best time to pick.
- As foliage falls from deciduous trees and shrubs, add it to the compost pile.
- Remove dead or dying branches, but continue to wait until late winter to do major pruning.
- Drain gas tanks and lubricate engines of power equipment left idle for the winter.
- Scrub pots and containers with a solution of 1 part laundry bleach to 10 parts water.
- Water only as needed, usually once or twice a week.
- In the greenhouse: Apply plastic for cold protection; bring in cold-sensitive plants; check heaters; sow vegetable and herb seeds for winter transplants; begin papaya transplants in containers. Feed plants sparingly and water only as needed.

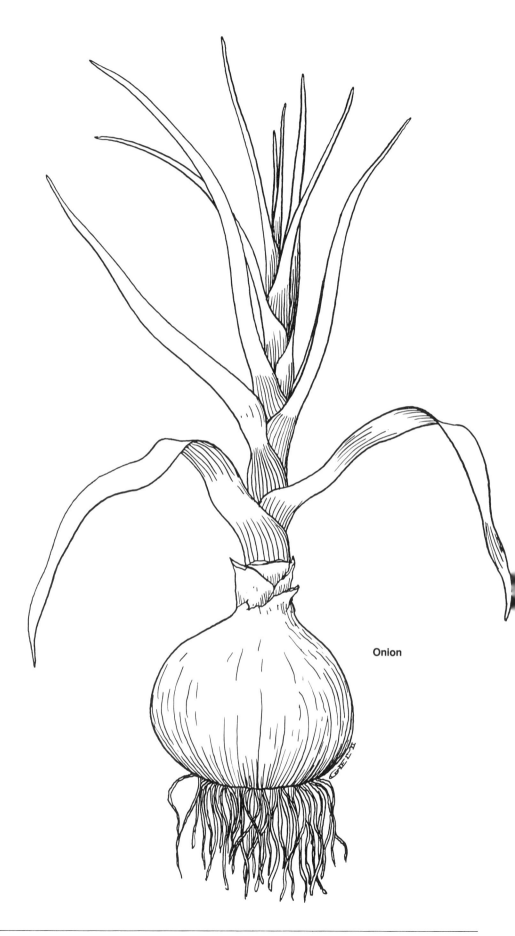

Onion

Appendix III

Resources you can use

GARDENING ENCOURAGES an ongoing education. With each plant grown, a new adventure begins, bringing an abundance of beauty and new problems. It's impossible to cultivate a garden, design a landscape or manage turf without the knowledge and help of others.

In Florida there are many individuals readily available to assist with plant culture. Use these resources to obtain the firsthand information needed to grow an attractive and productive landscape.

Cooperative extension service

All of Florida's 67 counties have cooperative extension service offices. In the past the service was known as the Agricultural Center or county agent's office.

These educational centers dispense plant culture information disseminated by the Institute of Food and Agricultural Sciences at the University of Florida, Gainesville.

Researchers, professors and extension agents work together to develop classes, bulletins and mass media programs to help gardeners.

Problems can be diagnosed and soil samples can be tested through the county extension service. It's one of the first resources gardeners should call upon for help. Most services are tax supported and only small fees may be charged to cover laboratory tests, a few publications and instructional materials. Find your county agent's office and give it a call.

Alachua County
2800 NE 39 Avenue
Gainesville, FL 32609-2658
(352) 955-2402

Baker County
Route 3 Box 1074b
MacClenny, FL 32063-9640
(904) 259-3520

Bay County
324 W 16 Street
Panama City, FL 32401-2616
(904) 784-6107

Bradford County
2266 N Temple Avenue
Starke, FL 32091-1028
(904) 964-6280

Brevard County
3695 Lake Drive
Cocoa, FL 32926-8699
(407) 633-1702

Broward County
3245 College Avenue
Davie, FL 33314-7798
(305) 370-3725

Calhoun County
340 E Central Avenue
Blountstown, FL 32424-2206
(904) 674-8323

Charlotte County
6900 Florida Street
Punta Gorda, FL 33950-5799
(813) 639-6255

Citrus County
3600 S Florida Avenue
Inverness, FL 34450-7369
(352) 726-2141

Clay County
2463 State Road 16 W
PO Box 278
Green Cove Springs, FL 32043-0278
(904) 284-6355

Collier County
14700 Immokalee Road
Naples, FL 33964-1468
(813) 353-4244

Columbia County
PO Box 1587
Lake City, FL 32056-1587
(904) 752-5384

Dade County
18710 SW 288 Street
Homestead, FL 33030-2309
(305) 248-3311

DeSoto County
PO Drawer 310
Arcadia, FL 33821-0310
(813) 993-4846

Dixie County
PO Box 640
Cross City, FL 32628-1534
(352) 498-1237

Duval County
1010 N McDuff Avenue
Jacksonville, FL 32254-2083
(904) 387-8850

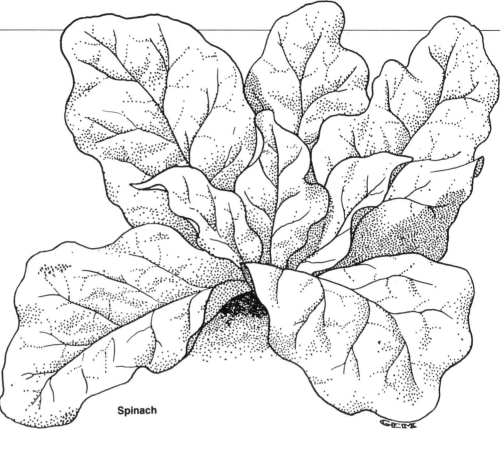
Spinach

Escambia County
PO Box 7154
Pensacola, FL 32534-7154
(904) 477-0953

Flagler County
150 Sawgrass Road
Bunnell, FL 32110-0308
(904) 437-7464

Franklin County
33 Market Street
Suite 305
Apalachicola, FL 32320-2310
(904) 653-9337

Gadsden County
2140 W Jefferson Street
Quincy, FL 32351-1905
(904) 627-6315

Gilchrist County
PO Box 157
Trenton, FL 32693-0157
(352) 463-3174

Glades County
PO Box 549
Moore Haven. FL 33471-0549
(941) 946-0244

Gulf County
200 E 2 Street
PO Box 250
Wewahitchka, FL 32465-0250
(904) 639-3200

Hamilton County
PO Drawer K
Jasper, FL 32052-0691
(904) 792-1312

Hardee County
507 Civic Center Drive
Wauchula, FL 33873-1288
(941) 773-2164

Hendry County
PO Box 68
Labelle, FL 33935-0068
(941) 674-4092

Hernando County
19490 Oliver Street
Brooksville, FL 34601-6538
(352) 754-4433

Highlands County
4509 W George Boulevard
Sebring, FL 33872-5803
(813) 386-6540

Hillsborough County
5339 State Road 579
Seffner, FL 32584-3334
(813) 744-5519

Holmes County
201 N Oklahoma Street
Bonifay, FL 32425-2295
(904) 547-1108

Indian River County
1028 20th Place
Suite D
Vero Beach, FL 32960-5360
(407) 770-5030

Jackson County
4487 Lafayette Street
Marianna, FL 32446-3412
(904) 482-9620

Jefferson County
275 N Mulberry
Monticello, FL 32344-2249
(904) 342-0187

Lafayette County
Route 3 Box 15
Mayo, FL 32066-1901
(904) 294-1279

Lake County
30205 SR 19
Tavares, FL 32778-4052
(904) 343-4101

Lee County
3406 Palm Beach Boulevard
Ft. Myers, FL 33916-3719
(813) 338-3232

Leon County
615 Paul Russell Road
Tallahassee, FL 32301-7099
(904) 487-3003

Levy County
PO Box 219
Bronson, FL 32621-0219
(352) 486-5131

Liberty County
PO Box 369
Bristol, FL 32321-0368
(904) 643-2229

Madison County
900 College Avenue
Madison, FL 32340-1426
(904) 973-4138

Manatee County
1303 17th Street W
Palmetto, FL 34221-2998
(813) 722-4524

Marion County
2232 NE Jacksonville Road
Ocala, FL 34470-3685
(352) 620-3440

Martin County
2614 SE Dixie Highway
Stuart, FL 33494-4007
(407) 288-5654

Monroe County
5100 College Road
Key West, FL 33040-4364
(305) 292-4501

Nassau County
PO Box 1550
Callahan, FL 32011-1550
(904) 879-1019

Okaloosa County
5479 Old Bethel Road
Crestview, FL 32536
(904) 689-5850

Okeechobee County
501 NW 5 Avenue
Okeechobee, FL 34972-2573
(813) 763-6469

Orange County
2350 E Michigan Street
Orlando, FL 32806-4996
(407) 836-7570

Osceola County
1901 E Irlo Bronson Highway
Kissimmee, FL 34744-8947
(407) 846-4181

Palm Beach County
559 N Military Trail
West Palm Beach, FL 33415-1311
(407) 233-1712

Pasco County
36702 State Road 52
Dade City, FL 33525-5198
(352) 521-4288

Pinellas County
12175 125 Street N
Largo, FL 34644-3695
(813) 582-2100

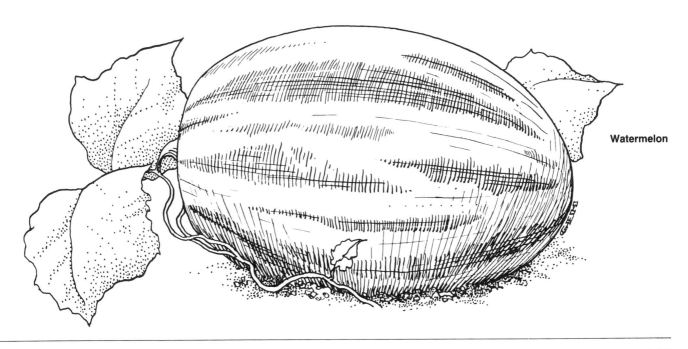

Watermelon

Polk County
1702 Highway 17-98 S
Bartow, FL 33830-6694
(941) 533-0765

Putnam County
111 Yelvington Road
Suite 1
East Palatka, FL 32131-8892
(904) 329-0318

St. Johns County
3125 Agriculture Center Drive
St. Augustine, FL 32092-0572
(904) 824-4564

St. Lucie County
8400 Picos Road
Suite 101
Ft. Pierce, FL 34945-3045
(407) 462-1660

Santa Rosa County
6051 Old Bagdad Highway
Room 116
Milton, FL 32583-8944
(904) 623-3868

Sarasota County
2900 Ringling Boulevard
Sarasota, FL 34237-5397
(941) 316-1000

Seminole County
250 W County Home Road
Sanford, FL 32773-6197
(407) 323-2500

Sumter County
PO Box 218
Bushnell, FL 33513-0218
(352) 793-2728

Suwannee County
1302 11th Street SW
Live Oak, FL 32060-3696
(904) 362-2771

Taylor County
203 Forest Park Drive
Perry, FL 32347-6396
(904) 838-3508

Union County
25 NE 1 Street
Lake Butler, FL 32054-1701
(904) 496-2321

Volusia County
3100 E New York Avenue
DeLand, FL 32724-6497
(904) 822-5778

Wakulla County
PO Box 40
Crawfordville, FL 32326-0040
(904) 926-3931

Walton County
732 N 9th Street
Suite B
DeFuniak Springs, FL 32433-1655
(904) 892-8172

Washington County
800 W Jackson Avenue
Chipley, FL 32428-1615
(904) 638-6180

Garden centers and seed companies

Every community has its nursery, plant store or garden center. Many of the supplies needed to cultivate a garden or landscape can be found locally.

Plants for sale at garden centers are the right choices for Florida conditions. Garden centers also are staffed with knowledgeable individuals waiting to help with a problem or give advice on a new crop. Many will test soil and identify insects found in the landscape.

Seed companies are mail-order garden centers. Each year gardeners await the arrival of the catalogs so they can plan the new season's garden.

Most catalogs serve as gardening guides with pictures and cultural information. Many companies offer transplants, trees, shrubs, pesticides and equipment as well as seeds.

Few gardeners would be caught without a stack of catalogs after the new year. Most are sent free, but some companies charge a small fee to cover the cost of printing.

Some companies that offer mail-order sales for difficult-to-find supplies are:

Rhubarb

Brudy's Exotics
PO Box 820874
Houston, TX 77282-0874
Tropical fruits.

Burgess Seed & Plant Co.
904 Four Seasons Road
Bloomington, IL 61701
General vegetables, herbs, minor vegetables.

W. Atlee Burpee Co.
300 Park Ave.
Warminster, PA 18991-0003
General vegetables, herbs, minor vegetables, organic gardening and irrigation supplies.

Chestnut Hill Nursery
Route 1 Box 341
Alachua, FL 32615
Florida fruit trees, shrubs & vines

The Cook's Garden
PO Box 535
Londonderry, VT 05148
General vegetables, minor vegetables.

DeGiorgi Seed Co. Inc.
6011 North St.
Omaha, NE 68117
General vegetables.

Ed Hume Seeds, Inc.
PO Box 1450
Kent, WA 98035
General vegetable, herbs.

Farmer Seed & Nursery
818 NW 4th St.
Monroe, IN 55021
General vegetables.

Ferry-Morse Seed Co.
600 Stephen Beale Dr.
PO Box 488
Fulton, KY 42041-0488
General vegetables, herbs, minor vegetables.

Florida Market Bulletin
545 East Tennessee St.
Tallahassee, FL 32308
Free publication offering Florida fruit and vegetables.

Gardens Alive
5100 Schenley Place
Lawrenceburg, IN 47025
Organic gardening supplies

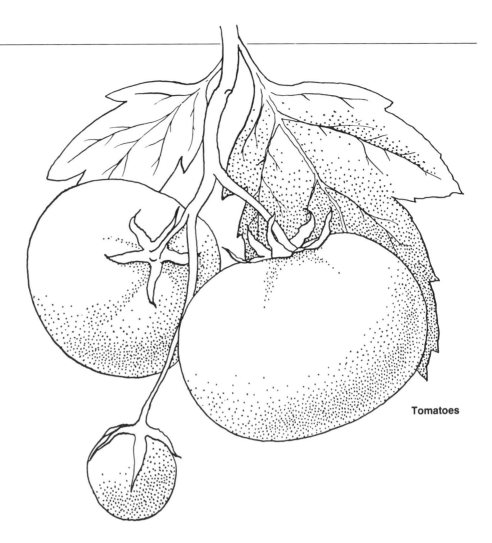

Tomatoes

Gardener's Supply Company
128 Intervale Rd.
Burlington, VT 05401
Organic gardening and irrigation supplies.

Gurney's Seed & Nursery Co.
110 Capital St.
Yankton, SD 57079
General vegetables, minor vegetables, organic gardening and irrigation supplies.

Henry Field's
415 N. Burnett St.
Shenandoah, IA 51602
General vegetables, herbs, gardening supplies.

Harris Seeds
PO Box 22960
Rochester, NY 14692-2960
General vegetables, herbs.

Johnny's Selected Seeds
310 Foss Hill Rd.
Albion, ME 04910-9731
General vegetables, minor vegetables, herbs.

Jung Seed Co.
335 S. High St.
Randolph, WI 53957-0001
General vegetables, organic gardening & irrigation supplies.

Kilgore Seed Co.
1400 W. First St.
Sanford, FL 32771
General vegetables, herbs.

Liberty Seed Co.
PO Box 806
New Philadelphia, OH 44663
General vegetables.

Mellinger's
2310 W. South Range Rd.
North Lima, OH 44452-9731
General vegetables, minor vegetables, herbs, organic gardening & irrigation supplies.

Nichols Garden Nursery
1190 N. Pacific Hwy.
Albany, OR 97321-4580
General vegetables, minor vegetables, herbs.

Park Seed
1 Parkton Ave.
Greenwood, SC 29647-0001
General vegetables, minor vegetables, herbs, irrigation supplies.

Peaceful Valley Farm Supply
PO Box 2209
Grass Valley, CA 95945
Organic gardening supplies.

Ronninger's Seed Potatoes
PO Box 1838
Orting, WA 98360
Potatoes

Santa Barbara Heirloom Nursery
PO Box 4235
Santa Barbara, CA 93140
General vegetables, minor vegetables, herbs.

Shepherd's Garden Seeds
30 Irene St.
Torrington, CT 06790
General vegetables, minor vegetables, herbs.

R.H. Shummway's
PO Box 1
Graniteville, SC 29829
General vegetables, herbs, irrigation supplies.

Stokes Seeds
1904 Stokes Building
PO Box 548
Buffalo, NY 14240-0548
General vegetables.

Stokes Tropicals
PO Box 9868
New Iberia, LA 70562-9868
Bananas

Sunrise Enterprises
PO Box 1960
Chesterfield, VA 23832
Oriental vegetables

Superior Seeds
PO Box 4873
Homestead, FL 33032
General vegetables, herbs.

Terrritorial Seed Company
PO Box 157
Cottage Grove, OR 97424
General vegetables, herbs.

Thompson & Morgan
220 Farraday Ave.
PO Box 1308
Jackson, NJ 08527-0308
General vegetables, herbs, Oriental vegetables.

Tomato Growers Supply Company
PO Box 2237
Fort Myers, FL 33902
Tomatoes & peppers.

Totally Tomatoes
PO Box 1626
Augusta, GA 30903
Tomatoes

Vermont Bean Seed Co.
Garden Land
Fair Haven, VT 05743
General vegetables

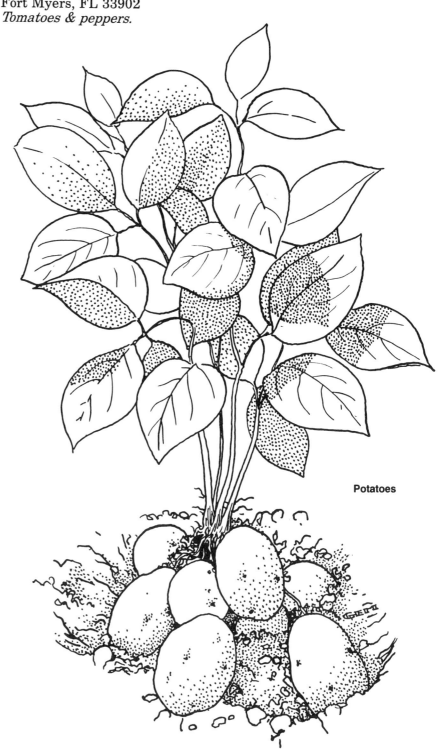

Potatoes

More help

Libraries are terrific resources for references on gardening. Learn how to grow a plant, build a greenhouse or make compost by drawing from the experience of horticulturists from around the world. Many books can be checked out, but larger and more costly editions will have to be used at the library.

Newspapers and magazines can keep gardens up-to-date. Gardening techniques change rapidly. There are also new products, societies and pests. These, plus monthly plant care hints, are good reasons to check the gardening section of a newspaper or subscribe to a magazine devoted to gardening.

One magazine just for gardeners of the sunshine state is *Florida Gardening*. Write to *Florida Gardening* at PO Box 500678, Malabar, Florida 32950 for subscription information.

A library is a good place to discover which magazine fits your horticultural needs.

Glossary

Acid citrus: Catchall term for highly acidic fruit, including lemons and limes.

Alternate bearing: A pattern of heavy production one year followed by a year of light production. Common with some varieties of oranges and other fruit.

Blanching: A cultural technique used on cauliflower to encourage development of a pure-white head. When the head grows to the size of a quarter, it is protected from direct sun by fastening leaves over it. A similar procedure using soil is performed on celery and leeks.

Chilling hours: Total number of hours below 45 degrees needed to break flower bud dormancy of some fruiting plants. These include peaches, apples and pears. This cold must occur fairly continuously over a period of time, normally during the winter months.

Chlorotic: Abnormal condition in plants in which the green parts lose their color or turn yellow as a results of a lack of chlorophyl production caused by disease, lack of fertilizer or insufficient light.

Clean cultivation: Keeping the area around the base of trees or plants free of weeds or other plants. Typically recommended for citrus to minimize chances of disease.

Cover crop: Sowings of ryegrass, hairy indigo or similar crops over vacant land to preserve available nutrients. The plants usually are mowed and plowed under to increase the organic matter content of the soil and return nutrients to the soil.

Cuttings: A vegetative propagation method of rooting a piece of the parent plant in soil or vermiculite.

Damping off: A condition caused by fungal rots that can prevent seedlings from emerging or allows them to grow a few inches tall, then die.

Deciduous: Refers to the annual shedding of leaves during the fall or winter season by many trees and shrubs.

Drip line: An imaginary line on the ground parallel with the outer canopy of a tree; drip refers to where rainfall drops from leaves to wet soil. Fertilizer often is spread beyond the drip line to ensure adequate feeding of the tree.

Fillers: The fillers, called transition plantings by landscapers, can be annuals and perennials or additional shrubs.

Foliar feeding: A technique of spraying plants with dilute liquid fertilizer; typically used to provide a special boost or to compensate for deficiencies in minor nutrients such as iron, manganese and zinc.

Foot rot: A disease that often affects citrus; it flourishes on damp or wet trunks, which is why clean cultivation is recommended.

French intensive: A technique for planting a vegetable garden in which plants are set in hexagonal patterns within wide rows.

Fumigation: Chemical treatment often used to eradicate nematodes from a planting site. The chemical Vapam is applied to the soil and allowed to work for about a month before the garden can be planted. Once in the soil, the chemical turns into a gas and controls not only nematodes but other soil problems including insects, diseases and weeds.

Grafting: Vegetative propagation techniques that unite two portions of closely related plants, splicing them together. Often used on fruit trees to ensure a plant that bears the desired variety of fruit.

Gynoecious: Vegetable varieties that primarily produce female flowers. These plants have greater potential for fruit production.

Hands: Clusters of bananas that form along a stalk after flowering. Many hands will develop along a single flower stalk.

Hardening off: A process of acclimating indoor-grown transplants to outdoor conditions by gradually exposing them to sun, bright light and wind over a period of one to two weeks.

Lifting: As the plants grow and leaves reach 8 inches in height, a cultural process called lifting must be performed to grow smooth roots free of side growths. Remove soil from the upper end of the main root and trim away small side roots. When trimming is completed, mound the soil up to its original level. Repeat the procedure in a few weeks. Typically used on horseradish plants.

Lime: Chemical used to raise pH of soil, making it less acidic. Dolomitic or agricultural lime is recommended for use in gardens; hydrated, brunt or pickling limes can damage crops.

Loam: A soil composed of approximately equal parts clay, sand and organic matter. Florida soils seldom form a good loam because of the predominance of sand.

Muck: Peats partially decomposed into basic soil components. May be the main soil type in some portions of the state. Very rich in nitrogen and quite acid. Usually moist and found in poorly drained locations.

Node: Area on plant branch where leaves are attached; in rooting cuttings, this portion should be stripped of leaves and placed in the rooting medium because growth typically occurs here.

Nubbins: Small, imperfect fruit on deciduous trees often caused by too-cold winter temperatures.

Parthenocarpically: The ability to produce fruit without being pollinated.

Parts per million (ppm): Formula by which salt content of water is measured. Water with levels above 1,000 ppm generally is considered much too salty for most common crops.

Peat: Partially decomposed wetland plants that include mosses, reeds and woody vegetation. Used to enrich sandy and clay soils by adding some nutrients while improving aeration and water-holding ability. All peats may be hard to wet if they become dry.

Peat moss: Partially decomposed plant portions similar to basic peat. Peat moss usually is dried from sphagnum moss with a fibrous, water-absorbent quality. Mainly used in potting mixtures and for improving garden soil.

Perfect-flowered: Refers to plants that in bloom have both male and female portions present. Varieties are self-fertile, needing no other variety for pollination.

Perlite: A white, porous volcanic rock ground into small particles. It is used to improve porosity and water-holding ability of planting mixtures.

Predacious insects: Beneficial insects that prey upon plant-damaging insects.

Respiration: The burning of foods by plants that drives the growth process within the cells.

Ringspot: A visual symptom used to describe a disease usually caused by fungal or viral organisms. The organism produces one or more rings of either yellow or brown color in a green leaf or fruit.

Root-knot nematodes: Microscopic roundworms that invade root tissue and cause galls or knots to form. Roots swell and lose their ability to remove water and nutrients from the soil; typically leads to stunting or death of plants. A major pest problem in Florida.

Rootstock: A plant onto which is grafted a more desirable variety; rootstocks are used to provide plants with resistance to diseases and other problems. Typically used on citrus and other fruit.

Seed pieces: Stem portions cut into sections with one or more buds present to propagate a plant when sown in the soil. Often used with potatoes.

Side dressing: Technique of feeding established plantings by spreading nutrients such as manure or fertilizer around the base of the plants. Sometimes referred to as top dressing.

Soil pH: An indication of the acidity of soil measured on a scale of 0-14, with 7 neutral; above 7, alkaline; below 7, acid. Most crops thrive when the soil pH is about 6.5. Sometimes pH levels can be changed by the addition of sulfur, to make the reading more acidic, or lime, to make the soil less acidic.

Soilless mix: A soil substitute made by combining peat moss, perlite, vermiculite and similar ingredients. Lime may be added to adjust pH and nutrients may be included to begin feeding the plants. Soilless mixes are used to avoid insects, diseases and nematodes typically found in garden soils. They also are used in container plants because they are lightweight.

Soil solarization: A technique of eradicating root-knot nematodes and other pests from the soil by using the heat of the sun to bake them away. The planting site is first watered, then covered with plastic and allowed to sit for at least four weeks. Effective only in the summer, when temperatures become high enough to bake away the pests.

Sphagnum moss: A coarse-textured wetland plant that is harvested fresh and dried for horticultural uses. The stringy leaves and stems are absorbent and rot resistant when used to line wire baskets, for air layers and serve as a medium for ferns and orchids. Ground sphagnum moss sometimes is marketed as a germination medium.

Sphagnum peat moss: Peat specifically formed from the partially decomposed sphagnum moss, a wetland plant. The fibrous brown particles form a well-aerated and water-absorbent addition for soils and potting mediums.

Sticker-spreader: A wetting agent typically mixed with pesticides or fungicides to ensure better adhesion of the product on plant and tree leaves.

Stratify: To prepare seeds for propagation by placing in a moist growing medium of peat moss or sand, then refrigerating for several weeks. Performed for many types of fruit tree propagation.

Topsoil: Commonly considered the uppermost few inches of native soils, often dark-colored and enriched with organic matter. Florida topsoil often is sand and low in organic matter. Soils that have been tilled or moved during construction probably will lack a true topsoil.

Trace elements: Also called minor elements, these are nutrients such as iron, manganese and zinc that often are incorporated into fertilizer formulations.

Trap crops: Plants that enable root-knot nematodes to hatch but, because they are not host plants, cause the nematodes to starve.

Vermiculite: A brown, micaceous clay that when heated expands to absorb moisture. Used to give aeration and moisture-holding ability to propagation or potting soil mixtures.

Index

Bold type indicates main reference.

A

Acid citrus, **125-126**
Anise, **97**
Aphids, 179
Apples, **130-131**
    container grown, 166
    fertilizing, 131
    harvest time, 72
    pest control, 130
    pH required, 130
    pruning, 130
    varieties, 130
Asparagus, **191-192**
Assassin bug, 178
Avocados, 147, **148-150**, 165
    container grown, 166, 167
    harvest time, 72, 150
    fertilizing, 149
    pests, 149
    starting from seed, 108
    varieties, 148-149

B

Bacillus thuringiensis, 96, **178**, 180
Bananas, **150, 151**, 167
    cold protection, 150
    fertilizing, 150
    harvest time, 72, 150
Basil, 93, **97**
Bay laurel, **97**
Beans, lima, **193-194**
Beans, snap, **195-196**
Bean tepee, 110
Beets, **197-198**
Beetles, 179
Blackberries, **131**
    harvest, 131
    pH, 131
    varieties, 131
Blights, 185, 186
Blueberries, 129, **131-132**, 163, 165
    fertilizing, 132
    pH, 132
    pruning, 132
    varieties, 131
Borage, **97**
Borers, 130
    apple, 130
    peach, 138
Braconid wasps, 177
Broccoli, 163, **199-200**
Brown rots, 186
Brussels sprouts, **201-202**
Budding, 38
Bush beans, 165

C

Cabbage, **203**
Calabaza, **78**
Cantaloupes, 71, 72, **205-206**
Carambola, 147, 148, **151**
    fertilizing, 151
Carrots, 165, **207-208**
Cassava, **78**
Caterpillars, 142, 177, 179
Catnip, **98**
Cauliflower, 163, **209-210**

Nectarines

Celery, **211-212**
Central Florida region, 14-**16**
Chard, Swiss, 163, **267-268**
Chayote, **79**
Chervil, **98**
Children's garden projects, **105-115**
    avocado trick, 108
    bean tepee, 110
    child's own garden, 113
    citrus from seed, 108
    edible sprouts, 106
    family fruit tree, 114
    forest in a jar, 106
    Halloween pumpkin, 111
    new pineapple plant, 107
    rooting cuttings, 111
    root-top gardens, 107
    seed view jars, 106
    sky-high sunflowers, 115
    square-foot garden, 112
    starting transplants, 109
    sweet potato vine, 107
    worm farm, 113
Chilling hours, 16, 129, **145**
    kiwis, 152
Chinese cabbage, **213-214**
Chip bud graft, 38-39
Chives, 94, **98**
Citrus, **117-127**
    care of, 120-121
    container grown, 166
    damaging temperatures, 118
    fertilizing, 120
    harvest time, 71, 72, **126**
    history of, 117, 122, 123, 124
    pest control, **126-127**
    pH for best growth, 118
    site selection, 118
    tree selection, 118

    types:
        acid citrus, **125-126**
        grapefruit, **124-125**
        mandarins, hybrids, **123-124**
        oranges, **121-122**
    planting techniques, 119
    varietal selection, 120
        acid citrus, 125
        grapefruit, 124
        mandarins and hybrids, 123
        oranges, 122
Cleft bud graft, 40
Cocoyam, **79**
Cold protection, **68-69**, 75, 147
    bananas, 150
    papayas, 157
    patio gardens, 165
    pineapples, 159
Collards, **215**
Comfrey, **98**

Borage

Compost, **22-24**
    herbs, 95
    how to make, **23**
    materials, 22
        nutrient values, 24
    as mulch, 65
    why use, 14, 24
Container gardens, 48, 67, **163-173**
    bags of soil, 172-173
        care of, 172
        drip irrigation for, 172
        fertilizing, 173
        what to plant, 172
    carrots in, 165
    fertilizing, 164, 166
    greenhouses, 167-170
    herbs, 94, 165
    hydroponics, 170-172
    patios, 164-167
    pests, 164
    pineapples, 159
    radishes in, 165
    soil mix for, 164, 168
    tomatoes in, 165
    tropical fruit, 148
    windows, 163-165
Coriander, **98**
Corn, sweet, **217-218**
County extension service, **282-286**
Cover crops, **27**
Cucumbers, 164, 165, **219-220**
    harvest time, 72
Cucuzzi, **80**
Cumin, **99**
Cuttings, **43**, 111
Cutworms, 177

D

Dasheen, **80**
Deciduous fruit:
  see "Fruit, deciduous"
  and individual entries
Design:
  edible landscape, 2-3
  formal vegetable garden, 47-55
  four-season garden, 19
  square-foot garden, **51**, 112

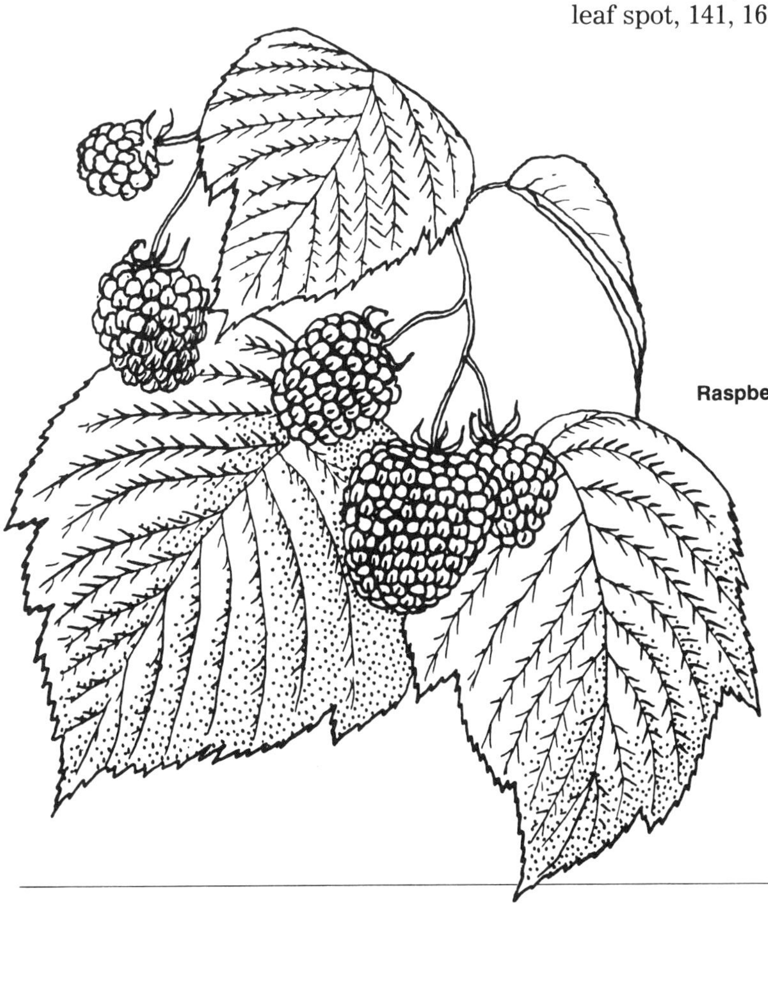

Dill, **99**
Diseases, **175-187**
  chemical controls of, 183
  common types:
    blights, 185, 186
    brown rot, 186
    downy mildew, 183, 184
    galls, 185, 187
    fig rust, 133
    fire blight, 130, 139, 183, 185
    fruit rots, 184
    fusariam wilt, 184, 185
    leaf spot, 141, 160, 184, 186
    mango anthracnose, 156
    Pierce disease, 134, 135
    powdery mildew, 183
    ringspot, 157
    rusts, 183
    seedling blights, 183, 184
    watery core, 131
  protection from, 182
Double cropping, 50
Downy mildew, 183, 184
Drainage problems, 8, 50
Drip irrigation, 60
  container gardens and, 165, 173
  how to install, 60
  problems with system, 61

E

Edible landscapes, **1-5**
  accents, 4
  advantages, 1
  designs, 2-3
  how to plan, 2-4, 8
  shrubs, 3
  substitutes, 2
  trees, 3
Eggplant, **221-222**
Endive/escarole **223-224**
Exotic fruit, **147-162**;
also see individual entries
  avocados, **148**
  bananas, **150**
  carambolas, **151**
  guavas, **151-152**
  kiwis, **152-153**
  loquats, **153-154**
  lychees, **154-155**
  mangoes, **155-156**
  papayas, **156-157**
  passion fruit, **157-158**
  pineapples, **158-159**
  pomegranates, **160**

Raspberries

Exotic fruit, cont'd

    Surinam cherry, **160-161**
Exotic vegetables, **77-91**
    calabaza, **78**
    cassava, **78**
    chayote, **79**
    cocoyam, **79**
    cucuzzi, **80**
    dasheen, **80**
    garlic, **81**
    horseradish, **82**
    husk tomato, **83**
    Jerusalem artichoke, **83**
    jicama, **83-84**
    luffa, **84**
    Malabar spinach, **84**
    momordica, **85**
    New Zealand spinach, **85**
    novelty beans, **86**
    pigeon pea, **87**
    pokeweed, **87**
    radicchio, **88**
    roselle, **88**
    rouquette, **89**
    Seminole pumpkin, **89**
    soybeans, **90**
    tamarillo, **90**
    vegetable spaghetti, **91**
    yam, **91**

F

Fennel, **99**
Fertilizer, 24-26, 51, 52, 64-65
    application techniques, 64
    apples, needs, 130
    chemical, **25-26**, 65
    citrus, needs, 120
    foliar feeding, 65
    frequency of feeding, 26
    how to read labels, **25**
    organic, 65
    manures, **24-25**
    recommended amounts, 26, 52
    for seedlings, transplants, 33, 34
    side dressing, 25, 64
Figs, **133-133**, 165
    fertilizer, 133
    fig rust, 133
    from cuttings, 133
    harvest, 133
    varieties, 133
Fire blight, 130, 139, 183, 185
Florida Market Bulletin, 78, 90, 148
Foliar feeding, 65
    guavas, 152
Frost dates, average, 14, 15
Fruit crop yields, 5
Fruit, deciduous, **129-145**
    types:
        apples, **130**
        blackberries, **131**
        blueberries, **131-132**, 165
        figs, **133**, 165
        grapes, **134-137**
        nectarines, **137**
        peaches, **137**
        pears, **139**
        pecans, **141-142**
        persimmons, **142-143**
        plums, **143**
        raspberries, **144**
Fruit propagation techniques, 42; see individual entries
Fruit rots, 184
Fruit trees, planting, 114
    see individual entries
Fumigation, 10, **26-27**, 66
Fungus gnats, 177
Fusariam wilt, 184, 185

G

Garden, design, 47
Galls, 185, 187
Garlic, **81**,236
Geometric spacing, 52
Geraniums, scented, **99**
Ginger, **99**
Ginseng, **100**
Grafting, **37-45**
    definition, 37
    care of graft, 40

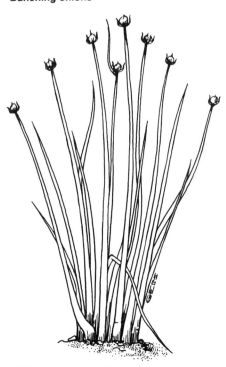

Bunching onions

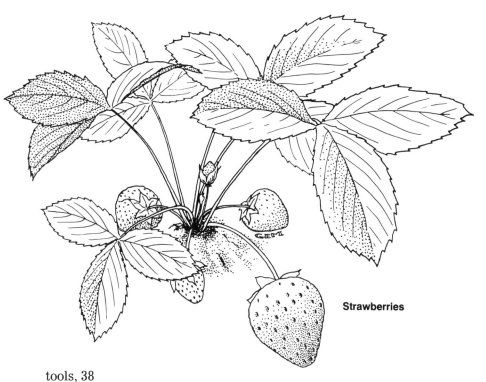
Strawberries

tools, 38
types:
    budding, 38
    chip bud, 38-39
    cleft, 40
    hanging bud, 39
    shield bud, 39
    side-veneer, 41
    whip, 40
uses for, 37
when to, 38
Grapefruit, **124-125**
Grapes, 129, **134-137**
    bunch, 134-135
    care of, 135-136
    fertilizing, 135, 136
    harvest time, 72, 74
    muscadine, 135
    pest control, 136
    pH for, 135
    pruning, 136
    uses for, 135
    varieties, 134
Greenhouses, **167-170**
    heat requirements, 168
    light requirements, 167
    materials selection, 167-168
    pests in, 170
    planting schedule, 168
    ventilation, 168
Greens, harvest time, 71, 73
Green lacewings, 177
Grubs, 177
Guavas, **151-152**
    fertilizing, 152
    harvest time, 72, 152
    from seed, 152

H

Hand watering, 58
Hanging bud, 39
Hardening off, 34
Harvest time, **71-75**
    apples, 72, 130
    avocado, 72
    bananas, 72
    blackberries, 131
    blueberries, 132
    calabaza, 78
    cantaloupes, 71, 72
    cassava, 78
    citrus, 71, 72, **126**
    chayote, 79
    cocoyam, 80
    cucumbers, 72
    cucuzzi, 80
    dasheen, 80
    figs, 133
    garlic, 82
    grapes, 72, 74
    greens, 71, 73
    guavas, 72, 152
    herbs, 71
    honeydew melons, 73
    horseradish, 82
    husk tomato, 83
    Jerusalem artichoke, 83
    jicama, 84
    luffa, 84
    Malabar spinach, 84
    momordica, 85
    New Zealand spinach, 85
    novelty beans, 86
    papayas, 74, **157**
    peaches, 71, 72
    pears, 74, 140
    persimmons, 74
    pineapples, 72, 159
    pigeon pea, 87
    pokeweed, 87
    radicchio, 88
    roselle, 89
    rouquette, 89
    Seminole pumpkin, 90
    soybeans, 90
    summer squash, 72-73
    Surinam cherries, 161

Harvest time, cont'd

    tamarillo, 91
    tomatoes, 71, 73
    vegetable spaghetti, 91
    watermelons, 73
    yam, 91

Hedge:
    blueberry, 132
    Surinam cherry, 160

Herbs, **93-103**
    container plantings, 94, 165
    in-ground plantings, 95
        care of, 96
        site preparation, 95
        soil pH, 95
        when to plant, 103 and individual entries
    fertilizing, 94
    gathering and storing, 96-97
    harvest time, 71, 103
    history of, 93
    pests common to, 96
    propagation:
        by cuttings, 95-96
        by division, 96
        from seeds, 95
    soil mixes for, 94
    sun requirements of, 164
    types:
        anise, **97**
        basil, 93, **97**
        bay laurel, **97**
        borage, **97**
        catnip, **98**
        chervil, **98**
        chives, 94, **98**
        comfrey, **98**
        coriander, **98**
        cumin, **99**
        dill, **99**
        fennel, **99**
        scented geraniums, **99**
        ginger, **99**
        ginseng, **100**
        horehound, **100**
        lavender, **100**
        lemon balm, 93, **100-101**

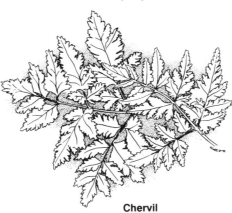

Chervil

        lovage, **101**
        marjoram, **101**
        mint, 93, 94, **101**
        oregano, 93, 94, **101**
        parsley, 94, 101
        rosemary, 93, **101-102**
        sage, 93, **102**
        savory, **102**
        tarragon, 93, **102**
        thyme, 93, **102**
        watercress, **103**
    windowsill plantings, 94

Hickory shuckworm, 142
Honeydew melons, harvest time, 73
Horehound, **100**
Horseradish, **82**
Husk tomato, **83**
Hydroponic gardens, **170-172**
    how to build, 171
    nutrient solutions, 170-172
        Hoagland solution, 171
        trace element solutions, 171
    starting plants, 172

I

Ichneumond wasp, 178
Insects, see "Pest control" and individual entries
    common pests, 179
        aphids, 179
        beetles, 179
        caterpillars, 179
        mealybugs, 180
        mole crickets, 177, 180
        scales, 180
        slugs and snails, 180
        spider mites, 181
        stink bugs, 181
        thrips, 181
        weevils, 181
        whiteflies, 181
    controls, natural, 178-179
    Bacillus thuringiensis, **178**
    control, non-chemical, 176-178
        entrapment, 177
        handpicking, 176
        mechanical barriers, 177
        predacious organisms, 177
            assassin bug, 176, 178
            braconid wasps, 177
            green lacewings, 177
            ichneumon wasp, 178
            ladybugs, 177
            mites, 177
            praying mantid, 177
            steinernematid, 177

identifying, 176
synthetic insectides, **179**
    safety with, 179-187
types:
    borers, 130
    caterpillars, 142, 177
    cutworms, 177
    fungus gnats, 177
    grubs, 177
    hickory shuckworm, 142
    nut casebearer, 142
    papaya webworm, 157
    papaya whitefly, 157
    pecan weevil, 142
    root weevils, 177
Intensive gardening, 51, **52**, 165
Iron chlorosis, 132

J

Jerusalem artichoke, **83**
Jicama, **83-84**

K

Kale, **225-226**
Kiwis, **152-153**
    fertilizing, 153
    from seed, 153
    pruning, 153
Kohlrabi, **227-228**

L

Ladybugs, 177
Lavender, **100**
Layering:
    air, 44, 45
    simple, 44
Leaf spot diseases, 141, 184, 186
Leeks, 236
Lemon balm, 93, **100-101**

Lemons, **125**
Lettuce, 163, **229-230**
Light requirements:
    greenhouses, 167
    herbs, 164
    outdoor gardens, 8, 48
    seedlings, 33
    vegetables, 164
    windowsill gardens, 163

Lime, agricultural or dolomitic, **22**
Limes, **125,** 165, 167
Loquats, **153-154**, 165
    fertilizing, 153
    pests, 153
    pruning, 153
    varieties, 153
Lovage, **101**

Spinach

Lychee, 147, 148, **154-155**
    fertilizing, 154-155
    varieties, 154
Luffa, **84**

M

Maintaining the garden, **63-75**
    citrus care, 120-121
    cold weather protection, **68-69**
    fertilizer, 64, 120
    mulching, 65, 66
    pests, 68, 96, 126-127
    supports for plants, 67
    water, 63-64
    weeding, 66-67
Malabar spinach, **84-85**
Mandarins and hybrids, **123-124**
Mangoes, 147, 148, **155-156**
    container grown, 166, 167
    fertilizing, 156
    from seed, 155
    harvest time, 156
    pests, 156
    varieties, 155
Manures:
    as fertilizers, **24**
    nutrient values, **24**
Marjoram, **101**

Mealybugs, 180
Microsprinklers, 61, 68-69
Minisprinklers, 61
Minor elements, 22
Mint, 93, 94, **101**
Mites, 177
Mole crickets, 180
Momordica, **85**
Mulch, 65, 66
Mustard greens, **231-232**

N

Nectarines, **137**
    care of, 137
    varieties, 137
Nematodes, 10, **26-27**, 134
    definition, 26
    symptoms, 26
    controls:
        cover crops, **27**
        fumigation, **26-27**, 48
        solarization, **27**, 66
New Zealand spinach, **85**
Novelty beans, **86**
Nut casebearer, 142
Nutrient values:
    compost materials, **24**
    manures, **24**
    natural, organic fertilizers, **25**, 65
North Florida region, 14, 15, **17**

Seminole pumpkins

O

Okra, **233-234**
Onions, 164, **235-236**
Oranges, **121-122**
Oregano, 93, 94, **101**
Organic:
    fertilizer, 25, 65
    pest control, 176-179
    matter, 22, 95
    nutrient values of materials, 25
    nutrient values of manures, **24**
    soils, 52
    techniques, 14

P

Parsley, **237-238**
Papayas, 148, **156-157**
    cold protection, 157
    crosses, 156
    fertilizing, 157
    harvest time, 74, 156
    pests, 157
        papaya webworm, 157
        papaya whitefly, 157
    varieties, 156
Parsley, 94, 101, **237-238**
Passion fruit, 148, **157-158**
    fertilizing, 158
    harvest, 158
    pH, 158
    propagation from cuttings, 158, 167
    varieties, 157
Patio gardens, 164-166
Peaches, 129, **137-139**
    care of, 138
    chilling hours needed, 137
    fertilizing, 138
    harvest time, 71, 72
    pest control, 138

pruning, 138-139
varieties, 137
Peanuts, **239-240**
Pears, 129, **139-141**
   care of, 139-140
   diseases, 139, 140, 141
   fertilizing, 139
   harvest, 74, 140
   pest control, 140-141
   varieties, 139
Peas, English, **241**
Peas, Southern, **243-244**
Pecans, **141-142**
   care of, 142
   fertilizing, 142
   pest control, 142
   pruning, 142
   varieties, 141
Pecan weevil, 142
Peppers, 164, **245-246**
Persimmons, **142-143**
   care of, 143
   fertilizing, 143
   harvest time, 74
   pruning, 143
   varieties, 142
Pest control, 15, 68, 96, **175-187**;
   also see "Insects" and individual pest entries
   identifying insects, 176
   natural chemicals, 96, 97, 175, 178-179
   non-chemical methods, 96, 177-178
   synthetic insecticides, 179
      safety with, 179-187
pH, soil, **22**
   altering, 22
   for herbs, 95
   citrus, 118
Pigeon pea, **87**

Blackberries

Pineapples, 105, **159**, 167
   cold protection, 159
   fertilizing, 159
   harvest time, 72, 159
   pH for, 159
   starting plants, 107, 159
   varieties, 158
Planting,
   methods:
      citrus trees, 119
      double cropping, 50
      geometric, 52
      group plantings, 54
      long rows, 49, 53
      raised beds, 9, 50
      small spaces, 51, 53, 112
      wide rows, 50
   near trees, 48

schedules, 17, 18, 19, 49, **275-282**
site preparation 8, 21
spacing, 51, 52
supports for plants, 67
Plums, **143**
   care of, 143
   varieties, 143
Pokeweed, **87**
Pomegranates, **160**
   fertilizing, 160
   pests, 160
   pH, 160
   propagation, 160
   varieties, 160
Potatoes, **247-248**
Potatoes, sweet, 107, **249-250**
Potting mixes, 30, 33
Powdery mildew, 183
Predacious organisms, 176-177
Praying mantid, 177
Propagation techniques:
   see "Grafting" and individual plant entries
   cuttings, general, 111
   cuttings, herbs, 96
   division, herbs, 96
   for fruit, 42
   for pineapples, 159
   for pomegranates, 160
   seeds, herbs, 95
Pumpkin, 111, **251-252**

R

Radicchio, **88**
Radishes, 105, **253-254**
Radishes, winter, **255-256**
Rainfall, average, 14, 17
Raised beds, 9, 50
Raspberries, **144**
   care of, 144

Raspberries, cont'd
  fertilizing, 144
  pruning, 144
  varieties, 144
Regions, **14-17**
Resources, **286-288**
Ringspot, 157
Rhubarb, **257-258**
Roselle, **88**
Rosemary, 93, **101**
Rouquette, **89**
Rusts, 183

S

Sage, 93, **102**
Salt-tolerant vegetables, 11
Salt-tolerant loquats, 153
Saltwater intrusion, 11, 57
Savory, **102**
Scales, 180
Seedlings:
  care of, 31-32
  fertilizer needs, 33, 34
  in greenhouse, 167
  light requirements, 33
  problems, **30-31**
    seedling blights, 183, 184
  protection of, 32
  transplanting, 33-34
Seed pieces, 248
Seeds, **29-35**
  care of seedlings, 31-32,
    see "Seedlings" entry above
  citrus, 108
  herbs, 95
  how to save, **35**
  problems with seedlings, **30-31**
  selection, 29-30
  sowing for transplants, 30, 33

sowing in garden, 52-53
sowing medium, 30
trees from, 34
Seminole pumpkin, **89**
Shallots, 236
Shield bud graft, 39
Shrubs, 3, 18
  spacing, 7
Side dressing, 25, 64, 65
Side-veneer graft, 41
Slugs and snails, 180
Soil:
  composition, 32
  drainage problems, 8
  pH, **22**
    altering, 22
  preparation, **21-27**
  soilless mixes, 30, 33, 168
  solarization, 27, 66
  quality, 14
Solarization, 27, 66
South Florida region, **16**
Soybeans, **90**
Spider mites, 181
Spinach, 163, **259-260**
Sprinkler types, 58, 59
Squash, summer, 72-73, **261-262**
Squash, winter, **263-264**
Steinernematid, 177
Sticky boards, 96, **177**
Stink bugs, 181
Stratification, **34**
Strawberries, **265-266**
Suckers, offshoots, **44-45**
Sulfur, **22**
Sunflowers, 115
Supports for plants, 67
Surinam cherries, 147, **160-161**
  care of, 161
  harvest, 161
  pruning, 161

varieties, 160
Sweet potatoes, see "Potatoes, sweet"
Swiss, chard, 163, **267-268**

T

Tangelos, **123**
Tangerines, **123**
Tamarillo, **90**
Tarragon, 93, **102**
Temperatures, average, 14
Thrips, 181
Thyme, 93, **102**
Tomatoes, 49, 105, 163, 164, 165, **269-270**
  harvest time, 71, 73
Trees, 3, 7, 18
  planting under, 48
  spacing, 7
  see "Grafting" entry

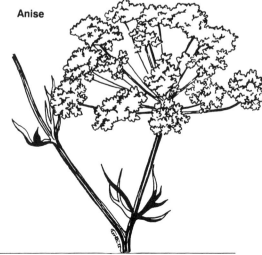

Anise

Transplants:
   buying, 55
   care of, 33-34, 55
   greenhouse grown, 167
   planting, **54-55**
   shading, 55
   starting, 109:
      avocado, 108
      citrus, 108
      sweet potato, 107
Tropical fruit, see "Exotic fruit" or individual entries
Turnips, **271-272**

V

Vapam, **26**
Vegetables, see individual entries:
   crop yields, 5
   garden site selection, 10
   four-season garden plan, 18, **19**
   salt-tolerant, 11
   water requirements, 10
Vegetable spaghetti, **91**

W

Water, **57-61**
   aid in cold protection, 69
   how to, 61
   importance of, 57, 63
   requirements, vegetables, 10
   saltwater intrusion, 11, 57
   from wells, 57
   when to, 61
Watercress, **103**
Watering, checklist, 59
Watering, container gardens, 58, 172
Watering, techniques, 10-11:
   drip irrigation, 59-61
   hand watering, 58
   microsprinklers, 61
   minisprinkers, 61
   overhead, 58
   pulsating sprinklers, 59
   soaker hoses, 58-59
Watering transplants, 55
Watermelons, 73, **273-274**
Weeds, 66-67
Weevils, 181
Whip graft, 40
Whiteflies, 181
Wide rows, 50
Wilting, 10, 63-64

Y

Yam, **91**
Yields, fruit, 5
Yields, vegetables, 5